Prayer
Book
Spirituality

Illustration from a
Book of Common Prayer, 1815.

Prayer
Book
Spirituality

A Devotional Companion to the
Book of Common Prayer
Compiled from
Classical Anglican Sources
Edited by

J. Robert Wright

THE CHURCH HYMNAL CORPORATION, NEW YORK

The Church Hymnal Corporation
800 Second Avenue
New York, NY 10017

5 4 3

The Illustrations

Examples of contemporary art
taken from some of the books from
which excerpts have been used in
this volume are reproduced opposite
the title page and chapter headings.
They are intended to provide
a representative visual component
showing how the spirituality
of the Prayer Book would have
appeared to the eyes of its users
in earlier editions.

The Type

We have attempted to match
the use of CAPITALS,
SMALL CAPITALS,
bold and *italics*
in the original editions.

Table of Contents

CHAPTER FOUR
The Daily Office

CHAPTER FIVE
The Litany

CHAPTER SIX

Christian Initiation

CHAPTER SEVEN

The Holy Eucharist

CHAPTER EIGHT

Marriage

CHAPTER NINE

Reconciliation of a Penitent

CHAPTER TEN

Ministration to the Sick

CHAPTER ELEVEN

Burial of the Dead

CHAPTER TWELVE

Ordination

CHAPTER THIRTEEN
Catechetical Instruction and Preaching

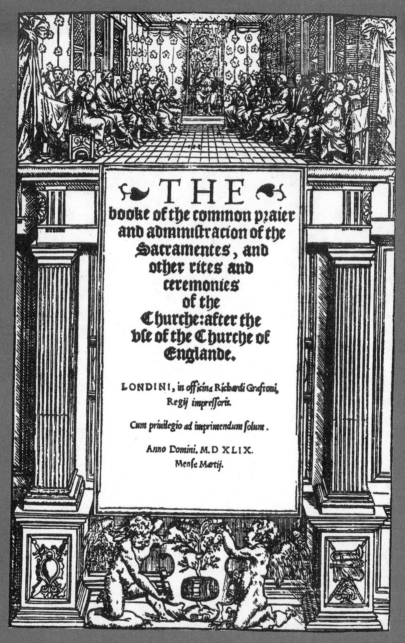

Illustration: Title page to *The First Book of Common Prayer*, edition of 8 March 1549.

Introduction

Revision of *The Book of Common Prayer* in the latter half of the twentieth century, while seeking to provide modernized and updated forms of worship for Anglican churchpeople, has at the same time also stimulated in them a desire to know and to participate more fully in the classical tradition of Prayer Book devotion. Over the centuries since the First Book of Common Prayer in 1549, numerous Anglican writers from many perspectives have produced variously related works that can be seen as, in effect, devotional commentaries on the nature and function of Prayer Book worship. The purpose of this present undertaking is to bring together basic selections from the most important of these earlier writings and to render them accessible to modern readers in one volume that can serve as both compendium and companion to the spiritual and devotional nature of Prayer Book worship. It is intended to accompany and supplement any Book of Common Prayer used anywhere in the Anglican Communion. The contents need to be read selectively in any order that may be desired; indeed, for most readers, the book will be better "dipped into" than read through from beginning to end. In showing how Anglicans since the Reformation have understood and interpreted their public worship, this anthology should also be of considerable assistance to non-Anglicans who want to understand the feature that is, ecumenically, most characteristic of Anglicanism.

More than a hundred selections from some fifty works of nearly forty different authors are excerpted for inclusion in this

15

volume, ranging from the later sixteenth to the mid-nineteenth centuries, with sources on both sides of the Atlantic, although the preponderance is, understandably, from England. It is regretted by the editor that no woman writer on the Prayer Book from this time-span could be found. The collection makes no pretense at being complete, for the length would be prohibitive, although it does claim to be comprehensive and broadly representative for the classical period that spans roughly the first three hundred years of independent Anglican history. The selections begin, soon after Anglicans at the Reformation received their first Prayer Book, with the Second Book of Homilies, followed by the classical works of Jewel and Hooker and a few others. Hooker, it has well been said, "established the principle underlying the whole work of the school; the principle that the prayer of individual Christians and the corporate prayer of the Church in the liturgy are two distinct things."[1] Writings on the spirituality of the Prayer Book flourished during the later seventeenth century. Anglicans, after the Restoration, sensed the need not only for domestic Prayer Book instruction but also for defense on two fronts: defense against the Roman Catholic claim that the Church of England had substituted an insular and vernacular liturgy in place of the historic Latin rite of the Western Church, and also for defense against the Puritan dislike of any set forms for public worship.[2] During the period of the Commonwealth and Protectorate, from 1645 to 1660, the Prayer Book had been proscribed and even the use of the Lord's Prayer forbidden by Puritan zealots.

The following decades, however, may be called a golden age of Prayer Book Spirituality. *The Whole Duty of Man,* which first appeared just before the Restoration of 1660, has been

---

[1] G.W.O. Addleshaw. *The High Church Tradition: A Study in the Liturgical Thought of the Seventeenth Century* (London, 1941), p. 32.

[2] Ibid., pp. 20–22; C.J. Stranks, *Anglican Devotion: Studies in the Spiritual Life of the Church of England between the Reformation and the Oxford Movement* (London, 1961), pp. 149–150.

16

estimated "the most popular book of devotion that England has known," appearing in many editions, and its title often imitated by others.[3] *A Rationale upon the Book of Common Prayer of the Church of England* by Anthony Sparrow, who had been ejected from his benefice for loyalty to the Prayer Book but later became Bishop of Norwich, was even reissued in the nineteenth century at the request of leaders in the Oxford Movement[4] (as was also the early seventeenth-century *Godly Meditations* of Christopher Sutton). *A Companion to the Temple* by Thomas Comber, Precentor of York Minster and afterwards Dean of Durham, is the most monumental of all these works. It was written in grandiloquent prose style and enormously popular in its own day, intended to provide devotional instruction on Prayer Book worship that churchpeople could use in preparation for the public services of the Church.[5] Simon Patrick (writing in language almost as noble as that of Comber), William Beveridge, and still others all contributed to make the late seventeenth century indeed a golden age of Prayer Book Spirituality. Of this age C.J. Stranks has remarked, "It was round the Prayer Book that the main body of Anglican piety was made to centre. England was to become a nation of churchmen once more. It was felt that if only people could be got to understand the nature and purpose of the Church's services they would come to love them and find them in every way sufficient."[6] For instruction in the Methodist societies as well, it was to *The Christian Sacrament and Sacrifice* by Daniel Brevint, Dean of Lincoln, that John and Charles Wesley turned, publishing it in a condensed version and basing many of their hymns on its teaching. Devotion and instruction was the aim of

---

[3.] J. Wickham Legg. *English Church Life from the Restoration to the Tractarian Movement* (London, 1914), p. 338.

[4.] Stranks, op. cit., pp. 150–154.

[5.] Addleshaw, op. cit., pp. 34–35; Stranks, op. cit., pp. 155–159.

[6.] Stranks, op. cit., p. 172.

all these writers, and in the following two centuries our series of commentators continues with the layman Robert Nelson, the various anonymous "Companions to the Altar," Samuel Seabury, John Henry Hobart, the evangelical Charles Simeon, and, one herald of a new age, F.D. Maurice, as the last of the authors chosen. To say more about them here, would be to deny the reader's rights to enjoy them on their own terms.

It should be noted that the words "Classical Anglican" in the present book's subtitle are not intended to limit the book's contents to any one century or school of thought (as, for example, some modern historians use the phrase "Classical Anglican" to prescribe their own definitions of "Anglicanism"[7]). For reasons of length and space, I have defined "classical" broadly as constituting roughly the first three hundred years of independent Anglican history and establishing a chronological boundary or terminus at the Oxford Movement about one hundred and fifty years before the present time. I do not intend the term "classical" to be doctrinally limiting, however, beyond the obvious restriction of sources to post-Reformation Anglican works from the late sixteenth to the mid-ninteenth centuries that comment on the Prayer Book and its contents. The middle of the nineteenth century, in a way, inaugurated the "modern" period of Prayer Book Spirituality whose writers' works, still being sifted, could require yet a second volume of their own.

The Book of Common Prayer and the tradition of Anglican worship and spirituality have stimulated many different sorts of writings, and so it should also be made clear at the outset what sort of writing has been generally excluded from the present compendium. This is not a comprehensive anthology of Anglican doctrine, or even of every type of Anglican spirituality.

[7.] Further see my essay, "Anglicanism, *Ecclesia Anglicana,* and Anglican: An Essay on Terminology," in *The Study of Anglicanism,* ed. Stephen Sykes and John Booty (London and Philadelphia, 1988), pp. 424–429.

This is a devotional companion to the Prayer Book, not an academic commentary upon it, and so the great tradition of scholarly commentaries and learned studies on the Prayer Book (such as those of J.H. Blunt or Charles Wheatly, now largely outdated) is not amply represented. Likewise, because the present volume is intended to be a supplement to the Prayer Book, not a substitute for it, very little from the great legacy of related private prayers and paraphrases, not to mention poetry and hymnody, has been included. (An occasional exception has been made for some work of Thomas Comber, where acts of meditation are integral to his exposition.) Nor will one find here examples of the many polemical passages, especially against the worship of Roman Catholics and of Jews, that often characterized Anglican apologetic in ages that were less ecumenical or conscious of liturgical renewal than our own. Direct theological writing has also been restricted, especially when it is more stimulative of controversy than of devotion. And, finally, because the focus of this companion is upon the public worship set forth in the Prayer Book itself, works of strictly private devotion or advice have also been omitted from consideration. Overall, the selections that I have chosen are, in my opinion, the best of those that were originally intended to turn the heart and mind towards God on the basis of the public worship set forth in the Prayer Book. They show an amazing depth and continuity of devotion even as, at the same time, they reveal a basic substance of Anglican theology and doctrine in the subjects treated. They exhibit, apart from the writers on marriage, a strikingly contemporary appeal. Collectively, I think it may be said, they constitute a strong tradition of Prayer Book Spirituality that flows even into modern Prayer Book revisions and thus possesses a renewed foundational significance for our own time.

There follows at the end a chronological list of the Anglican commentators on Prayer Book devotion that have been selected and excerpted for inclusion in this volume. Each personal name is followed by a most characteristic description of the author, even though he may not have held that particular position at the time of writing the work that is listed.[8] The date given is generally the earliest publication of the work listed, although in many cases, for various reasons, the excerpt may in fact be quoted from a later edition. To accommodate a wider reading public, the punctuation, capitalization, italicization, paragraphing and spelling have, to some extent, been standardized by the publisher and footnotes made consecutive where material is omitted, although it has not proved feasible to alter the texts for the purpose of inclusive language. Ellipsis marks (three dots) usually indicate omissions or exclusions, generally of outdated academic or polemical material, based on the editorial principles given above. Scholarly apparatus has been kept to an absolute minimum, since the purpose of the present work is to be a devotional compendium, not a scholarly edition. The table of contents follows the contents of standard Books of Common Prayer with a few additions, and under each chapter the selections are arranged by authors in approximate chronological order. The chapter on the Eucharist is understandably the longest, as it concerns the principal act of Anglican worship at the present, but it may also be the most interesting place to begin reading. The various contemporary illustrations are intended to provide a representative visual component, showing how the spirituality of the Prayer Book would have appeared to the eyes of its users in earlier centuries. There is a table of source references with full bibliographical information at the end.

I wish to thank my editorial assistant, Joseph Britton, whose considerable help has always been forthcoming and who has shared with me the joy of reviewing this wonderful collection of

---

[8.] More extensive biographical sketches for most of these authors may be found in *The Oxford Dictionary of the Christian Church* (Second edition, ed. F.L. Cross and E.A. Livingstone, London, 1974), and in *Anglicanism: The Thought and Practice of the Church of England, illustrated from the Religious Literature of the Seventeenth Century,* ed. Paul Elmer More and Frank Leslie Cross (London, 1935), pp. 785–811.

material. This volume is dedicated to the memory of three persons who early schooled me in the devotional tradition of Prayer Book Spirituality and who all entered God's eternity in the year 1985: my mother, Ruth M. Wright, who gave me birth and brought me up and gave me to the Episcopal Church; my catechist, Mary Woolley, who taught me much of the Prayer Book by heart; and my first priest, Donald Henning, who presented me for Confirmation and whose liturgical style made the Prayer Book beautiful.

J. Robert Wright, *D.Phil. (Oxon.), D.D., F.R.Hist.S.,*
St. Mark's Professor of Ecclesiastical History
The General Theological Seminary
New York City.

A RATIONALE
upon the
BOOK
or
Common-Prayer
of the
CHVRCH of ENGLAND
By Anth: Sparrow DD
Now Lord Bp of Excon
Printed for R Pawlet
at yͤ Bible in Chancery
Lane

Illustration from Anthony Sparrow,
A Rationale Upon the Book of Common Prayer,
edition of 1672.

CHAPTER ONE

On Prayer
In Common

(1) Richard Hooker
*Master of the Temple, Rector of Bishopsbourne (Kent),
chief apologist for Anglicanism under Queen Elizabeth I*
Of the Laws of Ecclesiastical Polity, book V
1597

Between the throne of God in heaven and his Church upon earth here militant if it be so that Angels have their continual intercourse, where should we find the same more verified than in these two ghostly exercises, the one Doctrine, and the other Prayer? For what is the assembling of the Church to learn, but the receiving of Angels descended from above? What to pray, but the sending of Angels upward? His heavenly inspirations and our holy desires are as so many Angels of intercourse and commerce between God and us. As teaching bringeth us to know that God is our supreme truth; so prayer testifieth that we acknowledge him our sovereign good. . . .

This holy and religious duty of service towards God concerneth us one way in that we are men, and another way in that we are joined as parts to that visible mystical body which is his Church. As men, we are at our own choice, both for time, and place, and form, according to the exigence of our own occasions in private; but the service, which we do as members of a public body, is public, and for that cause must needs be accounted by so much worthier than the other, as a whole society of such condition exceedeth the worth of any one . . .

When we publicly make our prayers, it cannot be but that we do it with much more comfort than in private, for that the things we ask publicly are approved as needful and good in the judgment of all, we hear them sought for and desired with common consent. Again, thus much help and furtherance is more yielded, in that if so be our zeal and devotion to Godward be slack, the alacrity and fervour of others serveth as a present spur. "For even prayer itself" (saith St. Basil) "when it hath not the consort of many voices to strengthen it, is not itself." Finally, the good which we do by public prayer is more than in private can be done, for that besides the benefit which here is no less procured to ourselves, the whole Church is much bettered by our good example; and consequently whereas secret neglect of our duty in this kind is but only our own hurt, one man's contempt of the common prayer of the Church of God may be and oftentimes is most hurtful unto many. . . .

A great part of the cause, wherefore religious minds are so inflamed with the love of public devotion, is that virtue, force, and efficacy, which by experience they find that the very form and reverend solemnity of common prayer duly ordered hath, to help that imbecility and weakness in us, by means whereof we are otherwise of ourselves the less apt to perform unto God so heavenly a service, with such affection of heart, and disposition in the powers of our souls as is requisite. To this end therefore all things hereunto appertaining have been ever thought convenient to be done with the most solemnity and majesty that the wisest could devise. It is not with public as with private prayer. In this rather secrecy is commended than out-

24

ward show, whereas that being the public act of a whole society, requireth accordingly more care to be had of external appearance. The very assembling of men therefore unto this service hath been ever solemn.

And concerning the place of assembly, although it serve for other uses as well as this, yet seeing that our Lord himself hath to this as to the chiefest of all other plainly sanctified his own temple, by entitling it "the House of Prayer," what pre-eminence of dignity soever hath been either by the ordinance or through the special favour and providence of God annexed unto his Sanctuary, the principal cause thereof must needs be in regard of Common Prayer. For the honour and furtherance whereof, if it be as the gravest of the ancient Fathers seriously were persuaded, and do oftentimes plainly teach, affirming that the house of prayer is a Court beautified with the presence of celestial powers; that there we stand, we pray, we sound forth hymns unto God, having his Angels intermingled as our associates; and that with reference hereunto the Apostle doth require so great care to be had of decency for the Angels' sake; how can we come to the house of prayer, and not be moved with the very glory of the place itself, so to frame our affections praying, as doth best beseem them, whose suits the Almighty doth there sit to hear, and his Angels attend to further?

---

(2) **George Herbert**
Rector of Fugglestone with Bemerton (Wilts.)
A Priest to the Temple, or The Country Parson
1633/1652

The Country Parson hath a special care of his Church, that all things there be decent, and befitting his Name by which it is called. Therefore first he takes order, that all things be in good repair; as walls plastered, windows glazed, floor paved, seats whole, firm, and uniform, especially that the Pulpit, and Desk, and Communion Table, and Font be as they ought, for those great duties that are performed in them. Secondly, that the Church be swept, and kept clean without dust, or Cobwebs, and at great festivals strawed, and stuck with boughs, and perfumed with incense. Thirdly, that there be fit, and proper texts of Scripture everywhere painted, and that all the painting be grave, and reverend, not with light colors, or foolish antics. Fourthly, that all the books appointed by Authority be there, and those not torn, or fouled, but whole and clean, and well bound; and that there be a fitting, and sightly Communion Cloth *of fine linen, with an handsome, and seemly Carpet of good and costly Stuff, or Cloth, and all kept sweet and clean, in a strong and decent chest, with a Chalice, and Cover, and a Stoop, or Flagon; and a Basin for Alms and offerings; besides which, he hath a Poor-man's Box conveniently seated, to receive the charity of well-minded people, and to lay up treasure for the sick and needy.* And all this he doth, not as out of necessity, or as putting a holiness in the things, but as desiring to keep the middle way between superstition, and slovenliness, and as following the Apostle's two great and admirable Rules in things of this nature: The first whereof is, *Let all things be done decently, and in order:* The second, *Let all things be done to edification.*

For these two rules comprise and include the double object of our duty, God, and our neighbor; the first being for the honor of God; the second for the benefit of our neighbor. So that they excellently score out the way, and fully, and exactly contain, even in external and indifferent things, what course is to be taken; and put them to great shame, who deny the Scripture to be perfect.

(3) Herbert Thorndike
Rector of Barley (Herts.), Fellow of Trinity College,
Cambridge, Prebendary of Westminster
The Service of God at Religious Assemblies
1642

The most eminent work that men are able to tender to the honour of God, is His public service at the assemblies of Christians. That supernatural tincture which the faith of Christ and His grace infuseth into the best of our actions, seemeth to consist in the obedience to God, out of which they are done; and the intention of His glory and worship, to which they are addressed;—That the reason of them is derived from the will and pleasure of God, and the intent of them directed to His honour and service. Whereas all the men of this world can do nothing but out of love to themselves, taking the rise and motive of their doings from that which concerneth their particulars, and aiming at nothing else in their intentions. All sorts of Christian men's actions, as they proceed from such considerations as these, are capable to be qualified "the service of God." But that which is called His public service professeth the exercise of nothing else, neither is capable to be accounted otherwise, unless it be counterfeit. For what consideration can common sense fasten upon that which we do, when we assemble ourselves for religious service, but the conscience of our subjection to God, the acknowledgment of our want of His direction and assistance, and our desire and affection to the good which we expect at His hands? . . .

Many men may think that they need not go to Church for those offices which they do at home: but they ought to think what the common sort of Christians might do if assemblies were not held: as the matter is, the service which the best are able to yield unto God is much improved by joining with the

27

rest of His members—but should we not assemble for that purpose, the hearts of plain simple members, which now are most acceptable to God, would be able to move little in this work, the order of the congregation not guiding them in it. Last of all, be it considered that this is the employment of the other world: when men's desires are all satisfied, and all the subject of prayers possessed, the Angels, the elders about the throne of God, and all the people of Jews and Gentiles which encompass it, *Rev*. 7:9, cease not to join in the praises of God, when the Church is become perfectly one.

---

(4) **Anthony Sparrow**
Bishop of Norwich
A Rationale upon the Book of Common Prayer
of the Church of England
1655/1657

The *Christians* set apart and consecrated with great solemnity of religious Rites and holy Prayers, Churches and Oratories for the same solemn service and worship. Nor can it with reason be thought needless or superstitious to use solemn religious Rites and Prayers, at the Consecration and setting of those Houses apart to religious uses and services. For as St. *Paul* argues in another case, *Doth not even nature teach you,* that it is unseemly for any man to go about the building of an house to the God of Heaven with no other appearance, than if his end were to rear up a Kitchen or a Parlor for his own use? Did not this light of Nature teach the *Patriarchs* in the state of Nature, when they erected Altars for God's service, to consecrate and set them apart with religious solemnities? And did not *Moses,* by the direction of the God of Nature, consecrate the Tabernacle and

28

Altar, with the like solemnities? And *Solomon* after consecrated the Temple, with religious Prayers and Rites, without any particular direction from God, that we find, only by the Light of Nature and right reason, which teacheth, that it is fit, that the House which is dedicated and given up to God, should be solemnly surrendered into his possession, and by religious Rites guarded and defended from Sacrilegious usurpation.

Again, Nature teaches us by these solemnities, that the House so consecrated, is to be no more used to Common and profane employments, but set apart to holy and religious services, such as those are, with which it is consecrated. These things, those pious Christians in Primitive times did not account superfluous. They knew how easily that which was meant should be holy and sacred, might be drawn from the use whereunto it was first provided. They knew how bold men are to take even from God himself; how hardly those Houses would be kept from impious profanation: they knew, and right wisely therefore endeavoured by such solemnities to leave in the minds of men that impression, which might somewhat restrain their boldness, and nourish a reverend affection towards the House of God. Thus therefore they built and set apart to God's holy service and worship by religious solemnity, Churches and Oratories, which they called *Dominicas, the Lord's Houses,* and *Basilicas, Royal and Kingly houses;* because Sacrifices and holy worship were offered up there to the great King of all the world. And when persecutors at any time destroyed those holy places, as soon as the storm was over, those blessed Souls, the first thing they did, rebuilt, and rebeautified them, that they might worship God, according to the Psalmists rule, *in the beauty of holiness.*

Thus to offer up God's public service and worship in separate and dedicated places, which we call Churches, is most fit; both for the honour of God, and our own profit. It is for the honour of God to have a House of his own, for his service alone, where flesh and blood hath no right or interest, where no common or profane thing may be done.

29

Again, it is for our profit many ways; for First, it begets and nourishes in us, dull flesh, a reverence and awe to God and his service, to offer it up thus in places set apart to that purpose, and so helps devotion. Besides, our prayers and public services are most readily accepted, in such holy separate places, 2 *Chron.* 7: 15. *Now mine eyes shall be open, and mine ears attent unto the prayer in this place.* This promise of acceptance of our prayer was there, indeed, made directly to the House which *Solomon* built, but belongs to any place so Dedicated and Consecrated unto God for his holy service and worship: For that is the reason that God gives of his gracious readiness to hear the prayer of that holy place; *For now have I chosen and sanctified this house, that my name may be there.* Now that it is dedicated and solemnly set apart by religious rites and prayers to my service, *Now have I chosen* or accepted *it for mine,* to be call'd by my name, St. *Mt.* 12: 13, to be for *a house of prayer,* and therefore *mine eyes and my heart shall be there.* Then, by the Rules of Logic, *a quatenus ad omne valet consequentia;* if because he hath so sanctified this place and accepted it for his, therefore his eyes and ears shall be open to the prayer of that place; by the like reason, whatsoever place shall be dedicated to him and accepted by him, shall have his eyes open, and his ear attentive to the prayer of it. And God Almighty promises as much, *Ex.* 20: 24. *In all places, where I record my name, I will come unto thee, and I will bless thee.* In all places dedicated to me and my service, and so made mine, *called by my name (Gen.* 28: 22.) *I will come and bless thee.* And such are all Consecrated Churches and Chapels. And therefore holy Church wisely orders that the prayers and public services of God shall be offered up there, in *the accustomed place of the Church, Chapel, or Chancel.* . . .

(5) **Thomas Comber**
Dean of Durham
A Companion to the Temple,
or A Help to Devotion in the Use of the Common Prayer
1672–76/1684

There are two principal ends of the Worship of God, *The Glory of him that is Worshipped, and the Benefit of the Worshippers.* . . . But whether we look on them single or conjoined, no part of *Divine Worship* doth so much express and advance God's glory, nor so directly tend to Man's good as *Public Prayer;* in which we make the most universal solemn acknowledgments of our Obligations unto, and Dependence upon, the Supreme Lord of all the World; and by which all the Servants of God in all times, places and circumstances, do with heart and voice, by common consent reveal their wants, and obtain supplies for them. So that we may call this the *Life and Soul of Religion,* the *Anima Mundi,* that universal Soul which quickens, unites and moves the whole Christian World. Nor is the case of a private Man more desperate, when he breathes no more in secret Prayer, than the condition of a Church is, where public Devotions cease. . . .

Objection 1. [Common, written prayer] *is said to be a Form, and therefore a hindrance to zealous praying by the spirit.*

Answer. Whoever makes this Objection, and affirms we cannot pray by the Spirit in the words of a Form, must beware his ignorance betray him not into a dangerous uncharitableness, and perhaps blasphemy. For the *Saints* of the *Old Testament* prayed by *Forms,* and so did *Christ* himself in the *New,* and he taught his Apostles a *Form* to pray by, and dare any say they prayed not by the Spirit? Have not all Churches, since the Apostles times to our days had their *Forms* of Prayer? And did

31

not the devoutest Men of all Ages compose and use such? Was ever *Extempore* Prayer heard of in public (till of late) unless on special occasions; and do we think no Church nor no Persons prayed by the Spirit, till now? To come nearer still: Have not *France* and *Geneva* their *Forms?* And did not learned *Calvin* (and the best reformed Divines) use a *Form* before their Sermons? And is not an unstudied Prayer a Form to the People, who are confined to pray in the Speaker's words? And will you say these all pray without the Spirit of God? But sure we hug the Phrase of *Praying by the Spirit,* not attending the Sense. For the meaning doubtless is, to be so assisted by the Holy Ghost, that (our Thoughts being composed, our Souls calmed, and our Hearts deeply affected with our Wants, and the Divine All-sufficiency) we can pray with a strong Faith, and a fervent Love: When we are so intent upon our Requests that we duly weigh them, and pursue every Petition with pressing Importunity, ardent Desires, and vigorous Affections, this is the *Spirit of Prayer.* And thus we may better **pray by the Spirit** in the words of a *Form,* than we can do, when our Mind is employed in inventing new expressions. For having a *Form* (which custom hath made familiar) we have all things set down to our *Hands* which we or others want; and we are at leisure to improve the good Motions of the Spirit; having no more to do but to join our Souls and Affections to every Petition, and follow them up to Heaven in most passionate and zealous wishes that God would grant them: Whereas in *Extempore Prayer* the Petitions expire into Air in a moment, for neither Minister nor People knew them before, nor can remember them afterwards; the one being busy in inventing, the others in expecting a pleasing novelty. And, methinks, it argues more of the Spirit of God, when we can attend the old Prayers with Zeal and Love, than when we need Variety and novel Expressions, to screw us up into a Devotion too much like Artifice, and seeming rather to be moved by the pleasure of the Fancy, than the actings of Desire. We may judge of the effects of God's Spirit rather by disposing our Hearts to join in a well-composed Form, than by filling our Heads with new Prayers, or opening our Mouths in fluent Expressions; both which may be done without the help of the Spirit, but to be devout without it is most impossible. To which we shall only add, that many truly good Men, and sound Members of our Church, do daily use these Prayers with as much Spirit and Life, with as serious and sincere Devotion, as any in the World can do. And this they account a demonstration that the Spirit doth assist them in this Form. And so it may assist these mistaken Persons, *if they will* lay down their groundless prejudice, and strive to serve God thus as well as they can. So would the good Spirit assist their Prayers, and make up our differences, giving us one Mind and one Spirit, that with one Heart and one Mouth we might glorify one God.

Objection 2. But it is farther urged, *That these Prayers, though good in themselves, will grow flat and nauseous by daily use, and consequently become an impediment to Devotion.*

Answer. We come not to the House of God for Recreation, but for a supply of our wants; and therefore this might be a better reason of an empty Theatre, than a thin Congregation. We come to God in Public, to petition for the relief of our own general Necessities, and those of the whole Church, *viz.* for Pardon of Sin, Peace of Conscience and succours of Divine Grace, and a Deliverance from Sin and Satan, Death and Hell: As also for Food and Raiment, Health and Strength, Protection and Success in all our concerns; and more generally for the Peace of the Kingdom, the Prosperity of the Church, the Propagation of the Gospel, and the success of its Ministers. Now these things are always needful, and always the same, to be prayed for every day alike. Wherefore (unless we be so *vain* as to fancy God is delighted with *Variety* and *Change* as well as we) what need is there to alter the Phrase every day, or what efficacy can a new model give to our old Requests? Particular wants and single Cases must be supplied by the Closet-devotions, for the Public (whether by *Form* or *Extempore)* can never reach all those which are so numerous and variable. Wherefore one Form may fit all that ought to be asked in the Church; and why then should we desire a needless and infinite Variety and Alteration?

. . .

But having thus cleared the way to all indifferent and disinterested Persons, it is time to speak briefly of the Design of the following *Discourses;* which is to make it evident that our Excellent Prayers do deserve all possible Love and Esteem, and contain in them a rich Treasury of all that can make our Devotion lively and useful. And if we be assisted by God's Spirit, and come desirous to pray with Zeal and Sincerity, here is (without calling in any aid but that of *Heaven*) a curious *Order*, clear *Method*, significant *Phrases*, and strong *Arguments* to quicken our Affections, and enlarge our Souls in holy and fervent Wishes, Desires and Meditations, which is the Prayer of the Inward Man, the Life and Soul of this Duty. All which we teach Men to do by giving a natural and facile *Analysis* of the Method, and by making plain and practical *Observations* on the Parts, together with a literal *Paraphrase* of the Whole. By which none can imagine I should give a borrowed lustre to the Prayers, which they had not of their own: For I only prove they had it before, and I find all in them, that I observe from them; which I hope will be so plain, that all Men will see the inference, and be able in their own Devotions to find out much more. Now in this *Essay* I shall hope to serve three sorts of Persons.

1. The Ignorant, who may be instructed hereby to *pray with understanding.* Not that we suppose these Offices so obscure as to need a Comment (for nothing can be more plainly expressed, nor is it possible to invent words more universally understood) but many that understand the *Sense* of the Words, have not Art enough to discern the *Order, Method* and *Connection* of the Prayers, nor skill to find out the *Arguments* that press every Request; or the Places of Scripture which furnish these Devotions with significant Phrases, nor Judgment to describe what disposition of Soul doth suit the several parts of them. And if we consider, that the greatest number are such, we shall

34

think it seasonable to help them with a plain and easy *Explication.* Besides, there are many (in other things) knowing Persons, who rather for want of Consideration than Judgment, never took notice of the natural dependences of these Prayers, nor the true and full import of the Expressions, nor of the Graces to be exercised in the several Parts, because they only attended the words, but took no care to expatiate into holy Meditations. And if the former need a *Master,* these want a *Monitor,* lest they offend in a worse kind: For **Negligence** is worse than simple **Ignorance.** But, I hope, though all that is here be obvious, yet something will be found which either was not known or not observed before, and those things also such as may elevate the Affections, and make the Prayers more pleasing and more profitable.

2. *The Devout Servants of God,* and *Obedient Sons of the Church,* whose care it is to pray daily in Public, and whose Desire and Endeavour is to do it well. . . . It hath been my Care to suggest not always the most Critical, but the most Practical Sense, which most directly tended to help Devotion, for these Men's sake; who no doubt have in their own Hearts made many of these Observations before, and I hope they will like them no worse, for I shall like them better, in hopes the same Spirit directed me and them. But I hope that what I have done will (besides its present assistance) suggest a way to all devout Souls for making pathetical and pious Enlargements, more and better than are to be found here; that so our daily Offices may be full of Life and Pleasure; and every day court us with new Delights. And I must affirm, I have rather opened the top than searched the bottom of this rich Mine. But sure I am we had need to quicken our Devotion all we can, not only for our own good, but that our flames might thaw the Hearts and lighten the Eyes of the rest of the Congregation; which scarce ever mind either Words or Sense, but are either sleepy or tired, to the dishonour of *God,* the discomfort of the *Minister* and the ruin of their *own* Souls. How happy should we be, if by my Endeavours and your Examples, we awaken such into a Sense

of their Duty; that these excellent Prayers might everywhere be said with an excellent Spirit, for the benefit of particulars, and the good of the whole Church?

3. The mistaken Dissenters: Who hereby may be convinced (and perhaps persuaded) that we can pray by this Form with as much *Zeal* and more *Knowledge,* with as much *Spirit* and more *Truth,* than by any other kind of Prayer. And then it must appear, that this *Venerable Liturgy* hath been falsely represented by such, who would not have it seen truly, lest it should be loved really. But if they are so much their own Masters, as that they dare to read the Prayers seriously, and view this Book with as much *Charity* as it was written with, I shall hope either for their *Company* at Prayers, or at least to escape their *Censures* for going thither. For unless they be foolishly obstinate they must either love them, or cannot hate them. If they would love them, and pray with us, we shall be *Friends;* and if only the second be obtained, we shall be *quiet,* and even that is desirable. That these are the designs which began and encouraged this Undertaking, the *Author's* own Conscience doth testify; and he hopes even those who approve not the Means, must confess the End of this *Work* is good. And if it be successful in any of these kinds, he will not repent his pains. If in one, he is not the first that hath failed of accomplishing good intentions. However he will have satisfaction in the Peace of a *good Conscience* and may say with that noble *Roman* [Brutus], *If the Success answers his Sincerity, it must be a cause of universal Joy; if not, he can rejoice in his cordial Intentions to do good.* For the Censures of furious *Zealots,* or the scoffing of profane *Ishmaels,* he doth not value them, being only unwilling to offend Authority, or true Piety. Wherefore he doth humbly submit these Pages to the Judicious Correction of the *Reverend Fathers of the Church,* desiring nothing may be said which dissents from the Doctrine and Discipline now established; for if it do, it is without the *Author's* Knowledge and against his Judgment. And now 'tis time to conclude this *Preface* with a twofold Request.

First, To my Brethren of the *Clergy,* that they will read these

Prayers so *frequently,* that such as have leisure may never want opportunity thus to serve God; and so *fervently,* that those who do attend them, may be brought into a high esteem of them. It was a great end of God's instituting the Priest's Office, and a principal motive to our pious Ancestors in their liberal Provisions for it; That there might be an Order of Men on purpose, to *Pray daily* for all Mankind, especially for such as could not daily attend *Divine Service:* So that if we neglect this *daily Sacrifice,* we neither answer the Designs of God, nor of our Benefactors: And as we are not excused by, so we ought not to be discouraged at the People's slowness in coming to *daily Prayers,* for their Presence is indeed a Comfort to us, and an Advantage to themselves, but their Absence doth not hinder the Success, nor should it obstruct the Performance of our *Prayers.* The Promise of *Jesus* is made to *two or three;* and since our Petitions are directed to God, we need not regard who is absent, so long as he is present to whom we speak: For he accepts our Requests, not by the *Number,* but the *Sincerity* of those that make them. Let our Congregation therefore be great or small, it is our Duty to read these Prayers daily: And every day to do it with such *Fervency* and *Reverence,* as may declare that our Affections keep pace with our words, while we are presenting so excellent Requests to so infinite a Majesty, upon so weighty Occasions. And also we must recite them with such *Gravity* and *Deliberation,* as may afford sufficient time both for ourselves and our People to consider every Petition, and Press it with devout Affections, and a holy Importunity, which is the *Life of Prayer.* And if any use these comprehensive Forms without such pious enlargements, it is not for want of matter in the Offices (as I have demonstrated) but for want of Devotion and Zeal in their own Hearts. 'Tis only such as have no true sense of Piety who say the *Liturgy* without Affection; and I am very confident the rude and hasty repeating thereof hath contributed more to the making *Common Prayer* odious and contemptible, than the Arguments or the Aspersions of its most malicious Enemies; whereas if we our selves would show that we are sincerely affected and concerned while we pray by it, we may expect it will be acceptable to God, and of high esteem among all People. So that I wish it may not be said of any of us, as once of *Eli's* Sons, *Their Sin was very great, for they made Men abhor the offering of the Lord* [1 *Sam.* 2: 17].

Secondly, I shall make it my earnest Request to all the *People* of this Church, not to judge of these Prayers by the Character that *Ignorance* and *Atheism, Prejudice* and *evil Interests* fasten on them; but to consider them very well, and then they will find the *Liturgy* to be plainer and more methodical in itself, more comprehensive and more suitable to a public Congregation, than the best *Extempore* Effusion, which makes more noise and show, but is emptier, and of far less weight in the esteem of *God* and all *Judicious Men.* Let none therefore think it a needless and unprofitable waste of time to go to the House of God only to hear *Common Prayer;* for Prayer is the proper Duty of that place, which is called *the House of Prayer;* and it is a Duty that is of all others the highest and hardest, and yet the most profitable, if it be devoutly and well performed. So that I cannot but pity and lament the *Stupidity* of those, who either sleep or sit by heedless and unconcerned, while so great and so advantageous a Scene of Duty lies before them. And I must (for their own sakes) beseech all that are present at these Devotions; *First,* to compose their Bodies into those most reverent Postures which the Church hath suited to every part of Duty, *Kneeling* at the *Confession, Absolution* and *Prayers; Standing* at the *Gloria Patri, Hymns* and *Creeds,* and *Bowing* at the Holy *Name of Jesus;* for a general uniformity in these things doth declare, that there is in us a due sense of the Divine Presence, a humble obedience to our Governors, and a sweet harmony between our Bodies and Souls in the Worship we pay to the Creator of both. *Secondly,* To make their Responses with a loud and audible voice.

. . .

The *Church of England* not only allows this primitive Privilege to her Sons, but commands it; and surely none will forbear to answer out of Laziness, that consider the Honour and Benefit thereof; nor ought any to be silent out of modesty or shame, it being no shame that Men should hear us Pray in *the House of Prayer,* for we came on purpose to Pray, and the only shame is, to be mute and silent. *Thirdly,* Let me entreat them to Ponder the Divine All-sufficiency, and their own great Necessities, before they begin; and to keep their Heart close to every Petition as they go along, and they will find them all so fit to be asked, and so likely to be obtained; so agreeable to their own wants, and to the necessities of all Mankind; that it will be pleasant to ask them, and delightful to expect a gracious answer to them. And if they daily come, and constantly use the *Common Prayer* in this manner, they will neither be tired with the Length, nor wearied with the frequent Repetition thereof; for it will appear to be the most noble and comfortable exercise that Religion doth afford; it will increase their Graces, multiply their blessings, and fit them for the never-ceasing Service of the *Heavenly Choir. May the God of Peace therefore reconcile us to these Prayers, and to one another, giving us pious and zealous* Priests, *devout and well-disposed* People, *that we may have full* Churches, *frequent* Prayers, *and fervent* Charity; *than which nothing will more conduce to the public Happiness of this Nation, and the Salvation of all our Souls; the Good Lord grant it therefore, for Jesus' sake.* Amen.

---

(6) **Daniel Brevint**
Dean of Lincoln
The Christian Sacrament and Sacrifice
1673

The Sacrament instituted by Christ at the Eve of his Passion, which St. *Paul* calls the *Lord's Supper,* is without Controversy one of the greatest Mysteries of Godliness and the most solemn

Festival of the Christian Religion. The holy Table, or Altar, which presents the sacred Banquet, may, as well as the old Tabernacle, take to itself the Title of *Meeting:* since there the People must appear to worship God, and there certainly God is present to meet and to bless his People. At the Place, and during the whole Act of this *Meeting* with God, the Christian Communicants are in a special manner invited to offer up to God their Souls, their Bodies, their Goods, their Vows, their Praises, and whatsoever they can *give.* And God on the other side offers to us the Body and Blood of his Son, and all those other Blessings withal, that will assuredly follow this sacred Gift. For this must be granted, that the holy Communion is not only a *Sacrament* that the Worshiper is to come to for no other purpose than to *receive,* nor a *Sacrifice* only, where he should have nothing else to do but to *give,* but it is as the great Solemnity of the antient Passover was, whereof it hath taken the Place, a great Mystery consisting both of *Sacrament* and *Sacrifice;* that is, of the Religious Service, which the People owe to God; and of the full *Salvation,* which God is pleased to promise his People.

---

(7) **Anthony Horneck**
Vicar of All Saints, Oxford,
Chaplain to William III,
Prebendary of Westminster
The Crucified Jesus, or, A Full Account of the Nature, End,
Design and Benefits of the Sacrament of the Lord's Supper
1686

That the Public Church is the most proper, most warranted, and fittest Place, to celebrate and eat the Lord's Supper in seems to have been the constant belief of the Christian Church. They have grounded their belief on the Apostle's Expostulation with the *Corinthians*, *1 Cor. 11:20,22*. where, speaking of their coming together into one place, and distinguishing private Houses from the Church of God, he imitates a known custom in that Age, to meet in certain Oratories, or places appointed for public Worship, and there to receive the holy Symbols. That which is commonly objected, of the great improbability of public Buildings, and Edifices in times of Persecution, such as the Apostles and the Christians for the first three Centuries had sad experience of, seems to carry greater weight, than really it doth; for though we speak of places appointed for public Worship, no person of common sense can imagine that we mean they had such stately and magnificent Buildings as our Churches are at this day. The effects of Ease and Peace and Plenty, these came not in till *Constantine* procured the Churches respite and freedom from their former bondage. Yet we may justly enough suppose that even in those days of trouble and calamitous times, they either converted some spacious upper Room in a charitable Believer's House into a Church, or some good Christian gave and dedicated his house for that religious use, or the Believers, by common consent, turned it into a place of public Worship. Which is the reason that the Disciples are said to have met in an upper Room, *Acts. 1: 13,* possibly the same that Christ celebrated the *Eucharist* in; and who knows not, that mention is sometimes made of a Church in such a Man's House? as Col. 4: 15.

· · ·

The succeeding Churches observed this very religiously and therefore called the Holy Communion *synaxis* or a *Convocation,* because they judged it meet, the whole Church should be together when it was administered: For this reason it was also called *leitourgia, Liturgy,* which properly imports, *Public Administration of an Office,* and therefore applied, *Rom, 15:27,* to public distribution of Alms, to the Magistrates executing of his Office, *Rom. 13:4.* and to the Office of Teaching, and Prophesying in the public Congregation, *Acts. 13:2.*

. . .

The public eating of the Lord's Supper doth certainly best represent the end, for which *Christ* died; and that is, the public good.

. . .

Many things are by Men pretended to be done for the public good, but what they call public, is either for the good of a Family or Corporation, or Parish or City, or a certain Territory, or a Kingdom. But the death of Christ spread its virtue infinitely wider, not confining its benefits to a Province, or a part of the World, but the whole Race of Mankind was concerned in the favour so that nothing was ever done so truly for the public good, as Christ's suffering and dying, and whoever remembers it in public testifies his esteem and value of it, not only by his inward sense and admiration of it, but by the very place in which he doth remember it, The truth is, *Christ* was crucified publicly in the face of the Sun and before huge multitudes both of Jews and Proselytes, who were come to give their attendance at the Passover: Both Jews and Gentiles beheld the spectacle, and Men of all sorts and conditions crowded to see so dreadful a shew, which was an *Item,* that the remembrance of it should be in the most public place, *the Church,* the rather because this public remembrance doth best promote Christ's Glory, as multitudes joining together in Confessions and Praises must necessarily advance it more than the *Hallelujahs* of two or three in private.

---

(8) **Robert Nelson**
layman and philanthropist
***The Practice of True Devotion, in Relation to the End,
as well as the Means of Religion***
1698

Thus some lay the great *Stress* upon *Hearing* of *Sermons,* as if the Knowledge of their Duty were the one Thing necessary. Others are so entirely *devoted* to the *Prayers* of the *Church,* that they have but a mean Opinion of those Instructions that are delivered by the Priests of the Lord, *whose Lips are to preserve Knowledge;* as if desiring God to make us good, were sufficient, without the Knowledge of the Way and Manner of being so. Some depend upon their *private Devotions,* for mortifying the *Deeds* of the *Flesh,* even to the Contempt of *Fasting,* as a Piece of Will-worship, tho' it is a *Christian Duty,* enjoined for the bringing under our Bodies. Others are punctual in their *bodily Exercises,* but neglect those *Prayers* which are necessary to make them effectual. And those who are engaged in the Use of some, or all of these Means, yet live in a most *shameful Neglect* of *Receiving* the *Holy Sacrament,* as if that were no ways necessary to enable them to grow in Grace; whereas it was instituted to that very End and Purpose, that the Benefits of Christ's Death might thereby be conveyed to them. Therefore, if ever we sincerely desire to *succeed* in our *holy Purposes,* we must constantly and diligently make use of *all* those *Means* which God has ordained towards the obtaining Eternal Life; since it is by the joint Use of them *all,* that we are *made meet to be Partakers of the Inheritance of the Saints in Light.*

There is another *Extreme,* which I hope is the Case of but few; but since it is incident to those who make the greatest *Pretenses* to *Spirituality,* it ought to be taken Notice of; which is, from a Purpose of *greater Perfection,* to lay aside the *ordinary Means of Grace,* which God has established: They *frequent* not the *Instructions* of *God's Ambassadors,* because they find themselves more enlightned from their own Meditations: They approach not frequently the *Holy Communion,* to feed themselves with the *Bread of Life* there distributed, because they feel not those *Raptures,* which they are supplied with from their own *Contemplations:* They seem to have a *mean Opinion* of all the holy *Functions* of the *Priesthood,* because the Men that exercise them are not *animated* with their *Spirit.*

Now that this is a great *Delusion,* is apparent, because it contradicts that *Order* and *Method* that *God* has *revealed* for the attaining everlasting Happiness. He has set apart an *Order* of *Men* under the *Gospel,* on purpose to assist us in the great *Business* of our *Salvation;* He has given them *Power* to declare to us the *Terms* upon which it is to be obtained; they are the *deputed Ministers* of Reconciliation, and therefore we ought to attend their Instructions: He has farther *Authoriz'd* them to administer *Sacraments,* that we might be made *Members* of *Christ's Body,* and nourish'd with all *Goodness;* these holy Actions receive their *Efficacy* from the *divine* Institution, which we must keep close to, if we pretend to receive the *Influences* and *Assistances* of God's Holy *Spirit.* To enlighten our *Understandings* in the Knowledge of our Duty, to influence our *Wills* in the Practice of it, he has *revealed* to us the holy *Scripture,* which, as it lays down the best Method for the attaining that *Perfection* we are capable of in this Life; so it furnishes us with the best *Arguments* for the Prosecution of it; and though I am satisfied, that the Spirit of God does farther *direct* and *excite* those that seriously and reverently apply themselves to the Use of this Rule of *Belief* and *Practice;* yet they that lay it aside, under Pretence of *Inspirations* of equal *Authority,* have reason to *doubt* their own *Inspirations.* For if they proceeded from the Spirit of God, they would put the greatest *Stress* and highest *Value* upon what has been *stamped* with his *Mark,* by being *confirmed* by the Testimony of Miracles, the Demonstration of the Spirit, and what has been received by the *Catholic Church,* as the undoubted Word of God. Besides, since it is agreed that we are *unable* of ourselves to do any Thing that is good; and that the Grace of God is necessary to strengthen our *Weakness,* and to assist us in the Performance of our *Duty;* how can we expect the Influences of his Holy Spirit, if we *neglect* the Use of those Means which are prescribed by *divine Institution,* to convey to us the Benefits and Advantages of it.

It is certain, therefore, that as we should not so rely upon any *outward Performance,* as to neglect the *Improvement* of our *Minds,* lest our *Fasting* become an *unprofitable* Trouble, and our

Prayers a *vain* Lip-Labour; so neither should we pretend to *inward Perfection,* by slighting the *outward* Observances of *Religion,* lest our *Thoughts* grow *proud* and *fantastic,* and all our Arguments prove but a *Cover* for *Delusion.* A Man may be a bad Man, and use them all; and yet there is no being good without them.

---

(9) **William Beveridge**
Bishop of St. Asaph
**The Great Necessity and Advantage of Public Prayer and
Frequent Communion, designed to revive
Primitive Piety, with Meditations, Ejaculations, and
Prayers before, at, and after the Sacrament**
1708

Here then is the great Task we have to do in all our *public Devotions,* even to keep our Spirits or Hearts in a right Posture all the While that we are before GOD, who sees them, and takes special Notice of their Motions: That we may *pray with the Spirit, and pray with the Understanding also,* as St. *Paul* did, 1 *Cor.* 14:15. I call this a great Task, because I know it is the hardest Work we have to do. Our *Thoughts* being so very quick and nimble, so unconstant and desultory, that it is difficult to keep them close to the Work we are about, so as to serve the Lord without Distraction. But it is a Thing that must be done, if we desire to receive any real *Benefit* and *Comfort* from our Devotions. And blessed be GOD, by his Assistance we may all do it, if we will but set ourselves in good earnest about it, and observe these few Rules, which may be very helpful unto us in it.

First, When you go to the House of GOD *at the Hour of Prayer,* be sure to leave all worldly Cares and Business behind you, entertaining yourselves, as ye go along, with these, or such like Sentences of Scripture: *Like as the Hart desireth the Water-brooks, so longeth my Soul after Thee, O God, My Soul is athirst for God, yea, even the Living God. When shall I come to appear before the Presence of God? Ps* 42:1, 2. *O how amiable are Thy Dwellings, thou Lord of Hosts! My Soul hath a Desire and Longing to enter into the Courts of the Lord. My Heart and my Flesh rejoice in the Living God, Ps.* 84:1, 2. *We will go into His Tabernacle, and fall low on our Knees before his Footstool, Ps.* 132:7.

WHEN ye come into the Church, say with *Jacob, How dreadful is this Place! This is none other but the House of God; and this is the Gate of Heaven, Gen.* 28:17. or something to that Purpose. And as soon as ye can get an Opportunity, prostrate yourselves upon your *Knees* before the Master of the House, the great GOD of Heaven, humbly beseeching Him to unite your Hearts unto Himself, to cleanse your Thoughts by the Inspiration of His Holy Spirit, to open your Eyes, and to manifest Himself unto you, and to assist you with such a Measure of Grace in offering up these your *Spiritual Sacrifices,* that they may be *acceptable* to Him by JESUS CHRIST.

AND now set yourselves, in good Earnest; as in GOD's Sight, keeping your Eye only upon Him, looking upon Him as observing what you think, as well as what you say or do, all the while you are before Him.

WHILE one or more of the *Sentences* out of GOD's Holy Word (wherewith we very properly begin our Devotions to Him) are *reading,* apprehend it as spoken by GOD Himself at first, and now repeated in your Ears, to put you in mind of something, which He would have you to believe or do upon this Occasion.

WHILE the *Exhortation* is reading, hearken diligently to it, and take particular Notice of every Word and Expression in it, as contrived on purpose to prepare you for the Service of GOD, by possessing your Minds with a due Sense of His special Presence with you, and of the great Ends of your Coming before Him at this Time.

WHILE you are *confessing* your Sins with your Mouth, be sure to do it also in your Hearts, calling to Mind every one, as many as he can, of those particular Sins which he hath committed, either by *doing what he ought not to do,* or *not doing what he ought,* so as to repent sincerely of them, and steadfastly resolve never to commit them any more.

WHILE the Minister is pronouncing the *Absolution* in the Name of GOD, every one should lay hold upon it for himself, so as firmly to believe, that upon true Repentance, and Faith in CHRIST, he is now discharged and *absolved* from all his Sins, as certainly as if GOD Himself had declared it with His own Mouth, as He hath often done it before, and now, by His Ministers.

WHILE you, together with the Minister, are repeating the *Psalms* or *Hymns,* to the Honour and Glory of GOD, observe the Minister's Part as well as your own; and lift up your Hearts, together with your Voices, to the highest Pitch you can, in acknowledging, magnifying and praising the Infinite Wisdom, and Power, and Goodness, and Glory of the most High GOD in all His Works, *the Wonders that He* hath done, and still *doth, for the Children of Men,* and for you among the rest.

WHILE GOD's *Word* is *read* in either of the Chapters, whether of the *Old* or *New Testament, receive it not as the Word of Men, but (as it is in Truth) the Word of God, which effectually worketh in you that believe,* 1 *Th.* 2:13. And therefore *hearken* to it with the same Attention, Reverence and Faith, as you would have done, if you had stood by Mount *Sinai,* when GOD proclaimed the *Law,* and by our Savior's Side, when He published the Gospel.

WHILE the *Prayers* or *Collects* are reading, although you ought not to repeat them aloud, to the Disturbance of other People; yet you must repeat them in your Hearts, your Minds accompanying the Minister from one Prayer to another, and from one Part of each Prayer to the other, all along with Affections suitable to the Matter sounding in your Ears, humbly adoring and admiring GOD according to the Names, Properties or Works, which are attributed to Him at the Beginning of each *Prayer,* earnestly desiring the good Things which are asked Him in the Body of it, for yourselves or others. And steadfastly believing in *Jesus Christ* for His Granting of them, when He is named, as He is at the End of every Prayer, except that of St. *Chrysostom;* because that is directed immediately to CHRIST Himself, as promising, that *when Two or Three are gathered together in His Name, He will grant their Requests;* which is therefore very properly put at the End of all our daily Prayers, and also of the *Litany,* (most Part whereof is directed also to our Savior) that when we have made all our *Common Supplications* unto Him, we may act our Faith in Him again for GOD's granting of them according to His said *Promise.* And so may [we] be dismissed with, *The Grace of our Lord Jesus Christ, the Love of God the Father, and the Communion or Fellowship of the Holy Ghost;* under which are comprehended all the Blessings, that we have, or can desire, to make us completely happy, both now and forever.

AFTER the *Blessing,* it may be expedient still to continue for some Time upon your *Knees,* humbly beseeching Almighty GOD to pardon what He hath seen amiss in you, since you came into His Presence; and that He would be graciously pleased to hear the Prayers, and to accept of the Praises, which you have now offered up unto Him, thro' the Merits of *Jesus Christ* our only Mediator and Advocate.

THESE few *Directions* I thought good to lay before you, as being of great Use towards the right Performance of your public Devotions, so as that they may be both acceptable to GOD, and profitable to yourselves.

---

(10) **Anonymous**
The New Whole Duty of Man
1747

Having thus given you the several parts of prayer, the next thing to be considered is, Where we ought to pray: and here it will be found our duty to pray both in *public* and *private.* Those prayers are most acceptable to God, and most necessary for us, which are offered in *public assemblies;* because they have these advantages above private devotions, that God is most honoured and glorified by such addresses; and a sense of his majesty is maintained in the world, somewhat suitable to his most excellent greatness and goodness, when by outward signs and tokens we publish and declare the inward regard and esteem we have for his divine attributes. For private prayer is only piety confined within our breasts; but public prayer is piety exemplified and displayed in our outward actions: it is the beauty of holiness made visible; our light shines out before men, and in the eye of the world; it enlarges the interest of godliness, and keeps up a face and sense of religion among mankind. Our Saviour promises his special presence to such assemblies, and hath appointed a particular order of men to offer up our prayers in such places of worship. Besides, we may expect greater successes, when our petitions are made with the joint and unanimous consent of our fellow Christians, and when our devotions receive warmth and heat from the exemplary zeal of pious ministers. Whoever thinks justly must be sensible, that private religion never did in fact subsist, but where some public profession of it was regularly kept up. He must be sensible, that if public worship was once discontinued, a universal forgetfulness of that God would ensue, whom to remember is the strongest sense and preservative against vice; and that the bulk of mankind would soon degenerate into mere savages and barbarians, if there were not stated days to call them off from the common business of this life, to attend to what is the most important business of all, their salvation in the next. These considerations should make all good Christians frequently attend the public worship of the house of God. Therefore it is to be wished, that they who have opportunities, and are not lawfully hindered, should endeavour so to regulate their time, as to be able constantly to attend on prayer at church; for, as those who have leisure cannot better employ it, so they must have but little concern for the honour and glory of God, who neglect such opportunities of declaring and publishing his praise before men. In a word, public worship is the great instrument of securing a sense of God's providence and of a world to come; and a sense of God's providence and a world to come is the great basis of all social and private duties. One thing more I beg leave to mention. Though you should be a regular attendant on the service of the church; take care, that your deportment out of church be correspondent to your behaviour in it; otherwise, you will do religion more disservice, than if you were its open and avowed enemy.

---

(11) **Samuel Johnson**
*Priest and missionary in Connecticut from the Society
for the Propagation of the Gospel,
first president of King's College (Columbia University)*
**On the Beauty of Holiness in the Worship
of the Church of England**
1749

I must think it another great article of the beauty of our worship, that the people bear a uniform vocal part in it, insomuch that we do literally, with one mouth and voice, as well as one mind and heart glorify God our heavenly Father. For as there cannot be imagined a more beautiful sight than for a large number of worshippers to join together in worship with one heart and voice, like children in doing honor to a common parent; so it looks like a kind of holy strife, in our method of joint vocal worship, who shall do the greatest honor to our common heavenly parent, while, keeping the unity of the spirit in the bond of peace, we do, as it were, call upon one another (the minister and the people interchangeably), and admonish one another in the short responses, and in the Psalms and Hymns and spiritual songs, all with life and spirit chanting forth the high praises of God. I am sensible, to those who have been bred up in a contrary way, this method may seem at first to look like confusion; but let me assure those to whom it may so seem, that if they would only have each his Book, and see every thing with his own eyes, and come a little while into the custom, this objection would not only entirely vanish, but soon turn into the appearance of a very sensible beauty, and be found to be a solid advantage. For not only the eye, as I observed before, but also the ear would affect the heart, and it would not only animate a spirit of devotion towards God, but a spirit of charity towards one another, to find ourselves surrounded with our Christian neighbors and brethren, all joining together, and according to the pattern of the holy Apostles (*Acts* 4: 24), lifting up our voices with one accord in the prayers and praises offered up to Almighty God. My neighbor's voice will be so far from interrupting that it will rather animate my devotion, and give it the more life and spirit. This is what, I assure you, I find to be the case; and I believe I may appeal to the experience of all that have had an opportunity of coming into a habit of it. And let me farther assure you, that now after near forty years use of our excellent method of worship, upon this account, as well as the other reasons above mentioned, it is so far from growing tedious or a matter of formality, as some imagine, that every opportunity seems to add fresh life, and I see fresh beauties, and find further advantages in it from time to time. And one thing that makes it rather appear so amiable is, that in the use of it I am offering up, not the devotions of this or that assembly only, much less of this or that particular person or minister, but the prayers and praises of the whole English church and nation, enjoined by lawful authority, which every assembly is jointly offering up at the same time.

(12) **John Henry Hobart**
Bishop of New York, founder of The General Theological Seminary
A Companion for the Book of Common Prayer
1805 / 1827
(Footnotes are from the original text)

Of the Devout and Decent Performance of the Service

It is the duty of every person to attend to the whole of the public service of the Church. They who are not present at the commencement of the service lose the opportunity of confessing their sins, and the comfort of hearing their pardon declared. And, by coming into the church after the congregation have assembled, they interrupt and disturb the devotion of others. This irreverent and censurable practice should therefore be carefully avoided.

Every person also should constantly attend the service in that particular

Church

where he is accustomed to attend. He will thus give a commendable example of order, of punctuality, and of attention, which it is of the greatest consequence to preserve and inculcate.

At their entrance into church, the people should offer up a secret prayer to GOD for the aids of his HOLY SPIRIT, in the discharge of the solemn duties of public worship. They should impress their minds with the serious and constant recollection that they are in the presence of that Almighty Being who *searches the heart,* who *cannot be deceived,* and *who will not be mocked.* The sense of his holy presence should not only repress all

52

frivolous, careless, and irreverent behaviour; but should excite in their hearts the sentiments of profound humility and awe.

It should be their object, agreeably to the injunction of the Apostle, and the practice of devout men in every age, to *glorify* GOD not only with their *spirits,* but with their *bodies* also;[1] to accompany the devotions of the heart with corresponding

Gestures of the Body.

Accordingly, in the ascription of praise they should stand, but in the acts of confession and supplication they should humbly kneel.

It is much to be lamented, that the POSTURE of KNEELING, during the public prayers, is very generally neglected. In many churches, the boards provided for the purpose of kneeling, are used only as foot boards.[2] The general prevalence of the posture of sitting during the solemn acts of confession and supplication must be a subject of deep regret with all who esteem the *decent* and *devout* performance of public worship a matter of the first importance. The late excellent and exemplary Bishop of London, Dr. PORTEUS, in a letter which he addressed in May 1804 to the clergy of his Diocese, thus enforces the duty of kneeling during the performance of prayer: "For many years past, I have observed with extreme concern, in different churches and chapels, both in the metropolis and in various parts of the country where I happened to be present, a practice prevailing (and evidently gaining ground every day) of a *considerable part of the congregation sitting during those parts of divine worship where the rubric expressly enjoins every one to kneel.*

"It may be thought, perhaps, that the posture of body in offering up our prayers, is a circumstance too trivial to deserve

[1.] *I Cor.* 6:20.

[2.] In the construction of pews of Episcopal churches, care should be taken to furnish them with conveniences for kneeling. And in square pews where there are no kneeling boards, some other convenience for kneeling should be provided.

such serious notice as this. But can anything be trivial that relates to the Almighty Governor of the universe? Does not every one know, too, that the mind and the body mutually act upon and influence each other; and that a negligent attitude of the one will naturally produce indifference and inattention in the other? Look only at the general deportment of those who sit at their devotions (without being compelled to it by necessity), and then say whether this remark is not founded in truth and in fact. I shall be told, perhaps, that there are some denominations of Christians that *stand,* and others that *sit* at their devotions. It is very true, and they must be left to judge for themselves; but my concern at present is with members of the church. Our Church, in her admirable form of public prayer, allows, in different parts of the service, the different postures both of standing and sitting; which, with her usual wisdom and discretion, she adapts to the respective circumstances of those particular parts. But where the solemnity and importance of our supplications require it, there she positively enjoins the posture of kneeling; and to disobey that injunction is unquestionably an offence against the discipline and usage of that venerable Church to which we have the happiness to belong.

"It is also contrary to the practice of the best, and greatest, and wisest men, both before the promulgation of the Gospel and after it. The exhortation of king *David* in the 95th Psalm, which we have adopted into our Liturgy, is, 'O come, let us worship, and fall down, and *kneel* before the LORD our Maker.' When *Solomon* dedicated his magnificent temple to GOD, he *kneeled* down upon his knees before all the congregation of Israel, and spread forth his hands towards heaven, while he poured forth one of the most sublime and affecting prayers that ever fell from the lips of man. It was the custom of the prophet *Daniel* to *kneel* upon his knees three times a day, and pray and give thanks unto his GOD. Our SAVIOUR himself, in his last agony, *kneeled* down and prayed; *St. Stephen,* in his last moments, *kneeled down* and prayed for his murderers; and *St. Paul,* when he took his last solemn leave of his brethren, *kneeled* down

54

even on the seashore, and offered up his petitions to heaven for their everlasting welfare.

"After these injunctions of the Church, and these examples from Scripture, no one, I think, who calls himself a Christian, and a member of the Church, will (unless prevented by *illness* or *infirmity*) refuse to *kneel down* before the LORD his Maker. But if you perceive any part of your congregation[3] habitually neglecting so to do, I must request you to represent to them, in forcible terms, the great impropriety and indecency of such a practice. It is very possible that they may have fallen into it from mere thoughtlessness and inattention, and considered it as a matter of very little importance; but you will, I hope, endeavour to convince them that it is in reality a very serious offense against the Majesty of Heaven and the decorum and solemnity of public worship. It is evidently inconsistent with that profound reverence which is due to the great Creator of the universe, and that deep humility and contrition which become such wretched sinners as we all are, in a greater or less degree, in the sight of GOD. It strikes, in short, in my apprehension, at the very root of all true devotion; and ought therefor to be vigorously resisted before it has gained too much strength to be subdued. If it is not, if it is suffered to go on without control, there is too much reason to apprehend, from the progress it has made within these few years, that it will in a few years more become a universal practice, and that you will see the whole of your congregation sitting during every part of divine service."

To the performance of the service with proper solemnity and decorum, it is also necessary that the people should

Repeat Aloud the Responses

and the other parts of the service assigned to them. Unless this duty be attended to by the congregation, the intention of the

---

[3.] The reader will recollect that the Letter from which these extracts are taken, was addressed by the Bishop of London to his clergy.

service of the Church is defeated, and its beauty and solemnity entirely lost. It is not sufficient that a few faint voices be heard; the whole congregation should, as it were *with one heart and one mouth, glorify* GOD. Their united answers should resemble the *voice of many waters and of a great thunder;* by which forcible comparison St. *John* describes the worship of the blest above.

The repeating of the responses seems to be too generally considered as the peculiar duty of the person called the Clerk; who is, in fact, an officer unknown in the service of the Church. And, as the congregation too generally depend upon him to repeat the responses, it is perhaps much to be lamented that his office was ever introduced.

Let a regard for the honour of the Church, and for the glory of GOD who delights in order in his worship, awaken the zeal of every member of the Church. Let him preserve silence in the parts of the service performed by the minister; joining in them not with his voice, but with sincerity of mind and heart. Let him, however, consider it as a sacred duty to *repeat aloud* the parts in the service assigned to the people. He will thus have the satisfaction of performing his share in the important and honourable duty of worshiping GOD. Confession will be rendered more lively, supplication more animated, and praise more ardent when the people join in the service with their *voices* as well as with their *hearts.* Both minister and people thus faithfully performing the respective parts allotted to them, the service of the Church will be exhibited in all its majesty, beauty, and affecting solemnity; and the worship of the Sanctuary will ascend as acceptable incense to the LORD OF HOSTS.

"*Praise the* LORD, *O ye* SERVANTS OF THE LORD, *ye that wait in the courts of the house of our* GOD"

"*Let all the* PEOPLE *praise thee, O* GOD; *yea, let all the people praise thee.*"

"GOD, *even our own* GOD *will* then *give us his blessing.*"

Illustration from
*The New Week's Preparation for a Worthy
Receiving of the Lord's Supper,* 1821.

On Prayer
from a Book

(13) Richard Hooker
Master of the Temple, Rector of Bishopsbourne (Kent),
chief apologist for Anglicanism under Queen Elizabeth I
Of the Laws of Ecclesiastical Polity, book V
(1597)

But of all helps for due performance of this service the greatest is that very set and standing order itself, which framed with common advice, hath both for matter and form prescribed whatsoever is herein publicly done. No doubt from God it hath proceeded, and by us it must be acknowledged a work of his singular care and providence, that the Church hath evermore held a prescript form of common prayer, although not in all things everywhere the same, yet for the most part retaining still the same analogy. So that if the liturgies of all ancient churches throughout the world be compared amongst themselves, it may be easily perceived they had all one original mould, and that the public prayers of the people of God in churches thoroughly settled did never use to be voluntary dictates proceeding from any man's extemporal wit.

To him which considereth the grievous and scandalous inconveniences whereunto they make themselves daily subject, with whom any blind and secret corner is judged a fit house of common prayer; the manifold confusions which they fall into where every man's private spirit and gift (as they term it) is the only Bishop that ordaineth him to this ministry; the irksome deformities whereby through endless and senseless effusions of indigested prayers they oftentimes disgrace in most insufferable manner the worthiest part of Christian duty towards God, who herein are subject to no certain order, but pray both what and how they list: to him I say which weigheth duly all these things the reasons cannot be obscure, why God doth in public prayer so much respect the solemnity of places where, the authority and calling of persons by whom, and the precise appointment even with what words or sentences his name should be called on amongst his people.

---

(14) **Herbert Thorndike,**
Rector of Barley (Herts.), Fellow of Trinity College,
Cambridge, Prebendary of Westminster
The Service of God at Religious Assemblies
1642

That this perpetual practice of the Church of prescript forms of service is not against the principles of the reformation, or the judgment of chief reformers, a few words shall serve to conclude. In particular in this of England, for which I plead; that the principal of the clergy should be employed to advise the whole kingdom assembled to enact a form of service, to the purpose that those which could make no prayers of their own head might use it as cork to help them to swim with—not for any of these considerations expressed afore, especially the practice of it once enacted having been without interruption ever since—is a thing so far from common reason to conceive that it is hard to believe that those which speak it believe themselves in it. In Luther's reformation the question is not made, though there is no reason to be showed why their example should not be drawn into consequence here. As for the other, according to Calvin, so far as my lot hath been to know the practice of it, I confess it is a thing which hath made me much marvel to see them so punctual in practicing their form prescribed, that scarce anything came from the ministers themselves but that very short prayer afore the sermon, wherein they recommend themselves and their performance to the blessing of God, as you saw the fashion was in the ancient Church.

---

(15) **Anonymous**
(John Gauden, later Bishop of Exeter, and/or King Charles I)
Eikon Basilike
1648

For the manner of using set and prescribed forms, there is no doubt but that wholesome words, being known and fitted to men's understandings, are soonest received into their hearts, and aptest to excite and carry along with them judicious and fervent affections.

Nor do I see any reason why Christians should be weary of a well-composed Liturgy (as I hold this to be) more than of all other things, wherein the constancy abates nothing of the excellency and usefulness.

I could never see any reason why any Christian should abhor, or be forbidden to use, the same forms of prayer, since he prays to the same God, believes in the same Savior, professeth the same Truths, reads the same Scriptures, hath the same duties upon him, and feels the same daily wants for the most part, both inward and outward, which are common to the whole Church.

Sure we may as well beforehand know what we pray as to Whom we pray; and in what words, as to what sense. When we desire the same things, what hinders we may not use the same words? Our appetite and digestion too may be good when we use, as we pray for, *our daily bread.*

Some men, I hear, are so impatient not to use in all their devotions their own invention and gifts, that they not only disuse (as too many), but wholly cast away and condemn the Lord's Prayer; whose great guilt is, that it is the warrant and original pattern of all set Liturgies in the Christian Church.

I ever thought that the proud ostentation of men's abilities for invention, and the vain affectations of variety for expressions, or in public prayer, or in any sacred administrations, merits a greater brand of sin than that which they call coldness and barrenness. Nor are men in these novelties less subject to formal and superficial tempers (as to their hearts) than in the use of constant forms, where not the words but men's hearts are to blame.

I make no doubt but a man may be very formal in the most extemporary variety and very fervently devout in the most wonted expressions. Nor is God more a God of Variety than of Constancy. Nor are constant forms of prayer more likely to flat and hinder the spirit of prayer and devotion than unpremeditated and confused variety to distract and lose it.

Though I am not against a grave, modest, discreet, and humble use of ministers' gifts, even in public, the better to fit and excite their own and the people's affections to the present occasions, yet I know no necessity why private and single abilities should quite jostle out and deprive the Church of the joint

62

abilities and concurrent gifts of many learned and godly men, such as the composers of the Service Book were; who may in all reason be thought to have more gifts and graces enabling them to compose with serious deliberation and concurrent advice such Forms of Prayers as may best fit the Church's common wants, inform the hearers' understanding, and stir up that fiduciary and fervent application of their spirits (wherein consists the very life and soul of prayer, and that so much pretended spirit of prayer), that any private man by his solitary abilities can be presumed to have; which, that they are many times (even there, where they make a great noise and show) the affectations, emptiness, impertinency, rudeness, confusions, flatness, levity, obscurity, vain and ridiculous repetitions, the senseless and ofttimes blasphemous expressions (all these burdened with a most tedious and intolerable length) do sufficiently convince all men but those who glory in that Pharisaic way.

Wherein men must be strangely impudent and flatterers of themselves not to have an infinite shame of what they so do and say, in things so sacred a nature before God and the Church, after so ridiculous, and indeed, profane a manner.

Nor can it be expected that in duties of frequent performance, as Sacramental administrations and the like, which are still the same, ministers must either come to use their own forms constantly, which are not like to be so sound or comprehensive of the nature of the duty as forms of public composition; or else they must every time affect new expressions when the subject is the same, which can hardly be presumed in any man's greatest sufficiencies not to want (many times) much of that completeness, order, and gravity becoming those duties; which by this means are exposed at every celebration to every minister's private infirmities, indispositions, errors, disorders, and defects, both for judgement and expression.

A serious sense of which inconvenience in the Church unavoidably following every man's several manner of officiating, no doubt, first occasioned the wisdom and piety of the

Ancient Churches to remedy those mischiefs by the use of constant Liturgies of public composition.

The want of which I believe this Church will sufficiently feel when the unhappy fruits of many men's ungoverned ignorance and confident defects shall be discovered in more errors, schisms, disorders, and uncharitable distractions in Religion, which are already but too many, the more is the pity.

However, if violence must needs bring in and abet those innovations (that men may not seem to have nothing to do) which law, reason, and religion forbids at least to be so obtruded as wholly to jostle out the public Liturgy;

Yet nothing can excuse that most unjust and partial severity of those men who either lately had subscribed to, used, and maintained the Service Book; or refused to use it, cried out of the rigor of Laws and Bishops, which suffered them not to use the liberty of their consciences in not using it.

That these men (I say) should so suddenly change the Liturgy into a Directory, as if the Spirit needed help for invention, though not for expressions; or as if matter prescribed did not as much stint and obstruct the Spirit as if it were clothed in, and confined to, fit words—so slight and easy is that legerdemain which will serve to delude the vulgar;

That, further, they should use such severity as not to suffer without penalty any to use the Common Prayer Book publicly, although their consciences bind them to it, as a duty of piety to God and obedience to the Laws;

Thus I see no men are prone to be greater tyrants and more rigorous exacters upon others to conform to their illegal novelties than such whose pride was formerly least disposed to the obedience of lawful constitutions.

(16) **John Durel**
Minister of the French Church in the Savoy, Dean of Windsor
The Liturgy of the Church of England Asserted
1662

Our Liturgy is an admirable piece of Devotion and Instruction. It is the marrow and substance of all that the Piety and Experience of the first five Centuries of Christianity found most proper to Edification in the public Assemblies. It is a Compound of Texts of Scripture, of Exhortations to Repentance, of Prayers, Hymns, Psalms, Doxologies, Lessons, Creeds, and of Thanksgivings: of Forms for the Administration of Sacraments, and for other public duties of Christians in the Church. And of Comminations against impenitent sinners. And all this mixed and diversified with great care expressly to quicken devotion and stir up attention.

The Instructions consist in the order which is set for the reading of the Holy Scripture every day in the year: and in the choice made of certain Chapters of the Old Testament and of certain portions of the Gospel, and of the Epistles of the New for *Sundays* and for *Festival Days,* which are called *proper Lessons,* and the *Gospel* and the *Epistles* for the day. All this ordered with so wise an economy, that those who have Devotion and leisure enough to come to Church and be present at Divine Service every day, Morning and Evening, may hear the whole Bible read every year. The Old Testament once, and the New (wherein we ought to be more conversant) no less then thrice. And the Book of Psalms (which is so excellently useful for the Consolation, Sanctification, as also Instruction of all believers in any condition whatsoever, but especially in adversity) no less then twelve times. And for other places, where people cannot meet but upon Sundays and Holy Days, are extracted out of the Old Testament for the first Lessons Morning and Evening, all the most remarkable Histories and chief Prophesies of the same. And out of the New (besides the Instructions which our Savior gave to his Disciples in his Sermon upon the Mount, and his other Divine exhortations) are selected the most Illustrious Miracles of his Life, and these are called the *Gospels*. As also the principal places, either for Doctrine or Manners, of the Epistles of St. *Paul,* and of the rest of the Holy Apostles, and of the Revelation, which are termed the *Epistles.* And although the Church of *England* makes that distinction which ought to be made between Canonical Books and those which are called Apocrypha, declaring that no Article of Faith can be grounded upon them, but upon the first only; yet she hath selected certain Chapters, and even whole Books of the latter to be read after the former, which she holds to be alone of Divine inspiration, have been read in that order which I have now represented. But nevertheless she orders them to be read by reason they contain some Histories that are part of the History of the Jewish Church, and a continuation of the same. And as in the 39 Articles it is expressed: *For the example of life, and for the instruction of manners, and not to establish any Doctrine.* So as the Church of *England* causeth them to be read publicly only for the same reasons for which the Primitive Church read them, and for which they are commonly bound up in one Volume with the Canonical Books in the Reformed Churches of *France,* and in all others. . . .

To these we may also add the three *Creeds,* that of the *Apostles,* the *Nicene,* and that of *Athanasius,* which our Church orders to be publicly recited among other means which she useth for the instruction of believers. To the Apostles *Creed* is added that of *Nicaea,* because it doth more especially teach the Godhead of the Son, and of the Holy Ghost. And to these two she joins that of *Athanasius,* where in a wonderful manner is expressed whatsoever the Scripture doth teach concerning the incomprehensible mystery of the most glorious Trinity, and that of the Incarnation of the Son of God, the depth of which is no less unsearchable: because upon these two most wonderful mysteries the whole sum of Christianity doth depend, which in the said *Creed* are set out in as clear tearms as so sublime a subject can permit. All that this *Liturgy* contains besides is proper to teach humility, zeal, and devotion, especially the *Litany,* and all that is comprised in the several Lessons, Prayers, Confessions of sins, and in the forms of Thanksgiving which are appointed for the celebration of the Lord's Supper: but your own experience being better able to instruct you in these particulars than all I can say upon this subject, I shall only speak a word of the manner wherein the Church orders the recital of the *Decalogue.* He that pronounceth it must be a *Minister,* as another *Moses* sent from God, the whole Congregation devoutly kneeling all the while, making a serious reflection upon the commandments of God, upon the lack of care they have in time past been guilty of to obey the same, and upon their inability, as of themselves, to do better for the time to come. And thereupon they ought to beg God's pardon and implore his assistance, saying with a loud though humble voice, *Lord have mercy upon us, and incline our heart to keep this law:* there can be nothing more powerful to touch sinners to the quick, and to draw them from their evil courses, than the *Commination,* to which the whole Congregation is bound to say *Amen,* after every particular denunciation of God's curse upon all sorts of sinners who persist in their sins. Not to wish them cursed (as ignorant & contentious spirits affirm contrary to truth) but as it is expressly set down there *To the intent that every one being admonished of the great indignation of God against sinners may the rather be called to earnest and true repentance, and may walk more warily in these dangerous days, eschewing such vices for the which they affirm with their own mouths the curse of God to be due.* For the words are not *cursed be,* but *cursed is* he who commits such or such a sin. Which saying doth not import any imprecation of a *Curse,* but declares it only. And then the *Amen,* which everyone saith, is not an expression of any wish made that the thing may come to pass, but only an intimation that it is so. For in truth it signifies in this case, not *so be it,* as it usually does, but *so it is;* which would be so nevertheless though it were not pronounced. Our *Liturgy* hath also set forms of administring Baptism, Marriage, and for the visitation of the sick, all very proper and fitted to their subject. It hath also a form for the Confirmation of Children, which binds the Parents and the Ministers to bring them to their Bishop, to render him an account of their Faith when they are capable; to make a solemn and public profession that they will live and die in the belief, and observation of those things their Godfathers and Godmothers promised for them at their Baptisms, that they should believe and do, and after that to receive the blessing from their Pastor, who gives it them solemnly with the Imposition of hands, and with Prayers. . . . And as Children are the gift of God, and as they are formed in the Womb and come out of it into the light of the living, through his wonderful goodness, wisdom, and power; the Church commands that the Mothers, being risen out of Childbed, come upon their first going abroad into the public Assembly, there to return thanks to God for so signal a mercy, and prescribes the manner wherein to do it. Finally, it is therein ordered that the dead be buried in a decent and solemn manner, in hope of a blessed Resurrection. And to the intent that Ministers, who together with their relations and friends come to perform this their last duty to them, may not be silent in an occasion wherein so much may be said, and that they may comfort them who survive; and lay before them the shortness and vanity of this life, and exhort them to improve it to their best advantage while God suffers them to enjoy it. There are certain places of Scripture appointed, such as are fit for that purpose, which they are enjoined to read; whereunto they are to add certain Prayers, not for the dead, to whom they are useless, but for the living that they may profit by the example that is set before their eyes.

It is required of the people that they repeat aloud the *Confession of Sins,* that they may be the more sensibly affected therewith. . . .

In like manner we are enjoined by the Church to lift up our

voice to God with one accord, to the end that the *Confession* of our *Sins,* and the *Prayers* we join therewith, may obtain pardon for them, and produce the same effect in moving his tender compassions toward us. And these joint supplications of ours will infallibly have this effect, if the heart which sends them, and the mouth which utters them, doth at the same time stir up the bowels, and the whole man to a true compunction, according to the intention of our wise and pious *Reformers.*

The Prayers of our *Liturgy* are short for the most part (for a reason must also be rendered of this shortness, since some dislike it) and they do seldom comprise more then one thing, to the intent they may be the better comprehended and may cause the less distraction when they are made. And to the end the whole Congregation may be quickened up to a necessary attention, and that they may feel the secret motions of a holy joy, the Church hath thought fit they should bear a part in the rehearsal of the *Canticles of Praise;* as of this, *We praise thee O God, we acknowledge thee,* and of the like. The repeating of certain Prayers which contentious persons call *vain repetitions* are outward ejaculations, and productions of the inward zeal of a pious Soul, like unto that reiterating of our Savior's upon the Cross, *My God, my God;* and that of Saint *Thomas, My Lord and my God,* when, being surprised, he acknowledged his error. They are like to those Repetitions of the fifty-seventh *Psalm: Be merciful unto me O God, be merciful unto me.* And of the 123rd *Psalm, Have mercy upon us O Lord, have mercy upon us.* And to the raptures of the *Seraphims* when they cry out thrice, *Holy, Holy, Holy, Is.* 6. It is the fervent zeal for God's glory, and the holy ecstasies that men are seized with through the contemplation of his incomprehensible perfections: and it is the earnest longing that they have to be heard, which naturally causeth them to utter such repetitions. And when it was ordered by those who framed these parts of our *Liturgy* that they should be therein inserted, it was done partly out of a charitable supposition that that earnest zeal, and those holy raptures and vehement longings which beget them when they are in the heart, from whence they

69

ought to ascend into the mouth, would really place them there; and partly to stir them up and to beget them in the heart when they are not there, and to increase them when they are but faintly in it. As experience teacheth all truly devout and pious souls that these things contribute to the mutual production of one another. The zeal, the joy, and the fervent affection produce these Repetitions of *Praises* and *Prayers;* and these Reiterations beget a godly zeal, a spiritual rejoicing, and an earnest desire of being heard. I confess that these Repetitions are vain, if they are made without affection and attention; but then it is the vice and the fault of the persons, and not of the thing. If men fell into that error which our Saviour prohibits, when he saith, *Use not vain repetitions,* as often as they repeat the same word, or sentence, or prayer more then once, *David* among others had fallen into a very gross one, repeating in the 136th *Psalm* six and twenty times these words; *O give thanks unto the Lord, for his mercy endureth for ever.* And in the 150th where he repeats no less then thirteen times (though this *Psalm* contains but six verses, and those very short) *Praise the Lord.* And when these *Psalms* are sung in all the Reformed Churches of *Europe* according to the order therein established, do they not commit the same fault? We also have been guilty of it, as many of us as have at this day sung these words of the *Psalm, Let the people praise thee O God, let all the people praise thee,* and the same again a little lower.

But it were a small matter if the censure of contentious persons did only light upon us, and upon all the Reformed Churches. It were a light thing if it fell only upon Prophets, nay upon holy Angels, Seraphims, and Cherubins. But their censuring of us (which I conjure them seriously to consider) becomes a blasphemy against the Person itself of the Son of God, Jesus Christ our Lord, since it also lights upon him. For that gracious Redeemer being in his Agony, and praying to his Father, doubtless with most vehement affection, repeated three times the same Prayer. And again he went away and prayed, *and spake the same words,* as Saint *Matthew* and Saint *Mark* expressly observe in the faithful Narration of that mournful passage of his Life. And Saint *Luke* saith that the *last time he prayed more earnestly,* though he repeated the same words. If this great example doth not stop the mouths of all contentious persons as to this subject, all that remains for us to do in their behalf, is to commend them to God, and not to give over *repeating* our prayers for them, until we see them become more reasonable.

These Repetitions which I spake of but now, which follow one another either immediately or very near, are not, nor ought to be made (as the thing itself declares) but of certain words or sentences, or very short prayers. . . .

The public and solemn Service which we render to God in Church Assemblies, is intermixed (as I have already said) with Prayers, Lessons, Hymns, and Rehearsals of *Creeds,* so that we pray at certain several Returns. And as often as we bend our knees before God in Prayer, we join to our other Prayers either in the beginning, or middle, or end of them, that which our Savior himself hath taught us, and the which he hath sanctified with his own mouth. And such is our *custom,* both because our Savior, when he gave us this *Form of Prayer,* commanded us *to say it when we pray.* And because it is a most perfect Prayer, which comprehends all we can stand in need of, and which supplies whatsoever can be wanting and imperfect in those we make ourselves. . . .

The peoples saying *Amen* at the end of every prayer, in token of their attention, consent, and devotion, is grounded upon the express words of Saint *Paul,* I *Cor.* 14, and confirmed by the practice of the Primitive Church as stands upon Record in the Writings of the purest and most venerable Antiquity, *Justin Martyr. Apolog.* 2.

The Pastors inviting the people to join with them in celebrating the praises of God, and their Responses set together, make a sacred Harmony, imitating the manner wherein *Esay cap.* 6 and Saint *John (Revel.* 19) represent that Saints and Angels praise the Lord in Heaven, answering one another at several turns (among other things) *Holy, Holy, Holy, Amen, Hallelujah, Amen, Hallelujah,* that is to say, *So be it, praise the Lord, So be it, praise the Lord,* not believing that either they have, or that he can ever be, sufficiently praised. The frequent repetition of our *Glory be to the Father, and to the Son, and to the Holy Ghost,* is also an imitation of the same Doxology of these Triumphant Spirits. And it was introduced into the Church in opposition to the enemies of the Trinity of persons in the Godhead. And as there never wanted such pernicious Heretics, the use of it hath been still retained in the Church, and placed (as was judged most convenient) at the end of every *Psalm* and of some other *Canticles;* it being reasonably supposed that the words therein contained ought to excite and stir up all the faithful who heard, recited, or meditated there to praise the Lord and magnify his holy name.

---

(17) **William Beveridge**
Bishop of St. Asaph
A Sermon on the Excellency and Usefulness
of the Common Prayer
1681 / 1682

The words being thus briefly explained, I shall now apply them to our present purpose and show that that form of religious worship which is prescribed by our Church, established by the laws of the land, and therefore to be used now in this place, agrees exactly with this rule or canon of the Holy Apostle, even that *all things in it are done to edify.*

But before we prove that that form in particular which our Church has prescribed is agreeable to this Apostolical rule, it is necessary to prove first that the prescribing a form in general is so. For unless the prescribing a form in general be according to this rule, no form in particular that is prescribed can possibly agree with it. But now that this rule admits, yea, requires the prescribing of some form is evident from the rule itself; for the Apostle here commands the Church of Corinth, and so all provincial Churches, to take care that in their religious assemblies *all things be done to edify.* But how is it possible for any provincial Church to see that this be done, except she prescribes some certain form for the doing of it? If every minister of a parish should be left to his own liberty to do what he pleaseth in his own congregation, although some, perhaps, might be so prudent as to observe this rule as well as they could, yet, considering the corruption of human nature, we have much cause to fear that others would not; at least the Church could be no way secured that all would, and, therefore, must needs be obliged to consider of and appoint some such form to be used in all her congregations, by which she may be fully assured that this Apostolical rule is everywhere observed as it ought to be. And although we should suppose, what can never be expected, that all the clergy in every province should be as wise and as good as they ought to be, yet it cannot be supposed that every one of them should understand what is for the edification of the people as well as all together. And, therefore, it must needs be acknowledged that the surest way to have this rule observed is for the governors of every Church and the whole clergy to meet together by their representatives in a synod or convocation; and there, upon mature deliberation, agree upon some such form which they, in their prudence and consciences, judge to be according to this rule, which the Apostle here lays down before them.

And, besides that the prescribing a form in general is more for our edifying than to leave everyone to do what seems good in his own eyes, we have the concurrent testimony, experience, and practice of the Universal Church; for we never read or heard of any Church in the world, from the Apostles' days to ours, but what took this course. Though all have not used the same, yet no Church but have used some form or other. And, therefore, for any man to say that it is not lawful, or not expedient, or not to edify, to use a form of prayer in the public worship of God, is to contradict the general sense of Christianity, to condemn the Holy Catholic Church, and to make himself wiser than all Christians that ever were before him; which, whatsoever it may be thought now, was always heretofore reckoned one of the greatest sins and follies that a man could be guilty of.

Nay, more than all this too. For this is not only to make a man's self wiser than all Christians, but wiser than Christ Himself; for it is impossible to prescribe any form of prayer in more plain and express terms than He hath done it, where He saith, *When ye pray, say, Our Father Which art in Heaven,* etc. And I hope none here present but will acknowledge that Christ, by Whom alone we can be edified, knows better what is or what is not for our edification than we, or all the men in the world, can do. And therefore, seeing He hath not only prescribed a form of prayer for His Disciples to use, but hath expressly commanded them to use it, we, who profess ourselves to be His Disciples, ought to rest fully satisfied in our minds that using of a form of prayer is not only lawful but much more for our edifying than it is possible for any other way of praying to be.

The same may be proved also from the nature of the thing itself, by such arguments which do not only demonstrate that it is so, but likewise show how it comes to be so. For, first, in order for us to be edified, so as to be made better and holier, whensoever we meet together upon a religious account it is necessary that the same good and holy things be always inculcated and pressed upon us after one and the same manner. For we cannot but all find by our own experience how difficult it is to fasten anything that is truly good either upon ourselves or others; and that it is rarely, if ever, effected without frequent repetitions of it. Whatsoever good things we hear only once, or now and then, though perhaps upon the hearing of them they may swim for a while in our brains, yet they seldom sink down into our hearts so as to move and sway the affections, as it is

74

necessary they should do, in order for us to be edified by them. Whereas, by a set form of public devotions rightly composed, we are continually put in mind of all things necessary for us to know or do; so long as they are always done by the same words and expressions, which, by their constant use, will imprint the things themselves so firmly in our minds that it will be no easy matter to obliterate or raze them out; but, do what we can, they will still occur upon all occasions, which cannot but be very much for our Christian edification.

Moreover, that which conduceth to the quickening our souls and to the raising up our affections in our public devotions must needs be acknowledged to conduce much to our edification. But it is plain that for such purposes a set form of prayer is an extraordinary help to us. For if I hear another pray and know not beforehand what he will say, I must first listen to what he will say next; then I am to consider whether what he saith be agreeable to sound doctrine, and whether it be proper and lawful for me to join with him in the petitions he puts up to God Almighty; and if I think it is so, then I am to do it. But before I can well do that, he is got to another thing; by which means it is very difficult, if not morally impossible, to join with him in everything so regularly as I ought to do. But by a set form of prayer all this trouble is prevented; for having the form continually in my mind, being thoroughly acquainted with it, fully approving of everything in it, and always knowing before-hand what will come next, I have nothing else to do, whilst the words are sounding in mine ears, but to move my heart and affections suitably to them, to raise up my desires of those good things which are prayed for, to fix my mind wholly upon God whilst I am praising of Him, and so to employ, quicken, and lift up my whole soul in performing my devotions to Him. No man that hath been accustomed to a set form for any considerable time, but may easily find this to be true by his own experience, and, by consequence, that this way of praying is a greater help to us than they can imagine that never made trial of it.

To this may also be added, that if we hear another praying a prayer of his own composition or voluntary effusion, our minds are wholly bound up and confined to his words and expressions, and to his requests and petitions, be they what they will; so that, at the best, we can but pray his prayer. Whereas, when we pray by a form prescribed by the Church we pray the prayers of the whole Church we live in, which are common to the minister and people, to ourselves, and to all the members of the same Church, so that we have all the devout and pious souls that are in it concurring and joining with us in them; which cannot, surely, but be more effectual for the edifying, not only of ourselves in particular, but of the Church in general, than any private prayer can be.

---

(18) **William Beveridge**
Bishop of St. Asaph
***The Great Necessity and Advantage of Public Prayer and
Frequent Communion, designed to revive Primitive Piety, with
Meditations, Ejaculations, and Private Prayers before, at, and
after the Sacrament***
1708

This, therefore is that which I shall now endeavour to do. Not that I can pretend to search into all the *Reasons,* if they may be so called, which keep Men from our *daily Prayers.* Some, I believe, have none but their *own Wills,* with such it would be in vain to argue. But they which have any *Shadow of Reason* for it, though some have *one,* some *another,* as they themselves best know, yet I humbly conceive they may all be *reduced* to these *following Heads,* which I shall now consider.

First, therefore, some will not come to our Prayers because as they pretend, they do not *like* them. But why *do not* they like them? Is there any Thing in them contrary to the *Word of God,* or unbecoming His Service? That most of them, be sure, can't say; for they never *read* nor *heard* them in their Lives, nor are suffered to do it by those which have Power over them, lest they *should* see, as they certainly *would,* their *Error* or Mistake. And they, who have sometimes, perhaps, *read* or *heard* them, if they would but impartially examine them by God's *Revealed Will,* cannot but acknowledge them to be *exactly consonant* and *agreeable* to it. And some of them have *testified* the same by joining in with them *upon Occasion,* which, it is supposed, they would never have done, if they thought it *unlawful;* as it must needs be if there be any Thing in them *contrary* to *God's Word.* But why then do they not do it often? Why not *every Day?* The great Reason which they pretend is because our *Prayers* are *read* out of a *Book;* and they had rather hear a Man *pray* by heart, and *Extempore,* which they think to be more *edifying.* But the Contrary to that hath been often *demonstrated* beyond all *Contradiction;* together with the *many* and *great* Inconveniences which usually *follow* upon such *private extempore* Prayers in *Public,* not to be suffered in the Church of CHRIST, as they never were in any Part of it till of late Years, and then, too, nowhere else but in this Island. And therefore at present I would *only* desire *those* who separate from our *public* Prayers, not out of *Humor* or *Faction* but merely out of an *erroneous* and *misguided* Conscience, of which Sort I hope there are *some:* I would *desire* such to consider whether the great Promise which our Savior hath made to *public* Prayers can possibly be applied to their Way of *praying.* To me it seems impossible, in that they do not perform the *Condition* required in it. The Promise I *mentioned* before, it runs thus: *Again I say unto you, that if Two of you shall agree on Earth, as touching any Thing that they shall ask, it shall be done for them of my Father which is in Heaven, Mt.* 18: 19, It is plain that this Promise belongs to *public* Prayers, such as are made by several Persons together, at the least by *two.* And it is as plain also that it belongs to *public* Prayers, wherein those several Persons *agree* together *beforehand* what they shall ask or pray for. But where

77

the *Minister* useth only an *extempore* Prayer, how many People soever may be present at it, there are *no Two* of them who agree what they shall ask: That is left wholly to the *Minister,* none of the People so much as knowing what he intends to ask; nor himself neither before he hath asked it. They may perhaps agree to it after they have heard it, and perhaps not: But if they do, that is not the Thing which the Promise requires; for it is made *only* to *those* who *agree* touching any Thing that they shall ask; and so requires a previous Agreement upon the Matter of our *public* Prayers before we put them up to *Almighty God,* which they who use only *extemporary Prayers* can by no Means pretend to, nor, by Consequence, to this great Promise of *God's* granting what they ask.

BUT now in the *public* Prayers of the Church, we keep close to the *Conditions* of the Promise: We *ask* nothing but what we all agree beforehand shall be asked. All the *Clergy* in *England* by their *Procurators* in *Convocation* and all the *Commons* by their *Representatives* in *Parliament* agreed together touching every Thing that should be asked every Day in the Year. And so do all that come to the Prayers; they all know before what shall be then asked, and *accordingly* agree in the asking of it; and therefore have *sure Ground* to believe, that God, according to His Promise, will do it for them.

---

(19) **Thomas Bisse**
Preacher at the Rolls Chapel, Chancellor of Hereford Cathedral
The Beauty of Holiness in the Common Prayer
1716

Worship the Lord in the beauty of holiness

Since the worship of God is the greatest and most honourable among all the acts and employments of the children of men, from which as the meanest are not excluded, so neither are the greatest exempted; since the highest among men, even they that sit on thrones, must bow down before the altars of the Most High, and do never appear in so true glory in the eyes of God and of men, as when, like those above, they fall down before the throne, and *cast their crowns before the throne;* surely this universal work or duty of man ought to be set off with the greatest order and magnificence, with *the beauty of holiness.* When king David left instructions to Solomon for building the temple, he gave in charge that it should be *exceeding magnifical:* and the reason afterwards given is itself exceeding awful as well as just: *for,* saith he, *the palace is not for man, but for the Lord God.* As the house of God, so the worship performed in it should in like manner be *exceeding magnifical.* For it is a work of a superior and incommunicable nature: it is not a respect paid to our superiors; it is not an offering made to our governors; it is not a homage done to our princes; no—worship *is not for man, but for the Lord God.*

Upon this account, when God chose Israel for his peculiar people, we find that both in the first framing of their worship by the hand of Moses, and afterwards in the enlarging of it by the hand of David, he left nothing to the invention of man. For as the tabernacle, with all the vessels of the ministry, was made *according to the pattern* God *showed to* Moses *in the mount;* so when David gave to Solomon the pattern of the temple, to wit, of the porch, of the place of the mercy-seat, of the courts of the treasury of the dedicate things, also for the courses of the priests and levites, and for all the work of the service and for all the vessels of the service in the house of the Lord; *All this,* said David, *the Lord made me to understand in writing by his hand upon me, even all the works of this pattern.*

79

Now as this temple was made after the pattern of the tabernacle, though in much larger dimensions; so the Christian Church is built after the pattern of the Jewish, though of a much larger comprehension. Christ, the builder of it, was pleased to erect it upon the same plan, to retain the like essentials, like in nature and in number. For instance; as the entrance into the Jewish Church was by circumcision, so the entrance into the Christian Church is by baptism. Again, as every one that was circumcised, and thereby become an Israelite, was obliged to eat of the passover; so every one that is baptized, and thereby become a Christian, is bound to partake of the Lord's supper. These two sacraments, baptism and the Lord's supper, being ordained by Christ himself, are doubtless essential to his Church; insomuch that if there be any congregation that calls itself a Church of Christ while it retains not these essentials, we may pronounce of it that it *is none of his.*

Again, as in the Jewish Church there were appointed three orders in the priesthood, high priest, priests, and levites; so in the Christian Church are appointed bishops, priests, and deacons, in a like subordination. This ecclesiastical government in these three orders, which was appointed by Christ and planted by his Apostles, and so continued down in all churches of the saints, is no less essential to the Christian Church than the levitical priesthood in the like orders was to the Jewish. For as St. Paul asserts concerning this latter, there being a change of the priesthood, there is *of necessity a change also of the law,* that is, the whole Jewish polity; so may we not as strongly argue concerning the former—should there be a change of the priesthood, must not there be of necessity a change also of the Church, that is, the whole evangelical establishment? But however that be, however God may dispense with the breach of his own ordinance, yet let us pour out our daily thanks to him in the congregation, that these three orders are rightly retained and the two sacraments duly administered in our established Church.

Thus then the essentials of the Church of God were prescribed and commanded to us Christians, as they had been before to the Jews: but then as to the ceremonials, the modes, the times, and circumstances of worship, the habits of the priesthood, the courses of their ministry, the vessels of the sanctuary; in a word, *all that is for the work of the service in the house of the Lord*—all these things which were prescribed under the law are now under the gospel left at liberty, without any particular direction or restraint, but only that general rule or canon of the Apostles—*Let all things be done decently and in order.*

This apostolical canon hath been faithfully observed by those holy men who compiled the form of our established worship. Those *wise master builders,* who at the REFORMATION had the charge of that great work, contrived all its ceremonies with such significancy, placed all its offices in such regularity, that we may justly take up that boast of Tyrus concerning our Zion, that her *builders have perfected* her *beauty.*

My present undertaking shall be to vindicate and recommend the public service of our Liturgy or Common Prayer; that so all they who upon that account *have evil will at* our Zion *may be confounded;* and that all those who for the sake of her worship wish her prosperity, may be confirmed. To this end have I chosen this exhortation of holy David, that *man after* God's *own heart,* the first of men desirous to build a house for God, above all men zealous, above all men skilled in ordering all things in the offices thereof; and whom, as a peculiar reward of his pious zeal, God hath so highly honoured as that his language hath been the general language of God's Church even unto this day. Hearken therefore unto this exhortation, taken out of that psalm of thanksgiving which David delivered to the priests and levites, now first established into a choir, to be sung continually before the ark of the covenant of God, as we read in the beginning of this chapter—*Worship the Lord in the beauty of holiness.*

Which words contain two qualifications, the one absolutely necessary, the other highly fitting for the worship of God. The first is that it be holy; the second that it be also beautiful; and when both these are united, then may we be said to *worship the*

Lord in the beauty of holiness. And both these we hope to show to be in the most eminent degree contained in our Liturgy, that is, the form of common prayer established in our holy and renowned Church.

---

(20) **Samuel Johnson**
*Priest and missionary in Connecticut from the Society
for the Propagation of the Gospel,
first president of King's College (Columbia University)*
**On the Beauty of Holiness in the Worship
of the Church of England**
1749

Worship consists in a most serious and solemn address to the great creator, preserver, and governor of the world; testifying from the bottom of our hearts our dependence upon Him, and submission to Him; praising Him for every thing we enjoy, praying to Him for whatsoever we want, and devoting ourselves sincerely and entirely to his service. Now all these things are abundantly provided for in our forms, as I shall show you presently: and that in the best manner, which is certainly best done by public forms, established by lawful authority, and known and agreed to by all the worshippers. For how can I worship God with the full devotion of my soul, unless I have beforehand satisfied myself with what I am to offer up? And how can a worshiping assembly jointly and with one heart and soul, and with a full assurance of faith, offer up their prayers and praises to God, unless they have properly a Common Prayer, and are beforehand all satisfied that what is to be offered is both agreeable to the will of God, and suitable to their common necessities and occasions? And how can they otherwise offer up their public devotions agreeable to Christ's express instructions, who plainly requireth, they should be agreed touching what they would ask, as a condition of their receiving it? *Mt.* 18: 19. If two of you shall agree on earth, as touching any thing they shall ask, it shall be done for them of my Father which is in Heaven. If there were a number of us to ask a favor of an earthly prince or governor, we should be very careful and exact in composing our address; we should take great care that it be well ordered, and that we be all fully agreed beforehand, both in the matter and manner of our address. How much more when we are to address the great God of Heaven and earth, and that for the life, even the eternal life of our souls, how fit and necessary is it, that we should accurately compose our address, and be beforehand well agreed and satisfied, both in the matter and manner of it; so as to have nothing to do when we come to offer it, but to offer up our whole souls with it, and make it our most devout free act and deed?

. . .

How happy are we, my brethren, who have a most excellent form prepared for us, by some of the wisest and best men that ever lived, and many of whom underwent the fire of martyrdom for what they did? I say, that we have, by them an excellent form of public devotion compiled for us, chiefly out of the Word of God, and conformed to it, in which, therefore, if we believe the Scriptures, we must be perfectly agreed and satisfied; so that when we come to worship God in public, we have nothing else to do but to prepare our hearts, and give up our whole souls, and exert the utmost force of our minds and hearts in offering it up to our Heavenly Father; and so can with one mind and one mouth, glorify God, even the Father of our Lord Jesus Christ, as St. Paul requires, Rom. xv. 16. (which is scarcely possible in the extempore way) and which we plainly see to be a true method of worship, as it contains praises to God for every thing we enjoy, both temporal and spiritual and prayers for every thing we can want, either for soul or body, either for ourselves or others. Let us therefore be heartily thankful to God's good providence, that we have such an excellent method of public worship, and let us make a faithful use of it to the best purposes; in order to which, let each one have his Book, and keep it in his eye, the better to engage his attention, that avoiding all indecent gazing about, we may make it the business of our souls, in the House of God, to offer it up with the sincerest and most intense devotion.

---

(21) **Thomas Secker**
Archbishop of Canterbury
**Sermon XXIV, on the Lawfulness and Expediency
of Forms of Prayer**
c. 1758–1768

---

1 Cor. 14:15.

I *will pray with the spirit, and I will pray with the understanding also: I will sing with the spirit, and I will sing with the understanding also.* Some then apprehend that there is such a gift or spirit of prayer bestowed by the Holy Ghost on true Christians, and peculiarly on all that are worthy to be ministers of God's Word, as enables them to address themselves to Heaven on all occasions, copiously and suitably, in unpremeditated words of their own: which they think ought not be restrained by appointing forms, even for the public use of congregations. And sometimes the text is quoted in support of this opinion. But plainly, so far as it relates to words, it relates to words inspired; to which in the strict sense but few of these persons themselves lay any claim: for indeed it would be equaling their own compositions to the holy Scripture. And excepting this miraculous gift of inspired prayer, the word of God mentions no gift of ready expression in prayer: nor have we the least ground to consider it as coming from above, any otherwise than as *every good gift,* every natural ability which God had conferred upon us, and every improvement which he qualifies us to make by our own industry *is from above.* For evidently this talent is one of that sort: depending partly on the fluency of speech to which people are born, partly on the art and diligence which they use to increase it; and varying as their health and spirits vary. Nor therefore is there any more harm in restraining this faculty if good reasons require it than in restraining any other. Even the extraordinary gifts of the Spirit, you have seen, were frequently put under some restraints: much more than may one of our ordinary powers. And they who call it limiting and stinting the Spirit have no Scripture warrant, either for the phrase or the thing which they understand by it. Nay supposing the Holy Ghost did ever so peculiarly assist in directing the words of prayer, why should we not think him as likely to have assisted in the drawing up of the established forms as in the extempore performances of those who reject forms and trust to the sudden dictates of their own fancy?

The *spirit of prayer* and *praying in* or *by the spirit* are indeed Scripture terms: but, so far as they belong to the present age, they signify not being furnished with variety of phrases in prayer but a much more valuable blessing, having religious affections breathed into us by the Holy Ghost for the exercise of this duty. And *quenching the spirit,* in the only sense which can be applied to us, means extinguishing such affections by indulging sin, or suffering them to die away through negligence. God is no more delighted with change of expressions than with a repetition of the same: nor will ever be weary of a devout soul for want of new language. Common reason pronounces this: and the Bible confirms it. We find several forms of prayer prescribed on several occasions in the law of Moses. We find afterwards a whole book of forms, the Psalms of David. We find our Savior frequenting the Jewish synagogue, which constantly used a form, and a very mean one. We find him enjoining his

Disciples a form of his own composing for them: *When ye pray, say, Our Father,* and so on. Nay, at the very time when the gift of inspired prayer was common, there is a strong appearance in the fourth chapter of the Acts that the Apostles and their followers used a form there set down. For how else could *they lift up their voice, and say it with one accord,* as verse 24 assures us they did? Probably the very next age after them practiced this method of public worship, at least in a good measure: and for more than 1400 years past it hath been without question almost universally the only one. There is not at this day a Christian Church in the world but what uses in part of their service, if not throughout it, forms of human composition; excepting that of Scotland, which had one immediately upon the reformation, though it afterwards fell into disuse; and the dissenters from our own, who, notwithstanding, many of them sing in their assemblies hymns that are forms of human composition, without scruple. Yet if extempore prayers be required, extempore praises are too. For it is equally said, *I will pray with the spirit,* and *I will sing with the spirit.*

It may be replied indeed that supposing forms of prayer lawful, they are not however expedient. But if that be all, so long as the vastly greater, and the ruling part think otherwise, ought not the rest to acquiesce? Is it not much less expedient to make a separation and division in the church, when Christ and his Apostles have so strongly prescribed unity and submission?

But why are forms of prayer inexpedient? It is argued that they cannot be altered according to circumstances, which extempore prayers may. And with respect to private devotion, the argument is so far of weight that though even in this, forms well chosen are excellent directions, yet no one should confine himself closely to them when his condition, spiritual or temporal, requires him to depart from them: but should omit, or add, or vary, as he perceives occasion; in which he may well hope that God's Holy Spirit will guide him, so far as is needful. But the circumstances of whole congregations, taken together, are in the main almost always the same: and therefore may be expressed in the same words. Besides, public offices make a stated provision for the more usual accidents that happen: and public authority provides for the rest occasionally, from time to time. Indeed an established liturgy doth not allow the cases of private persons or families, or the situation, real or supposed, of national affairs, to be enlarged on to God, at the discretion of the minister: a thing never necessary, and seldom proper. It is very sufficient that they who desire the rest of the assembly to join with them in petitions or thanksgivings on fit subjects relating to themselves have opportunity afforded them of signifying their desire: and that general expressions in the service may be applied more especially to particular purposes by each member in his own mind, as he conceives there is need. If these things be carefully done, forms of prayer will be found not so often defective perhaps in the matter of uncommon and extraordinary wants or mercies, as extempore prayers in what is far more necessary, expressing common and ordinary ones.

But some insist that, whatever may be said, they experience that forms do not edify and excite devotion. And this may be true, while they are unaccustomed to them and come with prejudice against them. But would they make trial of them for some time, with a serious endeavour of receiving benefit from them, they would not fail to find that true spirit of piety raised by them in their own hearts, of which we hope they would see many instances in their fellow worshipers. It is true, a form doth not afford the entertainment of novelty. But that hath nothing to do with devotion. The hearer may be highly delighted, the speaker highly admired: and all this may be mere amusement of the fancy and no prayer in reality, offered up by him who is best pleased with it. What alone deserves that name is a reverent application to God, from a deep sense of our necessities and blessings and his power and goodness: which a form deliberately precomposed by the joint counsels of a number of persons whom the public wisdom hath chosen for that end is surely more likely both to excite and to express fitly than the hasty produce of each private minister's invention: especially as he is expected by his people to vary even this continually, though it be for the worse.

One man will doubtless excel another in this way: and some perhaps may, really or seemingly, surpass at some times the public forms. But what multitudes would there be who through inability, carelessness, want of memory, diffidence, or imprudence would fall vastly short of them, were every minister in the nation to use, every time he officiates, a new prayer of his own devising upon the spot? How often doth it happen, were we to know the truth, among the small number of our dissenters, that the person praying hesitates and is at a loss, omits things necessary or useful, expresses himself obscurely, improperly, irreverently, works himself into gestures and accents by no means edifying, not to say worse? All which must grievously hurt the devotion of those who desire to pay God a *reasonable service,* and bring thoughts into their minds extremely unsuitable to the work in which they are engaged. Then what danger is there in this way that men may fill their public addresses to Heaven with their own private, it may be absurd and pernicious, notions and opinions: that national prayers may change, like fashions and fancies, and the faith of Christians change along with them, which the weight and authority of an established liturgy greatly contributes to keep steadfast and preserve from noxious errors? What danger is there also, that persons, either by ill design or ill-judging zeal, may mix their interests, their passions, their party attachments of various kinds with the requests and thanksgivings which they utter in the name of the congregation; may inflame one part of the neighborhoood, one part of their fellow subjects, against another; stir up some to mischief under colour of its being the cause of God; and by so doing make his worship abhorred by the rest? I am far from charging the body of those among us who use extempore prayer with being guilty of these things now. I am only representing what evils a more general use of it would be likely to produce, especially in times of public discord. Indeed most of them, if not all, it formerly hath produced: and preventing them is much easier and every way better than punishing them.

But supposing these inconveniences avoided, another, very considerable, would remain. Let their dislike of forms be ever so great, the words of their minister in praying are as absolutely a form to them for the time as the words of a national liturgy: but with this unhappy difference, that his expressions being continually varied, possibly the most judicious, at least the slower and more ignorant may often doubt of their meaning; and the scrupulous, of their fitness: and though, upon consideration, they should be satisfied, yet he in the meanwhile is gone on to something else. And thus they may follow after him through the whole of a prayer, and be able to overtake and really join with him in but a small part of it: whereas a form may always be examined beforehand; and when it is once understood and found to be right, our judgment and affections will go together in the use of it, without let or hindrance; and we shall be edified, not in imagination but reality.

Upon the whole, the reasons for a public liturgy are so strong that Calvin, the most universally esteemed by our dissenting brethren of all the reformers, in a letter to the protector of England, under Edw. VI. hath these words. *"As to a form of prayer and of ecclesiastical rites, I highly approve that it should be certain, from which it may not be lawful for any minister to depart: as well in consideration of the weakness and ignorance of some, as that it may more plainly appear, how our churches agree amongst themselves; and lastly, that a stop may be put to the giddiness of those, who affect novelties."*

Still I am sensible that some of the arguments which I have urged against devotions composed by the minister may seem to lie equally against sermons composed by him; and to require that instruction be in a constant form, as well as prayer. But besides that one hath been the *custom of the churches of God,* the other not; prayer is the voice of the people to their Heavenly Father, and should therefore be preserved, with singular caution, from every thing which they ought not to say, or may not

89

immediately comprehend or approve; else, in such parts of the service, either they do not pray at all or they pray amiss. But preaching is the voice of the minister to the people, which they may weigh and judge of at their leisure: and even should they fail of learning their duty from thence, they may learn it from a much higher authority, the lessons of Scripture read to them. Further, where a fixed form of worship is appointed, instruction may be left at liberty more safely; because it will be observed if the latter contradicts the former: and also very usefully, because a much greater variety of things is requisite to be said to the people in sermons than is needful for them to say to Heaven in their prayers. But how proper soever it may be to have some form, they who dissent from us apprehend there are such great imperfections and faults in the established form that if they must *pray with the Spirit and with the understanding* they must not pray by that. Now imperfections will be found in everything human: and if these be a sufficient objection against our prayers, it will hold against their own and all prayers, excepting that of our blessed Lord. From everything unlawful we are ready to prove that our service book is entirely free. But the faults of extempore devotions, which are different in every congregation and every time of meeting in the same congregation, easily escape the notice of such as are prejudiced in their favour, who alone hear them: and when observed, it is only by a few, and they are soon forgotten; while those that are charged on a public printed liturgy lie open constantly, year after year, to the censure of every one. And were it possible that the several prayers offered up in any one day in the several dissenting assemblies of this kingdom could be written down and examined half so narrowly for a short space as ours have been for two centuries together: can it be imagined that many times more and worse omissions and improprieties would not be found in almost every one of them than they have pretended to find in our Common Prayer? Still we are far from saying it is incapable of any alteration for the better. Yet this we must say, that most of the alterations proposed by some persons have been thought by others, every way their equals, if not superiors, by no means to be amendments. And as eminent a nonconformist as ever was, Mr. Baxter, hath long since owned that almost every church on earth hath a worse liturgy, than ours.

There hath indeed been *a railing accusation,* even of Popery, brought against it: though it was first compiled, then reviewed and approved, by confessors and martyrs for the Protestant cause; and several articles of Popery are as flatly contradicted in it as can be. Some parts of it, we acknowledge, were in the Romish offices before: but not one-tenth of the whole, as a very diligent person hath computed. Most of this tenth part also was in much ancienter offices, before the Romish corruptions were introduced. And had it not; as even these prayers are entirely free from those corruptions, where can be the harm of using them? Had our reformers rejected them, they would have been in reality never the farther distant from the Papists. And by retaining them, they had a prospect of bringing many of the Papists over to themselves: by showing that they did not act from passion and prejudice, but reason and consideration; that they respected the ancient offices and usages of the purer ages of the Church, and departed only from modern abuses and errors.

It hath also been alleged that we wear the habits of the Papists in offering up these prayers. But indeed, though it were no way material if we did, ours are very different from theirs. And if wearing any which are not in common use be condemned, what cause is there for it? why may not sacred, as well as civil offices of dignity and importance, be made somewhat more solemn by vestments appropriated to them? The fitness of it hath been confessed by the constant practice of mankind, and particularly of the Christian Church in early ages, and of our Dissenting Ministers themselves; who change their dress a little when they officiate. And where is the harm, if we change ours a little more? After all, if the wearing of such garments by the clergy were a fault, it would be entirely our own fault: and seeing us wear them could surely hurt nobody.

But besides these general objections, there are several made against particular passages, which ought to be confuted. This therefore I intend, God willing, to do in a proper number of discourses on all the stated offices of our Liturgy: and not only to vindicate what is blamed, but explain also what too many may possibly not understand; and direct your notice to what may not be sufficiently observed. All these things will very well come under the head of which I promised at first to treat,

That we should be very solicitous rightly to apprehend the sense and fitness of what we say and do in God's presence. For though censuring without reason is worse, yet esteeming without reason is not the part of wise men. And some perhaps are mighty zealous for our liturgy who yet know but very imperfectly what good reason they have to be zealous for it. Indeed, amongst many advantages of public forms of prayer there seems to be one disadvantage; that the words of them being in the main continually the same, and thus becoming well known and familiar, we often hear them, and even speak our share of them, with scarce any attention to them. But then it is equally true that we often hear sermons, though they are new to us, with just as little regard; and therefore should be likely very soon to hear extempore prayers also with no less negligence: which fault our liturgy is in several respects peculiarly calculated to prevent, as I shall hereafter show you. But still the danger is great enough to demand our utmost care to guard against it. For however good our public offices are in themselves, they convey no good to us farther than we comprehend the import of them and mind it: which, the better they are, the more they deserve from us. And on the other hand, were they ever so mean, this would be no excuse for omitting to get all the benefit we could from them; but a powerful motive, though a very unhappy one, to endeavour it most earnestly. Yet thinking them defective and blameable where they are not, or to a degree in which they are not, as multitudes have done, will naturally discompose, or deaden at least, our minds in the use of them: and therefore should be avoided as far as it can. Now persons may indeed, by their own private consideration, enter very competently both into the meaning and the grounds of most things contained in the liturgy. They who are able to purchase a few books may likewise receive much additional information from the several very useful paraphrases and commentaries upon it that are extant. And they are much to blame if they wilfully neglect either of these things. But still many cannot, and others are not likely to do them. To such therefore I shall attempt to give some instruction concerning the service in which we join so often. The fewer need it, the better: but those who do, it is of importance to assist. For with the more understanding we pray, with the more pleasure and earnestness we shall pray. And as on our praying, as we ought, depends our obtaining God's grace and blessing; so on that depends our only true comfort in this world and our eternal happiness in the next.

---

(22) John Henry Hobart
Bishop of New York, founder of The General Theological Seminary
A Companion for the Festivals and Fasts
of the Protestant Episcopal Church
1804

Q. *Since our Church has prescribed a form of prayer, or Liturgy, for the public service of the Church, state some of the particular advantages of forms of prayer.*

    A. When a form of prayer is used the people are previously acquainted with the prayers in which they are to join, and are thus enabled to render unto God a reasonable and enlightened service. In forms of prayer the greatest dignity and propriety of sentiment and expression may be secured. They prevent the particular opinions and dispositions of the minister from influencing the devotions of the congregation; they serve as a standard of faith and practice; and they render the service more animating by uniting the people with the minister in the performance of public worship. . . .

Q. *What are the peculiar excellences of the Liturgy prescribed by our Church?*

A. In the Liturgy of our Church there is an admirable mixture of instruction and devotion. The Lessons, the Creeds, the Commandments, the Epistles and Gospels contain the most important and impressive instruction on the doctrines and duties of religion; while the Confession, the Collects and Prayers, the Litany and Thanksgivings lead the understanding and the heart through all the sublime and affecting exercises of devotion. In this truly evangelical and excellent Liturgy the supreme Lord of the universe is invoked by the most appropriate, affecting, and sublime epithets; all the wants to which man, as a dependent and sinful being, is subject are expressed in language at once simple, concise, and comprehensive; these wants are urged by confessions the most humble, and supplications the most reverential and ardent. The all-sufficient merits of Jesus Christ, the Savior of the world, are uniformly urged as the only effectual plea, the only certain pledge of divine mercy and grace; and with the most instructive lessons from the sacred oracles and the most profound confessions and supplications is mingled the sublime chorus of praise, begun by the minister and responded with one heart and one voice from the assembled congregation. The mind, continually passing from one exercise of worship to another, and, instead of one continued and uniform prayer, sending up its wishes and aspirations in short and varied collects and supplications, is never suffered to grow languid or weary. The affections of the worshiper ever kept alive by the tender and animating fervour which breathes through the service, he worships his God and Redeemer in spirit and in truth, with reverence and awe, with lively gratitude and love; the exalted joys of devotion are poured upon his soul; he feels that it is good for him to draw

94

near unto God, and that a day spent in his courts, is better than a thousand passed in the tents of the ungodly.

---

(23) John Henry Hobart
Bishop of New York, founder of The General Theological Seminary
A Companion for the Book of Common Prayer
1805/1827
(Footnotes are from the original text)

Forms of prayer possess many important advantages. When public worship is conducted according to a prescribed form, the people are previously acquainted with the prayers in which they are to join, and are thus enabled to render unto GOD a reasonable and enlightened service. In forms of prayer that dignity and propriety of language, so necessary in supplications addressed to the infinite Majesty of Heaven, may be preserved. They prevent the particular opinions and dispositions of the minister from influencing the devotions of the congregation. They serve as a standard of faith and practice, impressing on both minister and people, at every performance of public worship, the important doctrines and duties of the Gospel. And they render the service more animating by uniting the people with the minister in the performance of public worship.
. . . Thus, then, we see how excellent and superior in all respects is the Liturgy of our Church; and how admirably she has provided for the two important objects of the public service, instruction and devotion. The lessons, the creeds, the commandments, the epistles and gospels contain the most important and impressive instruction on the doctrines and duties of religion. While the confession, the collects, and prayers, the litany and thanksgivings, lead the understanding and the heart through all the sublime and affecting exercises of devotion. In

this truly evangelical and excellent Liturgy the Supreme LORD of the universe is invoked by the most appropriate, affecting, and sublime epithets: all the wants to which man, as a dependant and sinful being, is subject are expressed in language at once simple, concise, and comprehensive; these wants are urged by confessions the most humble, and supplications the most reverential and ardent. The all-sufficient merits of JESUS CHRIST, the Savior of the world, are uniformly urged as the only effectual plea, the only certain pledge of divine mercy and grace; and with the most instructive lessons from the sacred oracles and the most profound confessions and supplications is mingled the sublime chorus of praise begun by the minister, and responded with one heart and one voice from the assembled congregation. The mind, continually passing from one exercise of worship to another, and instead of one continued and uniform prayer sending up its wishes and aspirations in short and varied collects and supplications, is never suffered to grow languid or weary. The affections of the worshiper ever kept alive by the tender and animating fervour which breathes through the service, he worships his GOD and his Redeemer in spirit and in truth, with reverence and awe, with lively gratitude and love; the exalted joys of devotion are excited in his soul; he feels that it is *good for him to draw near unto* GOD, and that *a day spent in his courts is better than a thousand passed in the tents of the ungodly.*

Thus, delightful and edifying will every person find the service who joins in it with sincerity; who unites his heart with his voice in the parts of the service assigned to the people; and who accompanies the minister in thought and affection through the supplications and prayers, lifting up his heart in secret ejaculations corresponding to the public addresses of the minister to the throne of GOD. A person who thus sincerely offers his devotions according to the Liturgy of the Church, may be satisfied that he is worshiping GOD "with the spirit and with the understanding also." The more frequently and seriously he joins in the service, the more will he be impressed with its exquisite beauties, which tend at once to gratify his taste and to quicken his devotion. That continual change of language in prayer which some persons appear to consider as essential to spiritual devotion, it would be impossible to attain, even were every minister left to his own discretion in public worship. The same expressions would necessarily recur frequently in his prayers. They would soon sink into a form destitute of that propriety and dignity of sentiment and language, of that variety, that simplicity, and affecting fervour which characterize the Liturgy of the Church. . . .

The *length* of the service has been sometimes a subject of complaint. But let every person who thus objects to the length of the service seriously consider whether this objection does not arise, in a considerable degree, from an indisposition to discharge the duties of public worship and from laying too much stress on *preaching*, which, though an appointed mean of grace, ought certainly ever to be subordinate to the more important duty of worshiping GOD. It is worthy of remark also, that the service is not entirely occupied with prayer. The reading of portions of the Holy Scriptures and the reciting of the Psalms constitute no inconsiderable part of it. The blending of instruction and devotion; the transition from prayer to praise and from one short supplication to another; the mingling of the responses of the people with the addresses of the minister afford an interesting *variety* in the service, which is one of its most excellent and valuable characteristics.

Long then may the Church preserve a form of service which is calculated to cherish in her members a spirit of devotion equally remote from dull and unprofitable lukewarmness on the one hand, and from blind, extravagant, and indecent enthusiasm on the other—a form of service which has ever served to brighten the pious graces of her members, and, in the season of declension and error, to preserve the light of divine truth and the genuine spirit of evangelical piety. With such sacred and commendable caution does the Episcopal Church in America guard the Book of Common Prayer that she exacts from all her ministers, at their ordination, a solemn promise of conformity to it; and, in one of her canons, enjoins the use of it "before all sermons and lectures, and on all other occasions of public worship," and forbids the use of any "other prayers than those prescribed in the said book."

Where indeed a form of prayer is provided, the introduction of extempore prayers would appear liable to the charges of being unnecessary and presumptuous—unnecessary because it is to be supposed that the Church has fully provided in her service for every subject of prayer; and presumptuous because it carries the idea that it is in the power of an individual to compose prayers for the congregation superior to those prepared by the united wisdom and piety of the Church. Equally presumptuous would be any attempt in an individual minister to alter the language of prayers universally admired for their correctness and their simplicity—prayers in the language of which the most eminent divines and the first scholars in every age have esteemed it an honour and a privilege to express their devotions.

If these wholesome restraints which confine the clergy to the prescribed form were removed, and every minister allowed at pleasure to alter the service, to depart from the rubrics, and to introduce prayers not approved by the Church; that uniformity of worship which constitutes one peculiar excellence of the Episcopal Church would be destroyed. No limits could be set to a liberty peculiarly liable to abuse. There would be reason to apprehend that the spirit of irregular enthusiasm, which experience proves is seldom satisfied with its encroachments or soothed by indulgence, would fundamentally change, and perhaps finally subvert that Liturgy, which is now at once the glory and safeguard of the Church, the nurse of evangelical truth and spiritual and sober devotion.[1]

[1.] A distinguished Bishop of our Church, in a sermon at a consecration thus bears his forcible testimony against all unlicensed alterations of the service: "We cannot, however, but have observed with the most poignant sorrow, that even our desire of extending the kingdom of the Redeemer, has been a door of admission to the ministry,

Against an event thus to be dreaded, let every friend of vital piety, of primitive order, of evangelical worship, most solicitously guard. Let him repress in himself and in others all tendency to innovation, all disposition to find fault with a service which has been deemed, through a long course of time, in the judgment of some of the wisest and best of men, to be the most perfect of human compositions.[2] Above all, since we enjoy "such an excellent form of prayer, let us reverence it accordingly; resort to it frequently; attend to it devoutly; accompany it not only with our *lips* but with our *hearts;* repeat what we are to repeat; and answer what we are to answer; join in every prayer of the minister with our mind, and in every response and Amen with our voice; and in all respects behave like those who are in the more immediate presence of GOD." Then will "the words of our mouths, and the meditations of our hearts, be always acceptable in thy sight, O LORD, our strength and our Redeemer."

Let every one who has received authority to minister in the sanctuary and to present the prayers of the people at the throne of GOD, let him consider it as his most sacred duty to

of persons who *disdain whatever restraints may be imposed by public reason on private fancy.* And, indeed, it gives us one of the most melancholy views which can be taken of human nature, to find evils of this magnitude arising out of a combination of extraordinary apparent piety, with *a disregard of the most explicit promises which can be made, in one of the most solemn acts to which religion can give her sanction."* Bishop White, in this last sentence, alludes to the vows at ordination, which, in the most solemn manner, bind every minister to conform to the doctrine, discipline, and worship of the Church.

2. Worthy of the serious observation of all, both ministers and people, is the judicious advice of the excellent Archbishop Secker in one of his sermons on the Common Prayer: "Supposing we should any of us apprehend that anything in the service might have been better ordered; yet we should always think of the judgment of *others* with proper *deference,* and of our *own* with *modesty.* And so long as nothing is required of us contrary to our duty, we should remember, that our concern is much more to improve by everything, than to object against anything; by which last, unless done very discreetly, we may hinder, more than a little, our own edification, and that of others." It is only on this principle of modest deference for the judgment of the Church, and of submission to her injunctions, when they do not prescribe anything sinful, that she can be saved from perpetual changes and innovations, and that unity and order preserved, so essential to her prosperity, and so frequently and earnestly inculcated by our Savior and his Apostles.

perform the service with that dignity and correctness of manner, and, above all, with that solemn and fervent spirit of piety, which, proceeding unaffectedly from his own heart, will always find its way to the hearts of the people and engage them with him in the sublime exercises of devotion.

"Let thy priests, O LORD, be clothed with salvation, that the people may rejoice."

---

(24) Thomas C. Brownell
Bishop of Connecticut
The Family Prayer Book
1823
(Footnotes are from the original text)

Of the advantages of forms of prayer for public worship.

The Protestant Episcopal Church in the United States of America, following *ancient, primitive,* and, until within these few centuries, *universal* usage, has prescribed a FORM OF PRAYER, or LITURGY, for public worship. This form she has received, and with few and unessential alterations adopted, from the Church of England, "to whom she is indebted under God, for her first foundation, and for a long continuance of nursing care and protection."[1]

She conceives that forms of prayer are justified by many particular and important *advantages,* as well as by *Scripture and ancient and primitive usage.*

Forms of prayer possess many *important advantages.* When public worship is conducted according to a prescribed form,

---

[1] Preface to the Book of Common Prayer of the Prot. Epis. Church.

100

the people are previously acquainted with the prayers in which they are to join, and are thus enabled to render unto God a *reasonable and enlightened* service. In forms of prayer, that *dignity and propriety of language* so necessary in supplications addressed to the infinite Majesty of Heaven, may be preserved. They prevent the *particular opinions and dispositions* of the *minister* from *influencing* the devotions of the *congregation*. They serve as a *standard of faith and practice,* impressing on both minister and people, at every performance of public worship, the important doctrines and duties of the Gospel. And they render the service more *animating,* by *uniting* the *people* with the *minister* in the performance of public worship.

The peculiar advantages of forms of prayer are thus forcibly displayed by an eminent prelate of the Church of England.[2] "A prescribed form of worship is not subject to the same inconveniences with extemporary effusions. If there should be nothing *absurd* and *unbecoming* in them, yet the audience must first endeavour to understand the words; and then they must weigh and consider the sense and meaning; and then they must deliberate whether such requests are proper for persons in their condition before they can lawfully join in them; and by that time the minister is passed on to some other subject, which requires the like attention and consideration; and so their *curiosity* may be raised and they may exercise their *judgment,* but there can scarce be any room left for *devotion.*

"A precomposed form of prayer is so far from obstructing or quenching our devotion, as is pretended, that it *assists* and *inflames* it; the matter and the words are both prepared to our hands; we know before what is to follow that we may lawfully join in it; and no other attention is required but to raise our affections. And let me ask, is not the spirit of the congregation equally stinted, whether the minister pray in an extemporary or in a composed regular form? And which is the more fit and

---

2. Bishop Newton, the learned author of the Dissertations on the prophecies. See his sermon on forms of prayer in the 3d vol. of his works.

proper for the people to receive, a form of prayer from the wisdom and authority of the whole Church, or to depend upon the discretion of every single minister?

"But a precomposed form of prayer is not only liable to no just objection; but hath besides several advantages to recommend it. It is more for the *honor of Almighty God,* expresses more reverence and devotion, preserves greater propriety and decency of language. It is likewise more for the *edification of men* as well as for the honor of God. For who can question which is likely to be most instructive and edifying, hasty conceptions or studied compositions; the productions of an individual, or the wisdom of the Church prepared and digested into form and order? It is better not only for the people, but for the *Ministers* too; for as it prevents any vain ostentation of their talents in the more learned, so it supplies the more ignorant with what, perhaps, they could ill compose of themselves. Moreover it better establishes and secures the *unity of faith and worship;* hinders the heterodox from infusing their particular notions in their prayers, which is, perhaps, the most artful and plausible way of infusing them; reduces all the Churches to a *uniformity,* prevents any disagreement or contradiction in their petitions, and instructs them, as they worship the same God, to worship him with the same mind and voice."

The use of precomposed forms of prayer for public worship is also justified by *Scripture* and the *practice of the primitive Church.* The public service of the Jews was conducted according to prescribed forms. The Levites who were appointed by David[3] "to stand every morning to thank and praise the Lord, and also at even," must have performed this duty according to some set form, in which they could all join. The book of Psalms was indited by the Holy Ghost, with the view of supplying forms of prayer and praise for the joint use of the congregation.[4] Our *Savior,* by joining in communion with the Jewish

---

[3.] 1 *Chr.* 23–30.

[4.] See Prideaux's Conn. B. 6. Part 1. Sec. 2.

Church, and particularly by giving to his disciples the form of prayer called the Lord's Prayer, testified in the strongest manner his approbation of *set forms*. The *Apostles* and *disciples* no doubt joined, until our Lord's ascension, in the Jewish worship, which was conducted according to a prescribed form. In the writings of the earliest Fathers, we find the expressions, *common prayers, constituted prayers;* from which it is evident that the primitive Christians had forms of prayers.

· · ·

Thus, then, we see how excellent and superior in all respects is the liturgy of our Church; and how admirably she has provided for the two important objects of the public service: *instruction* and *devotion*. The *lessons,* the *creeds,* the *commandments,* the *epistles* and *gospels* contain the most important and impressive instruction on the doctrines and duties of religion: While the *confession,* the *collects* and *prayers,* the *litany* and *thanksgivings* lead the understanding and the heart through all the sublime and affecting exercises of devotion. In this truly evangelical and excellent liturgy, the supreme Lord of the universe is invoked by the most appropriate, affecting, and sublime epithets: all the wants to which man, as a dependant and sinful being, is subject are expressed in language at once simple, concise, and comprehensive; these wants are urged by *confessions* the most *humble,* and *supplications* the most *reverential* and *ardent.* The *all-sufficient merits* of Jesus Christ, the Savior of the world, are uniformly urged as the only *effectual plea,* the only *certain pledge* of divine *mercy* and *grace;* and with the most *instructive lessons* from the sacred oracles and the most profound *confessions* and *supplications* is mingled the sublime *chorus* of *praise* begun by the Minister and responded with one heart and voice from the assembled congregation. The mind, continually passing from one exercise of worship to another, and, instead of one continued and uniform prayer, sending up its wishes and aspirations in short and varied collects of supplications, is never suffered to grow languid and weary. The affections of the worshiper ever kept alive by the tender and animating fervor which

103

breathes through the service; he worships his God and Redeemer in spirit and in truth, with reverence and awe, with lively gratitude and love; the exalted joys of devotion are poured upon his soul; he feels that it is *good for him to draw near unto God, and that a day spent in his courts is better than a thousand passed in the tents of the ungodly.*

Thus delightful and edifying will every person find the service who joins in it with sincerity; who unites his heart with his voice in the parts of the service assigned to the people; and who accompanies the minister in thought and affection through the supplications and prayers, lifting up his heart in secret ejaculations corresponding to the public addresses of the minister to the throne of God. A person who thus sincerely offers his devotions according to the liturgy of the Church may be satisfied that he is worshiping God "with the spirit and with the understanding also." The more frequently and seriously he joins in the service the more will he be impressed with its exquisite beauties, which tend at once to gratify his taste and to quicken his devotion. That *continual change of language* in prayer which some persons appear to consider as essential to spiritual devotion would be impossible to attain, even were every minister left to his own discretion in public worship. The same expressions would necessarily recur frequently in his prayers. They would soon sink into a form destitute of that propriety and dignity of sentiment and language, of that variety, that simplicity, and affecting fervor which characterize the liturgy of the Church.

. . .

If the charge of dull uniformity may with propriety be urged against the prayers of the Church, it may with equal justice be urged against that exalted and inspired composition the Lord's prayer. And yet we can surely offer no prayer more acceptable to God than the one prescribed by his blessed Son. A lively glow of the fancy and animal spirits may be excited where there is little of the spirit of true devotion, where the understanding and the feelings are not deeply and permanently interested.

104

The *novelty* that is sought for in extempore effusions tends to occupy the imagination with the words that are employed, and thus diverts the mind from the proper business of devotion. He who with sincerity and humility makes it his regular business to worship God according to the solemn forms of the liturgy may be assured that he renders unto God an acceptable service, even if he should not always feel those lively and ardent emotions which depend in no inconsiderable degree upon constitutional temperament, upon the state of health, and various external circumstances.

"It is the true and sincere devotion of the heart only that can make our prayers acceptable unto God. It is this only which gives life and vigor and true acceptance to all our religious addresses unto him. Without this, how elegantly and moving soever the prayer may be composed, and with how much seeming fervor and zeal soever it may be poured out, all is as dead matter and of no validity in the presence of our God. It is true, a new jingle of words and a fervent delivery of them by the minister in prayer may have some effect upon the auditors, and often raise in such of them as are affected this way a devotion which otherwise they would not have. But this being wholly artificial, which all drops again as soon as the engine is removed that raised it, it is none of that true habitual devotion which alone can render our prayers acceptable unto God."[5]

. . .

To the above remarks we add the following commendations of the Liturgy, which are not less distinguished for their justness than for their eloquence. They are from the pens of Bishop Newton, Bishop Jeremy Taylor, and Dean Comber.

"Our Liturgy," says Bishop Newton, "was not the production of this or that man—the compilers of it were not only the *best and wisest men* of that age in this nation, but they consulted likewise the most eminent of the divines abroad and had their

---

5. Dean Prideaux, Con. of Old and New Testament, Book 6. Part 1.

approbation of it, and approved it yet farther themselves by dying in its defence.

It was composed principally out of *Scripture,* or out of ancient liturgies and fathers. Even where entire *parts* and *passages* are not borrowed, and the very words of *Scripture* or of the fathers are not taken or applied, yet their *spirit* and *manner,* their style and character are still preserved; and perhaps there is scarce any collect in our liturgy, scarce any sentiment or expression that may not be justified by the authority of one or other of them. What a comfort and satisfaction should it be to us that we are such a sound part of the Holy Catholic Church that we thus maintain the communion of saints; that we worship God in the same manner as the Martyrs and the Confessors and best of Christians did in the purest ages; and the spirit of their Liturgies, like the *spirit* of Elijah upon Elisha, hath descended in "a double portion" upon ours.

Our prayers are addressed to the *proper object* through the *proper mediator;* to the one God through the "one Mediator between God and man, the man Christ Jesus." Each collect begins with a solemn invocation of the one, and concludes with the prevailing merits and intercession of the other.

It is besides a great excellence of our service to have so many *short distinct* petitions. They are thus rendered more fit and easy to be remembered and repeated. Our Liturgy in this respect may be compared to a string of pearls, every one valuable but altogether almost inestimable. If the whole was disposed in one continued prayer, though it might not be tedious yet it would keep our minds upon the stretch too long together; whereas these breaks and pauses give relief, our souls recover breath as it were, and we return to worship again with new spirit and vigour.

The variety of our service is another excellence in the composition of it, and contributes much to the keeping up of our attention and devotion. A sameness in anything soon satiates and wearies us; and it is as difficult to keep the mind as it is the body long in one posture. But by the beautiful intermixture of *prayer* and *praise,* of *supplication* and *thanksgiving,* of *confession* and *absolution,* of *hymns* and *creeds,* of *psalms* and *lessons,* our weariness is relieved, our attention is renewed, and we are led on agreeably from one subject to another. The frame of our Liturgy is somewhat like the frame of the world; it is order in variety and, though all the parts are different, yet the whole is consistent and regular.

What renders it more excellent is its *comprehensiveness.* There is nothing that relates either to ourselves or others, nothing that concerns us either as men or members of society, nothing that conduces to our happiness in this world or in the world to come but is comprehended in some or other of the petitions. It is easy, while the minister is reading it, to appropriate and apply any passages to ourselves and our own case. A great deal is *expressed* but more is *implied;* and our devotions in our closets and in our families, we cannot better perhaps express than in the words of our Liturgy; it is so suited to all ranks and conditions and adapted to all wants and occasions.

The *congregation* have particular reason to be pleased, as they have a *larger share* in our service than in any other whatever: and the *minister* and *people* mutually raise and inflame each others' devotions. It is a singular privilege, therefore, that our people enjoy of bearing so large a part in our service; and it is this that properly denominates ours, what really none else is, a book of COMMON *prayer.*

In a word, our Liturgy is in every respect excellently contrived, and fitted to promote *true devotion.* The *language* is so *plain* as to be level to the capacities of the *meanest,* and yet the *sense* is so *noble* as to raise the conceptions of the *greatest.* The *manner* too in which our service is performed is worthy of the *matter;* our *vestments* are suitable and becoming and the very emblem of holiness, for as St. John saith, "the *fine linen* clean and white is the righteousness of the saints"; our *ceremonies* neither too many nor too few, such as may excite and cherish, and not such as may distract and dissipate our devotions. All things are done as the Apostle would have them done, "de-

107

cently and in order," and if our piety is not eminent and conspicuous in proportion to our advantages it is because we are wanting to ourselves, not because our church has been wanting in making proper provision for us." [*Bishop Newton.*]

"The Liturgy of the Church of England," says Bishop Jeremy Taylor [in *An Apology for Authorized and Set Forms of Liturgy*], "hath advantages so many and considerable, as not only to raise itself above the devotions of other Churches, but to endear the affections of good people to be in love with Liturgies in general. To the Churches of the Roman Communion we can say that ours is Reformed: to the Reformed Churches we can say that it is orderly and decent. For we were freed from the impositions and lasting errors of a tyrannical spirit, and yet from the extravagances of a popular spirit too. Our Reformation was done without tumult and yet we saw it necessary to reform: we were zealous to cast away the old errors; but our zeal was balanced with consideration and the results of authority. We were not like women and children when they are affrighted with fire on their clothes; we shook off the coal indeed, but not our garments; lest we should have exposed our Church to that nakedness which the excellent men of our sister Churches complained to be among themselves. And indeed it is no small advantage to our Liturgy that it was the offspring of all that authority which was to prescribe in matters of religion. So that it was not only reasonable and sacred, but free both from the indiscretion and, which is very considerable, even from the scandal of popularity. That only in which the Church of Rome had prevaricated against the word of God, or innovated against apostolic tradition, was pared away. Great part of it consisted of the very words of Scripture, as the Psalms, Lessons, Hymns, Epistles, and Gospels: and the rest was in every particular made agreeable to it, and drawn from the Liturgies of the ancient Church. The Rubrics of it were written in the blood of some of the compilers, men famous in their generations; whose reputation and glory of martyrdom hath made it immodest for the best of men now to compare themselves with them. And its composition is so admirable that the most industrious wits of its enemies can scarce find out an objection of value enough to make a doubt, or scarce a scruple, in a serious spirit. There is no part of religion, but is in the offices of the Church of England. For if the soul desires to be humbled, she hath forms provided of confession to God before his Church: if she will rejoice and give God thanks for particular blessings, there are forms of thanksgiving for all the solemn occasions which could be foreseen and for which provision could by public order be made. If she will commend to God the public and private necessities of the Church and single persons, the whole body of collects and devotions supplies them abundantly: and if her devotions be high and pregnant, and prepared to fervency and importunity of congress with God, the Litany is an admirable pattern of devotion, full of circumstances proportionate to a quick and earnest spirit. When the revolution of the anniversary calls on us to perform our duty of special meditation on and thankfulness to God for the glorious benefits of Christ's incarnation, nativity, passion, resurrection, and ascension, etc., then we have the offices of Christmas, the Annunciation, Good-Friday, Easter, and Ascension, etc.; and the offices are so ordered that, if they be summed up, they will make an excellent creed and the very design of the day teaches the meaning of an Article. The life and death of the saints, which are very precious in the sight of God, are so remembered that, by giving thanks and praise, God may be honoured; the Church instructed by the proposition of their examples; and we give testimony of the honour and love we pay to religion by our pious veneration and esteem of those holy and beatified persons. To which, if we add the advantages of the whole Psalter, which is an entire body of devotion by itself and hath in it forms to exercise all graces by way of internal act and spiritual intention, there is not any ghostly advantage which the most religious can need or fancy but what the English Liturgy, in its entire constitution, will furnish us withal." [*Bishop Jeremy Taylor*]

Though all the Churches in the world have, and ever had,

forms of prayer, yet none was ever blessed with so comprehensive, so exact, and so inoffensive a composition as ours: which is so judiciously contrived that the wisest may exercise at once their knowledge and devotion: and yet so plain that the most ignorant may pray with understanding; so full that nothing is omitted which is fit to be asked in public; and so particular that it compriseth most things which we would ask in private; and yet so short, as not to tire any that hath true devotion. Its doctrine is pure and primitive; its ceremonies so few and innocent that most of the Christian world agree in them; its method is exact and natural; its language significant and clear, most of the words and phrases being taken out of the holy Scriptures and the rest are the expressions of the first and purest ages; so that whoever takes exception at these must quarrel with the language of the Holy Ghost and fall out with the Church in her greatest innocence. And in the opinion of the most impartial and excellent Grotius (who was no member of, nor had any obligation to, this Church), the English Liturgy comes so near to the primitive pattern that none of the reformed Churches can compare with it.

And if anything external be needful to recommend that which is so glorious within; we may add that the Compilers were [most of them] men of great piety and learning; [and several of them] either martyrs or confessors upon the restitution of Popery; which as it declares their piety, so doth the judicious digesting of these prayers evidence their learning. For therein the scholar may discern close logic, pleasing rhetoric, pure divinity, and the very marrow of the ancient doctrine and discipline; and yet all made so familiar that the unlearned may safely say Amen. 1 Cor. 14: 16.

Lastly, all these excellencies have obtained that universal reputation which these prayers enjoy in all the world: so that they are most deservedly admired by the eastern Churches, and had in great esteem by the most eminent Protestants beyond the sea, who are the most impartial judges that can be desired. In short, this Liturgy is honoured by all but the Romanist, whose interest it opposeth, and the Dissenters, whose prejudices will not let them see its lustre. Whence it is that they call that which the Papists hate because it is Protestant, superstitious and popish. But when we consider that the best things in a bad world have the most enemies, as it doth not lessen its worth so it must not abate our esteem because it hath malicious and misguided adversaries.

How endless it is to dispute with these the little success of the best arguments, managed by the wisest men, do too sadly testify: wherefore we shall endeavour to convince the enemies by assisting the friends of our Church devotions: and by drawing the veil which the ignorance and lack of devotion of some, and the passion and prejudice of others have cast over them, represent the Liturgy in its true and native lustre: which is so lovely and ravishing that, like the purest beauties, it needs no supplement of art and dressing but conquers by its own attractions, and wins the affections of all but those who do not see it clearly. This will be sufficient to show that whoever desires no more than to worship God with zeal and knowledge, spirit and truth, purity and sincerity, may do it by these devout forms. And to this end may the God of peace give us all meek hearts, quiet spirits, and devout affections; and free us from all sloth and prejudice that we may have full churches, frequent prayers, and fervent charity; that, uniting in our prayers here, we may all join in his praises hereafter, for the sake of Jesus Christ our Lord. Amen. [*Dean Comber*]

THE
LITURGY
of the
Church of England
Adorn'd with Fifty six
New Historical Cuts.

LONDON,
Sold by Richard Ware, at the Bible and Sun in
Warwick-Lane at Amen-Corner. Likewise Sells all
Sorts of Bibles, Common-Prayers & Testaments etc.

illustration from a
Book of Common Prayer, 1724.

CHAPTER THREE

The Calendar
and Liturgical Year

(25) **Richard Hooker**
Master of the Temple, Rector of Bishopsbourne (Kent),
chief apologist for Anglicanism under Queen Elizabeth I
Of the Laws of Ecclesiastical Polity, book V
1597

The sanctification of days and times is a token of that thankfulness and a part of that public honour which we owe to God
for admirable benefits, whereof it doth not suffice that we keep
a secret calendar, taking thereby our private occasions as we
list ourselves to think how much God hath done for all men,
but the days which are chosen out to serve as public memorials
of such his mercies ought to be clothed with those outward
robes of holiness whereby their difference from other days may
be made sensible. But because time in itself as hath been already proved can receive no alteration, the hallowing of festival
days must consist in the shape or countenance which we put
upon the affairs that are incident unto those days.

"This is the day which the Lord hath made," saith the prophet David; *"let us rejoice and be glad* in it." So that generally offices and duties of religious *joy* are that wherein the hallowing of festival times consisteth. The most natural testimonies of our rejoicing in God are first His praises set forth with cheerful alacrity of mind, secondly our comfort and delight expressed by a charitable largeness of somewhat more than common bounty, thirdly sequestration from ordinary labours, the toils and cares whereof are not meet to be companions of such gladness. Festival solemnity therefore is nothing but the due mixture as it were of these three elements, Praise, and Bounty, and Rest.

---

(26) **Anthony Sparrow**
Bishop of Norwich
A Rationale upon the Book of Common Prayer
of the Church of England
1655/1657

Holy in Scripture phrase is all one with separate or set apart to God, and is opposed to common. *What God hath clean'd, that call not thou common, Acts* 10: 15. Holy days then are those which are taken out of common days and separated to God's holy service and worship, either by God's own appointment or by holy Church's Dedication. And these are either Fasting and Penitential days (for there is a holy Fast, *Jl.* 2, as well as a holy Feast, *Neh.* 8: 10) such as are *Ash Wednesday, Good Friday,* and the whole week before *Easter* commonly called the *Holy week,* which days holy Church hath dedicated to God's solemn worship, in religious fastings and prayers. Or else holy Festivals which are set apart to the solemn and religious commemoration of some eminent mercies and blessings of God. And

114

among those Holy days, some are higher days than others, in regard of the greatness of the blessing commemorated and of the solemnity of the Service appointed to them. . . .

This sanctification or setting apart of *Festival days* is a token of that thankfulness and a part of that public honour which we owe to God for admirable benefits; and these days or Feasts so set apart are of excellent use, being, as learned *Hooker* observes, the

1. Splendor and outward dignity of our Religion.
2. Forcible witnesses of ancient truth.
3. Provocations to the exercise of all Piety.
4. Shadows of our endless felicity in heaven.
5. On earth, everlasting records teaching by the eye in a manner whatsoever we believe.

And concerning particulars. As the *Jews* had their *Sabbath*, which did continually bring to the mind the former World finished by Creation; so the *Christian* Church hath her *Lord's* days or *Sundays* to keep us in perpetual remembrance of a far better World begun by him who came to restore all things to make Heaven and Earth new. The rest of the holy Festivals which we celebrate have relation all to one Head, CHRIST. We begin therefore our Ecclesiastical year (as to some accounts, though not as to the order of our service) with the glorious *Annunciation* of his Birth by Angelical message. Hereunto are added his blessed *Nativity* itself, the mystery of his *legal Circumcision,* the Testification of his true Incarnation by the *Purification* of his blessed Mother the Virgin *Mary:* his glorious *Resurrection* and *Ascension* into Heaven, the admirable sending down of his *Spirit* upon his chosen.

Again, for as much as we know that CHRIST hath not only been manifested *great in himself,* but *great* in other *his Saints also;* the days of whose departure out of this world are to the Church of Christ as the birth- and coronation days of Kings or Emperors. Therefore, especial choice being made of the very flower of all occasions in this kind, there are annual selected times to meditate of Christ glorified in *them,* which had the honour to suffer for his sake, before they had age and ability to know him, namely, the blessed *Innocents.* Glorified in them which knowing him, as St. *Stephen,* had the sight of that before death, whereinto such acceptable death doth lead. Glorified in those *Sages of the East,* that came from far to adore him and were conducted by *strange light.* Glorified in the second *Elias* of the World, sent before him to prepare his way; glorified in everyone of those *Apostles* whom it pleased him to use as founders of his kingdom here; glorified in the Angels, as in St. *Michael;* glorified in *all* those *happy souls* that are already possessed of bliss.

Besides these, be four days annexed to the Feasts of *Easter* and *Whitsunday,* for the more honour and enlargement of those high solemnities. These being the days which the Lord hath made glorious, *Let us rejoyce and be glad in them.* These days we keep not in a secret Calendar, taking thereby our private occasions as we lift ourselves to think how much God hath done for all men: but they are chosen out to serve as public memorials of such mercies, and are therefore clothed with those outward robes of holiness, whereby their difference from other days may be made sensible, having by holy Church a solemn Service appointed to them.

Part of which Service are the *Epistles* and *Gospels:* of which in the first place we shall discourse, because these are peculiar and proper to each several Holy day, the rest of the Service for the most part being common to all.

Concerning these, two things are designed:

1. To show the Antiquity of them.

2. Their fitness for the day to which they belong, or the reason of their choice.

Concerning the Antiquity of *Epistles* and *Gospels,* it will be sufficient once for all to show that the use of them in the Christian Church was ancient. Concerning the antiquity of the days themselves to which the Epistles and Gospels appertain, it will be fit to be more particular.

That the use of Epistles and Gospels peculiar to the several Holy days was ancient appears first by ancient Liturgies: Sec-

116

ondly by the testimony of the ancient Fathers. Let St. *Augustine* testify for the Latin Church. . . .

Now let St. *Chrysostom* testify for the Greek . . .

The fitness of the Epistle and Gospel for the day it belongs to and the reason of the choice will plainly appear if we observe that these holy Festivals and Solemnities of the Church are, as I have touch'd before, of Two Sorts; The more high days, or the rest. The *First* commemorate the signal Acts or Passages of our Lord in the Redemption of mankind, his incarnation and Nativity, Circumcision, Manifestation to the Gentiles, his Fasting, Passion, Resurrection, and Ascension, the sending of the Holy Ghost, and thereupon a more full and express manifestation of the Sacred Trinity. The *Second* sort is of Inferior days that supply the Intervals of the greater, such as are either the remaining Sundays wherein, without any consideration of the sequence of time (which could only be regarded in great Feasts), the holy Doctrine, Deeds, and Miracles of our Lord are the chief matters of our meditations; or else the other Holy days of which already hath been spoken. And for all these Holy Times we have Epistles and Gospels very proper and reasonable, for not only on high and special days, but even in those also that are more general and indifferent, some respect is had to the season and the holy affections the Church then aims at, as Mortification in Lent, Joy, Hope, newness of Life, &tc., after Easter; the Fruits and Gifts of the Spirit and preparation for Christ's Second coming in the time between Pentecost and Advent. But these things I shall show in the Discourse of the Holy days severally. As for the Lessons, although they have another Order, and very profitable, being for each day of the week, following usually the method of Chapters and taking in the Old Testament also (the Communion dealing chiefly with the New as most fit for the nature of that Service), yet in them also regard is had to the more solemn times by select and proper readings as hath been show'd. This being the Church's Rule and Method (as she hath it from the Apostle) *that all things be done unto edifying,* that we may be better acquainted with God and with ourselves, with what hath been done for us, and what is to be done by us. And this Visible as well as Audible preaching of Christian Doctrine by these Solemnities and Readings in such an admirable Order is so apt to infuse by degrees all necessary Christian knowledge into us, and the use of it to the ignorant is so great, *that it may well be feared* that *When the Festivals and Solemnities for the Birth of Christ and his other famous passages of life, and death, and Resurrection, and Ascension, and Mission of the Holy Ghost, and the Lessons, Gospels (and Collects) and Sermons upon them, be turned out of the Church together with the Creeds also, 'twill not be in the power of weekly Sermons on some head of Religion to keep up the knowledge of Christ in mens hearts, &tc.* And no doubt for this and other good Reasons it was that the primitive Christians were so exact and religious in these Solemnities and Meditations on the occasions of them, and therefore the Sermons of the Fathers were generally on the Readings of the Day, as hereafter is showed.

---

(27) John Durel
Minister of the French Church in the Savoy, Dean of Windsor
The Liturgy of the Church of England Asserted
1662

As for our *Holy Days* . . . if we thought that by spending those days partly in idleness, partly in superstitious devotions, we merited of God: if we believed that the cessation from the works of our ordinary employments were in itself a thing acceptable to God, and made part of his service: if upon those *Holy Days* which bear the names of the blessed Virgin, or of the holy Apostles, or of the blessed Martyrs we did offer up Vows or Supplications unto them, or did *yield unto* them any part of that honour which is due to God alone. But thanks be to the

Lord, we do no such thing. All that we do is that we set apart those days for the meditation of the Mysteries of our Redemption, and the commemoration of the Graces of God which did shine in the life, in the conversation, and in the departure of those blessed souls: Reading publicly, and sweetly revolving in our minds what the Scripture tells us of them, or what they themselves have left in writing in that Sacred Volume; and praying to God that he be pleased to enable us to imitate them, and to profit every way by their holy instructions, and by their good example. And such is the observation of those Festivals which are marked in the Calendar of our Liturgy, which doth not teach us to set a higher value upon one day than upon another, as if there were some inherent holiness in it; but only directs us to do that upon certain days and in a certain Order which it were to be wished we did, or could do, incessantly every day in the year, and which, notwithstanding, most men would never do were it not for this good order which binds and as it were compels them to it by a gentle and holy Law.

---

(28) **Thomas Comber**
Dean of Durham
A Companion to the Temple,
or A Help to Devotion in the Use of the Common Prayer
1672–76/1684

A Meditation for the Communion at Christmas

Welcome thrice blessed Day! the desire of all Nations, whose distant glories made the Father of the Faithful to rejoice, and whole approachs filled the World with wonder and expectation: Thou wert ushered in with Angelic Hymns and celebrated

119

ever since with Anthems of Praise because thou didst bring forth Joy and a Redeemer to Mankind. Happy am I that I have a Sacrifice of Thanksgiving in my Hand to express the delight which my Heart doth feel. This Holy Table is the Altar upon which I offer my acknowledgments for all Mercies, and oh how many, how great are those which this day brings to my remembrance! So infinite they cannot be expressed, and yet so excellent they must not be forgotten: This Day hath reconciled Heaven and Earth and made contradictions friends, to find a way to help us as if nothing might disagree when Man was at peace with God. O my Soul, summon all thy Powers to admire and worship: For all is Miracle and the height of Wonder: Eternity begins to be, the Maker of all is made himself, an infinite Majesty is shrunk into the dimensions of a span: The Word is made Flesh and God becomes Man yet remains God still. Here is a Mother who knew no Man, a Son that had no Father on Earth, a Child of *Adam* untainted with the Contagion that infects all his Posterity, an Infant honoured with a new and glorious Star, adaged by Kings, worshiped by Angels, yet born in the condition of the meanest fortune. All hail, sweetest Savior, how lovely is thy condescension, how honourable thy abasement? Thou hast more splendour in the Rags of thy Humility than all the Grandeurs of this World could give thee; thou art more a King because thou wouldest be like a Slave for our sakes, and conquerest more Hearts by thy stupendous Love and unparalleled Self-denial: O how shall I celebrate this great Solemnity? Wherewithal shall I set forth my gratitude for this most auspicious Day? I will receive the Cup of Salvation and with Faith and ravishments of delight feast upon that precious Body and Blood which Jesus did this day assume for me. It is not enough, dearest Lord, that thou wast born for me, unless thou art also born again in me, and (as it were) become incarnate in my Heart. In thy Birth thou wast made one with us; thou didst put on Flesh and wert a partaker of our humanity. And thou hast appointed this Holy Sacrament that I might be one with thee, be replenished with thy Spirit and a partaker of thy Divine Nature. Nor is it any incongruity if I remember thy Passion and praise thee for thy Incarnation at once; for as soon as thou wast Born thou didst begin to die, and the Life which was here begun (compared to that glorious Life which thou didst leave) was itself a very Death. But therefore thou wast Born that thou mightest be capable to suffer that Death for us which thy Divinity could not feel, and thus thy Nativity was the first Scene of thy Passion, for it introduced thy Death and that effected our Salvation, so that I will remember both together. For in both thou hast most admirably humbled thyself to the depth of Misery; and yet I doubt not but thou wouldst have stooped lower if it had been either necessary or possible: But there needs no more testimonies of thy Love. Blessed Jesus! I am already overwhelmed with these which are so strange and undeserved, so sweet and ravishing that my Soul could not contain, if it did not vent itself in thy Praises. **Therefore with Angels, &tc.**

A Meditation for the Communion at Easter

O my Soul, adorn thyself with the garments of gladness, prepare thy most triumphant Hymns to go forth and meet this great returning Conqueror. Thou didst rejoice when he was pleased to undertake the Combat, and didst celebrate his entrance into the Lists with Praises; how then will it ravish thee to behold him come off with such success and honour? His warfare is now accomplished and he hath passed through the scorn and cruelty of Men, the malice and rage of Devils, the just but severe anger of God, yea the Shadow of Death and the Regions of Eternal Horror, and after all this thy surety is set at liberty, for he hath paid all thy Debts and canceled all those dismal Bonds by which thou wert forfeited to eternal Ruin. Thy Champion is Victorious, and as the Trophies of his Conquest he hath the Keys of Death and Hell and leads them both in triumph vanquished and disarmed. Blessed be he that cometh in the

Name of the Lord: We receive thee dearest Savior as born to us a second time, and this shall be thy Birthday also, the Nativity (though not of our Emperor yet) of thy Empire, thy Restoration to a state of Immortality. Thy former Birth did show thee to be the Son of Man, but this declares thee to be the Son of God, and now we know that our Redeemer liveth, he that loved us so infinitely as to die for us, doth now ever live to intercede on our behalf; he that expressed such kindness to us in his Passion, hath so fully demonstrated his own Power in his Resurrection that we are sure he is as able as willing to deliver us. Let the Heavens rejoice and the Earth be glad for this is the Day that the Lord hath made, a Day to be had in everlasting Remembrance, a Time destined to Jubilee and Rejoicing. Behold how Nature is raising itself from the Grave of Winter, and seems annually to celebrate the memory of her Lord's Resurrection in her green and fresh attire: A season chosen by God for Festival, Three thousand Years ago, and observed ever since by Jews or Christians, or both, with the greatest Solemnity. See how those blinded Jews rejoiced over their Paschal Lamb (in the midst of all their Calamities) for the Deliverance of their Fathers. But we have a nobler Passover, for a greater deliverance: Christ our Passover is sacrificed for us; therefore let us keep the Feast, and that upon the precious Body and Blood of the Lamb of God who was slain but is alive again, and behold he lives for evermore. Wherefore I will go to thy Altar with Joy, and tell out thy works with gladness, O most Mighty Savior, who hast not only died for my Sins but risen again for my Justification: And indeed what comfort could I have found in this memorial of thy Death if it had not been for thy Resurrection? This Sacrament would have only remembered thy sufferings and renewed my sorrow to think that so excellent a Person had perished in the attempt of my deliverance; but now it is become a Feast of Joy: Because it is an assurance of thy Resurrection, as well as a Commemoration of thy Passion. And since thou livest, sweet Jesus, we live also; thy Resurrection raised our Hearts from sad despair: it gives a New Life to our

Hopes, it makes our Sorrows light, our Labours easy, our Lives cheerful, and our Death advantage, because it hath lost its Sting and is become the Gate into Immortality: We can charm all our Fears and Troubles with these words, *The Lord is risen,* yea, *the Lord is risen indeed.* For thou hast washed us in thy own Blood, and made us Kings and Priests to God, to offer up at this thy Altar never ceasing Praises. **Therefore with Angels, &tc.**

A Meditation for the Communion on Whitsunday.

I will go to thy Altar, O Lord, with a new Sacrifice of Praise, because thou hast given me a fresh instance of thy Love this day; thou art slow to punish thy Enemies but speedy to comfort thy Servants! For no sooner was thy Misery changed into Glory but we received the greatest demonstration of thy Affections: No sooner didst thou put on thy Crown in Heaven but the Earth felt the bounty of thy dispensations: For it was not possible for thee, sweet Jesus! to let thy promise remain long unperformed, or the sad expectations of thy Disciples unsatisfied. Being assembled therefore this Day with one heart in one place, they are suddenly surprised with wonder and inspired with a Heavenly Power such as they had never felt before; vigorous as a mighty wind, cheering as the morning light, inflaming their hearts with zeal and filling their mouths with Anthems composed in the Languages of all the World. O wonderful change! their ignorance is turned into learning, their mistakes into infallibility, their fear into courage, their weakness into strength, their sorrow into joy, and they in a moment made able to confound the Arts and conquer the oppositions of the Heathen World, and in spite of all the devices of Satan to set up the Kingdom of the Lord Christ. And shall not we praise thee for these miraculous dispensations by which the Gospel was made known even to us in these utmost corners and last of times? Yes, holy Jesus, we will also meet with one accord at thy Table, not doubting but thou wouldst give us the same measures of thy spirit there, if our duty or our necessity did require it. It is enough to us that thou knowest our needs; more than will supply them we dare not ask, less thou wilt not give: Thou hast given us thy self, wherefore we believe thou wilt not deny us thy spirit without which we can have no interest in thee nor benefit from thee. We come not, gracious Lord, with the carnal Jews to devour thy Flesh, but to partake of thy Spirit which only giveth Life; the Flesh profiteth nothing. Behold thy Spirit hath converted Millions; let me therefore together with thy precious Body receive here such proportions of thy Holy Spirit as may suppress my evil affections, revive my dead heart, comfort my dejected mind, and turn my ignorance into knowledge, my knowledge into practice, and make that practice so sweet and easy that this may be a day of joy to me also, solemnized in the white garments of sanctification and rejoicing. And finally, Let not this Heavenly Inspiration be only expressed in ecstasies and holy fervours this day; but let thy Spirit rest upon me and dwell in me forever; So shall I always have cause to bless thee for so incomparable a gift. Methinks I feel already the force thereof, bearing down my corruptions, and its bright beams driving away the Mists of Sin and Error. I find its flames warming my heart with zeal and charity, and its quickening Power opening my sealed lips to show forth thy praise. **Therefore with Angels,** &tc.

---

(29) **Robert Nelson**
layman and philanthropist
A Companion for the Festivals and Fasts
of the Church of England
1703

Q. What do you mean by festivals?

A. Days set apart by the Church, either for the remembrance of some special mercies of God, such as the birth and resurrection of Christ, the descent of the Holy Ghost, &tc.; or in memory of the great heroes of the Christian religion, the blessed Apostles and other saints who were the happy instruments of conveying to us the knowledge of Christ Jesus by preaching his gospel through the world; and most of them attesting the truth of it with their blood.

Q. Of what authority is the observation of these festivals?

A. They are of ecclesiastical institution; agreeable to Scripture in the general design of them, for the promoting of piety; consonant to the practice of the primitive Church, as appears by the joint consent of antiquity.

. . .

Q. What may be pleaded for such days, from the design of their institution?

A. It being not only good but a great duty to be grateful, and to give thanks to God for the blessings we receive from Him, it must be not only lawful but commendable, upon the account of gratitude, to appoint and observe days for the particular remembrance of such blessings and to give thanks for them: the sanctifying of such days being a token of that thankfulness, and part of that public honour which we owe to God for his inestimable benefits.

Q. But do not these festivals restrain the praises of God to certain times, which ought to be extended to all times?

A. No duty can be performed without the circumstance of time: and that there is a certain time allotted for this duty tends only to the securing of some time for the exercise of the duty, against the frailties of men and the disturbances of the world which might otherwise supplant and rob it of all. And though the days of solemnity, which are but few, must quickly finish that outward exercise of devotions which appertains to such times; yet they increase men's inward disposition to virtue for the present, and by their frequent returns bring the same at length to great perfection. What the Gospel enjoins is a constant disposition of mind to practice all Christian virtues, as often as time and opportunity require, and not a perpetuity of exercise and action; it being impossible at one and the same time to discharge a variety of duties.

. . .

Q. But doth not the abuse of festivals to intemperance and luxury, make it necessary to have them abolished?

A. I think this a very terrible objection, somewhat of the nature of that of the scandalous lives of Christians against the efficacy of the Christian religion: but as that is an objection not so strong against Christianity as it is shameful to Christians, so this perverting of holy seasons shows only the great depravity of mankind in turning their food into poison, and no ways reflects upon the prudence and piety of the institution. For as they who are intemperately disposed do upon these occasions turn feasting, designed for hospitality and charity, into luxury and excess, so the same men treat the Lord's day with as little respect, and make the advantage of rest and leisure from their worldly affairs only an instrument to promote their pleasure and diversions. But I wish Christians would lay this seriously to heart and retrieve the honour of such holy seasons by the exercise of piety and charity; lest our spiritual governors should be forced to lay these festivals aside, as it is certain the ancient Church was to abolish even some apostolical rites, viz. the agape and kiss of charity, through men's obstinate abuse of them.

. . .

Q. How ought we to observe the festivals of the Church?

A. In such a manner as may answer the ends for which they were appointed: that God may be glorified by a humble and grateful acknowledgment of his mercies; and that the salvation of our souls may be advanced by firmly believing the mysteries of our redemption, and by imitating the examples of those patterns of piety that are set before us.

Q. What manner of keeping these days answers these ends?

A. We should constantly attend the public worship and partake of the blessed Sacrament if it be administered. In private we should enlarge our devotions and suffer the affairs of the world to interrupt us as little as may be. We should particularly express our rejoicing by love and charity to our poor neighbors. If we commemorate any mystery of our redemption or article of our faith, we ought to confirm our belief of it by considering all those reasons upon which it is built; that we may be able to give a good account of the hope that is in us. We should from our hearts offer to God the sacrifice of thanksgiving and resolve to perform all those duties which result from the belief of such an article. If we commemorate any saint, we should consider the virtues for which he was most eminent and by what step she arrived at so great perfections; and then examine ourselves how far we are defective in our duty, and earnestly beg God's pardon for our past failings; and beg his grace to enable us to conform our lives for the time to come to those admirable examples that are set before us.

. . .

[On Christmas Day]

Q. What thoughts are proper to entertain our minds upon this festival?

A. Great admiration of the stupendous love of God towards mankind in sending no less a person than his own Son, and no less dear to Him than his only-begotten Son, out of his mere grace and goodness, to accomplish our salvation who were enemies to God by our evil works. Great thankfulness to the blessed Jesus for his wonderful humility and condescension when He undertook the work of our redemption. He who lodged in the bosom of his Father came into the world "and had not where to lay his head." He, who had heaven for his throne, was contented to be born in a stable, to be laid in a manger, to be wrapped in swaddling clothes. Great transports of gratitude; that, for our sakes, He would be pleased to be made miserable that we might be made happy; to be poor that we might be enriched; to die that we might live forever. Great

127

trust and confidence in the mercy of God, who hath showed such tenderness and compassion towards us and done such great things for our salvation.

Q. How ought we to express our thankfulness for the incarnation of our blessed Savior?

A. We ought to join with the heavenly host and the pious believing shepherds in hymns of praise and thanksgiving. To comply with the great design of this wonderful love "by denying all ungodliness and worldly lusts, and by living soberly, righteously, and godly in this present world." To propound this pattern of love for our own imitation and, because God hath so loved us, to love one another; and to stoop to the lowest offices of charity for the relief of our neighbour. Never to despise the poor for the meanness of their circumstances, since it is what our Savior chose for our sakes; but to cherish and assist them as his lively representatives here upon earth, especially because all the kindness we show to them He reckoneth as done to Himself.

. . .

[On Whitsunday]

Q. What may we learn from the observation of this festival?

A. To thank God for those miraculous gifts which He bestowed upon the Apostles to fit them to convert the world, and for inspiring the sacred penmen of holy Writ; whereby He hath given such abundant testimony of the truth of our religion and such firm grounds for our faith. To live according to the holy precepts of that Gospel which hath received so convincing a testimony. Earnestly to beg of God the gift of his Holy Spirit which is so necessary to enable us to run the ways of his commandments, and which God is ready to grant to our hearty and fervent prayers. To support ourselves under all the difficulties of our Christian warfare which arise either from our own weakness or the power of our spiritual enemies, by considering that He that is in us is greater than he that is in the world; and that we may "do all things through Christ that strengtheneth" us. To attribute all the good that is in us, as well as the perfections and abilities we enjoy, to the Holy Spirit, whose free gift they are; and to employ them to the benefit and advantage of our neighbors, they being therefore given that we might profit with them.

. . .

Q. How is a day of fasting to be observed by serious Christians?

A. Not only by interrupting and abridging the care of our bodily sustenance, but by carefully inquiring into the state of our souls; charging ourselves with all those transgressions which we have committed against God's laws, humbly confessing them with shame and confusion of face, with hearty contrition and sorrow for them; deprecating God's displeasure and begging Him to turn away his anger from us. By interceding with Him for such spiritual and temporal blessings upon ourselves and others as are needful and convenient. By improving our knowledge in all the particulars of our duty. By relieving the wants and necessities of the poor, that our humiliation and prayers may find acceptance with God. If the fast be public, by attending the public places of God's worship.

Q. What ought we chiefly to beware of in our exercise of fasting?

A. We ought to avoid all vanity and valuing ourselves upon such performances; and, therefore, in our private fasts, not to proclaim them to others by any external affectations, that we may not appear unto men to fast. Not to despise or judge our neighbor who doth not and, it may be, hath not the same reason to tie himself up to such methods. Not to destroy the health of our bodies and thereby make them unfit instruments for the operations of our minds or the discharge of our worldly employments.

(30) Anonymous
The New Whole Duty of Man
1747

The ends for which the sabbath was originally instituted, and for which the command was from time to time renewed, were principally as follows. That men might continually commemorate the works of creation: which original reason of the institution of the sabbath is of eternal and unchangeable consideration. Another reason of this commandment is that the poor laborer and the servant and even the cattle may have a time of rest: this reason likewise, as well as that of commemorating the creation, is of a moral and perpetual nature. And a third reason, which was added upon occasion of renewing this institution to the Jews, was that they might commemorate their deliverance out of the land of Egypt, which to that people was as it were a new creation. . . . Then, instead of the Jewish sabbath, there succeeded, by the appointment and practice of the apostles, the commemoration of our Lord's resurrection: which coming to pass upon the first day of the week, the Christian Lord's day, was accordingly from that time kept on the first day of the week, which we call *Sunday.* Therefore one day in seven must be yielded unto the Lord and set apart for the exercise of religious duties, both in public and private.

For we must not only rest from the works of our calling, but our time must be employed in all such religious exercises as tend to the glory of God and the salvation of our own souls. We must regularly frequent the worship of God in the public assemblies, from which nothing but sickness or absolute necessity should detain us; and there we are not to talk or gaze about us but to join in the prayers of the church, hear his most holy word, receive the blessed sacrament when administered, and contribute to the relief of the poor if there be any collection for their support; that we may thereby openly profess ourselves Christians, which is one great end of public assemblies in the service of God. We ought, in private, to enlarge our ordinary devotions and to make the subject of them chiefly consist in thanksgivings for the works of creation and redemption, recollecting all those mercies we have received from the bounty of Heaven through the course of our lives. We ought to improve our knowledge by reading and meditating upon divine subjects; to instruct our children and families; to visit the sick and the poor, comforting them by some seasonable assistance; and if we converse with our friends and neighbors, to season our discourse with prudent and profitable hints for the advancement of piety; and to take care that no sourness or moroseness mingle with our serious frame of mind. In a word, it is to be spent in works of necessity and in works of charity; and in whatever tends without superstition and without affectation to the real honour of God, and to the true interest and promotion of religion and virtue in the world. The extremes to be avoided are, on the one hand, that habit of spending a great part of the Lord's day in gaming and in other loose and debauched practices, which has to numberless persons been the corruption of their principles and the entire ruin of their morals; on the other hand, an affected judaical or pharisaical preciseness, which usually proceeds from hypocrisy or from a want of understanding rightly the true nature of religion.

And hence we may collect the great advantages of a religious observance of the Lord's day: it keeps up the solemn and public worship of God, which might be neglected if left to depend upon the will of man; it preserves the knowledge and visible profession of the Christian religion in the world when, notwithstanding the great differences there are among Christians in other matters, they yet all agree in observing this day in memory of our Savior's resurrection; and it is highly useful to instruct the ignorant by preaching and catechizing and to put those in mind of their duty, who in their prosperity, are apt to forget God. Moreover, by spending this day in religious exercises, we acquire new strength and resolution to perform God's will in our several stations for the future.

Beside this weekly day of the Lord there are other principal times or days set apart by the church, either for the remembrance of some special mercies of God, such as the birth and resurrection of Christ, the coming down of the Holy Ghost from heaven, &tc., or in memory of the blessed apostles and other saints who were the happy instruments of conveying to us the knowledge of Christ Jesus by preaching his gospel through the world, and most of them attesting the truth of it with their blood. These days ought to be observed in such a manner as may answer the ends for which they were first appointed: that God may be glorified by a humble and grateful acknowledgment of his mercies; and that the salvation of our souls may be advanced by believing the mysteries of our redemption and imitating the examples of those primitive patterns of piety that are set before us. Therefore we should be so far from looking upon them as common days, or making them instruments of vice and vanity, or spending them in luxury and debauchery, intemperance, excess, and sensuality, as the manner of some is who look upon a *holiday* as designed for a loose to their passions and unbounded pleasure. Our greatest care should be to improve our time in the knowledge and love of God, and of his son Jesus Christ our Lord, by constantly attending the public worship and partaking of the blessed sacrament if it be administered; and in private by enlarging our devotions and withdrawing ourselves as much as possible from the affairs of the world, particularly expressing our joyfulness by love and charity to our poor neighbour. If the holiday is such as is intended for our calling to mind any mystery of our redemption, or article of our faith, we ought to confirm our belief of it by considering all those reasons upon which it is built, that we may be able to give a good account of the hope that is in us. We should from our hearts offer to God the sacrifice of thanksgiving, and resolve to perform all those duties which arise from the belief of such an article. If we commemorate any saint, we should consider the virtues for which he was most distinguished, and by what steps he arrived at so great a perfection; and then examine ourselves how far we are wanting in our duty and earnestly beg God's pardon for our past failings, and his grace to enable us to conform our lives to those admirable examples which the saints have left for our imitation.

As we are thus to express our thankfulness to God for mercies received and the good examples set before us for our imitation, we are with the same view of honoring God by acts of humiliation and repentance to keep holy those *fast days* set apart by the church or by civil authority or by our own appointment; to humble ourselves before God in punishing our bodies and afflicting our souls in order to a real repentance; by outward tokens testifying our grief for sins past, and by using them as means to secure us from returning to those sins for which we express so great a detestation. And this must be done, not only by interrupting and abridging the care of our body, but by carefully inquiring into the state of our souls; charging ourselves with all those transgressions we have committed against God's laws, humbly confessing them with shame and confusion of face, with hearty contrition and sorrow for them; praying that God will not suffer his whole displeasure to arise and begging him to turn away his anger from us; by interceding with him for such spiritual and temporal blessings upon ourselves and others as are needful and convenient; by improving our knowledge in all the particulars of our duty; by relieving the wants and necessities of the poor that our humiliation and prayers may find acceptance with God.

(31) John Henry Hobart
Bishop of New York, founder of The General Theological Seminary
A Companion for the Book of Common Prayer
1805/1827

The first day of the week, called *Sunday,* is devoted by Christians to the celebration of the goodness of GOD in the creation, but more especially in the redemption of the world. Certain days are also appointed by the Church for the celebration of the leading events and mysteries of our redemption, and for the commemoration of the Apostles and primitive disciples. The Church designs by these FESTIVALS and FASTS not only to instruct her members in the history and doctrines of their redemption, but also to excite them to celebrate the infinite love of CHRIST by which this redemption was effected; and to imitate the faith and piety of those primitive saints by whom the glad tidings of salvation were proclaimed. The Jews had not only festivals and fasts of divine but of human appointment, which our Savior sanctioned by his presence.

The reading of the EPISTLES and GOSPELS on festivals and fasts, as well as on Sundays, is a very ancient usage of the Church. It is thought the Collects, Epistles, and Gospels now in use were framed and selected by the famous St. *Jerome* in the fourth century.

For the more judicious arrangement of the Epistles and Gospels, the Church has divided the year into *two parts:* the former takes in the period from Advent to Trinity Sunday, and the latter comprises all the Sundays from Trinity to Advent.

The design of the *former* portion of the year is to commemorate CHRIST's living among us. Beginning at Advent, we first celebrate his incarnation in general and, after that, the several particulars of it in their order: his nativity, circumcision, and manifestation to the Gentiles; his doctrine and miracles; his

134

baptism, fasting, and temptation; his agony and bloody sweat; his cross and passion; his precious death and burial; his glorious resurrection and ascension; and his sending the HOLY GHOST to comfort us. As during this period, therefore, it is the design of the Church to celebrate the agency of the blessed Trinity in the work of our redemption, the chief end of the Epistles and Gospels is to make us remember what unspeakable benefits we receive from the FATHER, first by his SON, and then by the HOLY GHOST; accordingly, this portion of the year is concluded on Trinity Sunday by giving praise and glory to the whole blessed Trinity.

The design of the *latter* portion of the year is to instruct us to *live after the example of Christ.* Having in the first part of the year learned the mysteries of our religion, we are taught in the second what we are to practice that we may build upon our faith a holy and virtuous life. The Epistles and Gospels, therefore, for this portion of the year are designed to instruct us in the practical duties of the Gospel.

Illustration from
The Devout Christian's Companion, 1715

CHAPTER FOUR

The Daily Office

(32) **Lancelot Andrewes**
Bishop successively of Chichester, Ely, and Winchester
Sermons on the Lord's Prayer,
probably given at Cambridge in the
1580s

[from Sermon VII, on "Our Father"]
That which we learned *in lege credendi,* that God is the Father Almighty, is here taught again *in lege supplicandi,* where we are instructed in our prayers to ascribe both these unto God; first, that He is "our Father," secondly, "our heavenly Father."

The consideration of these two are the pillars of our faith, and there is no petition wherein we do not desire that God will either show us His goodness or assist us with His power, and no psalm or hymn that is not occupied in setting forth one of these.

The titles which express God's goodness have two words: the one a word of faith, the other a word of hope and charity.

Of both these words of *Pater* and *noster* Basil saith that here *Lex supplicandi non modo credendi sed operandi legem statuit*, "The law of prayer doth not only establish and confirm the law of belief, but of working also"; for where in the word "Father" is expressed the love of God to us, it comprehendeth withal the love we bear to Him.

Where we call God "our Father," and not "my Father," therein is contained our love to our neighbor, whom we are to love no less than ourselves: "Upon these two hang the Law and the Prophets." (*Mt.* 22:40)

Again, the word "Father" is a word of faith, and "our," a word of charity; and the thing required of us in the New Testament is *fides per charitatem operans*, "faith which worketh by charity." (*Gal.* 5:6)

So that in these words, "Our Father," we have a sum both of the Law and the Gospel.

Christ might have devised many more magnificent and excellent terms for God; but none were apt and fit for us, to assure us of God's favour. Our Savior saith, that earthly fathers which many times are evil men have notwithstanding this care for their children, that if they ask them bread they will not give them a stone: "much more shall our Heavenly Father give us the Holy Spirit if we ask it." (*Lk.* 11:13)

Wherefore Christ teaching us to call God by the name of "Father," hath made choice of that word which might serve most to stir us up unto hope; for it is *magnum nomen sub quo nemini desperandum*, "a great name under which no man can despair."

. . .

[from Sermon IX, on "Hallowed be thy Name"]

Here Christ tells us that no other name is to be sanctified but the name of God, whereof we should be so careful that we ought to pray that God's name may be sanctified by others if not by ourselves; though we in our own persons cannot hallow it, yet *sanctificetur Nomen Tuum*, "let Thy Name, O Lord, be sanctified."

Hereby, as we pray for the gift of "the fear of God," which

is one of the seven virtues which are set down because we do truly sanctify God when we make Him "our fear and dread," so we pray against the vice of pride which is the contrary to the virtue of fear; so shall we obtain the blessings, "Blessed are the poor in spirit," &tc. And upon this petition is grounded not only whatsoever hymn or psalm is sung of the congregation, but even the end of all assemblies is to ascribe holiness to God, and to sanctify His name for His benefits bestowed upon us. (*Is.* 11:2, 8:13; *Mt.* 5:3)

And in this they acknowledge, first, their own unworthiness; secondly, they bless Him for His goodness extended toward them; thirdly, they do not acknowledge it in themselves but do tell it forth as the Psalmist speaketh, "O come hither and hearken all ye that do fear God, and I will tell you what He hath done for my soul." Fourthly, to this end they lift up their voices in singing, "to the end they make the voice of His praise to be heard." (*Ps.* 66:16, 8)

And among other benefits, we are to praise and bless His name for the benefits of sanctification, which we have in the name of the Lord Jesus; secondly, for the means whereby this sanctification is offered and wrought in us, which is the word, as Christ saith, "O Father, sanctify them in Thy truth." For the perfection of sanctification that we shall have after this life, when we shall be "partakers of the inheritance of the saints in light," when we shall continually sing with the heavenly angels, "Holy, Holy, Holy, Lord God of Hosts." (*Jn.* 17:17; *Col.* 1:12; *Is.* 6:3)

And howsoever, when we desire of God that His name may be sanctified, we seem like natural children to forget our own necessities in respect of the care we have to God's glory; yet even then we pray no less for ourselves than for God, for the Lord hath promised, "Them that honour Me I will honour"; and Christ saith, "that if the name of the Lord Jesus be glorified in us, we also shall be glorified in Him." *Et sanctificando nomen adveniet regnum,* In sanctifying His name His kingdom shall come, as the next petition is. (I Sam. 2:30; II Thes. 1:12)

If while we remain on earth our whole desire be to sanctify God's name, we shall at length come to the place where we shall day and night sing as the Cherubims do, and with the heavenly host of Angels sing, "Glory to God on high"; we shall fall down before His Throne, saying always, "Thou art worthy, O Lord, to receive glory and honour and praise for ever." (*Is.* 6:3; *Lk.* 2:14; *Rev.* 4:11)

---

(33) **Richard Hooker**
Master of the Temple, Rector of Bishopsbourne (Kent),
chief apologist for Anglicanism under Queen Elizabeth I
Of the Laws of Ecclesiastical Polity, book V
(1597)

[The Psalter]

The choice and flower of all things profitable in other books the Psalms do both more briefly contain and more movingly also express by reason of that poetical form wherewith they are written. The ancients when they speak of the Book of Psalms used to fall into large discourses, showing how this part above the rest doth of purpose set forth and celebrate all the considerations and operations which belong to God; it magnifieth the holy meditations and actions of divine men; it is of things heavenly a universal declaration, working in them whose hearts God inspireth with the due consideration thereof, a habit or disposition of mind whereby they are made fit vessels both for receipt and for delivery of whatsoever spiritual perfection. What is there necessary for man to know which the Psalms are not able to teach? They are to beginners an easy and familiar introduction, a mighty augmentation of all virtue and knowledge in such as are entered before, a strong confirmation to the most perfect among others. Heroical magnanimity, exquisite justice, grave moderation, exact wisdom, repentance un-feigned, unwearied patience, the mysteries of God, the sufferings of Christ, the terrors of wrath, the comforts of grace, the works of Providence over this world, and the promised joys of that world which is to come, all good necessarily to be either known or done or had, this one celestial fountain yieldeth. Let there be any grief or disease incident into the soul of man, any wound or sickness named, for which there is not in this treasure house a present comfortable remedy at all times ready to be found. Hereof it is that we covet to make the Psalms especially familiar unto all. This is the very cause why we iterate the Psalms oftener than any other part of Scripture besides; the cause wherefore we accustom the people together with their minister and not the minister alone to read them as he does other parts of Scripture.

---

(34) **Anthony Sparrow**
Bishop of Norwich
A Rationale upon the Book of Common Prayer
of the Church of England
1655 / 1657

The Lord be with you.

This Divine Salutation taken out of Holy Scripture, *Ru.* 2:4, was frequently used in Ancient Liturgies before Prayers, before the Gospel, before the Sermon, and at other times. . . .

It seems as an *Introit* or entrance upon another sort of Divine Service, and a good Introduction it is, serving as a holy excitation to Attention and Devotion by minding the people what they are about, namely such holy Services as without God's assistance and special grace cannot be performed, and therefore when they are about these Services the Priest minds them of it by saying, **The Lord be with you.** And again, it is a most excellent and seasonable Prayer for them, in effect thus much, The Lord be with you to lift up your Hearts and raise your Devotions to his Service. The Lord be with you to accept your Services. The Lord be with you to reward you hereafter with eternal life.

The people Answer, **And with thy Spirit.** Which form is taken out of 2 *Tim.* 4: 22. and is as much as this, Thou art about to Offer up Prayers and spiritual Sacrifices for us, therefore we pray likewise for thee, that He without whom nothing is good and acceptable may be with thy spirit while thou art exercised in these Spiritual Services, which must be performed with the Spirit, according to St. *Paul,* 1 *Cor.* 14: 15. Thus the Priest prays and wishes well to the people, and they pray and wish well to the Priest. And such mutual Salutations and Prayers as this and those that follow, where Priest and people interchangeably pray each for other, are excellent expressions of the Communion of Saints. Both acknowledging thus that they are all one body and each one members one of another, mutually caring for one another's good, and mutually praying for one another, which must needs be, if well considered, and duly performed, excellent *Incentives* and provocations to Charity and love one of another; and . . . if these solemn mutual Salutations were religiously performed, it were almost impossible that Priest and people should be at Enmity. . . .

The Divine Service may be said privately

We have seen the reason of the Church's command that the holy Service should be offered up in the Church or Chapel, &tc. But what if a Church cannot be had to say our Office in? Shall the Sacrifice of Rest, the holy Service be omitted? By no means. If a Church may not be had, **The Priest Shall say it Privately** says the same Rubric 2. And good reason; for God's worship must not be neglected or omitted for want of a circumstance. It is true, the Church is the most convenient place for it and adds much to the beauty of holiness. And he that would neglect that decency and, despising the Church would offer up the public worship in private, would sin against that Law of God that says *Cursed is he that having a better Lamb in his flock, offers up to God a worse:* For God Almighty must be served with the best we have, otherwise we despise him. He that can have a Church and will offer up the holy Service in a worse place, let him fear that curse: but if a Church cannot be had, let him not fear or omit to offer up the holy Service in a convenient place in private, having a desire to the Church, looking toward the Temple in prayer, 2 *Chr.* 6: 28ff., for it will be accepted, according to that equitable rule of St. *Paul,* 2 *Cor.* 8: 12. *If there be a willing mind, God accepts according to that a man hath, and not according to that he hath not.*

Agreeable to this command of holy Church . . . let every man say *the Office in private* by himself. Let every Layman say this Morn and Even Office, his Psalter, leaving out that which is peculiar to the Priest, Absolution, and solemn benediction; and let him know that when he prays thus alone he prays with company, because he prays in the Church's communion, the Common prayer and vote of the Church. But let not the Priest of all others fail to offer this service of the Congregation . . . toward *the mercy seat of the holy Temple,* having in his *soul a desire and longing to enter into the Courts of the Lord,* praying with *David,* that he may go unto *the Altar of God, the God of our joy and gladness,* to offer up his service there, and it will be acceptable.

· · ·

This public service is accepted of God, not only for those that are present and say *Amen* to it, but for all those that are absent upon just cause, even for all that do not renounce Communion with it and the Church, for it is the Common service of them all. Commanded to be offered up in the names of them all and agreed to by all of them to be offered up for them all, and therefore is accepted for them all, though presented to God by the Priest alone . . . a sweet smelling savour, a savour of *rest,* to pacify God Almighty daily and to continue his favour to them, and make him dwell with them.

Good reason therefore it is, that this sweet smelling savour should be daily offered up to God *Morning* and *Evening,* whereby God may be pacified and invited to dwell among his people. And whatsoever the world think; thus to be the *Lord's Remembrancers* putting him in mind of the people's wants. *Being as it were the Angels of the Lord,* interceding for the people and carrying up the daily prayers of the Church in their behalf, is one of the most useful and principal parts of the Priest's office.

---

(35) **John Pearson**
Bishop of Chester
An Exposition of the Creed
1659

I believe in God the Father

Now, although the Christian notion of the divine Paternity be some way peculiar to the evangelical revelation; yet wheresoever God hath been acknowledged he hath been understood and worshiped as a Father: the very Heathen Poets so describe their gods, and their vulgar names did carry Father in them as the most popular and universal notion.

This name of Father is a relative; and the proper foundation of Paternity, as of a relation, is Generation. As therefore the phrase of generating is diversely attributed unto several acts, of the same nature with generation properly taken or by consequence attending on it: so the title of Father is given unto divers persons or things, and for several reasons unto the same God. *These are the generations of the heavens and the earth, when they were created, in the day that the Lord God made the earth and the heavens,* saith Moses. So that the creation or production of any thing by which it is, and before it was not, is a kind of generation, and consequently the creator or producer of it a kind of Father. *Hath the rain a Father? or who hath begotten the drops of dew?* By which words Job signifies, that as there is no other cause assignable of the rain but God, so may he as the cause be called the Father of it, though not in the most proper sense, as he is the Father of his Son: and so the Philosophers of old, who thought that God did make the world, called him expressly, as the Maker, so the Father of it. And thus *to us there is but one God, the Father, of whom are all things;* to which the words following in the Creed may seem to have relation, *the Father Almighty, Maker of heaven and earth.* But in this mass of Creatures and body of the Universe some works of the creation more properly call him Father, as being more rightly Sons: such are all the rational and intellectual offspring of the Deity. Of merely natural beings and irrational agents he is the Creator; of rational, as so, the Father also; they are his Creatures, these his Sons. Hence he is styled *the Father of Spirits,* and the blessed Angels, when he laid the foundations of the earth, his Sons; *When the morning stars sang together, and all the sons of God shouted for joy:* hence Man, whom he created after his own image, is called his *offspring,* and Adam, the immediate work of his hands, the *Son of God:* hence may we all cry out with the Israelites taught by the Prophet so to speak, *Have we not all one Father; hath not one God created us?* Thus the first and most universal notion of God's Paternity, in a borrowed or metaphorical sense, is founded rather upon Creation than Procreation.

• • •

Born of the Virgin Mary

The necessity of believing our Savior thus to be *born of the Virgin Mary* will appear both in respect of her who was the mother and of him who was the son.

In respect of her it was therefore necessary that we might perpetually preserve an esteem of her person proportionable to so high a dignity. It was her own prediction, *From henceforth all generations shall call me blessed;* but the obligation is ours, to call her, to esteem her so. If Elizabeth cried out *with so loud a voice, Blessed art thou among women,* when Christ was but newly conceived in her womb; what expressions of honour and admiration can we think sufficient now that Christ is in heaven and that mother with him! Far be it from any Christian to derogate from that special privilege granted her, which is incommunicable to any other. We cannot bear too reverend a regard unto the *mother of our Lord* so long as we give her not that worship which is due unto the Lord himself. Let us keep the language of the primitive Church: Let her be honoured and esteemed, let him be worshiped and adored.

In respect of him it was necessary, first, that we might be assured he was *made* or *begotten of a woman,* and consequently that he had from her the true nature of man. *For he took not on him the nature of angels,* and therefore saved none of them who, for want of a redeemer, are *reserved in everlasting chains under darkness unto the judgment of the great day.* And man once fallen had been, as deservedly, so irrevocably condemned to the same condition, *but* that *he took upon him the seed of Abraham.* For being we are *partakers of flesh and blood,* we could expect no redemption but by him who *likewise took part of the same:* we could look for no Redeemer but such a one who by consanguinity was our brother. And being there is but *one Mediator between God and man, the Man Christ Jesus,* we cannot be assured that he was the Christ or is our Jesus except we be first assured that he was a man. Thus our Redeemer, the Man Christ Jesus, was born of a woman that he might redeem both men and women; that both sexes might rely upon him, who was of the one, and from the other.

(36) **Thomas Comber**
Dean of Durham
A Companion to the Temple,
or A Help to Devotion in the Use of the Common Prayer
1672–76 / 1684

[On Morning and Evening Prayer]

Prayer is not only an excellent means to obtain all Blessings, but the very act itself is an Elevation of the Soul to contemplate the Beauties of the Divine Nature, that by beholding such transcendent Perfections it may learn to love, desire to please, and delight to imitate so great and exact a Pattern; and consequently it is a Duty of the highest involvement: For it is an Honour and a Benefit to us, and yet it is accepted by God as our Homage and the Testimony of our Observance. It is a high Favour to be admitted to have *familiar Converse* with the King of Kings, and a huge Advantage to have so frequent Access to the Fountain of all Goodness. But then it is difficult as well as fair, and requires so much Attention and Serenity, Zeal and Vigour, Faith and Love, Reverence and Humility that it can neither be well done nor kindly accepted without some preceding Preparation. For these Souls of ours are so clogged with Corruptions, disturbed with Passions, and so constantly entertained with the Vanities which our Senses present us with that we find our Minds pressed down when we would lift them up to God. But as those Fowls whose wings are not proportionable to the weight of their Bodies do usually run some Paces before they can rise from the Earth to begin their flight; so the Church directeth us first to prepare our hearts before we begin to pray. The Jews are taught when they enter their Synagogues to stand silently a while in the posture of Prayer before they begin their Devotion; And one of their Masters told his Scholars this was the way to obtain Eternal Life. The Primitive Christians had a preparatory Preface to their Public Prayers as long ago as the time of the famous St. *Cyprian.* And we are appointed to exercise our Souls in the Meditation of these *Sentences of Scripture* with the *Exhortation* subjoined that we may thereby become more fit to pray. That illustrious Heathen Temple had this Inscription in Letters of Gold, *know thyself,* that the Worshipers, by a true consideration of themselves, might approach with all humility to their supposed Deities. And surely it is more requisite for us who worship the true God to reflect upon the vast disproportion between ourselves and Him, which is as great as between finite and infinite, holy and impure; and so we may be convinced of the necessity of being most lowly and reverent before him. The Frailties of our Bodies and the Infirmities of our Nature, the Defects of our Faculties and the Misery that cleaves both to Soul and Body doth command us to be humble in the Presence of God. But that which should lay us lowest of all in our own thoughts is the remembrance of our sins, which do alone alienate us from God; for he that pitieth our Miseries hateth our sins, and he that caused the Leper to be banished out of the City, admitted the lame Man to the beautiful Gate of the Temple. *Joshua* himself could not be heard till the sin of *Israel* was taken away, and he meets with a Check in his Devotion for presuming to pray before he had removed the accursed thing, *Jos.* 7: 10. Wherefore our Spiritual Guides present us with these *Admonitions* to Repentance before we begin to pray, lest we should stumble at the Threshold and pray in vain while we remain impenitent; for there is a moral impossibility such Prayers should prevail. The Petitions of Sinners are either a heap of Contradictions or a fabric of Indignities against the God of Heaven; for such men bewail that with their mouth which they love in their heart, and ask forgiveness where they are neither sensible of an offence, nor will own the pardon as a favour. They accuse themselves for that which they did willingly and never condemned themselves for but will reiterate upon the first opportunity: They require things that they hope he will not give, and if they ask anything seriously it is either inconsiderable or with evil designs, and so becomes a provocation. Now can an All-seeing Eye discern this without Indignation? Will not an Almighty Hand be lifted up to destroy them who both delude themselves and mock the King of Glory? But lest we should experience the truth of this in our eternal Ruin, we are advised to a serious Repentance which will be the best Harbinger for all our Petitions; for if we see our Sins and feel their weight (it is to be hoped) we shall draw near with low apprehensions of ourselves and strong desires after God, with a high opinion of him and a hearty love to him, with many fears and yet many hopes; and who can be more fit to pray? What better foundation for those Prayers, which must reach as high as Heaven, than Humiliation and Repentance?

Now the better to dispose us to pray in this manner, God himself is brought in speaking to us from sundry places of Holy Scripture: The voice of God brought our first Father to repentance, *Gen.* 3: 9, and it will surely have the same effect on us, for who dare refuse when he invites that can pardon or punish, save or destroy? He begins first to speak to us in his Holy Word, to whom we are about to speak in our Prayers; so that those who expect God should hear their Prayers must hearken to his Word, especially where the matter is so excellent and of so great concern to us as in these invitations to repentance from the mouth of God himself. It was therefore most prudently ordered that we should begin with Holy Scripture; and for the particular Sentences I may say they are the plainest and most pertinent that can be found in the whole book of God, which though it be divine in every part, yet that care is well bestowed which selecteth such portions thereof as are suitable to the occasion: And thus the Reverend Composers of the *Liturgy,* like Skillful Physicians, have walked in this Garden of God which is stored with remedies of all kinds, and have gathered the choicest and most useful, different in operation but having the same effect, *viz.* To bring us to Repentance. They have chosen many, yet they leave it to the discretion of the succeeding Physicians of Souls to use such a Sentence every

149

day as may suit best with their own and their people's hearts.

. . .

[On the General Confession]

"That we may hereafter." The very Method of this exact Confession directs us in our Repentance to look three ways successively. 1. Inward, for Humiliation. 2. Upward, for Pardon. And 3. Onward, for Amendment. Which Order we must not break, nor disjoin the Connexion: For he that first looks up to God before he hath seen his sin will but mock the Almighty; he that first looks forward will but deceive himself and not be able to proceed. Again, he that looks inward and not upward will despair, he that looks upward and not inward will presume; and if he do both see his sin and seek for Mercy, but looks not onward to amend, he doth but dissemble; and of all the rest we must be careful of what we are to do *hereafter,* because the discovery of sin and the hopes of forgiveness are only to engage to a future Reformation.

. . .

"To the glory of thy holy Name." This Conclusion may either have respect to all the Petitions before, or it may particularly be applied to the last: In the *first* sense it is a Declaration, that (though we shall be happy in having all these Prayers heard, yet) we are not so devoted to our own advantage as to aim no higher, but we believe it will tend to God's Glory as well as our good. Nothing by us can be added to make his Perfections more glorious in themselves, but by such incomparable testimonies of Grace and Mercy his Goodness will be more clearly manifested to us and all men; for we consider that his delivering us from Death to Life, retrieving us from Fears of Hell to Hopes of Heaven, his changing us from Sin to grace, and doing all this for rebellious Wretches that he could easily destroy; this will be a great Manifesto of his Glory to all the World. For all that see will admire and be encouraged to repent and turn to this most merciful God, and we ourselves shall ever remember with joy and delight that we have found in him a generous propensity to pity the miserable, unspeakable kindness to help the unworthy, and omnipotent power to rescue the perishing from the Jaws of eternal Ruin. And with these holy thoughts the flames of gratitude will ever be preserved upon the Altar of our Hearts, and from thence daily will ascend a cloud of hearty Praises and Gratulations. Or, *secondly,* it may be annexed to the last Petition, *viz.* That we may not only do good but do it well, having an eye to his Glory, *Rom.* 14: 5, 6, not to our own estimation or to obtain the Praise of Men. That we may live *godlily, righteously,* and *soberly,* not to our own Credit but his *Glory.* And when we have done all, may in gratitude cast all at his Feet, to let all the World see by whose Long-suffering we are spared, by whose Mercy we are forgiven, and by whose Grace we are reformed: And that our holy Lives hereafter may show that we are so in love with God and his ways that we esteem it our chiefest Happiness to be like him, and walk in them all our days.

· · ·

[On "Glory be to the Father, and to the Son, and to the Holy Ghost: As it was in the beginning, is now, and ever shall be, world without end. Amen."]

It is our Duty to praise the Father for our Creation, the Son for our Redemption, the Holy Ghost for our Sanctification. The Father hath sent us into the World and preserves and provides for us in it. The Son hath lived with us and died for us, and being returned to his Glory is still mindful of us. The Holy Ghost doth come to us and stay with us as a Guard and a Guide, a Comforter and an Advocate: clearing our Minds, cleansing our Hearts, quickening our Affections and enforcing our Prayers. And shall we not then be highly ungrateful if we pay not a particular tribute to every person in special as well as to all in general? Remember the Angels sang Praise to the undivided and ever-blessed Trinity in the morning of the Creation, in the beginning of all time, *Job* 38: 7, and they and all the World do it *now,* and both Men and Angels shall continue in this Jubilee to *Eternity.* As long as Goodness endures, Gratitude and Praise

151

cannot cease. This *was,* and *is,* and ever shall be done in all Ages and Generations, *Ps.* 145: 4. The Patriarchs and Prophets did in the beginning and first Ages of the World; the Apostles and Martyrs in the first planting of the Gospel. And all these, though removed to Heaven, continue to sing Praises to the Triune God there as we and all pious Christians do here; and there will never want Tongues in Heaven and earth to sing this gratulatory Hymn for all Generations. Observe farther the comprehensiveness of these few words, which extend to all things as well as to all times and persons; and present at once to our view all the Mercies of God, past, present, and to come. They are an acknowledgment that all the good that ever was or shall be done, with all that is now enjoyed in Heaven and Earth, hath proceeded from this All-sufficient and everflowing Fountain to whom this tribute of Praise is, and was, and ever will be due. Behold then, O pious Soul, a glorious Choir of Angels, Patriarchs, Prophets, Apostles, Saints and Martyrs in Heaven, with all holy Men and Women in all the World, at once with united Voices and joyful Hearts singing this triumphant Song. Let this inspire thee with holy Raptures and Ecstasies of Devotion whilst thou singest thy part here on Earth, and when thou art taken hence thy place shall be supplied by the succeeding Generations, and thou shalt be advanced to a state as endless as his Mercy where thou shalt praise him to Eternity. What better Form can we have to glorify God by than this, which is a declaration of our Faith and a discharge of our Homage, in which we acknowledge his former Mercies, confess his present Favours to us and all the World, and glorify him for both? We hope in him for those that are to come, expecting all from him and promising those returns of Eucharist which we will forever make to him. How can this be done too often or repeated too frequently? Surely his Mercies are more frequent than our Praises can be.

· · ·

[On the Daily use of the Psalms in Morning and Evening Prayer]
The Book of *Psalms* seems to be a Collection of those devout

Hymns wherewith Holy Men did praise God upon public or private occasions, being fitted to all Conditions of the Church, and of particular persons also. They are Divine Prayers and Praises indited by the Spirit of God with such admirable variety that we may easily Collect a Form from thence either to Petition for anything we need or to glorify the Name of God for any mercy we have received. Wherefore they are used and commended by Christians, Jews, and Mahometans also. And although we have many differences among the several Parties that are called Christians, yet all agree to make use of these incomparable and sacred Anthems. . . . This joint Consent and universal Approbation will make it needless to spend much time to commend what all admire. Yet it were easy to reckon up those excellent Titles and honourable Characters which have been given them. They are called the instrument of Virtue, the marrow of Divinity, the Storehouse of Devotion, the Epitome of Holy Scripture. They contain excellent Forms to bless the People, to praise God, to rejoice in his Favour, to bewail his Absence, to confess our Faith, to crave Pardon of our Sins, deliverance from our Enemies, and all Blessings for the Church of God. In the use of them we ought to exercise all Graces, Repentance and Faith, Love and Fear of God, Charity to all men, and Compassion to the miserable. The Composition of them declares they are fitted for Men of all Ages and Degrees, in all Estates and Conditions, young and old; Kings, Priests, and People; in Prosperity and Adversity; here they may find that which so exactly suits them all, as if their Condition had been foreseen and particularly provided for. And if any who grant this shall except, That many of the *Psalms* are not applicable to their Condition, I shall confidently affirm That as devout Men in their enjoyment of the Divine Favour can be humbled in using the Complaints for want of it, which were uttered by better Men, and thereby be moved to see what they deserve and to consider what many of their Brethren want: So on the contrary, a Pious Man under trouble of Spirit can, by the Spiritual rejoicings there described, behold the goodness of God to others and foresee his own deliverance, receiving thereby additions to his Faith, Hope and Patience.

. . .

[On the Lessons from Scripture]

Before we begin to read or hear the Holy Scriptures, it will be useful that we consider, *First,* their own Excellence, to engage our Love to them. *Secondly,* The Providence of God in the composing and preserving them, to excite our Reverence. *Thirdly,* The care of the Church in fitting them to our use, to encourage our Diligence. *First,* The Scripture must needs be excellent, because it is the Revelation of the whole Will of God, so far as is necessary for our Salvation. We believe as God hath taught us, and as it was believed in the Primitive Church, that it is the complete Repository of all Divine Truths that concern Faith or Manners; and therefore we own it to be the Rule of our Lives and the Foundation of our Faith; and in all our considerable Controversies we place it in the Throne (as the Councils of *Ephesus* and *Aquileia* did) for the Moderator and Determiner of such doubts and differences. This is the guide of our Consciences, the ground of our Hopes, the evidence of our Inheritance, and the Law by which we shall be judged at the last day, *Jn.* 5: 45; *Rev.* 20: 12. Wherefore it is the Duty (*Jn.* 5: 39) and interest (2 *Tim.* 3: 15) of every Christian to be conversant in them, according to the command of Jesus, and the example of all God's Servants, who studied them more than any other Writings. . . . And if it were possible, we should exercise ourselves in them *day and night,* that is, always. But however we must spend so much time upon them that we may be always furnished with Precepts to direct, Promises to encourage, and Examples to quicken us to do all good; and also with Prohibitions to restrain, Threatenings to affright, and precedents to warn us from all evil. And being so constantly useful, and so able to show us all that is necessary to be known, believed, or to be done, we should love them and delight to hear and know them, because ignorance of these sacred Oracles will lay us open to errors in Judgment, (*Mk.* 12: 24) and wickedness in

154

Practice (*Ps.* 119: 3), and finally prove the ruin of our Souls.

· · ·

[On the Magnificat]

"My Soul doth magnify the Lord, and my Spirit hath rejoiced in God my Savior." The blessed Virgin (whom God chose to be the Instrument of the greatest Blessing that ever the World had) by the fruit of her lips, as well as of her womb, hath given apparent testimony of the extraordinary presence of the Divine Spirit with her and in her. For this sacred Hymn breathes forth such lovely mixtures of Faith and Fear, Humility and Love, Charity and Devotion, that it appears she was *full of grace* as well as *highly favoured.* And it should be our wish and endeavour to repeat it with the same Affections and holy Fervors with which she indited it. Perhaps we think we have not the same occasion; 'tis true, God the Word took Flesh in her Womb and that was her peculiar Privilege. But if we receive the Word of God, and the Motions of the Holy Spirit that attend it, we may turn that Word into Flesh by Faith and Obedience; if we so hear as to practice, we do conceive Christ by Faith. He is formed in us by the overshadowing power of the Holy Ghost in a pure heart, and he is by Holiness brought forth; for Christ himself calls such, *Mt.* 12:50, by the name of his *Mother.* We are to *rejoice with all that do rejoice:* But especially when we are sharers in the mercy and advantage which occasions that Joy; wherefore we are most of all obliged to rejoice with the blessed Virgin, both as she was the Mother of our Redeemer according to the Flesh, and because we may be so according to the Spirit. The *Lesson* we have heard is out of the *Old Testament;* and as there we find the Records and Examples of the Divine Mercy to the pious and humble, and of his Vengeance upon the proud and arrogant, so here we find a Form of Praise for those Dispensations of God's Providence. And since all the Deliverances of God's People there related are either founded on this mercy of our Redemption, flow from it, or are directed to it, this Hymn will teach us to turn the Old Testament into Gospel, and with the holy Patriarchs ever to apply all to this great Salvation, of which

155

all other Mercies were but Types. Behold then the Mother of Jesus saying to you, *O praise the Lord with me, Ps.* 34:3, *and let us magnify his Name together:* Let us show forth the greatness of his Power and Goodness, for we cannot set out his Perfections with any advantage, nor represent him greater than really he is (as we often magnify one another). But then we *magnify the Lord* when we declare how great he really is; and let us advance his Glory as high as is possible, for here is no danger of exceeding. Our Praises will be short but they must be real; wherefore before we can bear a part in this Anthem we must get our *Souls* affected with a sense of his infinite Power, and our minds exalted with the belief of his excellent Mercy. So our Praise shall be no Complement, but our *Soul* and *Spirit* shall bear their part and our Thanksgiving shall be real as his Favours are; Let his admirable Love present itself to our Affections until it excite our Wonder and Joy, our Hopes and Desires. And then let us still behold it, till these Passions begin to be moved by the Divine Love, and then they will carry a lovely Notion and fair Idea of it to the mind, and so effectively recommend it that the whole inward man shall be ravished with the beautiful Prospect and every Faculty of the Soul, every one of the Affections, shall unite into a devout Celebration of the Divine Mercy. Behold the holiest of Women; observe where she fixes her Eye, and whither she directs her Praises: She *rejoiceth* not in her own Excellencies, nor doth she *magnify* herself but *God* her *Savior;* which may check our vanity, who are so apt in a prosperous Success and unexpected Exaltation to sacrifice to our own deserts, to crown ourselves, though we snatch it from the head of Heaven's King. But sure, since he gives the Blessing he deserves the Honour, and he that pays it not is a double Thief and steals the Gift and the Glory also; for both are God's. She that was the Mother of Jesus after the Flesh thinks it no disparagement to confess her Son to be her *Savior,* but rejoices that he was so. Let not us then think we can be saved from temporal Evils, much less from eternal Death, without him; and let us esteem it a greater honour to us, and a surer ground of our rejoicing that the most High God is become our Salvation, than if we had our Strength in our own hands.

· · ·

[On the Apostles' Creed]

The place of this Creed in our Liturgy may be considered with respect to what goes before and that which follows it. (1.) That which goes before it is *The Lessons* taken out of the Word of God, for *Faith comes by hearing, Rom.* 10:17, and therefore when we have heard it, it is fit we should profess our Belief thereof, thereby setting (as it were) our Seals to the Truth of God, especially to such Articles as the Chapters now read unto us have confirmed. . . . We hope it may profit us, who as soon as we have heard it, do make *Confession of our Faith.* (2.) That which follows the Creed is *The Prayers,* which are grounded on it, "Faith is the Fountain of Prayers" (saith St. *Augustine*), whence the Apostle saith, *"How shall they call on him whom they have not believed?"* therefore that "we may pray, let us first believe." So that the reciting our Creed before we pray is the laying a Foundation whereupon to build our Requests: We believe in One Almighty God who is distinguished into Three Persons, the Father our Creator, the Son our Redeemer, the Holy Ghost our Sanctifier, by whom we and the whole Church may have Remission of Sins and the hopes of a blessed Resurrection to Eternal Life. Wherefore we may very reasonably pray to God the Father, in the Name of the Son, by the Assistance of the Spirit, in Fellowship with the Saints, for the Forgiveness of our Sins and a joyful Resurrection. Now for these reasons our Creed ought to be used as often as we do either solemnly read or pray, that is, in all Public Assemblies.

· · ·

[On the Versicles and Responses
before and after the Lord's Prayer]

Q. "The Lord be with you."
A. "And with thy Spirit."

If we have sincerely repeated our Creed together, we have professed our Faith in God and declared our Unity and Agree-

157

ment with one another; and then we have cause to hope our Prayers will prevail, since they were ushered in by Faith and Charity, the best Preparatives to that Duty. We have all owned that we have one Lord and one Faith, and now we are preparing as Brethren and Fellow Soldiers to unite our Requests and to send them to the Throne of Grace. But first, in token of our mutual Charity, the Church appoints (instead of the ancient *Kiss of Peace*) a hearty Salutation to pass between the Minister and People, he beginning in the phrase of *Boaz* to his Reapers, *The Lord be with you, (Ru.* 2: 4; *Ps.* 129:8) which was after drawn into common use as a form of Salutation to all, and used by St. *Paul* in his Epistles (2 *Th.* 3:16). To which the People are to return a good wish for their Minister, in a form taken from the same Apostle (2 *Tim.* 4:22; *Gal.* 6:18) desiring *the Lord may be with his Spirit:* Which is no invention of our own, . . . But sure it never had a fitter place than in our excellent Service, where it succeeds the Creed as the Symbol and Bond of Peace. St. *John* forbids us to salute (or desire *God to be with*) any that cleave not to the right Faith, 2 *Jn.* 5: 10, 11. But when the Minister hath heard everyone profess his Faith in the same words with himself, how cheerfully and without scruple may he salute them as Brethren, and they requite his affection with a like return? 'Tis too sadly true that little Differences in Religion make wide Separations and the most incurable Animosities. Why then should not our exact agreement be as forcible a uniter of all our hearts, since the Profession of the same Faith hath ever been reputed the firmest Bond of Charity. Wherefore, when those endearing Offices have warmed our hearts with mutual Love, these expressions will not barely signify the Affections between the Minister and his People, but may be used as the exercise of their Charity by way of Prayer for one another. Let the Spiritual man meditate how often *Satan* is among the Sons of God; how many of his flock which now are preparing to join with him are oppressed with hard hearts or disturbed with vain thoughts; and then let him earnestly pray *the Lord* may *be with them,* that his Prayers be not in vain for them. Let the People also remember how comfortable and advantageous it will be to them that he who is their Mouth to God may have a pure heart and fervent spirit; and with these thoughts let them most heartily requite their Pastor's Prayer by desiring *the Lord to be with his Spirit,* that both may (by acknowledging their Insufficiency and declaring their Charity) obtain a Blessing of God for each other, and find the benefit of these short Petitions in every part of the succeeding Offices.

· · ·

[On the Evening Collect for Peace]

"O God, from whom all holy desires, all good counsels, and all just works do proceed." This Collect hath the same title and seems to have the same subject with that in the *Morning Office.* And indeed Peace is so desirable a Blessing that we cannot pray for it too often, especially for different kinds of Peace, as it is in the present case if we well observe it. In the *Morning* we pray for external, in the *Evening* for internal Peace. In the beginning of the Day, being to conduct various affairs and converse with the World, we desire to be preserved from the injuries, affronts and designs of evil Men: In the close thereof we request that Tranquillity of mind that springs from the Testimony of a good Conscience, that when our Hearts lie as easy as our Heads, our sleep may be sweet and quiet. The first kind of Peace sometimes the best of Men cannot obtain, for the wicked will do wickedly; but even then this inward Peace will support them and make a calm within when the waves beat most furiously from without. So that this is the most necessary and most advantageous. Wherefore we are taught to ask this (which is called the *Peace of God)* from the *God of Peace,* who is here described to us as the Author and Finisher of all Holiness and Righteousness, which are the surest and only foundations for a true and lasting Peace. From which we may learn that there is an inseparable union between Righteousness and true Peace, and that we cannot have this Peace unless it spring from *holy desires, good counsels, and just works.* If the Grace of God work these in us, it is not all the slanders, the scorn nor injustice of

159

the World can hinder the serene reflexions and inward *Peace* of a good Conscience. He that doth not deserve reproach can nobly despise it; and he that hath not provoked his Neighbor to wrong him by any evil doing can easily bear the greatest of Injuries. Whereas if all the World be quiet and none disturb the wicked Man, he makes himself restless because there is an enemy within that upbraids him more loudly and wounds him more deeply than he can do the *holy* Man. Whoever therefore enquires for *true Peace,* let them here behold him, in and from whom are all the causes of it, with Love and Admiration. And let them acknowledge to his Glory and their own Comfort that he is the Author and Finisher of every good Work. He excites our Affections to desire that which is good, engageth our Will to choose it, and strengtheneth our Hands to perform it. There are no holy Thoughts in our minds, nor good Purposes in our Hearts, nor any righteous Actions in our lives but it is in, and by, and through him. To him then let us make our Supplications, that he will fill our Hearts with the motions of his Holy Spirit, the first seeds of all virtue; and by the continuing influence of the same Grace make these *holy desires* spring up into prudent and *religious counsels* and determinations; and by favourable circumstances and addition of strength ripen them into pious and *just works;* and the fruit hereof will be *Peace.* We may cheerfully hope and pray that he that planted the Root and sowed the Seed will give us the pleasure of the Fruit and comfort of the Harvest. And let us beware, since we confess this to be the fruit of Righteousness, that when we seem most earnest in our Prayers for this Peace we do not wilfully deprive ourselves of it and hinder our own wishes by stifling holy Thoughts and breaking pious Resolutions and neglecting *good Works.* For he that cuts the Root and lops off the Branches must not expect ever to eat of this Fruit; and if he complains, deserves to be silenced as the Author of his own Misery.

(37) **William Wake**
Archbishop of Canterbury
The Principles of the Christian Religion explained in a Brief Commentary upon the Church Catechism
1699

Q. Rehearse the Articles of your Belief.

A. I BELIEVE IN GOD THE FATHER ALMIGHTY, &tc.

Q. You said that those words, *I believe,* were not only the first words of your *Creed,* but the most material; as running in effect through every branch of it. Tell me, therefore, what do you mean when you say *I believe?*

A. To *believe,* in general, is to *assent to the truth of anything upon the sole authority of the person who delivers it:* if he be a man only, the assent which I give to what he says produces in me a *human faith;* if, as here, he be *God,* then the assent which I give to what is delivered by Him is properly a *divine faith.*

Q. What is the difference, with respect to us, between these two?

A. It is very great: for because a man, though never so wise and careful himself, may yet not be honest, and so impose upon me; or should he be never so upright, may yet, after all his care, be mistaken himself and thereby lead me into error; therefore, in assenting to what such a one proposes, I can, at the most, give but such a *belief* to it as is suitable to a mere *human testimony.* I may believe what he says to be *true,* but yet so as not to exclude a *possibility* of its being *otherwise.* Whereas God, being neither capable of being deceived Himself nor of imposing upon any other, when I give my assent to what He has revealed, I do it not only with a certain assurance that what I believe *is true,* but with an absolute security that *it cannot possibly be false.*

Q. But why do you say, *I believe,* and not *we believe;* as when you pray, you say, *OUR Father,* &tc.?

A. Because though one man may *pray,* yet one man cannot *believe* for another. And however in charity I may suppose every Christian to believe what is here delivered: yet since it is certain there are many *infidels* and *hypocrites* scattered up and down among the faithful, and I cannot certainly distinguish who are indeed believers and who not; neither can I, with an assurance of faith, say *we believe,* because I cannot certainly tell whether another man does truly believe those articles or no. Besides, that this Creed being intended to be the form upon the confession whereof persons should be admitted to baptism; and in that case every one was to make a distinct profession of his faith in order thereunto; it was fitting the Creed itself should be penned after such a manner as was most proper for the main end for which it was composed.

---

(38) **Samuel Johnson**
Priest and missionary in Connecticut from the Society for the Propagation of the Gospel, first president of King's College (Columbia University)
On the Beauty of Holiness in the Worship of the Church of England
1749

First, as to the negative part of holiness, which consists in hating and avoiding all sin and wickedness, which God hates; what can more effectually tend to this, than to begin with those declarations of holy Scripture, from whence we may abundantly learn the necessity of true repentance, the impossibility of pardon without it, and the assurance of God's pardon and mercy upon our true repentance? And what can better tend to this purpose, than the excellent exhortation which the minister thereupon makes, to put us upon the exercise of such a repentance, by confessing and forsaking our sins that we may obtain mercy? And what can more effectually tend to make us abhor our sins and reform our lives, than to begin our worship with such a serious solemn act of confession of sin, and imploring God's mercy and pardon in Jesus Christ, as is expressed in that excellent comprehensive form, which our holy mother, the church, hath put into our mouths; upon which the minister is directed to declare God's pardon to every true penitent. By which she teacheth all her children, that if they would look for the acceptance of all their following prayers and praises, they should begin with such a solemn act of renewing their repentance, in order to obtain God's pardon and acceptance, without which their worship will be but mocking God. For if they regard iniquity in their hearts, the Lord will not hear their prayers; and if they persist in their wickedness, without repentance, their prayers, and all their services are an abomination to him. On which account I beseech you, as far as possible, to make conscience of coming in season, that you may have opportunity, by such an act of repentance, to secure your pardon, and the acceptance of your following services in the other parts of worship; and in order thereunto, to perform this confession in the most serious and truly penitent manner. And that you may be the more affected with it, you are wisely directed, every one, to repeat it with his own mouth, that he may make it his own act and deed, recollecting in his mind, with true contrition, his own particular sins and infirmities.

And then secondly, as to the positive part of holiness, which consists in being devoted to God, to be like him, and that from a sense of duty, and in submission and obedience to his will; what can more tend to promote this, than all the other parts of our worship in their order? Particularly,

1. The Lord's Prayer, which is the most wonderfully comprehensive, and on every account the most excellent form of prayer that was ever composed in the world; and which our Lord hath made, as it were, the badge of his disciples. On

which account it cannot be sufficiently wondered at, that any that call themselves his disciples, should not think themselves obliged in conscience to use it, since he hath expressly commanded us, when we pray to say, Our Father, etc., especially since nothing can more effectually tend to promote universal holiness, than the frequent and serious offering it up in our devotions. For therein we address God, as our Heavenly Father, which strongly teaches and obliges us to be his holy and obedient children. Therein we pray for whatever may tend to promote his glory, and our own best good and happiness, both temporal and spiritual. Particularly, we pray that we and all the world may hallow, or do all the honor we possibly can to his holy name, both by word and deed. That his Kingdom may come, and rule in all our hearts, which is a Kingdom of universal holiness, into which no unclean or unholy thing can ever enter. And that we on earth, may all, in everything, learn to do and submit to his holy will, as the saints and angels do in heaven, that we may be forever holy and happy with them. We next testify our entire dependence upon God, by praying for our daily bread, *i.e.,* for our preservation, and whatsoever is needful for our comfortable subsistence; which sense of our dependence is a great principle of true holiness. We next pray for the forgiveness of all our sins, whereinsoever we have been unholy in heart or life; and that we may be qualified for God's pardon, it must be supposed that we have truly repented of them; and we are here taught to testify our hearty forgiveness of others, without which we dare not look for forgiveness from Him; which is another great article of that holiness, in imitation of him, without which no man shall see the Lord. We then pray that he would keep us from all temptation, to every kind of sin or unholiness; and that he would save and deliver us from all evil; both the evil of sin, and the evil of punishment; both from the power and guilt of sin here, and the wrath and displeasure of God hereafter, that we may be secure of his everlasting favor. And lastly, in dependence upon Him, and acknowledgement to Him for all that we ask of Him, we ascribe unto Him,

164

the kingdom, power and glory, for ever and ever. To which, as to all other prayers, according to the Scripture pattern we add a joint vocal *Amen.* Than all which, nothing can more abundantly tend to promote universal piety and holiness.

2. Having made this entrance on the public worship of God, we proceed to the celebration of his praises in the psalms of holy David, and other devout hymns, taken out of the New Testament, and that admirable Christian Hymn called *Te Deum,* between the lessons; all which breathe nothing but holiness, devotion and purity. For they do either celebrate the glories, perfections and operations of God, in his wonderful works of creation, providence, or redemption; or express our sense of our entire dependence upon Him, and innumerable obligations to his infinite goodness; our abhorrence of every thing displeasing to Him, or our resolution to be in all things obedient to his will; or explain the duty and happiness of every virtue, or the baseness, perverseness and misery of every vice; or open the glorious views both of God's kingdom of grace, and his kingdom of glory, and teach us in the practice and experience of all those heavenly graces which are necessary to qualify us for an interest in the glories, and felicities thereof. These, and such as these, are the noble subjects of those sublime odes, all which are in effect, nothing else but universal holiness to the Lord. So that the Psalms are a most copious storehouse of devotion, consisting of an endless and most beautiful variety.

3. After the Psalms, come the Lessons, taken out of the holy Scripture; and under this head, I may also mention the Epistles and Gospels, all being a variety of select and most instructive portions of the holy oracles, which are best adapted to instruct the people in the knowledge of divine and heavenly things, and to improve them in devotion and holiness; being all of them profitable for doctrine, for reproof, for correction, for instruction in righteousness, that not only the man of God, but even every Christian, may be perfect, thoroughly furnished to all good works. For in them, either some article of faith, or rule of life is explained and inculcated; or some ancient prophesy, or some Gospel fact correspondent to it, or some miraculous operation, or remarkable providence, or example is set before us, etc., all tending to confirm our faith and hope, and to train us up in the blessed trade of holy living, for a happy immortality, which is the whole design and business of this heavenly school, the House of God; to which the public reading of the Word of God is so admirably subservient, that it is extremely surprising that any Christians, for the sake of tedious long sermons, and extempore prayers, which are but mere human performances, should jostle out the Psalms, and reading the Scriptures, except here and there a little scrap of them. This sure, if any thing may be called imposing the inventions of men in the worship of God; for I believe it may be truly said (with regard to many of their assemblies at least) that there are twenty times as much Scripture in one of our services, as in one of theirs.

4. Next to the Lessons, I may mention the Creeds as another part of our public worship, which also vastly tend to promote piety and holiness, and therefore ought by all means to be openly recited when we worship God. For as with the heart, man believeth unto righteousness, so with the mouth, confession is made unto salvation. These Creeds are only brief summaries of the Christian doctrine, so that nothing can seem more strange than that any Christian should disapprove of them; and every article of our most holy faith, is either a motive or obligation to holiness. For what can more tend to make us holy, than to believe that we and all creatures in heaven and earth, do depend entirely on God the Father Almighty, for both our beings, and all we enjoy? What can more engage us to it, than to believe in Jesus Christ; his only Son, our Lord, who came into our nature, and taught us a most heavenly doctrine, and died a most bitter death, to kill the power and take away the guilt of sin; and arose from the dead, to confirm his doctrine, and ascertain our immortality, and that we might thereby be induced to arise to a new and holy life; and ascended into

Heaven, that we might thereby be taught and obliged to mortify our earthly members, and set our affections on things above, where Jesus is at the right hand of God? What can better tend to make us careful of all our behavior, than to consider that we must give an account of ourselves to him, when he shall return to judge the quick and the dead? Especially if we consider further, that he hath sent his Spirit, which is the Spirit of Holiness, to enable us to mortify our lusts and passions, and to live as it becomes the redeemed of the Lord, and to be as it were the universal soul of his Church, and the fountain of all spiritual life to our souls? And how can we think of any thing but true repentance, faith and holiness, when these are the qualifications indispensably requisite, to give us a place in the holy Catholic Church of God, and to entitle us to the forgiveness of our sins, and everlasting life, and happiness in his heavenly kingdom? Thus the repetition of the several articles of our holy faith still drive at the same blessed end, of promoting universal holiness; whether it be done in that short form of sound words, which is called the Apostles' Creed, as being a summary of the Apostles' doctrine; or in the Nicene Creed, which was agreed upon as a summary of the catholic doctrine, within 250 years after the Apostles' times, by a general council of bishops from all parts of the Christian Church; or in the other creed which was formed to bear testimony against the chief heresies, which infested the Church in those and the following ages.

---

(39) **Thomas Secker**
Archbishop of Canterbury
Sermon XXV, in Explanation and Defense
of the Liturgy of the Church of England
c. 1758–1768

The confession is directed to be said of the whole congregation, after the minister.

. . .

In the first words of the confession, we apply to God, as our *Father:* the author of our being, and therefore entitled to all honour and service from us; the adopter of us, after our forfeiture, into his family again through Jesus Christ, and therefore entitled to have it paid him with double gratitude. We acknowledge him *Almighty,* either to protect or punish; and therefore to be obeyed from interest as well as duty: we acknowledge him to be *most merciful;* and therefore in the highest degree unfit to have been offended, and fit to have pardon asked of him.

The expression, *We have erred and strayed from thy ways, like lost sheep,* is taken from Scripture. *I have gone astray, like a lost sheep: seek thy servant.* Again: *all we, like sheep, have gone astray; we have turned every one to his own way: and the Lord hath laid on him,* on Christ, *the iniquity of us all.* But to understand the full propriety of the phrase, it must be observed that both the likelihood of straying was much greater and the consequences of it much more fatal in open countries, full of wild beasts, as those of the East were, than in ours. And such *a great and terrible wilderness,* in the spiritual sense, is this world.

It hath been objected that our confession is too general. But it comprehends all sins, both of omission and commission. The particulars, each person's conscience, if it be duly tender, will represent to itself as far as is needful, or well can be, in public. And was every sin that men can fall into expressed by name, the catalogue would be too long; and such that many (it is to be hoped) could not with truth join in the whole: nor would it be proper that they who had, and had not, been guilty should confess all the same things; or that those about us should perceive which we did confess.

It hath been further objected that in our appointed form there is no acknowledgment of the original corruption of our

168

nature by the fall. Nor is there an explicit one even in the prayer of our blessed Lord. But surely, when we say that *we have followed too much the devices and desires of our own hearts,* it may well be part of our meaning that they are from the first irregular and depraved.

The words *and there is no health in us,* besides that they also profess our inward frame throughout to be more or less disordered, signify too that we have no power of our own, either to cure the spiritual diseases of which we are already sick, or to prevent the attacks of future ones. And therefore we apply to God that he would *heal our souls,* whom also, in the conclusion, we implicitly promise that whatever amendment shall be produced in us by the means which he prescribes, we will give the glory of it not to ourselves but to his holy name: *who hath blessed us with all spiritual blessings in Christ to the praise and glory of his grace.*

After the confession follows the absolution.

. . .

And as none but his ministers are commissioned to make this solemn proclamation of pardon on his behalf: it is fitly ordered that none should share with them in publishing it by repeating it along with them. And you will observe that wherever in the service the congregation are not directed to speak, but the minister only, their speaking the same words low, as many persons inconsiderately do, removes only part of the impropriety and leaves the rest. On this therefore, and the like occasions, you will remember that your business is only to hearken and assent with silent reverence: of which reverence, in the present case, continuing on your knees in token of your humble thankfulness to God is undoubtedly a suitable expression.

After the above-mentioned declaration, immediately follows an admonition to *pray for repentance and God's holy Spirit:* which may seem perhaps needless and unaccountable considering that we have just been professing to exercise repentance and have been assured of God's forgiveness upon it, of which the gift of his Spirit is a consequence. But if it be considered also that we are to repent, not only before but after pardon;

and even the more deeply for the mercy and love shown in our pardon else it would be justly revoked: and that the continuance of God's Spirit with us depends on the continuance of our supplications for his presence, which will also procure us greater degrees of it; there will be found no weight in this objection.

At the end of the absolution and of every prayer the people are directed to say *Amen:* which means, it is true; we do sincerely desire, or sincerely affirm, what hath been said. This was the practice of the Jewish Church: it was also that of the Christian in the Apostle's days. *How shall he that occupieth the room of the unlearned say Amen at thy giving of thanks, seeing he understandeth not what thou sayest?* And the subsequent ecclesiastical writers show that it used to be pronounced audibly and fervently: each expressing his own faith or desire, and animating that of his fellow worshipers. We should therefore by no means neglect to give this proof, amongst others, that we not only hear the service with attention but join in it with earnestness.

After the confession and absolution comes the Lord's Prayer: it being a very proper time to address God in that form which our Savior taught his Disciples, when we have approved ourselves his real disciples by repentance of sins and faith in the Gospel-offers of mercy. And as he directs, *When ye pray, say, our Father, &c.,* our liturgy accordingly directs that every one should say it. For so they did in the primitive Church: in which it was called the daily, the appointed, the public, the common prayer of Christians. Further: as our blessed Redeemer delivered it twice and we see it in St. *Matthew* with the doxology, *For thine is the kingdom,* &tc., and in St. *Luke,* without it; we sometimes use it one way, sometimes the other.

And now having presumed, in these solemn words, to claim God for our Father through Christ; for though his name is not mentioned in this prayer, it is to be understood by us in every article of it; we now proceed to vent the joy and thankfulness belonging to such a privilege. Which I observed to you before is the second part of our public service, as it was in the ancient

Church; where, St. *Basil* informs us, the people, after confession, rose from prayer and went on to psalmody. But to make the transition more natural and beneficial, we first beg that God would permit and assist us, unworthy as we are, to pay him this homage. *O Lord, open thou our lips; and our mouth shall show forth thy praise:* which are the words of David in his chief penitential psalm, the fifty-first. Guilt had shut up his mouth from the utterance of cheerful sounds, till humiliation and assurance of pardon gave him that liberty of speech again which, in his expressions, we pray it may give us. And some of the earliest liturgies used the same verse for the same purpose: as they did likewise that which follows here, and which is found in two different psalms, *O God, make speed to save us: O Lord, make haste to help us:* it being seasonable at all times to request that, as our danger is continual, he would be continually at hand to *save* us from sin and *help* us in our duty; especially when we are just advancing to so sublime a duty and one which requires such purity of heart. *For praise is not seemly in the mouth of a sinner,* but *it becometh well the just to be thankful.*

The way then being thus prepared, and having qualified ourselves with holy David to say, *My heart is ready, my heart is ready, I will sing and give praise,* we rise up from our knees and stand upon our feet. For so we read that when *the Priests and Levites praised the Lord, all Israel stood.* And we begin this good work with that summary of all our praises to which we shall often return in the course of them, and in which we shall conclude them: *Glory be* ascribed *to the Father, and to the Son, and to the Holy Ghost: as it was in the beginning* of time *by* angels, *when the morning stars sang together and all the sons of God shouted for joy.* As it hath been ever since by religious persons in succeeding ages, according to the degree of their light; as it *is now* by all the saints in earth and heaven, *and ever shall be,* not only throughout the present scene of things, by new Christians rising up in the place of those who die or fall away (whatever men or devils may do to prevent it), but after the final consummation, when all are united into one general assembly: whose triumphant acclamations to our Creator, our Redeemer, our Sanctifier, shall re-sound *world without end,* duration without period, in that blessed state which shall last to eternity.

And now having proposed the unspeakably great subject that we are to celebrate, we invite each other to enter upon it more particularly: the minister saying, *Praise ye the Lord;* which is the literal translation of *Alleluiah,* so often repeated in the Old Testament, in the New, in the liturgies of the universal Church; and the people answering with joyful approbation, *The Lord's name be praised.*

. . .

In this manner then we glorify God: beginning always with the 95th Psalm as the whole Christian Church did in early ages, and as the nature of the Psalm recommends to us: it being a distinct invitation to the several duties of praise, prayer, and hearing, with an awful warning of the danger of neglecting God.

. . .

When we call him, in this Psalm, *the strength of our salvation,* we mean that by his power alone we can be saved from the present and future evils. When we call him *a great King above all Gods,* we mean above all that have ever had that name ascribed to them: the princes of the nations, the false deities of the heathen Satan, *the God of this world* and the holy angels in Heaven. When we say that *in his hands are all the corners of the earth, and the strength of the hills is his also,* we mean that his presence and his influence extend to the remotest and most inaccessible places; and there is none where he cannot deliver or punish. When we call our-selves *the people of his pasture and the sheep of his hand,* we own our Maker to be likewise our preserver, supporter, and director; who feeds our souls by his word and his grace, as well as our bodies with daily bread, and guides us mercifully through this world to a better. *Today if you will hear his voice, harden not your hearts* is an affecting and alarming exhortation, that if we design ever to become his servants in earnest we should hearken im-mediately to his continual calls; else through a habit of disobe-

172

dience our minds may grow callous and *past feeling.* The words, *when your fathers tempted me,* which are put into the mouth of God himself, the Jews (for whom first this Psalm was composed) were to understand literally of their fathers according to the flesh. But we are to take them of those who have gone before us in the profession of religion: and whom we are not to resemble in *tempting and proving* God; that is, doubting and putting to unreasonable trials his omnipotence, his goodness and truth: lest . . . we also be excluded from what it prefigured, that eternal *rest* which *remains for the people of God* in Heaven.

At the end of this, and each Psalm that we repeat, of whatever nature it may be, we add the same doxology that we used at first: glory being due to God for everything he hath taught and everything he hath done, both in former times and present; for every affliction as well as every enjoyment. And therefore we do well to observe the Apostle's rule of *giving thanks always, for all things, unto God and the Father in the name of our Lord Jesus Christ.*

Then we proceed to rehearse the Psalms, in proper portions according to the days of the month: of which it will be needful to say much more than there is now time to say. I shall therefore conclude with only remarking in general that words of God's own inspiring are surely the fittest to praise him: in which, being so noble a duty, we should take peculiar care to perform it in the most unexceptionable, judicious, and affectionate manner. *When you glorify the Lord, exalt him as much as you can; for even yet will he far exceed: and when you exalt him, put forth all your strength and be not weary; for you can never go far enough.*

. . .

[Sermon XXVIII, on Evening Prayer]

THE liturgy of our Church has now been explained to you as far as the end of the Morning Prayer. The Evening Prayer hath nothing different from it; excepting the Hymns that follow the Lessons, and the two Collects after that for the day.

The Hymn after the first Lesson, called *Magnificat,* from the word with which it begins in the Latin, was used anciently by the Western Church; and continues to be used by the Protestants abroad. It is the song of the blessed Virgin, recorded by St. *Luke,* on the confirmation which she received at Elizabeth's house of what the angel had told her, that she should become the mother of our Lord by the operation of the Holy Ghost: and it expresses most naturally the transport which on that occasion she must feel; but like the Hymn of Zacharias, in phrases of the Old Testament to be interpreted from the New: of which matter I have already spoken.

My soul doth magnify the Lord, doth acknowledge the infinite greatness of his power and mercy: *for he hath regarded the lowliness of his handmaiden;* that is, the *low estate;* for so the original signifies and so it is expressed in our Bibles; not the humility of mind which the Holy Virgin was too humble to ascribe to herself. *From henceforth all generations shall call me blessed:* as we do accordingly, both by repeating this Hymn and in our common speech. *For he, that is mighty, hath magnified me,* hath raised me to great honour: *and holy is his name;* his truth, his justice, his mercy, his concern for the goodness as well as happiness of his creatures, are gloriously manifested in this wonderful dispensation. *He hath showed* in times past, and will as certainly now as if it were done already, *strength with his arm,* supernatural deeds performed by his power for the erection of the kingdom of his Son: and hath often, and will again, *scatter* and defeat *the proud* opposers of it by means of those very *imaginations of their hearts* in which they exult. *The mighty* . . . shall be put down from their seat, and humble and meek Christians *exalted* in their stead. *They that hunger and thirst after righteousness* shall be *filled with* spiritual *good things; and the rich,* that rely on the vain and false treasures of their own wisdom and merit, he will convict of being *poor and blind and naked, and* so *send* them *empty away. He hath helped his servant Israel,* all that by obeying him, become his people *as he promised to our forefathers: Abraham* the father of the faithful *and his* true *seed;* thus *remembering his* covenanted *mercy,* which shall last *forever.* This is the triumph of the holy Virgin: and every part of it should be our own likewise. For God *hath regarded our low estate,* together with her's, and *magnified* us and made us *blessed.* And we should magnify and bless him continually for it.

Instead of this hymn, our Prayer Book tells us, the 98th Psalm may be used, and in some places it frequently is: in which we exhort one another to *sing unto the Lord a new song;* words denoting, in the book of Revelation, Gospel praises: and we foretell that *all lands* shall join in it *with trumpets and shawms* (another instrument of wind-music which in our Bible is called a cornet): whence we may conclude, if it needed proof, that musical instruments are lawful in Christian worship. This future time of universal thanksgiving is described to be when God shall *remember;* that is, shall give evidence that he hath never forgot *his mercy and truth towards the house of Israel,* according to the flesh; and not only they but *all the ends of the world shall see his salvation.* No wonder that even the irrational and inanimate parts of nature are called upon by a lofty figure of speech to celebrate that glorious day: *the sea* to *make a noise, and all that therein is; the floods* to *clap their hands, and the hills to be joyful together before the Lord:* partly for the present happiness of that period, in which possibly the lowest of God's works may share; but chiefly for the approach of the next and concluding scene of Providence, when he shall *come* finally *with righteousness to judge the world and the people with equity.*

After the second lesson is appointed another hymn used by the ancient Church, in their private devotions at least; and by the present Greek and foreign reformed, as well as ours and the Romish, in their public ones; and called from the Latin beginning of it, *Nunc dimittis.* It expresses the gratitude of good old Simeon, *a just man and devout* as we read in St. *Luke, and waiting for the consolation of Israel; to whom it was revealed that he should not die till he had seen the Lord's Christ.* Accordingly *he came by the spirit into the temple; and when the parents brought in the child Jesus he took him up in his arms* (image to yourselves the scene, I beg you) *and blessed God and said: Lord, now lettest thou thy servant depart in peace,* that is, in comfort, *according to thy word; for mine*

175

eyes have seen thy salvation which thou hast prepared to set *before the face of all people.* And the following sentence hath a strong appearance of being designed by the Holy Ghost to intimate (whether the speaker of it perceived the design or not) that contrary to the expected and natural order of things, Christ should first *be a light to lighten the Gentiles;* then, afterwards, *the glory of God's people Israel.* To perceive the fitness of Simeon's thanksgiving for our use, it needs only be remembered, and ever should in repeating it, that we also *have seen the Lord's salvation.* For though we have not yet beheld our Savior with our bodily eyes, to that of faith he is exhibited continually in the Gospel history and sacraments; we may meet him in his church, we may converse with him in our private meditations. And this we should think happiness enough for us here, whatever else we want or suffer; and be always prepared and always willing to *bless God* and *depart in peace.*

For this hymn we are allowed to use, and sometimes do, the 67th Psalm: which is a prophetic prayer that, through *the light of God's countenance,* his gracious illumination, *the way* of his providence and man's duty to him *may be known on earth; his saving health,* the means by which he heals and saves men's souls, *to all nations,* who are invited to *rejoice and be glad,* because *he shall judge the folk righteously;* shall govern and reward the people of the world (for so the word *folk* signifies and was not a low expression formerly) by the equitable and merciful rules of Christianity. For *then,* on our doing this, *the earth shall bring forth her increase* more plentifully, *and God, even our own God, shall give us his blessing* temporal and spiritual: *for godliness hath promise of the life that now is and of that which is to come.*

The former of the two Collects, peculiar to Evening Prayers, is taken from a Latin form at least 1100 years old. It begs for the greatest of blessings here below, that joyful peace of mind which our Savior promised his Disciples: *Peace I leave with you: my peace I give unto you: not as the world giveth, give I unto you.* And since it cannot be obtained but by *holy desires, good* and prudent *counsels* for the execution of them, *and just actions* done in consequence of both, so we petition him *from whom all* these *proceed* to grant it us by means of them: that *our hearts being set* by his grace *to keep his commandments,* and our ways *defended* by his Providence *from the fear of our enemies,* we may find *the work of righteousness, peace, and its effect, quietness and assurance forever.*

The latter Collect, taken in part from an office of the Greek Church, prays more particularly for the safety of the ensuing night: that God's favour may shine upon us and *lighten our darkness;* that is, protect us while we are unable to help ourselves, or even to know our danger. The same phrase is twice used in the book of Psalms: *Unto the godly there ariseth up light in darkness,* and again, *the Lord shall make my darkness to be light.*

---

(40) **John Henry Hobart**
Bishop of New York, founder of The General Theological Seminary
A Companion for the Book of Common Prayer
1805 / 1827
(Footnotes are from the original text)

Of the Order for Daily Morning and Evening Prayer

In the primitive ages of the Church it was customary to meet not only on Sundays, but *daily* for the public worship of God. Our Church, hoping that the time will come when the devotion of the people will admit of the restoration of this pious and primitive custom, continues to style her service the Order for *Daily* Morning and Evening Prayer. The service is performed daily in the Cathedrals and in some of the parish churches in England. Many of our churches are opened for public worship on Wednesdays and Fridays, which are the days on the which the litany is read, and also on the festivals and fasts. Every pious member of our Church should endeavour to attend regularly on these days; not only to enjoy the inestimable advantage and privilege of worshiping GOD "in the beauty of holiness"; not only for the purpose of commemorating the great events of redemption set forth in the festivals and fasts, and of celebrating the memories of the Apostles and first disciples of our LORD; but also with the view of contributing, by the force of example, to the revival of primitive piety, and to the more general attention to the solemn duty of public worship.

The Church, in her Book of Common Prayer, only acknowledges two daily services, the one for *morning,* and the other for the *evening,* or afternoon. In some congregations a third service has been introduced.[1] And in this case, when the appropriate evening service has been previously performed, the liberty sometimes is taken of forming another; but on these occasions in England, and in many in our own country, the regular evening prayer is used; and this appears the most proper course. But certainly, on all occasions of service after the customary hours of the appropriate evening service, when that service has not been previously performed, evident propriety dictates that it should be used without alteration or abridgment.[2] . . .

[1.] It is supposed by many judicious persons that a *third service on Sunday* or, as it is commonly called, an *evening lecture* is an innovation that does not subserve the real interests of religion. They are of opinion that the evening is not a proper reason to collect together a number of people for any serious purpose; that the multiplying of *sermons* tends to encourage the very prevalent error that religion consists principally in *hearing sermons;* and that the *old way* of spending the evening of Sunday in pious exercises in the family, in the religious instruction of children and servants, tended much more to advance the interests of piety. On the other hand, it is thought that, from the present relaxation of family discipline and neglect of family religion, Sunday evening, if not occupied with the public services of the Church, would probably be passed in an unprofitable, if not frivolous manner.

[2.] The use of the forms of *family prayer* on any occasion of public worship could certainly never have been contemplated by the Church, and would obviously be injudicious and improper.

It may not be amiss to state a form for a *third service,* which is used in the city of New York and has always had the sanction of the Bishops of that Diocese, under the canon empowering a Bishop to draw up a form of prayer for extraordinary occasions.

178

Explanation of the Service

The MORNING and EVENING SERVICES commence with some short SENTENCES from the Holy Scripture, which are read by the minister to impress on the people their guilt and unworthiness in the sight of GOD, and also his promises of pardon and forgiveness; in order that they may be excited to worship him with reverence and godly fear, and at the same time with humble faith and confidence.

The first three of these sentences are not in the English Prayer Book, as they are not of a penitential nature. They should not be read unless with some of the other sentences, otherwise, the connection between the sentences and the exhortation is broken and the minister cannot with so great propriety say that "the Scripture moveth us, in sundry places, to acknowledge and confess our manifold sins and wickedness," when he has not read the sentences which *"move"* to this necessary duty.

The design of

The Exhortation

which is to be recited by the minister alone, and not to be repeated by the people, is to apply the foregoing sentences and

---

The form of *evening* or afternoon prayer is pursued until the Psalms, when one of the *Selections* is generally used. Then a lesson taken from the Calendar, and appropriate to the season, followed by the *Deus misereatur,* or *Benedic, Anima mea,* the *Creed,* the *Versicles* before the Collects, the *Collect* for the day, and for *Aid against Perils,* the *Prayer for Christ's Church militant,* and one of the *short prayers* at the end of the *Communion Service,* concluded by the *Apostolic Prayer,* "The grace of our LORD JESUS CHRIST," &tc. There certainly is no authority for using, on any occasion, any service except the form of Morning and Evening Prayer, unless set forth under the authority of the Canon above referred to, which empowers the Bishop of every Diocese to compose forms of prayer for *extraordinary occasions,* which forms are to be transmitted to his clergy, and to be used by them. In those states where there is no Bishop, the form of prayer or thanksgiving composed by the Bishop of some other state is to be used. Canon 38th.

A *discretion* in the choice of Psalms and Lessons is allowed on days of fasting and thanksgiving, and on occasions of ecclesiastical conventions and charitable collections. See the order for reading the Psalms and Lessons, inserted immediately after the Preface to the Book of Common Prayer.

to excite the congregation sincerely and devoutly to join in the confession which follows.

The Church has with great propriety placed

The Confession

at the commencement of the service, in order that the guilt of the congregation being removed by penitence, they may with holy confidence supplicate GOD for his grace and praise him for his mercies. This confession is expressed in general terms suited to the state of all in the congregation; and is so humble, so simple, and affecting that the person must be insensible indeed who can repeat it, sentence by sentence after the minister, without feeling the most lively sorrow for his sins and the most earnest desire to be freed from their guilt and dominion.

The declaration of

Absolution

is placed after the confession. For GOD having committed to his ambassadors the *ministry of reconciliation,* the Church calls upon them to exercise it when the congregation have been humbled by the preceding confession. The *Priest* (for the absolution is not to be pronounced by a *Deacon,* much less by a *layman*), rising from his knees and standing up, declares for their comfort and support that "GOD pardoneth and absolveth all those who truly repent, and unfeignedly believe his holy Gospel." While the absolution is thus pronouncing, the congregation should continue upon their knees and hearken to it with perfect silence, not reading or repeating it along with the minister; for it is the minister's duty alone to make this declaration by authority from GOD, and in his name, as his ambassador. But every person ought humbly and thankfully to apply it to himself, so far as to be fully persuaded that if he really and heartily repent and sincerely trust in GOD's mercy through JESUS CHRIST, he will be discharged and absolved from all his sins as

180

certainly as if GOD himself had declared it; since God's minister has done it in his name and by his power.

The nature and effect of this declaration of absolution are thus accurately stated by WHEATLEY in his commentary on the Book of Common Prayer:—"Since the Priest has the ministry of reconciliation committed unto him by GOD, and hath both *'power* and *commandment,'* (as it is expressed by this form) *'to declare* and *pronounce* to his people, being *penitent,* the *absolution* and remission of their sins'; therefore, when he does by virtue of this power and commandment, declare and pronounce such absolution regularly in the congregation; those in the congregation who *'truly repent and unfeignedly believe* GOD's *holy Gospel,'* though the priest does not know who or how many there are who do so, have yet their pardon conveyed and sealed to them at that very instant through his ministration; it being the ordinary method of GOD with his Church to communicate his blessings through the ministry of the Priest.

"It is indeed drawn up in a *declarative* form, and considering it is to be pronounced to a mixed congregation it could not have been drawn up in any other. For the minister, not knowing who are *sincere* and who are feigned penitents, is not allowed to prostitute so sacred an ordinance amongst the good and bad promiscuously; but is directed to assure those only of a pardon who truly repent, and unfeignedly believe GOD's holy Gospel."

The power of declaring the remission of sins, as thus explained, is not liable to abuse. For it is not made essential to salvation, as in the Church of Rome, that every person should *privately confess his sins to a priest,* and receive *absolution.* Nor is this power exercised with certainty on any particular individual; it is effective only to those who repent and believe. And it is surely a great comfort to the humble and sincere penitent to have his pardon thus conveyed to him by GOD through the ministry of the Church.

The commission which our Savior gave to his Apostles immediately before his ascension is considered as the institution of the Christian priesthood. In this commission, as re-corded by St. *John,* the words are contained *Whose soever sins ye remit, they are remitted unto them, and whose soever sins ye retain, they are retained.* And that this power was not to die with the Apostles, but to be continued to their successors in the ministry, is evident from the words which, according to St. *Matthew,* our Savior added to the commission—"Lo, I am with you alway, even unto the end of the world."

Concerning this commission, Bishop ANDREWS observes—"It is not said by CHRIST, whose sins ye *wish and pray for, to be remitted;* but *whose sins ye remit.* To which he addeth a promise that he will make it good; and that his power shall accompany the power he has given them, and the lawful execution of it in his Church for ever."

The "excellent HOOKER," with his usual judgment and accuracy, thus defines the power of absolution and limits and guards the exercise of it:—"It is true that our Savior, by these words, *whose sins ye remit, they are remitted,* did ordain judges over our sinful souls, gave them authority to absolve from sin, and promised to ratify in heaven whatsoever they should do on earth in execution of this their office; to the end that hereby, as well his ministers might take encouragement to do their duty with all faithfulness, as also his people admonition, gladly with all reverence to be ordered by them; both parts knowing that the functions of the one towards the other have his perpetual assistance and approbation. Howbeit, all this with two restraints which every jurisdiction in the world hath; the one, that the practice thereof proceed in due order; the other, that it do not extend itself beyond due bounds; which bounds or limits have so confined penitential jurisdiction that although there be given unto it power of remitting sin, yet no such sovereignty of power that no sin should be pardonable in man without it."

The congregation, having thus confessed their sins and received the assurances of GOD's merciful forgiveness, are now prepared for approaching GOD as their reconciled Father with the humble confidence of children. The solemn business of supplication therefore very properly commences with

The Lord's Prayer

This prayer is not only used in the morning and evening prayer, properly so called, but also in the litany at the commencement of the communion service, and before sermon. These being considered as in some measure *distinct* services, the Church, with great propriety, assigns a place in each to the LORD's Prayer.

The Church now passes from prayer to the exercise of

Praise

and both minister and people previously implore the grace of GOD that their lips may be opened to show forth his praise. To denote the elevation of heart with which they should magnify the name of the GOD of their salvation, the minister and congregation now rise up and begin the delightful business of praise by repeating, standing, the sublime hymn called the GLORIA PATRI, in which the Church takes up the acclamations of triumph which, from the beginning and world without end, the host of heaven send forth to the Blessed and Glorious TRINITY.

Part of the 95th PSALM, styled VENITE, EXULTEMUS, with the addition of two appropriate verses from the 96th Psalm, is then alternately recited by both minister and people. This Psalm is, with propriety, called in the Latin service the *invitatory* because, in glowing and lively strains, it invites the people heartily to praise and devoutly to worship the LORD their GOD, who will finally come to judge the earth with righteousness. After this sublime Psalm, the

Psalms for the Day

are alternately recited. At the end of each Psalm in the service, as well as each Psalm for the day, the *Gloria Patri* is recited, by which the Psalms are applied in a spiritual sense to the use of the Christian Church. The *Gloria Patri* at the end of each Psalm for the day also very properly marks the transition from one Psalm to another. The American Church allows the GLORIA IN EXCELSIS [glory in the highest], which is taken from the Communion Service, to be substituted at the end of the whole portion of Psalms for the day, instead of the GLORIA PATRI.

The design of the alternate recital of the Psalms by the minister and people, and of the responses, is to excite the attention and to quicken the devotion of the congregation. Hymns and prayers were sung by COURSES in the ancient Jewish Church; and in all the old Christian liturgies there are short sentences, called RESPONSES, from the people *answering* the priest.

The PSALMS are divided into thirty portions, and are thus repeated once every month. The translation of the Psalms in the Common Prayer Book, is thought to be more smooth and flowing than that in the Bible. The American Church has provided Selections of Psalms that may be used instead of the portions appointed for the day.

The PSALMS were originally used in the service of the Jewish temple and have been thence transferred into the Christian Church. These divinely inspired compositions breathe the sentiments of penitence, of prayer, and of praise, in strains the most tender and sublime. By beautiful and interesting comparisons drawn from the works of nature and the customs of society, but principally by personal and ceremonial types and shadows, they display the excellence of Christian doctrine; the character, the offices, and the condition of the Savior, and the circumstances of his Church and its members. As the Psalms therefore have a spiritual application and meaning, and are thus frequently applied by CHRIST and his Apostles, it is no objection to the use of them that they contain sentiments and expressions applicable to the Jewish dispensation and to the particular circumstances of the king of Israel. Whatever the

184

Psalmist says of the excellences of the law; of the ark, the temple, and the holy city of Jerusalem, of the sacrifices on the Jewish altar; and of his own distresses, his temporal enemies, and signal deliverances, may be easily applied to the Gospel, which is the law fulfilled; to the Christian Church, which the ark, the temple, and Jerusalem prefigured; to that one great sacrifice of CHRIST still commemorated in the holy Eucharist, from which the Jewish sacrifices derived all their efficacy; and to the humiliation of the Savior to the enemies of his Church and people, and to the victories by which he wrought their redemption; all which were set forth in the humiliation, the enemies, and the victories of the frequently distressed and persecuted, yet finally triumphant, king of Israel.

Many of the Psalms, as now translated, contain bitter imprecations of David against his enemies. In these cases, however, the imperative form "Let them be confounded," &tc., may, according to the original, be rendered in the future "They shall be confounded," &tc., and the imprecations are thus changed into prophetic predictions. But even supposing, as an excellent and distinguished divine observes, "that these predictions are wishes, David might be directed by infinite wisdom to pronounce them, even against the opposers of his ruling over Israel, who opposed, at the same time, the known decree of Providence. Repeating them in this view, solely as his, must be innocent; and they strongly suggest an important admonition, not to *fight against* GOD. But perhaps in some of these, as well as other passages, he speaks in the person of the whole Church of GOD, against all its irreconcilable enemies whoever they be. Such was Judas; to whom, therefore, the two most dreadful of these Psalms are applied, *Acts* 1:20. And, with the *utmost tenderness to the whole of* GOD's *creation,* we *may* and *must* desire the overthrow of them who obstinately hate him and his laws. For though we ought much more to desire the repentance than the death of a sinner, as he himself doth; yet, if they will not repent, we ought to think and speak with approbation and satisfaction (yet mixed with an awful concern) of their punishments here and sentence hereafter; which last St. *Paul* represents good persons as joining to pronounce: *Do ye not know, that the saints shall judge the world?"*

But let us remember that the Psalms claim our reverence by the awful sanction of divine authority. Whenever we unfold the sacred volume, its awful sanctity as the word of GOD should repress all bold and irreverent criticism. He has made the path of duty plain before our face: yet he has permitted, in the sacred volume, things hard to be understood as the trial of our faith and humility, with the view of *bringing down every high imagination* and *everything that exalteth itself against him.*

Bishop HORNE, in his learned preface to his Commentary on the Psalms, unfolds with equal elegance and perspicuity their typical nature and establishes the principles by which their spiritual meaning is to be ascertained. In his explanation of the Psalms he applies them with inimitable tenderness, taste, and piety to the purposes of Christian faith and devotion. Every Christian should take this book as his guide to the spiritual meaning of the Psalms; and every Churchman should use it as a companion for the services of the sanctuary, that he may offer up with enlightened devotion those divine compositions in which, from the beginning the Christian Church has celebrated the praises of GOD.

While the PSALMS AND HYMNS are repeating, it will be the duty of the congregation to observe the minister's part, as well as their own, and to lift up their hearts together with their voices. While engaged in the exalted exercise of praise, they should *stand up,* not only to *signify* but to *assist* the lifting up of the heart at the same time.

The Lessons

with great propriety follow the PSALMS; the mind making an agreeable transition from active exertion in reciting the Psalms, to a state of more quiet attention during the reading of the lessons. As the Old Testament prefigures the New, the first

186

Lessons are taken from the former and the second Lessons from the latter. The two dispensations are thus made to harmonize, and what the one predicted the other shows fulfilled.

For the FIRST LESSONS on ordinary weekdays, the Church begins with the first chapter of Genesis, in the month of January, and continues till all the books of the Old Testament are read through, with the exception of certain omissions. The books of Chronicles are omitted because they are, for the most part, the same as the books of Samuel and Kings. The Song of Solomon is wholly omitted because it should be read with a disposition to understand it spiritually, and therefore is not a proper piece of writing for a mixed congregation. Isaiah is appointed for the time of ADVENT; this evangelical prophet being the best monitor to prepare us for a true faith in the mystery of CHRIST'S *incarnation* and *birth.* Several chapters in Ezekiel are omitted on account of the mystical visions in which they are wrapped.

In appointing the FIRST LESSONS for SUNDAYS, the Church pursues a very judicious method. From Advent to Septuagesima Sunday, the season which the Church devotes to the celebration of the incarnation of CHRIST and his manifestation to the Gentile world, some particular chapters are appointed out of the prophet Isaiah, who predicts, with more clearness and sublimity than any other prophet, those great events. For Septuagesima Sunday, and the following Sundays before Lent, and during that season, being the time of penance and mortification, the Church appoints out of the prophets chapters which declare the judgments of GOD against sin and excite to repentance and reformation. But on the Sundays toward the end of Lent, with a view to prepare for the proper celebration of GOOD FRIDAY and EASTER, the Church reads parts of some of the prophets which immediately refer to the death of CHRIST, and to his glorious completion of the work of redemption. On the Sundays succeeding EASTER, portions of Scripture to the same evangelical purport are read, until TRINITY Sunday when Genesis is taken up. And such chapters of this book, and of the

187

succeeding books of Scripture, as are deemed particularly instructive in piety and morals are continued to the season of ADVENT.

On SAINTS' DAYS the Church appoints LESSONS out of the *moral books* such as Proverbs, Ecclesiastes, &tc., which being full of excellent instruction are fit to be read on the days of Saints, whose exemplary lives and deaths are the causes of the Church commemorating them and commending them to our imitation. Other holy days such as CHRISTMAS, *Circumcision, Epiphany,* &tc., have PROPER LESSONS of their own, suited to the occasion. It may be proper to remark that there were *proper lessons* on all holy days appointed, even as early as the time of St. *Augustine.*

With respect to the SECOND LESSONS, the method is, on week days, to read generally the Gospels and the Acts of the Apostles in the morning and the Epistles in the evening, both in the order in which they stand in the New Testament. But on Sundays, Saints' days, and other holy days, *proper lessons* suited to the occasion are generally appointed.

By the above method of appointing the lessons, the Old Testament, with few exceptions, is read through once, and the New Testament twice in every year.

As the Scripture is not the word of man but the *word of* GOD, we should hearken to the lessons which are read either out of the Old or New Testament with the same attention, reverence, and faith as we would have done had we stood by Mount Sinai when GOD proclaimed the Law, or by our Savior's side when he published the Gospel. But we should hear in order to practice and be doers of the word, and not hearers only. We should, therefore, diligently observe, in those portions of Scripture which are read, what the particular *sins* are against which GOD warns us; what the *doctrines* which he requires us to believe; and what the *duties* which he commands us to perform.

HYMNS and PSALMS are intermingled with the lessons, to secure the people from weariness and to keep alive their devout affections. It is indeed highly proper that after we have declared, in the lessons, the wonderful works of GOD and his gracious dispensation of mercy, we should burst forth in ascriptions of praise and homage, and in expressions of thankfulness for the exalted blessings of his word.

The two HYMNS after the first lesson at morning prayer are that sublime Hymn the TE DEUM, *We praise thee O* GOD, &tc., which, it is generally believed, was composed by St. *Ambrose;* and the BENEDICITE, *O all ye works of the* LORD, &tc., which is an exact paraphrase of the 148th Psalm and was a Hymn in the Jewish Church and early adopted into the public devotions of Christians. This Hymn may very properly be used on Trinity Sunday, when the first lesson for the morning gives an account of the work of creation; immediately after which there appears great beauty in calling on all the *works of the* LORD *to bless and praise him.* The first Hymn after the first lesson at evening prayer is the 98th Psalm, styled CANTATE DOMINO, which may be applied to Christians, who are GOD's *spiritual Israel* and who are bound to praise him for their glorious deliverance from the bondage of *sin* and *death.* The second Hymn which may be used is part of the 92d Psalm, styled BONUM EST CONFITERI, and is a beautiful and affecting exhortation to the duty of *praise* to GOD *for all the operations of his hands.*

As the second LESSONS are all taken out of the New Testament, which conveys to us the glad tidings of salvation, the HYMNS which follow these Lessons all celebrate the goodness and mercy of GOD in our redemption. The first Hymn after the second Lesson in the morning is the 100th Psalm, styled the JUBILATE, which calls upon us to praise GOD, not only for his goodness and power manifested in our creation and preservation, but for that grace, mercy, and truth which in his everlasting gospel are set forth from generation to generation. The other Hymn, styled BENEDICTUS, was pronounced by Zacharias at the circumcision of his son, John the Baptist; and is a lively thanksgiving to GOD for the incarnation of CHRIST and for the unspeakable mercies of redemption. After the second Lesson in the evening service, the first Hymn, the 67th Psalm, styled DEUS MISEREATUR, is an earnest prayer of David for the *coming* of the *Gospel,* and the other Hymn, part of the 103d Psalm, styled BENEDIC, ANIMA MEA, is a sublime and animated act of thanksgiving for the mercies of redemption *actually conferred* on mankind.

As "faith comes by hearing," it seems proper that after the lessons which declare to us the word of GOD should follow the CREED, which is the profession of our faith; and after the Creed follow prayers, which are grounded upon faith.

Both minister and people join in repeating the Creed, because it is designed to be the profession of every one present, and also that they may the more expressly declare their belief of it to each other and to the whole Christian world with whom they maintain communion. It is to be repeated standing, to signify their resolution to maintain and defend it. At the second article of this Creed, when the name of JESUS is mentioned, the whole congregation make obeisance in compliance with an ancient custom of the Church, probably founded on the command of St. *Paul* that at the name of JESUS every knee should bow.

The Apostles' Creed is so called because the greatest part of it was derived from the very days of the Apostles; and the Nicene Creed is so called being for the most part drawn up by the first council of [Nicaea or] Nice. The Nicene Creed was designed to establish more fully the divinity of the Son and of the HOLY GHOST against the heresies which began to prevail in the Church. The 3d article of religion makes the same declaration with the Apostles' Creed that "CHRIST descended into hell," which declaration is founded on several passages of Scripture. There would be no impropriety in supposing that in the interval between his death and resurrection CHRIST went into the place of condemned spirits to proclaim, in the kingdom or residence of the great adversary and destroyer of men, the glorious triumphs of his cross. But CHRIST's descent into hell is with more propriety thought to mean his descent into the place where the souls of the faithful rest in hope till the resurrection. The word hell is expressed in the original by two words, one of which is used to denote the place of torment, and the other the place of departed spirits; and in this latter signification it is supposed to be used in the Creed.

The different parts of the service which have now been explained, are admirably calculated to prepare the people for the remaining part of divine worship, supplication and prayer.

After their consciences are absolved from sin, their affections warmed with thanksgiving, their understandings enlightened by the word, and their faith strengthened by a public profession of the Creed, they are prepared to enter on the remaining part of divine worship, supplication and prayer; "to ask those things which are requisite and necessary, as well for the body as the soul."

Since neither minister nor people can possibly pray to GOD aright without his grace and assistance, the minister first prays for the special presence of GOD with the people, saying, "the LORD be with you"; and they put up the same petition for the minister who is to be their representative before the throne of grace, answering, "And with thy spirit." The minister then says, "LET US PRAY." This form is several times repeated through the service. When it is first used after the Creed, it is designed to call the attention of the people to the solemn duty of prayer on which they are now to enter. When it is first used in the *Litany,* its design is to excite and to inflame to a still higher pitch the devotions of the people. In the ancient liturgies it was customary for the Deacon to cry aloud, "Let us pray vehemently"; and again, shortly after, "Let us pray more vehemently"; When it is used near the close of the Litany, it is designed, in addition to the foregoing purpose, to mark the transition from the alternate petitions of the minister and people to prayers by the minister alone.

The people being thus solemnly called to the duty of prayer, both minister and people proceed to address GOD in a few short VERSICLES taken from the Psalms, beseeching him to grant them those spiritual blessings of mercy and salvation, of inward purity and grace, which are the principal subjects of the

191

prayers that follow. These prayers are divided into

Short Collects

in order by this variety to quicken our attention; to impress on us more deeply the attributes of GOD with which every prayer commences, and the merits and mediation of CHRIST with which every Prayer concludes; and by the frequency of saying *Amen,* to warm our hearts and inflame the ardour of our supplications.

These short prayers are styled COLLECTS, most probably because in them the minister *collects* or comprises all the wants of the people and presents them unto GOD. The same reason will apply to the Collect for the day, which has always reference to some sentiments that may be *collected* from the Epistle and Gospel.

These COLLECTS are principally taken from the ancient Greek liturgies, particularly the sacramentary of St. Gregory the Great. When the Communion service is not read, the Collect for the day, which is *always* used in the evening, is used in the morning service. After this, follows in the morning the Collect for external, and in the evening the Collect for internal *peace.* Then succeeds in the morning a Collect for *grace* to avoid all temporal and spiritual evil through the day; and in the evening a Collect for *aid against the perils of the night.* Then follow prayers for the *civil authority,* for the *clergy and people,* and a solemn and pathetic *prayer for all conditions of men.* In the morning service on Sundays, Wednesdays, and Fridays, instead of these prayers the *Litany* is to be read.

. . .

Having in the collects or Litany prayed for all necessary blessings for ourselves and others, it is but fit that the congregation should praise GOD also for all temporal and spiritual mercies, and give thanks, not only in behalf of themselves but, according to the apostle's direction, for all mankind; this is done toward the end of the service in the

General Thanksgiving

This with inimitable tenderness sets forth the various subjects of thankfulness; and directs us to pray that the sense of the mercies of GOD may produce its proper effect by leading us to glorify him by a holy life.

There are

Occasional Prayers and Thanksgivings

for particular blessings and mercies; the former of which are generally used immediately before and the latter immediately after the general thanksgiving.

After the general thanksgiving succeeds the prayer of ST. CHRYSOSTOM; and then the minister alone concludes, still *kneeling,* with the prayer, *The grace of our* LORD JESUS CHRIST, &tc. In this prayer is embodied all we have desired, or can desire, to make us completely happy both here and hereafter.

After this prayer, which concludes the proper morning service, and also immediately before the sermon, some verses from the

Psalms in Metre

are sung. The Church, in the form of Ratification of the book of Psalms in metre, makes it the duty of the minister to "appoint the portions of Psalms that are to be sung; to give order concerning the tunes that are to be sung; and especially to suppress all light and unseemly music."

The singing of the praises of GOD is so important and delightful a part of public worship that it is the obvious duty of every person in the congregation to endeavour to perform it with propriety and devotion. The voice of melody is employed in its appropriate and most honourable duty when it shows forth the praises of the greatest and best of Beings. . . .

Prayer to be used on our first entrance into Church

ALMIGHTY GOD, who dost vouchsafe to dwell in temples made with hands, teach me now to act as in thy immediate presence; enable me to worship thee *in spirit and in truth.* By the gracious influences of thy HOLY SPIRIT, help my infirmities and dispose my heart to seriousness, attention, and devotion; that this opportunity of worshipping thee, my GOD, in thy holy temple may tend to the honour of thy holy name and the benefit of my soul, through JESUS CHRIST our LORD. Amen.

Prayer to be Used After Service

Blessed be thy name, O GOD, for this opportunity of worshiping thee in thy holy temple. Pardon my wanderings and imperfections. Hear and accept my prayers and praises. May the truths of salvation sink deep into my heart and bring forth the fruits of holiness and virtue. And may the worship and services of thy Church on earth prepare me for the exalted services of thy temple and Church eternal in the heavens, through JESUS CHRIST our Mediator and Redeemer. Amen.

---

(41) **Charles Simeon**
Fellow of King's College and Vicar of Holy Trinity, Cambridge
The Churchman's Confession, or, An Appeal to the Liturgy
1805/1813

We shall content ourselves with calling your attention to the Liturgy, and especially to that part of it which we call the general Confession. We will briefly state what doctrines we insist upon as necessary to be received; and under each we will compare our statements with what we "read" in the Scriptures and "acknowledge" in our prayers. And we trust that, after having done this, we shall be able to adopt the language of the text and say, "We write none other things unto you than what ye read and acknowledge."

• • •

We begin our confession with saying, *"We have erred and strayed from thy ways like lost sheep."* This is a peculiar expression that must not be overlooked. We apprehend it does not mean merely that we have departed from God, but also that we have never sought to return to him. For other animals will find their way back when they have wandered from their home; but it is rarely, if ever, known that the sheep traces back its footsteps to the fold from whence it has strayed; if it return at all, it is not by any foresight of its own. How just a picture does this exhibit of our fallen race! That we have departed from God is too plain to be denied: but in how few do we behold any solicitude to return to him! How few are there who search the Scriptures daily in order to find their way back! How few who implore help and direction from their God with an earnestness at all proportioned to the urgency of their case!

Is it inquired wherein we have so greatly erred? Our own acknowledgments contain the most satisfactory reply: *"We have followed too much the devices and desires of our own hearts."* How true is this! Look at all mankind; see them from infancy to youth, and from youth to old age. What are they all following? are they obeying unreservedly the commands of God? are they, in compliance with his will, mortifying every evil propensity and doing the things which are pleasing in his sight? Alas! nothing is further from their minds than this. Their pursuits indeed vary according to their age, their circumstances, their habits; but whatever they be, they are no other than the devices and desires of their own hearts. If in anything they appear to do the will of God, they do not act from a principle of love to him but from a desire to conform to the customs of their country and to lay a foundation for self-applause. The whole tenor of our lives is but too justly marked in those following acknowledgments,

"We have offended against thy holy laws; we have left undone those things which we ought to have done; and have done those things which we ought not to have done." Permit me to ask, Which of the laws of God have we not violated times without number? Shall we say we have not committed murder or adultery? How vain the boast if we interpret the commandments in their full latitude, and call to mind the declarations of our Lord that an angry word is murder, and a wanton look adultery! (*Mt.* 5:27, 28). To go into all our sins of omission, and comission were an endless task. Suffice it to say that in ten thousand instances "we have sinned, in thought, word, and deed, against the Divine Majesty" and have habitually neglected the interests of our souls.

Perhaps it may be said, "Our actions indeed have been evil, but our hearts are good." But how does this accord with that which in our Confession forms the summit of the climax, *"There is no health in us!"* Here our Church has taught us to trace all the evils of our life to the fountainhead, a corrupt and wicked heart. In this expression she evidently refers either to that confession of the Apostle, "In me, that is, in my flesh, dwelleth no good thing" (*Rom.* 7:18); or rather to that most humiliating declaration of the Prophet, "From the sole of the foot even to the head, there is no soundness in us, but wounds and bruises and putrifying sores" (*Is.* 1:5,6). The import of the words is plain: we confess before our God that we are altogether depraved; that we are disordered in every member of our body and in every faculty of our soul; that our understanding is darkened, our will perverse, our affections sensual, our memory treacherous, our conscience seared, and all our "members, instruments of unrighteousness and sin."

· · ·

What are the terms in which we address the Divine Majesty every time that we attend his worship? *"Do thou, O Lord, have mercy upon us, miserable offenders: Spare thou them, O God, which confess their faults: Restore thou them that are penitent."* Have we then been dissembling with God all our days; calling ourselves "miserable offenders" when we feel no misery at all; and when,

196

instead of bewailing our offenses, we think ourselves almost, if not altogether, as good as we need to be? In this prayer we do not presume even to expect mercy except as persons deeply penitent and contrite. And let it be remembered that these petitions are put into the mouths of all the congregation; there is not one form for one class of persons and another for another; but all profess to approach God as the repenting publican, "Smiting upon their breasts, and crying, God be merciful to me a sinner!" (*Lk.* 18:13). We mean not to say that no person can hope for mercy who does not feel such or such a measure of contrition (for all who pray in *sincerity* may hope for acceptance though their hearts be not so contrite as they could wish), but to show that all members of the church of England acknowledge that penitence is highly suited to their state.

· · ·

Let us attend to the supplications which we offer before God—*"Grant, O most merciful Father, for Christ's sake, that we may hereafter live a godly, righteous, and sober life, to the glory of thy holy name."* Here so far from putting godliness out of our thoughts, we profess to desire it in the first place; and justly do we ask that first, because, without that, all our acts of righteousness and sobriety would be no better than splendid sins; they would want the motives and principles which alone distinguish them from heathen virtues. Mark too the measure and degree in which we desire these virtues: we are not satisfied with that which shall gain us a name among men; we ask (and let it ever be remembered that without the influences of God's Spirit all our own efforts will be in vain) that we may be enabled to attain such a degree of piety, as that God may be glorified in us, and that the transcendant excellence of Christianity may be visibly exhibited in our lives.

We appeal then to all; What do we, or what can we ask of you more than this? And if these high attainments be not necessary, why do you ask of God for Christ's sake to give them to you? If, on the other hand, they are necessary, why are we deemed enthusiastic and over-righteous for requiring them at your hands? If in your prayers you mean what you say, you justify us; and if you do not mean what you say, you condemn yourselves, you confess yourselves to be hypocrites and dissemblers with God.

We have now finished our consideration of that truly scriptural prayer: and we will conclude with commending it to you as *a test* in a twofold view.

First, take it as *a test whereby to try the discourses which you hear.* As Members of the Church of England, we have a right to expect that the discourses of Ministers shall correspond with the Liturgy of our Church. Certainly, in the first instance, the holy Scriptures are to be our guide: but, as all profess to have the Scriptures on their side, let us bring to our aid that excellent compendium of religion which we have been considering (i.e., the Liturgy).

Are there any who discuss the dignity of our nature, the goodness of our hearts, and the rectitude of our lives? What appearance do such sentiments make when brought to the touchstone of this prayer? Are they not as opposite as darkness is to light? and should we not regard such statements as the effusions of pride and ignorance? should we not tremble for those who hear them, lest being "blind followers of the blind, they all together should fall into the ditch?" (*Mt.* 15:14).

Are there others who tell us that we are to be saved by our works, and who would thereby lull us asleep in impenitence and divert our attention from the Savior of the world? Let us not be deluded by the siren song. Let us turn to our own confessions, to refute such anti-Christian doctrines: Let us learn from them the necessity of humiliation and contrition, and of "fleeing to Christ, as to the refuge that is set before us." As for the idea that the founding of our hopes upon Christ and upon the promises made to us in him will lead to a neglect of good works, let us see what the Compilers of our Liturgy thought of that, and what they have put in the mouths of all believing penitents. Do not the very same persons who seek for mercy through Christ entreat of God that they may be enabled to "live a godly, righteous, and sober life, to the glory of his holy name"? And is it not notorious that the very persons who maintain most steadfastly the doctrines of faith are uniformly condemned for the excessive and unnecessary strictness of their lives?

In the same manner, if there be any who plead for a conformity to the world and decry all vital godliness as enthusiasm, we may see what judgment is to be formed of them also. They may call themselves Christians; but they have nothing of Christianity except the name.

Lastly, if there be any who separate the different parts of religion, inculcating some to the neglect of others, magnifying works to the exclusion of faith or establishing faith to the destruction of good works, or confounding faith and works instead of distinguishing them as the fruit from the root; if such, I say, there be, let their statements be contrasted with the order, the fullness, and the harmony of this prayer, and the erroneousness of them will instantly appear. We do not wish to produce critical hearers; but it is the duty of every man to "prove all things, and to hold fast that which is good" (1 *Th.* 5:21); and as we have the advantage of an authorized standard of divine truth, we invite all to search that, as well as the holy Scriptures. And we do not hesitate to say of this prayer in particular what the prophet speaks of the inspired volume, "To the law, and to the testimony; if Ministers speak not according to this word, it is because there is no light in them" (*Is.* 8:20).

Next, let us take this prayer as *a test whereby to try our own experience.* We may now discard from our minds all that this or that Minister may lay down as necessary to our salvation. We have here what no man can reasonably dispute, our own acknowledgments. We have here as beautiful, as just, as scriptural a summary of experimental religion as ever was penned from the foundation of the world. The man that from his inmost soul can utter this prayer is a real Christian. Whatever be his views with respect to some particular doctrines (those I mean which are distinguished by the name of Calvinism), his heart is right with God. Whether he admit or reject those abstruser points, he is accepted of God; and if he were to die this moment he would be in heaven the next; the termination of his warfare would be to him the commencement of everlasting felicity. But is this the experience of us all? Would to God it were! All will repeat the words: but it is one thing to repeat, and another to feel them. Let us then bring ourselves to this test; and never imagine that we are in a Christian state till we can appeal to God that this prayer is the very language of our hearts. In examining ourselves respecting it, let us inquire whether from our inmost souls we lament the numberless transgressions of our lives and the unsearchable depravity of our hearts? When we cry to God for mercy as miserable offenders, do we abhor ourselves for our guilt and tremble for our danger? Do we indeed feel that we deserve the wrath of Almighty God? Do we feel this not only on some particular occasions but, as it were, daily and hourly? Is the consciousness of it wrought into us and become the habit of our minds, so that we can find no peace but in crying unto God and pleading with him the merits of his dear Son? Is Christ, in this view, "precious" to our souls? (1 *Pet.* 2:7). Is HE "our wisdom, HE our righteousness, HE our sanctification, HE our complete redemption"? (1 *Cor.* 1:30). Having nothing in ourselves, do we make HIM our "all in all"? (*Col.* 3:11). Are we at the same time "renewed in the spirit of our minds?" Do we hate sin, not merely as it is destructive, but as it is defiling to the soul? Do we account "the service of God to be perfect freedom"; and instead of wishing his law reduced to the standard of our practice, do we desire to have our practice raised to the standard of his law? Is it our labour to "shine as lights in a dark world," and "to show forth in our own conduct the *virtues* of him that has called us"? (1 *Pet.* 2:9). Let us all put these questions to ourselves; and they will soon show us what we are. If this be not the state of our souls, we are in an awful condition indeed. Our very best services have been nothing but a solemn mockery: in

200

our prayers we have insulted, rather than worshiped, the Majesty of Heaven; we have come before our God "with a lie in our right hand" (*Is.* 44:20). O that it might please God to discover to us the heinousness of our guilt; and that we might all be "pricked to the heart" ere it be too late! Let us, the very next time we attempt to use this prayer, take notice of the frame of our minds: let us mark the awful incongruity between our professions and our actual experience: and let a sense of our hypocrisy lead us to repentance. Thus shall the returning seasons of worship be attended with a double advantage to our souls: in praying for what we ought to seek, we shall be stirred up to seek it in good earnest: and through the tender mercy of our God we shall attain the experience of those things which too many of us, it is to be feared, have hitherto hypocritically asked and ignorantly condemned.

---

(42) **Frederick Denison Maurice**
Professor of Theology at King's College, London;
Professor of Moral Philosophy at Cambridge
Sermons on the Prayer Book and the Lord's Prayer
1848–1849

The Paternoster is not, as some fancy, the easiest, most natural, of all devout utterances. It may be committed to memory quickly, but it is slowly learnt by heart. Men may repeat it over ten times in an hour, but to use it when it is most needed, to know what it means, to believe it, yea, not to contradict it in the very act of praying it, not to construct our prayers upon a model the most unlike it possible, this is hard. This is one of the highest gifts which God can bestow upon us; nor can we look to receive it without others that we may wish for less—sharp suffering, a sense of wanting a home, a despair of ourselves.

At certain periods in the history of the Church, especially when some reformation was at hand, men have exhibited a weariness of their ordinary theological teaching. It seemed to them that they needed something less common, more refined than that which they possessed. As the light broke in upon them, they perceived that they needed what was less refined, more common. The Creed, the Ten Commandments, the Lord's Prayer were found to contain the treasures for which they were seeking. The signs of such a period are surely to be seen in our day. We can scarcely think that we require reformation less than our fathers. I believe, if we are to obtain it, we too must turn to these simple documents; we must inquire whether there is not a wisdom hidden in them which we do not meet with elsewhere; whether they cannot interpret the dream of our lives better than all the soothsayers whom we have consulted about it hitherto.

I. Much of the practical difficulty of the prayer lies assuredly in the first word of it. How can we look round upon the people whom we habitually feel to be separated from us by almost impassable barriers; who are above us so that we cannot reach them, or so far beneath us that the slightest recognition of them is an act of gracious condescension; upon the people of an opposite faction to our own, whom we denounce as utterly evil; upon men whom we have reason to despise; upon the actual wrong-doers of society, those who have made themselves vile, and are helping to make it vile—and then teach ourselves to think that in the very highest exercise of our lives these are associated with us. That when we pray, we are praying for them and with them; that we cannot speak for ourselves without speaking for them; that if we do not carry their sins to the throne of God's grace, we do not carry our own; that all the good we hope to obtain there belongs to them just as much as to us, and that our claim to it is sure of being rejected if it is not one which is valid for them also? Yet all this is included in the word "Our": till we have learnt so much, we are but spelling at it; we have not learnt to pronounce it. And what man of us—the aptest scholar of all—will venture to say that he has yet truly pronounced it; that his clearest utterance of it has not been broken and stammering? Think how many causes are at work every hour of our lives to make this opening word of the prayer a nullity and a falsehood. How many petty disagreements are there between friends and kinsfolk, people dwelling in the same house—so petty that there is no fear of giving way to them, and yet great enough to cause bitterness and estrangement, great enough to make this "Our Father" a contradiction. How often does my vanity come into collision with another man's vanity, and then, though there be no palpable opposition of interests between us, though we do not stand in the way of each other's advancement, what a sense of separation, of inward hostility, follows! As the mere legal, formal distinctions of caste become less marked, how apt are men to indemnify themselves for that loss by drawing lines of their own as deep, and more arbitrary! As persecution in its ruder shapes becomes impossible, what revenge does the disputatious heart take under this deprivation by bitter manifestations of contempt for an adversary, by identifying him more completely with his opinions, by condemning him, if not for them then for the vehemence and bigotry with which he supports them! How many pretexts have the most tolerant amongst us for intolerance? How skillful are the most religious in finding ways for explaining away the awful command "Judge not, that ye be not judged"?

II. But when we say "Father," are we more in earnest? Do we mean that He whom we call upon is a Father actually, not in some imaginary metaphorical sense? . . .

"Our Father:" there lies the expression of that fixed eternal relation which Christ's birth and death have established between the littleness of the creature and the Majesty of the Creator; the one great practical answer to the philosopher who would make heaven clear by making it cold; would assert the dignity of the Divine Essence by emptying it of its love and

reducing it into nothingness. Our Father, *which art in Heaven:* there lies the answer to all the miserable substitutes for faith by which the invisible has been lowered to the visible; which have insulted the understanding and cheated the heart; which have made united worship impossible because that can only be when there is One Being, eternal, immortal, invisible, to whom all may look up together, into whose presence a way is opened for all. Whose presence is a refuge from the confusions, perplexities, and divisions of this world; that home which the spirits of men were ever seeking and could not find, till He who had borne their sorrows and died their death entered within the veil, having obtained eternal redemption for them, till He bade them sit with Him in heavenly places.

What I have said may have seemed to prove that this simple prayer is too high and too deep for creatures such as we are. Would you have it otherwise? Would you have a prayer which you can comprehend and fathom? I am sure the conscience and reason would reject such a prayer as a delusion, an evident self-contradiction. I have said nothing to show that this prayer is unsuitable to the wants and ignorance of any beggar in our streets. I have shown only that the wisest man, who will not use it as that beggar does, who will try it by his own narrow methods and measures, will find that he has never entered into the sense of it, that he is condemning himself in the repetition of it. And if, brethren, we all know that we have been guilty of this mockery again and again, how clearly do our consciences witness that it is after this manner and no other we must make our confession. What despair we should be in if our unbelief were indeed truth, and not a lie! If the word "Our" did *not* express the truth that we participate in the blessings as well as the curses of the whole race; if the word "Father" were a word merely, and not the expression of an eternal truth; if we might think of Him as not nigh but afar off; in a book, not as one in whom we are living and having our being; if He were subject to the changes of earth, not forever fixed in Heaven, whither could we turn under the overpowering sense of our own sinfulness and heartlessness? It is the full conviction that our misery has proceeded from ourselves, from our maintaining a resolute war with facts and reality, which can alone give us encouragement. For we know there is One who is willing to teach us how to pray this prayer in spirit and in truth; we know that there is One who is praying it. He who died for us and for all mankind, He who is ascended into Heaven, He who is true and in whom is no lie, did when He was here clothed with our mortality, does now in his glorified humanity say, in the full meaning of the words, for us and for his whole family above and below, "Our Father which art in Heaven."

Illustration from Anthony Sparrow,
A Rationale Upon the Book of Common Prayer,
edition of 1672.

CHAPTER FIVE

The
Litany

(43) **Anthony Sparrow**
Bishop of Norwich
A Rationale upon the Book of Common Prayer
of the Church of England
1655/1657

Concerning the Litany of our Church, we may boldly say, and easily maintain it, that there is not extant anywhere: 1. A more particular, excellent enumeration of all the Christians' either private or common wants; Nor 2. A more innocent, blameless form, against which there lies no just exception; Nor 3. A more Artificial Composure for the raising of our devotion and keeping it up throughout than this part of our Liturgy.

In the beginning it directs our *prayers* to the right object, the Glorious TRINITY. For necessary it is that we should know whom we worship. Then it proceeds to *Deprecations,* or prayers against evil; lastly, to *Petitions* for good. In the *Deprecations,* as right method requires, we first pray against sin, then against punishment; because sin is the greatest evil. From all which we pray to be delivered by the holy actions and passions of CHRIST, the only merits of all our good. The like good order is observed in our *Petitions* for good. First, we pray for the *Church Catholic,* the common mother of all Christians; then for *our own Church,* to which, next the Church Catholic, we owe the greatest observance and duty. And therein, in the first place for the principal members of it, in whose welfare the Church's peace chiefly consists. After this we pray particularly for those sorts of men that most especially need our prayers, such amongst others, as those whom the Law calls *miserable persons.*

The Litany is not one long continued prayer, but broken into many short and pithy Ejaculations: that the intention and devotion which is most necessary in prayer may not be dull'd and vanish, as in a long prayer it is apt to do; but be quickened and intended by so many new and quick petitions; and the nearer to the end, the shorter and livelier it is, strengthening our devotions by raising in us an apprehension of our misery and distress, ready, as it were, to sink and perish; and therefore crying out as the Disciples did, **Master, save us, we perish; O Lamb of God hear us; O Christ hear us; Lord have mercy upon us.**

---

(44) **Thomas Comber**
Dean of Durham
A Companion to the Temple,
or A Help to Devotion in the Use of the Common Prayer
1672–76 / 1684

Though we must call upon God at all times, yet we must do it more especially in the time of trouble, for then we are most fit to pray and he is most apt to hear us, who hath said, *Is any afflicted? let him pray, Jas.* 5:13. When we are in Misery, what should we seek but Mercy? That is the sum of all our Litanies, or the Prayers we make in trouble, for which cause *David* begins his great *Penitential* with *Have mercy on me, &tc., Ps.* 51: 1, and all the Litanies in the World do begin with this solemn word, **Lord have mercy.** And so doth ours also, only we repeat that great Request with a particular address to each person of the blessed Trinity, the Object of a Christian's Worship, and this we call the Invocation, being both a Confession of our Faith and a preparation to all following Petitions.

· · ·

There is nothing more comfortable in an afflicted state than to trust in the Divine Mercy; but if this Faith be not well grounded, nothing doth more dangerously deceive us at the last; wherefore we do here add to the former Petition this Request, that we may live holily as well as trust firmly, or else our Faith is presumption, and our confidence nothing else but a groundless expectation. For they only have just cause to trust and confide in the Divine Mercy who endeavour to observe his Laws and do his Will, and they only shall have their hopes accomplished. But they who dishonour God's Name and disobey his Commands, who take part with his Enemies and do not cease to Sin, no not in the time of their Troubles, these do as foolishly, as unjustly pretend to rely on his Mercy, for they have no right to his Promises nor reason to expect any deliverance from him whom they have abused. Let us therefore pray that our Holiness may be as firm as our Faith in the time of our Affliction.

(45) **Samuel Johnson**

*Priest and missionary in Connecticut from the Society
for the Propagation of the Gospel,
first president of King's College (Columbia University)*
**On the Beauty of Holiness in the Worship
of the Church of England**
1749

As to the Litany (which word means a supplication) nothing can be devised or imagined more conducive to promote devotion and holiness, than that most excellent, that most devout and comprehensive form of public devotion. For therein we pray, not only for deliverance from every sin and calamity, but also for grace to perform every duty; and we not only testify and exercise our devotion in praying for ourselves, for everything needful both for our souls and bodies, but also our charity for others, in praying for them, even for all men, whether friends or enemies; and at the same time we show our solicitous concern for the public weal, in praying both for the whole church, and for the king and all that are in authority, both in church and state, that under them we may lead quiet and peaceable lives in all godliness and honesty; and our tender concern for the distresses of our fellow Christians, in praying for all that are under any kind of affliction, whether in mind, body or estate. In a word, therein we pray for all orders of men, whether they be ministers of religion or justice, and for all conditions of men, whether they be in prosperity or adversity; so very particular and comprehensive are our supplications in the Litany, together with the prayers and thanksgiving annexed to it, both in general, and for a variety of particular occasions, so that it is scarce possible to conceive what the Church could have done more, that she hath not done, in providing for the public devotions.

(46) **Thomas Secker**
Archbishop of Canterbury
Sermon XXVIII, in Explanation and Defence of the
Liturgy of the Church of England
c. 1758–1768

Next to the Morning and Evening Service in our Prayer book stands the Litany, or more earnest supplication for averting God's judgments and procuring his mercy. This earnestness, it was thought, would be best excited and expressed by the people's interposing frequently to repeat with their own mouths the solemn form of *beseeching* God to *deliver* and to *hear* them; in which however the minister is understood to join equally; as the congregation are in every particular specified by him. Such Litanies have been used in the Church at least 1400 years. And they were appointed first for Wednesdays and Fridays, these being appropriated to penitence and humiliation, and for other fasts: but not long after for Sundays also; there being then the largest congregation, and most solemn worship; and our Litany is further directed to be used at such other times as the ordinary shall think proper. Originally it was intended for a distinct service; to come after the Morning Prayer, as the rubric of our Liturgy still directs, and before the Office for the Communion, at a proper distance of time from each: of which custom a few churches preserve still, or did lately, some remains. But in the rest, convenience or inclination hath prevailed to join them all three together: excepting that in some places there is a psalm or anthem between the first and second; and between the second and third almost everywhere: besides that the latter part of the Morning Prayer is, most of it, ordered to be omitted when the Litany is said with it. But still, by this close conjunction, several things may appear improper repetitions, which, if the offices were separate, would not. However, as it is, they who use extempore prayers in public have small right to reproach us on this head. For doth it not frequently happen that, during one assembly of theirs, different ministers praying successively, or the same minister in several prayers, or perhaps in one only, shall fall into as many repetitions as are in the different parts of our Liturgy, or more? But be that as it will, to these last all persons would easily be reconciled, if an interval were placed, in their minds at least, between the services; and they would consider each, when it begins, as a new and independent one just as if it were a fresh time of meeting together.

The Litany of our church is not quite the same as any other; but differs very little from those of the Lutherans in Germany and Denmark. It is larger than the Greek but shorter than the Roman, which is half filled up with the names of saints invoked: whereas we invoke, first the three persons of the holy Trinity, separately and jointly: then in a more particular manner our Redeemer and Mediator *to whom all power is given in heaven and earth.*

Him we pray that he would *not remember our offenses, nor the offenses of our forefathers:* which he may not only with justice permit to intercept from us (as they naturally often will) the blessings that we might else have inherited: but if we have imitated wicked ancestors instead of taking warning by them, he may with equal justice punish us more severely, not indeed than we deserve, but than he would have done otherwise, to prevent the contagion from growing general and inveterate. Accordingly the second commandment threatens to *visit the iniquities of the fathers upon the children:* and the Psalmist, according to the marginal, and perhaps righter translation, prays as we do: *O remember not against us the iniquities of them that were before us.*

The words *and be not angry with us for ever* beg that the corrections which he doth see fit to inflict on us (for surely we all feel some) he would in mercy shorten. It is common language to speak of afflictions that last any time as if they were endless. And the expostulation of David in the just-quoted

Psalm, *How long, O Lord? wilt thou be angry for ever?* fully vindi-
cates this petition, which was doubtless taken from thence.

Having, after this, besought our blessed Lord to deliver us
from all evil and mischief in general, that is from everything bad
and hurtful to us: we deservedly rank *sin* the foremost of such
things; and pray, first against the original cause of human wickedness, *the* secret *crafts and* open *assaults of the devil,* and its
dreadful consequences, *God's wrath and everlasting damnation;*
then against the principal transgressions of his laws by name,
subjoining, *and all other deadly sin.* By this we mean not to deny
that *the* just *wages* of every *sin is death* (though *there are,* as we
learn from St. *John, sins not unto death,* that is comparatively) but
only to pray against the peculiarly deadly with peculiar earnestness. But still, that we may leave out none, we petition lastly to
be delivered *from all the deceits of the world, the flesh, and the devil:*
every iniquity of every kind and degree.

Then we proceed to deprecate the present sufferings that
our sins have merited: and entreat our merciful Redeemer to
preserve us, both from such as God's immediate hand inflicts;
lightning and tempest, plague properly so called, *pestilence* or epi-
demic diseases of any sort, *famine and sudden death;* and from
such also as men's unreasonable passions produce: whether
they be temporal, as *battle and murder;* or spiritual, as *false doctrine* with its fruits *heresy and schism;* and what begets them all,
hardness of heart in regard to God's commands and *contempt of his
word,* which contempt was never so widely spread and infec-
tious as at present.

We have indeed been blamed for praying against *sudden
death.* But the whole Christian Church hath done it from ancient time: and nature and reason, as well as religion, direct us
to do it. Some, we own (and we wish they were many), may be
always prepared thoroughly, in all respects, to die at any time.
Yet even these may have cause to wish for warning of their
death on account of other persons. Their example under the
approach of it will usually be very instructive; and their dying
advice more than ordinarily beneficial to their friends, depen-

dents, and relations: whom also their being taken away at once may shock, to a degree, for which they would be extremely sorry whatever they might otherwise choose for themselves. But even on their own account, Christian humility would surely desire a little space for completer preparation. And they, who profess to wish the contrary, are they so very certain, as this implies, that every part, both of their worldly affairs and their eternal concerns, is in the best condition to which it can be brought? Or may not possibly this appearing readiness to die at any time arise either from a secret dread to think of dying at all or a secret unbelief, more or less, of what will follow after death? But whatever a few may imagine best for themselves, justly or unjustly; some previous notice is undeniably best for the generality: and common prayers must be adapted to common cases; always submitting it to God to make exceptions where he shall think proper.

Having thus expressed from what things we desire to be delivered, we earnestly entreat our good and gracious Lord to show this mercy to us, *by the mystery of his holy Incarnation* and so on: that is, by the means and for the sake of all that he hath done and suffered for us. The same manner of expression is used, not only in common speech on other occasions and in the liturgies of the ancient Church on this, but in the Scripture itself: where St. Paul *beseeches* Christians *by the mercies of God, by the meekness and gentleness of Christ, by his coming and their gathering together to him,* and Daniel intercedes with God thus, *According to all thy righteousness, let thine anger be turned away: defer not for thine own sake, O my God.*

As we have need of protection and deliverance continually, so we proceed to beg for it, not only *in all time of our tribulation* or adversity, but *in all time of our wealth* or prosperity: for when we seem in the most flourishing state we are often in the most danger of evil; and of sin, the worst evil. But as *the hour of death* is a season of peculiar trial and terror; *and the day of judgment* will determine our lot forever: we therefore entreat his more especial grace and favour at both. The former indeed fixes our

214

condition at the latter. But still, as the best life and death obtain acquittal and reward only through the pardoning goodness of our Judge; we have great cause to pray for ourselves, as St. Paul did for Onesiphorus, *that we may find mercy of the Lord in that day.*

Having thus represented our own necessities, we now enlarge the subject of our devotions; and *make supplications* as the Apostle *exhorts, for all men:* acknowledging that we are *sinners* and therefore unworthy, yet sensible that we are bound by his commands and encouraged by his promises to offer up such requests. And here, after praying in general for the Catholic Church, we pray in particular for the head and principal members, both spiritual and temporal, of that part of it to which we belong, and for the whole of God's people of this land. Then we extend our views further yet and apply for blessings, religious and civil, to all other nations in common with our own; and to all sorts of persons amongst them and ourselves, according to their respective distresses and wants of soul, body, or outward circumstances; and lastly conclude our intercessions with imploring God's *mercy upon all men,* whatever their country, their religion, their sins may be; but especially *on our enemies, persecutors, and slanderers,* whom we beg he would *forgive,* and in order to it, *turn their hearts* to a righter disposition.

Against some of our requests for others, objections have been made. One is that in beseeching God *to succour, help, and comfort all that are in danger,* we beseech him to assist malefactors in escaping justice. But doth not every one understand it of such *help and comfort,* as their case admits, consistently with common good? Another is that in praying him *to preserve all that travel by land or by water,* we pray for the preservation of robbers and pirates. But surely our intention is very plain: to beg that travelers on their lawful occasions may be secured from robbers and pirates, amongst other accidents: and if we add in our minds a further request that these wretches also may be preserved, that is from attempting any more injustice and violence, do we not act a very Christian part? The same cavil hath been raised against our praying for God's *pity to all prisoners,*

215

mercy upon all men: words which notoriously mean such pity and mercy as he shall judge not to be unfit. And writers and speakers never scruple to omit limitations, which every reader or hearer who is not perverse will of course supply.

After going through these petitions, we endeavour to excite our desires of a gracious answer to as much fervency as we can by short but affectionate sentences, uttered alternately in a sort of pious emulation between the minister and the people; and humbly importuning our Redeemer, as the eternal *Son* and spotless *Lamb of God,* the Lord's *Christ,* and the *Lord* of Christians, that he would *grant us* his promised *peace,* which includes all blessings, and *have mercy upon us* in bestowing what we have asked. For this purpose, it is acknowledged, we repeat several times the same words with very small variations. But such *repetitions,* far from *vain,* are most expressive ones: the natural, the almost constant language of earnestness. Hence our Savior, in his agony, reiterated the same words thrice, and David, in a transport of thanksgiving, even to the six and twentieth time, as you may see in the 136th Psalm. And these very repetitions which we use are warranted by the ancient offices of the Christian Church.

Having thus enlivened our devotion, we proceed to offer up what deserves the most lively efforts of it, that perfect summary of all our petitions, the *Lord's Prayer:* which, though it occurs several times in the several services of the morning, occurs but once in this; and cannot easily be recited too often, provided it be with attention and affection.

Hitherto the Litany hath dwelt on no single subject of prayer long; but included a surprising variety of the most needful articles in a very narrow compass. The remainder is of a different nature. It considers our state here, very justly, as furnishing perpetual ground of sad reflection to every thoughtful mind: and applies itself wholly to express to our heavenly Father the sentiments required in such a condition. The seemingly happiest persons in the world are very inconsiderate if they do not discern a great deal to mourn over in others and

216

themselves. Yet at the same time the most afflicted are to blame if they sink under either what they see or feel. But the common duty of both is *in every thing, by prayer and supplication, with thanksgiving, to make their requests known unto God.* And therefore this part of the Litany, though first introduced on occasion of extraordinary distresses lying heavy on Christendom 11 or 1200 years ago, will be too seasonable in every age, till one of truer piety and more tranquillity shall come, than hath yet been known or is likely soon to take place.

As the transgressions by which we offend God are the cause of our sufferings, these our supplications begin very properly with entreating in Scripture words that on humbling ourselves before him he would *not deal with us after our sins, neither reward us after our iniquities.* Next to this follows, as is repeated in the sequel, an exhortation, *Let us pray:* which may appear somewhat strange considering that prayers immediately precede in both places. But they are short ejaculations, not continued forms like those which follow. And besides, this redoubled admonition, toward the conclusion of the office, will very usefully remind those who may possibly be growing languid and inattentive in how important a work they are engaged. Something there was of this kind even in the heathen devotions. But in the old liturgies of Christian Greece, *Let us pray, let us pray earnestly, let us pray more earnestly,* often returns.

And the succeeding prayer, which is of ancient use in the Western Church, deserves our utmost earnestness. It begs of him who, as the Psalmist assures us, *will not despise a broken and contrite heart* (which phrase I have already explained to you) that *in all our troubles* he will both *assist us to make our prayers before him* as we ought, *and graciously hear us:* that so the designs of our enemies, visible and invisible, may be disappointed and we may feel and express a just gratitude for our deliverance. To this the congregation answer, not as usual, *Amen:* but in a short form of Scripture words, more strongly expressive of pious fervency. The minister instantly returns another Scriptural address to God; pleading with him, and suggesting to us *the noble works* done by him for his Church and people in general, and many good persons in particular, which, if we have not seen with our eyes, *we have heard with our ears:* holy Writ and other history hath related them: or *our fathers have declared them to us,* partly as performed *in their days,* partly *in the old time before them.* And since *his arm is not shortened that it cannot save; nor his ear become heavy that it cannot hear,* the congregation again petition him in the same words as before (only changing one for another still more pathetic) that he would *arise, help, and deliver them* for the *honour of his name:* not for our merits, but his own glorious perfections and the instruction of his creatures; that we and all men may learn to love and praise and serve him. Yet to this we are indispensably bound, even while the painfullest view of our sorrows and wants is before our eyes: and therefore in the midst of our supplications we proceed immediately to ascribe that glory to the sacred Three which ever hath been, is, and will be their due; whether infinite wisdom allots to us prosperity or adversity. Nor is the mixture of doxologies with complaints less common in acts of worship than it is reasonable. The Book of Psalms uses it frequently: the old Latin and Greek liturgies use it on this very occasion: and surely in our private devotions, even when most afflicted, we still give praise to God.

But though we own it our duty to glorify him in the severest sufferings if it be his will that we should undergo them: yet conscious of our weakness, we go on to beg his protection against them, or deliverance of us from them, in mutual ejaculations of the utmost warmth: not that moving expressions will any otherwise incline him to grant mercy than as they fit us to receive it by imprinting on us a just sense of our dependence; which, if used with sincerity, they naturally do.

Then we close this part of the Litany with a more continued form of address to our merciful *Father;* composed originally above 1100 years ago; corrupted indeed afterwards by entreating God to *turn from us all evils* for the sake of the intercession of his Saints; but reformed in our liturgy not only by leaving out that addition but by inserting for completer security a new clause: *Grant, that in all our troubles we may put our whole trust and confidence in thy mercy.* And thus it is that we borrow from the Church of Rome. By this prayer, so amended, we humbly confess our infirmities and unworthiness: yet beg that notwithstanding both we may, if God sees it proper, escape the afflictions which we fear. But if not, that being still assured of his goodness to us, we may, with Job, *though he slay us, trust in him,* and that for proof of this we may as faithfully do our duty under the heaviest pressures as the highest exaltation; *and evermore serve him in holiness and pureness of living, to his honour and glory;* saying with Job again, *shall we receive good at the hand of God, and shall we not receive evil? The Lord gave, and the Lord hath taken away: blessed be the name of the Lord.*

What remains of the Litany is the same with the conclusion of the morning and evening prayer: and therefore needs no separate explanation. May God give us grace to use these and all our devotions in so right a manner that from praying to him amidst the troubles and sorrows of this world we may be taken, in his good time, to praise him for ever amidst the joys of the next, through Jesus Christ our Lord. Amen.

---

(47) **John Henry Hobart**
Bishop of New York, founder of The General Theological Seminary
A Companion for the Book of Common Prayer
1805 / 1827

The Litany

is a GENERAL SUPPLICATION in which both minister and people, imitating the priests who *wept between the porch and the altar,* and the blessed Savior of the world who besought his Father with *strong crying and tears,* supplicate, with more than usual earnestness and ardour, deliverance from temporal and spiritual wrath, as well as all needful blessings for soul and body. . . . The Litany commences with solemn INVOCATIONS of the Trinity, followed by earnest DEPRECATIONS from evil; by ardent OBSECRATIONS or entreaties to the Redeemer to deliver us; by INTERCESSIONS and SUPPLICATIONS to GOD to hear us in behalf both of ourselves and others. In the close of the Litany, the minister and people join in the most pathetic addresses to the "Son of GOD," the "Lamb that taketh away the sins of the world," to grant them his mercy and peace. They reiterate in united invocations to the Savior, their entreaties for mercy. Subject as they are to the manifold afflictions of this mortal pilgrimage, to the persecutions of the ungodly, and to the assaults of their spiritual enemies, they implore their merciful LORD to "deliver them," to "pity their sorrows," and to "forgive their sins." And mindful of his Almighty Power to save, and of his past mercies, they burst forth in the animating strains of the *Gloria Patri.*

This Litany then, whether we consider its simple, chaste, sublime, and affecting language, or the importance and variety of the matter with which it abounds; the solemnity of the invocations of the sacred persons of the Trinity with which it commences; the earnestness of the deprecations which it contains of the punishment of sin, of all temporal and spiritual evil; the importunity of the affecting entreaties by which we implore the blessed Redeemer, the Lamb that taketh away the sins of the world, to hear and deliver us, to grant us his mercy and peace; the justness and variety of the intercessions and alternate supplications by which we implore for ourselves and others all necessary blessings both temporal and spiritual—in all these points of view this Litany may be pronounced one of the most sublime, affecting, and animating offices of devotion that can possibly be formed. By its variety, its force, and its penetrating fervour it is calculated to arrest the attention of the careless, to animate and exalt the devotions of the pious, and to engage all the powers of the soul in the most exalted acts of homage and supplication.

While the minister is offering up the prayers and the Litany, the people ought not to sit or place themselves in any irreverent posture, but should continue on their knees, being the posture which becomes sinful and unworthy creatures when addressing their great and almighty Creator. They ought not to *repeat* the prayers *aloud;* but should accompany the minister in their *mind* and *affections* from one prayer to another, and from one part of each prayer to the other. At the conclusion of every collect and prayer they are to testify their sincere joining in it and their earnest desire of the blessings contained in it by a solemn *Amen,* which signifies *so be it;* or, *thus I heartily pray* GOD *it may be.* And they are to join in the Litany by repeating *aloud,* with humble but earnest importunity, the several answers, "Good LORD deliver us," "We beseech thee to hear us, good LORD," and the other parts assigned to them.

---

(48) **Frederick Denison Maurice**
Professor of Theology at King's College, London;
Professor of Moral Philosophy at Cambridge
Sermons on the Prayer Book and the Lord's Prayer
1848–1849

Of all parts of our Service the Litany is the one which lies most open to the charge of being anthropomorphic, and which has oftenest incurred it. The Son of Man is distinctly exhibited in all the petitions. His acts upon earth are put forward as the very ground of prayer to him. He is addressed as one who feels for all the common outward sufferings and the bodily calamities of his saints here on earth. Moreover, the Litany belongs to what may be called, without injustice, the anthropomorphic period of Church history. In all probability it was not composed within those first four centuries, which some English divines regard with such exclusive veneration. It may have been formed upon older models; but Gregory the Great would seem to have cast it into its present shape.

. . .

I appeal from both to those who have tried and do try to pray these prayers; who know what they are, not from books of antiquity but from their own hearts. If there is a cure in earth or heaven for men who would turn prayer into a show, who would make it a part of the finery and ornament of life, not of its inner substance; who fancy we can train ourselves for devotion by putting on a dress or learning a tone, I should say this Litany must be the cure. What do you mean by saying it is so human but this: That it calls upon the Son of God as one who has actually entered into the depths of human sorrow; who has borne the agony and bloody sweat, the cross and passion, who has been dead, and buried, and has known the darkness of the unseen world? What do you mean by calling it human but this: That it speaks of the actual vulgar sorrows to which flesh is heir; that it supposes men to be praying who know them for themselves and for others, who are too much crushed by them to have any power except to lift up such a cry as this, "Good Lord, deliver us," "Lord, have mercy upon us"? It is in the press and tumult of life you learn the tones in which these prayers should be uttered; it is amidst the terrible realities of sickness and death, of conflict with flesh and blood and with principalities and powers that you are taught with what kind of garlands, in what measures, you shall approach the divine altar. Surely you cannot be thinking of plays and babyshows while you are crying out, "In the hour of death, in the day of judgment, deliver us." Or if you are—and who can say that the merest vanity and frivolity may not assault his mind at the most dreadful moment?—is not this one of the very temptations, the most tormenting, if not the most terrible, of all from which we come to seek deliverance? Are you not flying to Him who is all true, from your own follies and weaknesses and hypocrisies? Did you ever meet with words which expressed more distinctly, simply, passionately, the sense of that oppression and the hope of that refuge? From first to last the prayer supposes you to be surrounded with enemies; some visible, some invisible; both equally real; the secret pestilence no more than the drawn sword; the pride and malice and envy of our own hearts, no less than those of the persecutor and slanderer. Everything about this document is intensely practical. The man who utters it is alone in God's presence, yet he is speaking of evils that are common to thousands. He does not isolate himself from his fellows. Plagues and pestilences threaten the whole land; sin and death lay their hands on princes and beggars. You ask help for all nations, you beseech the Lord God to govern the whole Church in the right way. Not the less do you enter into every individual suffering and mode of suffering.

Illustration from a
Book of Common Prayer, 1781.

CHAPTER SIX

Christian Initiation

(49) **John Jewel**
Bishop of Salisbury
An Apology of the Church of England
1564

We allow the sacraments of the church, that is to say certain holy signs and ceremonies which Christ would we should use, that by them he might set before our eyes the mysteries of our salvation and might more strongly confirm the faith which we have in his blood, and might seal his grace in our hearts. And these sacraments, together with Tertullian, Origen, Ambrose, Augustine, Jerome, Chrysostom, Basil, Dionysius and other Catholic fathers, we call figures, signs, marks or badges, prints, copies, forms, seals, signets, similitudes, patterns, representations, remembrances, and memories. And we make no doubt, together with the same doctors, to say that these be certain visible words, seals of righteousness, tokens of grace. And we expressly pronounce that in the Lord's Supper there is truly given unto the believing the body and blood of our Lord, the flesh of the Son of God which quickeneth our souls, the meat that cometh from above, the food of immortality, of grace, truth, and life; and the same supper to be the communion of the body and blood of Christ by the partaking whereof we be revived, we be strengthened and fed unto immortality; and whereby we are joined, united, and incorporate unto Christ, that we may abide in him and he in us.

Besides, we acknowledge there be two sacraments which, we judge, properly ought to be called by this name; that is to say, baptism and the sacrament of thanksgiving. For thus many we see were delivered and sanctified by Christ, and well allowed of the old fathers Ambrose and Augustine.

We say that baptism is a sacrament of the remission of sins and of that washing which we have in the blood of Christ; and that no person who will profess Christ's name ought to be restrained or kept back therefrom; no, not the very babes of Christians; forsomuch as they be born in sin and pertain unto the people of God.

---

(50) **Richard Hooker**
Master of the Temple, Rector of Bishopsbourne (Kent),
chief apologist for Anglicanism under Queen Elizabeth I
Of the Laws of Ecclesiastical Polity, book V
1597

[On the necessity of outward Baptism]

For as we are not naturally men without birth, so neither are we Christian men in the eye of the Church of God but by new birth, nor according to the manifest ordinary course of divine dispensation newborn but by that baptism which both declareth and maketh us Christians. In which respect we justly hold it to be the door of our actual entrance into God's house, the first apparent beginning of life, a seal perhaps to the grace of Election, before received, but to our sanctification here a step that hath not any before it.

. . .

[On Confirmation.]

The ancient custom of the Church was after they had baptized to add thereunto imposition of hands, with effectual prayer for the illumination of God's most Holy Spirit to confirm and perfect that which the grace of the same Spirit had already begun in baptism.

For our means to obtain the graces which God doth bestow are our prayers. Our prayers to that intent are available as well for others as for ourselves. To pray for others is *to bless* them for whom we pray, because prayer procureth the blessing of God upon them, especially the prayer of such as God either most respecteth for their piety and zeal that way, or else regardeth for that their place and calling bindeth them above others unto this duty as it doth both natural and spiritual fathers.

With prayers of spiritual and personal benediction the manner hath been in all ages to use *imposition of hands* as a ceremony betokening our *restrained desires* to the party whom we present unto God by prayer.

---

(51) **Anonymous**
(? Richard Allestree, Regius Professor of Divinity
at Oxford, Provost of Eton)
The Whole Duty of Man
1657

It is true, that the Sacrament of Baptism being now administered to us when we are Infants, it is not to be expected of us that we should in our own Persons do anything either *Before* or *At* the Time of receiving it: those Performances were strictly required of all Persons who were baptized when they were of Years. But for us it suffices to give us this Right to Baptism; that we are born within the Pale of the Church, that is, of Christian Parents; and all that is required at that Time is what we can only perform by others, they in our Stead promising that when we come to Years we will perform our Parts of the Covenant. But by how much the less we are then able to do so much, the greater Bond lies on us to perform those after-duties required of us by which we are to supply the Want of the former.

Now if you would know what those Duties are, look over those Promises which your Godfathers and Godmothers then made in your Name, and you may then learn them. I cannot give you them in a better Form than that of our Church's Catechism, which tells us *That our Godfathers and Godmothers did promise and vow three Things in our Names:* first, *That we should forsake the Devil and all his Works, the Pomps and Vanities of this wicked World, and all the sinful Lusts of the Flesh.* Whereby the Devil is meant; first the worshiping of all false Gods, which is indeed but worshiping the Devil: A Sin which at the Time of Christ's Coming into the World was very common, most Part of Mankind then living in that vile Idolatry. And therefore, when Baptism was first ordained, it was but needful to make the forsaking of those false Gods a principal Part of the Vow. And tho' those false Worships are now much rarer, yet there was one special Part of them which may be feared to be yet too common among us; and that is all Sorts of Uncleanness, which tho' we do not make Ceremonies of our Religion as the Heathens did of theirs, yet the committing thereof is a most high Provocation in God's Eyes, such as drew him to destroy whole *Cities with Fire and Brimstone,* as you may read, *Gen.* 19; nay, *the whole World with Water,* Gen. 6; and will not fail to bring down Judgments, and strange ones, on any that continue therein; and therefore the forsaking them well deserves to be looked on as an especial Part of this Promise. Besides this, all Dealing with the Devil is here vowed against, whether it be by practicing Witchcraft ourselves or consulting with those that do, upon any Occasion whatever, as the Recovery of our Health, our Goods, or whatever else; for this is a Degree of the former Sin, it is a forsaking of the Lord and setting up the Devil for our God, whilst we go to him in our Needs for Help.

But we also renounce *all the Works of the Devil;* and those are either in general all those that the Devil tempts us to, or else those particular Kinds of Sin which have most of his Image on them; that is, those which he himself most practices. Such are Pride (which brought him from being an Angel of Light to the accursed Condition he is now in) and Lying: He is, as our Savior saith, *Jn.* 8:44. *A Liar, and the Father of it:* And such also are Malice and Envy, especially killing and destroying of others, for he was a *Murderer from the Beginning, Jh.* 8:44. But above all there is nothing wherein we become so like him as in tempting and drawing others to sin, which is his whole Trade and Business; and if we make it any Part of ours we become like that *roaring Lion, that goes about seeking whom he may devour,* 1 *Pet.* 5: 8.

The second Thing we vow to forsake is the *Pomps and Vanities of this wicked World.* By the Pomps and Vanities, there are several Things meant; some of them such as were used by the Heathens in some unlawful Sports of theirs wherein we are not now so much concerned, there being none of them remaining among us; but besides that there is meant all Excess, either in Diet, or Sports, or Apparel, when we keep not those due Measures which, either by the general Rules of Sobriety or the particular Circumstances of our Qualities and Callings, we are bound to. Next, by the wicked World, we may understand, First, the Wealth and Greatness of the World, which, tho' we do not so totally renounce that it is unlawful for a Christian to be either rich or great, yet we thus far promise to forsake them that we will not set our Hearts upon them nor either get or keep them by the least unlawful Means. Secondly, by the wicked World we may understand the Companies and Customs of the World which, so far as they are wicked, we here renounce. That is, we promise never to be drawn by Company to the Commission of a Sin, but rather to forsake the most delightful Company than to be ensnared by it; nor yet by Custom, but rather venture the Shame of being thought singular, ridiculous Persons, walking as it were in a Path by ourselves, than put ourselves into that *broad Way that leads to Destruction* by giving ourselves over to any sinful Custom, however common it be grown. If this Part of our Vow were but thoroughly considered, it would arm us against most of the Temptations the World offers us; Company and Custom being the two special Instruments by which it works on us.

A third Thing we renounce is *all the sinful Lusts of the Flesh;* where the Flesh is to be understood in that Sense wherein the Scripture often uses it, for the Fountain of all disordered Affections. For though those unclean Desires which we ordinarily call the Lusts of the Flesh are meant here, yet they are not the only Things here contained, there being divers other Things which the Scripture calls *the Works of the Flesh.* I cannot better inform you of them than by setting down the list St. *Paul* gives of them: *Gal.* 5:19,20,21: *Now the Works of the Flesh are manifest, which are these: Adultery, Fornication, Uncleanness, Lasciviousness, Idolatry, Witchcraft, Hatred, Variance, Emulations, Wrath, Strife, Seditions, Heresies, Envyings, Murders, Drunkenness, Revelings, and such like.* This, with those other Descriptions you will find scattered in several Places of Scripture, will show you there are many Things contained in this Part of your Vow, the forsaking all the sinful Lusts of the Flesh.

The second Thing our Godfathers and Godmothers promised for us was that *we should believe all the Articles of the Christian Faith.* These we have summed up together in that which we call the Apostle's Creed which, since we promise to believe, we are supposed also to promise to learn them, and that not only the Words but likewise the plain Sense of them; for who can believe what he either never heard of or knows not anything of the Meaning of it? Now by this Believing is meant not only the consenting to the Truth of them, but also the living like them that do believe: As for Example, our believing that God created us should make us live in that Subjection and Obedience to him which becomes Creatures to their Creator. The believing that Christ redeemed us should make us yield up ourselves to him as his Purchase, to be disposed of wholly by him and employed only in his Service; the believing a Judgment to come should give us Care so to walk that we may not be condemned in it; and our believing the Life everlasting should make us diligent so to employ our short Moment of Time here that our everlasting Life may be a Life of Joy not of Misery to us. In this Manner, from all the Articles of the Creed, we are to draw Motives to confirm us in all Christian Practice, to which End it is that our learning and believing of them tends; and therefore without it we are very far from making good this Part of our Vow, the *believing all the Articles of the Christian Faith.*

The last Part of our Vow is that we *should keep God's holy Will and Commandments, and walk in the same all the Days of our Lives.* Where by *our keeping God's holy Will and Commandments* is meant our doing of all those Things which he hath made known to us to be his Will we should perform; wherein he hath given us his holy Word to instruct us and teach us what it is that he requires of us, and now he expects that we should faithfully do it, without favouring ourselves in the Breach of any one of his Commands. And then in this entire Obedience we must walk *all the Days of our Lives;* that is, we must go on in a constant Course of obeying God; not only fetch some few Steps in his Ways, but walk in them, and that not for some Part of our Time but *all the Days of our Lives,* never turn out of them, but go on constantly in them as long as we live in this World.

Having now thus briefly explained to you this Vow made at your BAPTISM, all I shall add concerning it is only to remind you how closely you are concerned in the keeping it; and that, first, in respect of Justice; secondly, in respect of Advantage and Benefit. That you are in Justice bound to it, I need say no more but that it is a Promise; and, you know, Justice requires of every Man the keeping of his Promise. But then this is of all

231

other Promises the most solemn and binding, for it is a Vow, that is, a Promise made to God; and therefore we are not only unjust but forsworn whenever we break any Part of it.

But, secondly, we are also highly concerned to keep it in respect of our own Benefit. I told you before that Baptism entered us into Covenant with God. Now a Covenant is made up of two Parts; that is, something promised by the one Party and something by the other of the Parties that make the Covenant: And if one of them break his Part of the Covenant, that is, perform not what he hath agreed to, he can in no Reason look that the other should make good his. And so it is here; God doth indeed promise those Benefits before-mentioned, and that is his Part of the Covenant. But then we also undertake to perform the several Things contained in this Vow of Baptism, and that is our Part of it; and unless we do indeed perform them, God is not tied to make good his, and so we forfeit all those precious Benefits and Advantages. We are left in that natural and miserable Estate of ours, *Children of Wrath, Enemies to God, and Heirs of eternal Damnation.* And now what can be the Pleasure that any or all Sins can afford us, that can make us the least Degree of Recompense for such a Loss, the Loss of God's Favour and Grace here and the Loss of our own Souls hereafter? For as our Savior saith, *Mk.* 8:36, *What shall it profit a Man, if he shall gain the whole World, and lose his own Soul?* Yet this mad Bargain we make whenever we break any Part of this our Vow of Baptism. It therefore most closely concerns us to consider sadly of it, to remember that every Sin we commit is a direct Breach of this our Vow; and therefore when thou art tempted to any Sin, seem it never too light, say not of it as Lot did of Zoar, *Gen.* 19:20, *Is it not a little one?* But consider that whatever it is thou hast in thy Baptism vowed against it; and then be it never so little, it draws a great one at the Heels of it, no less than that of being forsworn, which whoever commits, God hath in the third Commandment pronounced *He will not hold him guiltless.* And that we may the better keep this Vow, it will be very useful often to repeat to ourselves the several

Branches of it, that we may still have it ready in our Minds to set against all Temptations; and surely it is so excellent a Weapon that if we do not either cast it aside or use it very negligently it will enable us, by God's Help, to put to flight our spiritual Adversary. And this is that Reverence we are to pay to this first Sacrament, that of Baptism.

---

(52) Simon Patrick
Bishop of Ely
Aqua Genitalis: A Discourse Concerning Baptism
1659

[On Baptism]

Let me beseech all the People of God to live in Love and Peace together. Let us not quarrel about every little Thing, nor make every petty Difference a cause of Trouble and Contention. For as the Apostle saith, 1 Cor. 12:13, *By one Spirit we are all baptized into one Body.* We are all by this made of the same Corporation, and taken by Baptism into the same Brotherhood, and therefore should not make them the Waters of Strife and so provoke the Lord to Anger against us. We are not baptized into this or that particular Opinion, nor received into a particular Church, but into the Belief of the Gospel and into the Church of God in general, and therefore should love all the Disciples and Followers of our Lord and embrace all of every Persuasion that live godlily in Christ Jesus. You were not baptized (saith the Apostle) into the name of *Paul;* therefore do not say, I am of *Paul,* I adhere to this Man or that: for whosoever did baptize you, it was not into the particular Love of him and his Opinions, but into the Communion of the whole Church of Christ who hold the Catholic Faith. Though a *Heretic* in ancient

Times had baptized any Man, yet did not the Christians therefore baptize him over again when he left those Men's Company; because being baptized into the Name of the Father, Son, and Holy Ghost, he was not received into the Profession of their particular Opinions but of the Truth of Christ universally believed by all good Christians.

And therefore let us live with them all as our Confederates, as those that are tied together in the same Bonds and united in the same Covenant and engaged in the same Cause against the common Enemies, the Devil, the World, and the Flesh; and let us never give these Enemies so much cause to rejoice, as an unhandsome word against any sincere Christian might administer. But let us endeavour to keep the Unity of the Spirit in the Bond of Peace; for as the Apostle speaks, *There is one Lord, one Faith, one Baptism, one God and Father of All, who is above all, and through all, and in you all.*

. . .

[On Confirmation]

If Baptism did at first admit us into the Enjoyment of many Privileges, surely we shall receive more of the Blessings of it when we do seriously reflect upon it and engage our Hearts by our own free Consent to God; because then we begin more solemnly to perform the Conditions that God requireth of us. When I first entered upon a Charge of Souls, I could think of no Course so anciently attested unto, so reasonable in itself, and so likely to be effective for Men's good, so free likewise from the just Exceptions of any Party, as to propose this to my People; That all those who had not yet communicated should freely and heartily profess to be sincere and constant in their Baptismal Covenant, and declare themselves Enemies to the Devil, the World, and the Flesh.

. . .

This Christian Duty hath long passed under the name of *Confirmation;* which is a word full and significant of the thing that I would express, and consists of two Parts. First, that a Person do undertake in his own name every part of the Vow made by others for him in Baptism, and so personally consent unto Christ to be wholly his, according to that Agreement. And so it is an act of *Confirmation* on our part; because we do hereby further ratify and establish that Contract which is between God and us, and by confessing of it to be valid and good bind ourselves faster still to him whose we were before. The second part of it is a receiving of God's Blessing and Grace by the Hands and holy Prayers of him that ministers, to strengthen us to perform our Engagement and make good our Word and Faith which we have plighted unto God; which many have taken to be the meaning of that place, *Heb.* 6:4, Where after Baptism follows laying on of Hands, which the *Jews* used in their Blessings.

And so it is an *Act of Confirmation* of the Person on the part of God, who confers a new Grace to strengthen and confirm in him these holy Principles and that good Resolution of which he hath made a faithful Profession, and to enable him to keep and persist in it. As in Baptism the Holy Ghost was conveyed as a Sanctifier, so herein as a Comforter and Strengthener, now that the Person is entering upon a great Contest and Conflict with himself, the World, and Principalities, and Powers, and spiritual wickedness in high places.

---

(53) **John Durel**
Minister of the French Church in the Savoy, Dean of Windsor
The Liturgy of the Church of England Asserted
1662

The *sign* of the *Cross* which is made upon the Forehead of Infants *after* Baptism is neither an addition to that Sacrament nor the institution of a new; nor yet a superstition as some imagine, I know not why. But rather are not such both *contentious* and *superstitious* together who, living in a Communion where it is in use, do notwithstanding reject it? It is no addition to the Sacrament of Baptism: for one of the Rubrics of our Liturgy, to wit, that which speaks of the Baptism of weaker Infants, declareth that an Infant baptized without this sign is *Lawfully and sufficiently baptized.* It is no new Sacrament either; for although it be a significant Ceremony (as we speak in this Country), such as are and such as ought to be all Ceremonies reasonable and proper to edification (otherwise it were impertinent to have or to observe any), yet it hath no invisible Grace accompanying it which is essential to constitute a Sacrament; neither do we pretend it hath. . . . Its only use (as the words which are spoken at the making of it expressly declare) is only to signify, as among the Primitive Christians. As when the King, having created those noble Knights of his Order, bestows upon them the Garter and the blue Riband as badges to be known by of others and to put them in mind of the great honour done unto them. In like manner, when an Infant hath by Baptism been enrolled in the *Militia* of the King of *Glory* Jesus Christ our Lord, this *sign* of the *Cross* is made upon his forehead to declare unto all such as are present and as many as shall thereafter know that he hath received it and to himself when he comes to years of understanding that he was consecrated to Christ crucified; that he *hath put on* his Livery and *wears* his Badge: that he is bound to crucify the *old man* and to bear the *Cross;* that to this he is called by our Savior; that he ought in all places and in the most dangerous occurrences boldly and openly own the name of his Redeemer, without ever being ashamed with bearing his reproach.

(54) **Thomas Comber**
Dean of Durham
A Companion to the Temple,
or A Help to Devotion in the Use of the Common Prayer
1672–76/1684

[On Baptism]

"Seeing now, Dearly Beloved Brethren, that this Child is regenerate; &tc." We must not presently turn our backs upon God so soon as the Holy Rite is finished, but complete the Solemnity by Thanksgiving and Prayer, and that we may do both not only with the Spirit but with Understanding, the Minister doth here teach us what must be the Subjects of our Praises and Petitions. I. Our Praises must look back upon the Grace already showed and the benefits which are already given to this Infant, which are principally two. 1. Internally it is Regenerated. 2. Externally it is grafted into Christ's Church; for which we must give hearty thanks to Almighty God. To which we must add, II. Our Prayers, which must look forward upon the Grace which will be needful to enable it to live answerable to this Estate into which it is admitted; and this we must beg of Almighty God also, or else the former Blessings will be altogether in vain.

. . .

[On Confirmation]

It is very fit we should praise God for the grace of *Baptism* before we beg that of *Confirmation;* especially because the washing of us from Original Sin in the Holy Laver did cleanse and prepare us that we might be pure Temples for the Holy Ghost to dwell in; the greater measures of the Spirit now begged are but in pursuance of the former mercy. The Lord did then consign us to the Spirit, and now we pray it may visibly exert itself: He then lifted us as his Soldiers, and ever since we have been *trained* by Catechising, *Gen.* 14:14, and now are going into

237

the Field against our Spiritual Enemies, so that we shall need more visible and more efficacious assistances. Wherefore we pray for all the gifts of the Holy Spirit, which in the old Greek and Latin Translations are reckoned up to be *seven, Isa.* 11:2, and from thence are transcribed into this Prayer; and these seven are put for all, because the Scriptures describe the gifts of the Holy Ghost by *Seven Spirits, Rev.* 1: 4; 4: 5; and 5: 6.

. . .

We must not be too curious in the particulars, since many of the Words seem to be synonymous, yet we may thus distinguish these seven Gifts. 1. The Spirit of being wise in Spiritual Things. 2. The Spirit of apprehending what we are taught. 3. The Spirit of prudent managing all our Actions. 4. The Spirit of Power to execute all our Religious purposes. 5. The Spirit of Discerning between Good and Evil. 6. The Spirit of Devotion in God's Service. 7. The Spirit of Reverence to be expressed towards God in our whole Conversation. These are the blessed Gifts for which the Bishop Prays, that we may be wise and apprehensive, prudent and couragious, discreet in our choice, devout in our Duties, and pious in our Lives; and if these can be obtained, we may be assured all Graces will spring from these Roots, Charity, and the Love of God, Humility and Watchfulness, Faith and Holiness, Meekness and Patience, Temperance and Chastity, and what not? Let us therefore *kneel reverently,* and join devoutly with the Holy Man, let us open our Hearts by earnest desires, and stretch out the Hands of Faith and Hope to receive these so much needed, these so inestimable Gifts; and let us not doubt but God will hear his own Servant and gratify our desires; Christ hath promised to give these Gifts to us, and others have received them in the use of this very means, so that if we ask heartily and believe firmly God will by the same means give them unto us also.

(55) John Henry Hobart
Bishop of New York, founder of The General Theological Seminary
A Companion for the Book of Common Prayer
1805 / 1827

In the Offices of Baptism, and also in that of Confirmation, the terms *regenerate* and *born again* are applied to those who are *baptized.* And this circumstance has given rise to the unfounded opinion that the Church does not maintain the necessity of any spiritual change but that which takes place in baptism. It appears, however, from these very Offices, that the Church does most strenuously insist, in the case of those who are baptized, on that "renewing of the mind," or that "renewing of the HOLY GHOST," to which in modern times the term *regeneration* is erroneously applied. The scriptural application of this term is to *baptism.* Thus the apostle speaks of the "washing of regeneration," evidently meaning *baptism;* and, as a distinct operation, "the *renewing* of the HOLY GHOST." Guided by this authority, the Church makes the same distinction, particularly in the collect for Christmas day—"grant that we, *being regenerate* and made thy children by adoption and grace, *may* daily *be renewed* by thy HOLY SPIRIT." Regeneration is always applied in the writings of the first ages of the Christian Church to baptism; and a different construction of this term in modern times to denote a change of heart and life has given rise to very erroneous opinions as to the views of the Church on this important subject. By regeneration she means—a *change of state* from our natural state, in which we have *no title* to the blessings of the Gospel covenant, to "a state of grace or salvation" in the Christian Church, in which we *have a title,* on the conditions or qualifications of repentance, and faith and evangelical obedience to the privileges of pardon and grace and eternal life which CHRIST purchased for his mystical body. In this sense it is, therefore, that in the Office of Confirmation, the Church speaks of those who are baptized as "regenerate with water and the HOLY GHOST, and having received the forgiveness of their sins." But this blessing, and all the other blessings of the Christian covenant conveyed and assured in baptism, suppose repentance and faith and evangelical obedience in the recipients; when they come of age in the case of infants, and actually in the case of adults. Without these qualifications—without the "renewing of the mind"—without "dying unto sin and living unto righteousness," for which the necessary grace is pledged in baptism, and in which also the most powerful motives, arising from the blessings of pardon and eternal life there proffered, are presented—the regeneration of baptism will only increase the guilt and condemnation of those who thus resist the grace and disdain the privileges there conferred.

That the Church does maintain and most earnestly urge on those who are baptized and regenerated,

A Change of Heart

and life from sin to holiness, which is properly styled *renovation, renewing, conversion, sanctification,* must be evident from the following language which she uses in the Offices of Baptism:— "O merciful GOD, grant that the old Adam in this child (or person) may be so buried, that the new man may be raised up in him."—"Grant that all sinful affections may die in him, and that all things belonging to the Spirit may live and grow in him."—"Grant that he, being dead unto sin and living unto righteousness, and being buried with CHRIST in his death, may crucify the old man and utterly abolish the whole body of sin."

"Baptism doth represent unto us our profession; which is to follow the example of our Savior CHRIST and to be made like unto him; that as he died and rose again for us, so should we who are baptized die from sin, and rise again unto righteousness; continually mortifying all our evil and corrupt affections and daily proceeding in all virtue and godliness of living."

240

And in the Office of Confirmation, the Church prays for those who are regenerated in baptism—"Strengthen them, we beseech thee, O LORD, with the HOLY GHOST, the Comforter; and daily increase in them thy manifold gifts of grace," &tc.— "lead them in the knowledge and obedience of thy word," &tc.

The Church then does maintain the necessity of *a change of heart,* of *spiritual renovation,* and points by her views of baptism the most powerful motives to it.

Illustration from Charles Wheatly, *A Rational-
Illustration of the Book of Common Prayer*, 1720.

CHAPTER SEVEN

The Holy Eucharist

(56) **Anonymous**
Second Book of Homilies
An Homily of the Worthy Receiving and Reverent Esteeming
of the Sacrament of the Body and Blood of Christ
(John Jewel)
1563/1571

The great love of our Savior Christ toward mankind, good Christian people, doth not only appear in that dear-bought benefit of our redemption and salvation by his death and passion, but also in that he so kindly provided that the same most merciful work might be had in continual remembrance, to take some place in us, and not be frustrate of his end and purpose. For, as tender parents are not content to procure for their children costly possessions and livelihood, but take order that the same may be conserved and come to their use; so our Lord and Savior thought it not sufficient to purchase for us his Father's favour again (which is that deep fountain of all good-

243

ness), and eternal life, but also invented the ways most wisely whereby they might redound to our commodity and profit. Among the which means is the public celebration of the memory of his precious death at the Lord's table: which although it seem of small virtue to some, yet, being rightly done by the faithful, it doth not only help their weakness, who be by their poisoned nature readier to remember injuries than benefits, but strengtheneth and comforteth their inward man with peace and gladness, and maketh them thankful to their Redeemer with diligent care of godly conversation. And as, of old time, God decreed his wondrous benefits of the deliverance of his people to be kept in memory by the eating of the passover with his rites and ceremonies, so our loving Savior hath ordained and established the remembrance of his great mercy expressed in his passion in the institution of his heavenly Supper: where every one of us must be guests and not gazers, eaters and not lookers, feeding ourselves and not hiring others to feed for us; that we may live by our own meat and not perish for hunger while others devour all. To this his commandment forceth us, saying, *Do ye thus, Drink ye all of this.* To this his promise enticeth us: *This is my body, which is given for you; This is my blood, which is shed for you.*

So then, as of necessity we must be ourselves partakers of this table and not beholders of others, so we must address ourselves to frequent the same in reverent and due manner; lest, as physic provided for the body, being misused, more hurteth than profiteth, so this comfortable medicine of the soul, undecently received, tends to our greater harm and sorrow. As St. Paul saith: *He that eateth and drinketh unworthily eateth and drinketh his own damnation.* Wherefore that it be not said to us as it was to the guest of that great supper, *Friend, how camest thou in not having the marriage garment?* and that we may fruitfully use St. Paul's counsel, *Let a man prove himself, and so eat of that bread and drink of that cup,* we must certainly know that three things be requisite in him who would seemly, as becometh such high mysteries, resort to the Lord's table: that is, a right and a

244

worthy estimation and understanding of this mystery; secondly, to come in a sure faith; and thirdly, to have newness or pureness of life to succeed the receiving of the same.

But, before all other things, this we must be sure of specially, that this Supper be in such wise done and ministered as our Lord and Savior did and commanded to be done, as his holy Apostles used it, and the good fathers in the primitive Church frequented it. For, as that worthy man St. *Ambrose* saith, "he is unworthy the Lord that otherways doth celebrate that mystery than it was delivered by him; neither can he be devout that otherways doth presume than it was given by the Author." We must then take heed, lest, of the memory, it be made a sacrifice; lest, of a communion, it be made a private eating; lest, of two parts, we have but one; lest, applying it for the dead, we lose the fruit that be alive. Let us rather in these matters follow the advice of Cyprian in the like cases; that is, cleave fast to the first beginning; hold fast the Lord's tradition; do that in the Lord's commemoration which he himself did, he himself commanded, and his Apostles confirmed.

If we use this caution or foresight, then may we see to those things that be requisite in the worthy receiver; whereof this was the first, that we have a right understanding of the thing itself. As concerning which thing, this we may assuredly persuade ourselves, that the ignorant man can neither worthily esteem nor effectually use those marvellous graces and benefits offered and exhibited in that Supper, but either will lightly regard them to no small offense or utterly disdain them to his utter destruction; so that by his negligence he deserveth the plagues of God to fall upon him, and by contempt he deserveth everlasting perdition. To avoid these harms then, use the advice of the Wise Man, who willeth thee, *when thou sittest at an earthly king's table*, to *take diligent heed what things are set before thee.* So now much more, at the King of kings' table, thou must carefully search and know what dainties are provided for thy soul: whither thou art come, not to feed thy senses and belly to corruption, but thy inward man to immortality and life; not to consider the earthly creatures which thou seest, but the heavenly graces which thy faith beholdeth. "For this table is not," saith Chrysostom, "for chattering jays, but for eagles," who flee *"thither, where the dead body lieth."* And, if this advertisement of man cannot persuade us to resort to the Lord's table with understanding, see the counsel of God in the like matter who charged his people to teach their posterity not only the rites and ceremonies of his Passover, but the cause and end thereof: whence we may learn that both more perfect knowledge is required at this time at our hands, and that the ignorant cannot with fruit and profit exercise himself in the Lord's Sacraments. But to come nigher to the matter: St. Paul, blaming the Corinthians for the profaning of the Lord's Supper, concludeth that ignorance both of the thing itself and the signification thereof was the cause of their abuse; for they came thither unreverently, *not discerning the Lord's body.* Ought not we then, by the admonition of the Wise Man, by the wisdom of God, by the fearful example of the Corinthians to take advised heed that we thrust not ourselves to this table with rude and unreverent ignorance, the smart whereof Christ's Church hath rued and lamented these many days and years? For what hath been the cause of the ruin of God's religion but the ignorance hereof? What hath been the cause of this gross idolatry but the ignorance hereof? What hath been the cause of this mummish massing but the ignorance hereof? Yea, what hath been, and what is at this day the cause of this want of love and charity but the ignorance hereof? Let us therefore so labor hard to understand the Lord's Supper, that we be no cause of the decay of God's worship, of no idolatry, of no dumb massing, of no hate and malice: so may we the more boldly have access thither to our comfort.

Neither need we to think that such exact knowledge is required of every man that he be able to discuss all high points in the doctrine thereof. But thus much he must be sure to hold, that in the Supper of the Lord there is no vain ceremony, no bare sign, no untrue figure of a thing absent but, as the Scrip-

246

ture saith, *the table of the Lord, the bread and cup of the Lord, the memory of Christ, the annunciation of his death,* yea, *the communion of the body and blood of the Lord* in a marvelous incorporation which, by the operation of the Holy Ghost, the very bond of our conjunction with Christ, is through faith wrought in the souls of the faithful, whereby not only their souls live to eternal life but they surely trust to win to their bodies a resurrection to immortality. The true understanding of this fruition and union, which is betwixt the body and the head, betwixt the true believers and Christ, the ancient Catholic fathers both perceiving themselves and commending to their people were not afraid to call this Supper, some of them, "the salve of immortality, a sovereign preservative against death"; other, "a divine communion"; other, "the sweet dainties of our Savior"; "the pledge of eternal health, the defense of faith, the hope of the resurrection"; other, "the food of immortality," "the healthful grace," and "the conservatory to everlasting life." All which sayings, both of the holy Scripture and godly men, truly attributed to this celestial banquet and feast; if we would often call to mind, O how would they inflame our hearts to desire the participation of these mysteries and oftentimes to covet after this bread, continually to thirst for this food; not as specially regarding the mundane and earthly creatures which remain, but always holding fast and cleaving by faith to the *Rock* whence we may *suck the sweetness of* everlasting *salvation.* And, to be brief, thus much more the faithful see, hear, and know the favourable mercies of God sealed, the satisfaction by Christ toward us confirmed, the remission of sin established. Here they may feel wrought the tranquility of conscience, the increase of faith, the strengthening of hope, the large spreading abroad of brotherly kindness, with many other sundry graces of God: the taste whereof they cannot attain unto who be drowned in the deep dirty lake of blindness and ignorance. From the which, O beloved, wash yourselves with the living waters of God's word, whence you may perceive and know both the spiritual food of this costly Supper and the happy trustings and effects that the same doth bring with it.

Now it followeth to have with this knowledge a sure and constant faith, not only that the death of Christ is available for the redemption of all the world, for the remission of sins, and reconciliation with God the Father, but also that he hath made upon his cross a full and sufficient sacrifice for thee, a perfect cleansing of thy sins; so that thou acknowledgest no other Savior, Redeemer, Mediator, Advocate, Intercessor but Christ only, and that thou mayest say with the Apostle that he *loved thee and gave himself for thee.* For this is to stick fast to Christ's promise made in his institution, to make Christ thine own and to apply his merits unto thyself. Herein thou needest no other man's help, no other sacrifice or oblation, no sacrificing priest, no mass, no means established by man's invention. That faith is a necessary instrument in all these holy ceremonies we may thus assure ourselves, for that, as St. *Paul* saith, *without faith it is impossible to please God.* When a great number of the Israelites *were overthrown in the wilderness,* "Moses, Aaron, and Phinees did eat manna, and pleased God, for that they understood," saith St. *Augustine,* "the visible meat spiritually: spiritually they hungered it; spiritually they tasted it; that they might be spiritually satisfied." And truly, as the bodily meat cannot feed the outward man unless it be let into a stomach to be digested which is healthsome and sound, no more can the inward man be fed except his meat be received into his soul and heart, sound and whole in faith. Therefore saith Cyprian, "when we do these things, we need not to whet our teeth, but with sincere faith we break and divide that holy bread." It is well known that the meat we seek for in this Supper is spiritual food, the nourishment of our soul, a heavenly refection and not earthly, an invisible meat and not bodily, a ghostly sustenance and not carnal. So that to think that without faith we may enjoy the eating and drinking thereof, or that that is the fruition of it is but to dream a gross carnal feeding, basely abjecting and binding ourselves to the elements and creatures; whereas, by the advice of the Council of Nicene, we ought to "lift up our minds by faith," and, leaving these inferior and earthly things, there seek it where the *Sun of righteousness* ever shineth. Take then this lesson, O thou that art desirous of this table, of Emissenus, a godly father, that "when thou goest up to the reverend Communion to be satisfied with spiritual meats, thou look up with faith upon the holy Body and Blood of thy God, thou marvel with reverence, thou touch it with thy mind, thou receive it with the hand of thy heart, and thou take it fully with thy inward man."

Thus we see, beloved, that, resorting to this table, we must pluck up all the roots of infidelity, all distrust in God's promises, we must make ourselves living members of Christ's body. For the unbelievers and faithless cannot feed upon that precious Body: whereas the faithful have their life, their abiding, in him; their union, and as it were their incorporation with him. Wherefore let us prove and try ourselves unfeignedly, without flattering ourselves, whether we be plants of that fruitful olive, living *branches of the true Vine, members* indeed *of Christ's mystical body;* whether God hath purified our hearts by faith to the sincere acknowledging of his Gospel and embracing of his mercies in Christ Jesu: so that at this his table we receive not only the outward Sacrament but the spiritual thing also; not the figure but the truth; not the shadow only but the body; not to death but to life; not to destruction but to salvation. Which God grant us to do through the merits of our Lord and Savior: to whom be all honour and glory forever. Amen.

The Second Part of the Homily of the Worthy Receiving and Reverent Esteeming of the Sacrament of the Body and Blood of Christ

In the Homily of late rehearsed unto you ye have heard, good people, why it pleased our Savior Christ to institute that heavenly memory of his death and passion, and that every one of us ought to celebrate the same at his table in our own persons and not by other. You have heard also with what estimation and knowledge of so high mysteries we ought to resort thither, you have heard with what constant faith we should clothe and deck ourselves that we might be fit and decent partakers of that celestial food. Now followeth the third thing necessary in him that would not eat of this bread nor drink of this cup unworthily, which is newness of life and godliness of conversation.

For newness of life, as fruits of faith, are required in the partaker of this table. We may learn by the eating of the typical lamb, whereunto no man was admitted but he that was a Jew, that was circumcised, that was before sanctified. Yea, St. Paul testifieth that, although all the people were partakers of the Sacraments under Moses, yet, for that some of them were still worshipers of images, whoremongers, tempters of Christ, murmurers, and coveting after evil things, God overthrew those in the wilderness, and that for our example; that is, that we Christians should take heed we resort unto our Sacraments with holiness of life, not trusting in the outward receiving of them, and infected with corrupt and uncharitable manners. For this sentence of God must always be justified: *I will have mercy, and not sacrifice.* "Wherefore," saith Basil, "it behooveth him that cometh to the Body and Blood of Christ, *in commemoration of him that died and rose again,* not only to be pure *from all filthiness of the flesh and spirit,* lest he eat and drink to his condemnation, but also to show out evidently a memory of *him that died and rose again for us,* in this point, that he be *mortified to sin* and *the world,* to *live* now *to God in Christ Jesu our Lord.*" So then we must show outward testimony in following the signification of Christ's death: amongst the which this is not esteemed least, to render thanks to Almighty God for all his benefits briefly comprised in the death, passion, and resurrection of his dearly beloved Son.

The which thing because we ought chiefly at this table to solemnize, the godly fathers named it Eucharistia, that is, Thanksgiving: as if they should have said, Now above all other times ye ought to laud and praise God; now may ye behold the matter, the cause, the beginning and the end of all thanksgiving. Now if ye slack, ye show yourselves most unthankful, and that no other benefit can ever stir you to thank God who so little regard here so many, so wonderful, and so profitable benefits. Seeing then that the name and thing itself doth admonish us of thanks, *let us,* as St. Paul saith, *offer always to God the host* or sacrifice *of praise by Christ, that is, the fruit of the lips which confess his Name.* For, as David singeth, *he that offereth to God thanks and praise honoureth him.* But how few be there of thankful persons in comparison to the unthankful! Lo, ten lepers in the Gospel were healed, and but one only returned to give thanks for his health. Yea, happy it were if among forty communicants we could see two unfeignedly give thanks. So unkind we be, so oblivious we be, so proud beggars we be, that partly we care not for our own commodity, partly we know not our duty to God, and chiefly we will not confess all that we receive. Yea, and if we be forced by God's power to do it, yet we handle it so coldly, so drily, that our lips praise him but our hearts dispraise him; our tongues bless him but our life curseth him; our words worship him but our works dishonour him. O let us therefore learn to give God here thanks aright, and so to acknowledge his exceeding graces poured upon us that they, being shut up in the treasure house of our heart, may in due time and season in our life and conversation appear to the glorifying of his holy Name.

Furthermore, for newness of life, it is to be noted that St. *Paul* writeth that *we being many are one bread and one body, for all be partakers of one bread;* declaring thereby not only our communion with Christ, but that unity also wherein they that eat at this table should be knit together. For by dissension, vainglory, ambition, strife, envying, contempt, hatred, or malice they should not be parted, but so joined by the bond of love in one mystical body as the corns of that bread in one loaf. In respect of which strait knot of charity the true Christians in the tender time of Christ's Church called this Supper Love; as if they would say none ought to sit down there that were out of love and charity, who bore grudge and vengeance in his heart, who also did not profess his kind affection by some charitable relief for some part of the congregation. And this was their practice. O heavenly banquet then so used! O godly guests who so esteemed this feast! But O wretched creatures that we be at these days, who be without reconciliation of our brethren whom we have offended, without satisfying them whom we have caused to fall, without any kind thought or compassion toward them whom we might easily relieve, without any conscience of slander, disdain, misreport, division, rancour, or inward bitterness; yea, being accombred with the cloaked hatred of Cain, with the long covered malice of Esau, with the dissembled falsehood of Joab, dare yet presume to come up to these sacred and fearful mysteries. O man, whither rushest thou unadvisedly? It is a table of peace and thou art ready to fight. It is a table of singleness and thou art imagining mischief. It is a table of quietness and thou art given to debate. It is a table of pity and thou art unmerciful. Dost thou neither fear God, the maker of this feast? nor reverence his Christ, the refection and meat? nor regardest his spouse, his beloved guest? nor weighest thine own conscience, which is sometime thine inward accuser? Wherefore, O man, tender thine own salvation; examine and try thy good will and love toward the children of God, the members of Christ, the heirs of the heavenly heritage; yea, toward the image of God, the excellent creature thine own soul. If thou have offended, now be reconciled. If thou have caused any to stumble in the way of God, now set them up again. If thou have disquieted thy brother, now pacify him. If thou have wronged him, now relieve him. If thou have defrauded him, now restore to him. If thou have nourished spite, now embrace friendship. If thou have fostered hatred and malice, now openly show thy love and charity; yea, be prompt and ready to procure thy neighbor's health of soul, wealth, commodity, and pleasure as thine own. Deserve not the heavy and dreadful burden of God's displeasure for thine evil will toward thy neighbor, so unreverently to approach to this table of the Lord.

Last of all, as there is here "the mystery of peace" and the

Sacrament of Christian society, whereby we understand what sincere love ought to be betwixt the true communicants, so here be the tokens of pureness and innocency of life, whereby we may perceive that we ought to purge our own soul from all uncleanness, iniquity, and wickedness, "lest, when we receive the mystical bread," as Origen saith, "we eat it in an unclean place, that is, in a soul defiled and polluted with sin." In Moyses's law the man that did eat of the sacrifice of thanksgiving with his uncleanness upon him should be destroyed from his people: and shall we think that the wicked and sinful person shall be excusable at the table of the Lord? We both read in St. Paul that the Church of Corinth was scourged of the Lord for misusing the Lord's Supper; and we may plainly see Christ's Church these many years miserably vexed and oppressed for the horrible profanation of the same. Wherefore let us all, universal and singular, behold our own manners and lives, to amend them. Yea, now at the least let us call ourselves to an account, that it may grieve us of our former evil conversation, that we may hate sin, that we may sorrow and mourn for our offenses, that we may with tears pour them out before God, that we may with sure trust desire and crave the salve of his mercy, bought and purchased with the blood of his dearly beloved Son Jesus Christ, to heal our deadly wounds withal. For surely, if we do not with earnest repentance cleanse the filthy stomach of our soul, it must needs come to pass that "as wholesome meat received into a raw stomach corrupteth and marreth all, and is the cause of further sickness," so we shall eat this healthsome bread and drink this cup to our eternal destruction. Thus we, and not other, must throughly examine, and not lightly look over, ourselves, not other men; our own conscience, not other men's lives: which we ought to do uprightly, truly, and with just correction. "O," saith St. Chrysostom, "let no Judas resort to this table; let no covetous person approach. If any be a disciple, let him be present. For Christ saith, *With my disciples I make my passover.*" Why cried the deacon in the primitive Church, "If any be holy, let him draw near"?

Why did they celebrate these mysteries, the choir door being shut? Why were the public penitents and learners in religion commanded at this time to avoid? Was it not because this table receiveth no unholy, unclean, or sinful guests? Wherefore, if servants dare not presume to an earthly master's table whom they have offended, let us take heed we come not with our sins unexamined into this presence of our Lord and Judge. If they be worthy blame who kiss the prince's hand with a filthy and unclean mouth, shalt thou be blameless which with a filthy stinking soul, full of covetousness, fornication, drunkenness, pride, full of wretched cogitations and thoughts, dost breathe out iniquity and uncleanness on the bread and cup of the Lord?

Thus you have heard how you should come reverently and decently to the table of the Lord, having the knowledge out of his word of the thing itself and the fruits thereof, bringing a true and constant faith, the root and wellspring of all newness of life, as well in praising God, loving our neighbour, as purging our own conscience from filthiness. So that neither the ignorance of the thing shall cause us to despise it, nor unfaithfulness make us void of fruit, nor sin and iniquity procure us God's plagues; but shall, by faith in knowledge and amendment of life in faith, be here so united to Christ our Head in his mysteries to our comfort that after we shall have full fruition of him indeed to our everlasting joy and eternal life. To the which he bring us that died for us and redeemed us, *Jesus Christ the righteous:* to whom with the Father and the Holy Ghost, one true and eternal God, be all praise, honour, and dominion forever. Amen.

---

(57) **John Jewel**
Bishop of Salisbury
An Apology of the Church of England
1564

We say that *Eucharistia*, the supper of the Lord, is a sacrament, that is to wit, an evident token of the body and blood of Christ, wherein is set, as it were, before our eyes the death of Christ and his resurrection, and what act soever he did whilst he was in his mortal body. To that end we may give him thanks for his death and for our deliverance; and that, by the often receiving of this sacrament, we may daily renew the remembrance of that matter, to the intent we, being fed with the body and blood of Christ, may be brought into the hope of the resurrection and of everlasting life and may most assuredly believe that the body and blood of Christ doth in like manner feed our souls, as bread and wine doth feed our bodies. To this banquet we think the people of God ought to be earnestly bidden, that they may all communicate among themselves and openly declare and testify both the godly society which is among them and also the hope which they have in Christ Jesus.

---

(58) **Richard Hooker**
Master of the Temple, Rector of Bishopsbourne (Kent),
chief apologist for Anglicanism under Queen Elizabeth I
Of the Laws of Ecclesiastical Polity, book V
1597

The grace which we have by the holy Eucharist doth not begin but continue life. No man therefore receiveth this sacrament before Baptism, because no dead thing is capable of nourishment. That which groweth must of necessity first live. If our bodies did not daily waste, food to restore them were a thing superfluous. And it may be that the grace of baptism would serve to eternal life were it not that the state of our spiritual being is daily so much hindered and impaired after baptism. In that life therefore where neither body nor soul can decay, our souls shall as little require this sacrament as our bodies corporal nourishment, but as long as the days of our warfare last, during the time that we are both subject to diminution and capable of augmentation in grace, the words of our Lord and Savior Christ will remain forcible, "Except ye eat the flesh of the Son of man and drink his blood ye have no life in you."

Life being therefore proposed unto all men as their end, they which by baptism have laid the foundation and attained the first beginning of a new life have here their nourishment and food prescribed for *continuance of life* in them. Such as will live the life of God must eat the flesh and drink the blood of the Son of man because this is a part of that diet which if we want we cannot live. Whereas therefore in our infancy we are incorporated into Christ and by Baptism receive the grace of his Spirit without any sense or feeling of the gift which God bestoweth, in the Eucharist we so receive the gift of God that we know by grace what the grace is which God giveth us, the degrees of our own increase in holiness and virtue we see and can judge of them, we understand that the strength of our life begun in Christ is Christ, that his flesh is meat and his blood drink, not by surmised imagination but truly, even so truly that through faith we perceive in the body and blood sacramentally presented the very taste of eternal life, the grace of the sacrament is here as the food which we eat and drink.

· · ·

If then the presence of Christ with *(the disciples)* did so much move, judge what their thoughts and affections were at the time of this new presentation of Christ not before their eyes but within their souls. They had learned before that his flesh and blood are the true cause of eternal life; that this they are not by the bare force of their own substance, but through the dignity and worth of his Person which offered them up by way of sacrifice for the life of the whole world, and doth make them still effectual thereunto; finally that to us they are life in particu-

256

lar by being particularly received. Thus much they knew, although as yet they understood not perfectly to what effect or issue the same would come, till at the length being assembled for no other cause which they could imagine but to have eaten the Passover only that Moses appointeth, when they saw their Lord and Master with hands and eyes lifted up to heaven first bless and consecrate for the endless good of all generations till the world's end the chosen elements of bread and wine, which elements made forever the instruments of life by virtue of his divine benediction, they being the first that were commanded to receive from him, the first which were warranted by his promise that not only unto them at the present time but to whomsoever they and their successors after them did duly administer the same, those mysteries should serve as conducts of life and conveyances of his body and blood unto them, was it possible they should hear that voice, "Take, eat, this is my body; drink ye all of this, this is my blood"; possible that doing what was required and believing what was promised, the same should have present effect in them and not fill them with a kind of fearful admiration at the heaven which they saw in themselves? They had at that time a sea of comfort and joy to wade in, and we by that which they did are taught that this heavenly food is given for the satisfying of our empty souls, and not for the exercising of our curious and subtle wits.

If we doubt what those admirable words may import, let him be our teacher for the meaning of Christ to whom Christ was himself a schoolmaster, let our Lord's Apostle be his interpreter, content we ourselves with his explication, My body, *the communion of my body,* My blood, *the communion of my blood.* Is there anything more speedy, clear, and easy than that as Christ is termed our life because through him we obtain life, so the parts of this sacrament are his body and blood for that they are so to us who receiving them receive that by them which they are termed? The bread and cup are his body and blood because they are causes instrumental upon the receipt whereof the *participation* of his body and blood ensueth. For that which produceth any certain effect is not vainly nor improperly said to be that very effect whereunto it tendeth. Every cause is in the effect which groweth from it. Our souls and bodies quickened to eternal life are effects the cause whereof is the Person of Christ, his body and blood are the true wellspring out of which this life floweth. So that his body and blood are in that very subject whereunto they minister life not only by effect or operation, even as the influence of the heavens is in plants, beasts, men, and in everything which they quicken, but also by a far more divine and mystical kind of union which maketh us one with him even as he and the Father are one.

---

(59) **Christopher Sutton**
Canon of Winchester and Lincoln
Godly Meditations upon the Most Holy Sacrament
of the Lord's Supper
1613/1630

Of the First Institution of this Most Holy Sacrament of the Lord's Supper

AMONG other parts of divine worship and religious duties of a Christian life which knit men in love and service unto God (for who should have the fruit but He that planted the tree), there is none more solemn, none more divine than is the celebration of the most Holy Sacrament of the Lord's Supper, in the due celebration whereof we present ourselves before God. We honour Him who hath honoured us (miserable sinners that we are), and thereby we become partakers of our greatest good.

Fasting humbleth, prayer beseecheth, repentance bewaileth, charity worketh, faith believeth; but the Holy Sacrament applieth all by Christ Jesus' merits to the salvation of our souls. . . .

258

Of the Love of Christ Showed unto Faithful Believers in Ordaining this Most Holy Sacrament of the Lord's Supper

FOR that this Sacrament is a Sacrament of love, and left unto us from the love of our beloved Savior, it is convenient that to put away the suspicion of ingratitude it be received and handled with love chiefly, seeing we can requite in no other thing the love declared in ordaining this Sacrament, so full of love, than by love. Of which love God would that we should dispose and so change it into what we see most pleasing to Him: whereupon, as Christ our Savior, while He giveth Himself to us for meat, giveth us a token of His highest love with His grace, with so many merits of His preachings, labours, fastings, prayers; so we, when we give our love to God do give Him all things which we have most precious. Hence it cometh that God doth more esteem, and that more worthily too, of this one love than of all other things in the world. Neither doth He require any other thing of us when elsewhere he saith, "My Son, give me thy heart," that is to say, the love which is thine. When Christ our Savior humbled Himself to be baptized of John Baptist, it made John more humble himself to Christ. His love should wound our hearts and make us love Him who is love itself; and this love of His is manifest to us by instituting this most Holy Sacrament. When Nathan the prophet would show King David what love the poor man bore to that ewe lamb which he nourished in his bosom, he gave him, saith he, of his own meat and drink of his own cup. Christ, to show His love toward us, hath given us of His own bread and of His own cup; nay, He hath given us His own Body as bread, His own Blood as wine, for the nourishment of our souls.

. . .

An Exhortation unto the Holy Communion, Moving Every Devout Christian to Repair Often Unto the Same

I HOPE, gentle reader, thou perceivest well, by that which hath been formerly spoken, how much more excellent and profitable a thing it is often to receive the most Blessed Body of Christ in the Eucharist than to abstain from a meat so healthful and nourishing unto life. One thing yet remaineth, that thou, thoroughly regarding the unspeakable favour and bounty of so great a King so cheerfully and so bountifully calling thee to His marriage feast, when He saith, "Take and eat, this is My Body," and again, "Do this in remembrance of Me," shouldest therefore with all speed and often repair unto this banquet, lest thou fall into the fault of ingratitude and be shut out of the Kingdom of Heaven (as those were who are mentioned in the Gospel to have been bidden to the wedding dinner) if thou absent thyself, thinking to excuse it.

This is the marriage feast of the King of Heaven: the Banquet is Spiritual, Whose Bread doth strengthen man's heart and Whose Wine doth inflame the soul with Heavenly joy; and the meat thereof is the flesh of Christ, Who says, "My flesh is meat indeed." This is that healthful food of Angels sent down from Heaven, having in it all delight and savoury sweetness. This is that fat bread which giveth pleasures for a king. This is the most plentiful bread of good nourishment above all that the earth yieldeth. This is the bread of the offering of the first fruits. This is the bread signified as well in the cakes which Abraham did set before the angels, as also in the shewbread; and this was likewise revealed in the bread and wine which Melchizedek brought forth. Lastly, this is that bread baked upon the coals in the strength whereof Elias did walk forty days and forty nights unto Horeb, the mount of God. This is that tree of life, planted by Almighty God in the midst of the earthly paradise, whose fruit being eaten would preserve bodily life. This is that Paschal Lamb without spot, by Whose blood dabbed upon the two posts and the lintel of the door, the children of Israel were in times past delivered from the hand of the angel that smote the Egyptians. This is that kid which Manoah offered unto the Lord upon the stone. This is also that honeycomb which Jonathan, dipping the tip of his rod therein, did put to his mouth and his eyes were enlightened. This is also that large flowing stream of water which suddenly issued out of the rock after Moses had stricken it with his rod.

Come freely therefore to this most sweet Banquet of Christ Jesus wherein is promised unto thee most assured life and salvation. For if the garments of Christ, and if napkins and partlets brought from Paul did even with the least touch thereof give health, how much more then shall the very Body of Christ, being worthily received, deliver thee from all thine infirmities and wicked afflictions! If, at Christ's only word, Lazarus, having been four days in the grave, was raised up from the dead, how much more shall Christ's Body, being eaten of thee, give life unto thee and purge thy conscience, quickening thee from the death of sin! Oh therefore, faithful soul, if thou be unclean, come to the fountain of purity; if thou be hungry, come and feed of the bread of life which fadeth not and filleth the hungry soul with goodness. Art thou sick? This will be a most sovereign medicine for thine infirmity. Hast thou an issue whereof thou canst not be cured by the physicians? Touch thou, in the full assurance of faith (as did the woman in the Gospel sick of the flux of blood), the hem of Christ's garment, even the most Blessed Sacrament, and thine issue shall be stayed. If thou feel thyself to be stung by the serpents of perverse temptations, look upon that brazen serpent in which there was no poison, even Christ hanging upon the Cross. Dost thou make thy moan that thou art blind, weak, and lame? Thou must then remember that such are bidden to the supper of the great King and are compelled to go in. But thou wilt say I am wavering, alas! and inconstant; yea, but this Bread doth strengthen the heart of man. Art thou sorrowful and in perplexity? This Wine doth make joyful the inward man. Do many things trouble thee? Cleave fast to Him Who calmed the waves of the sea when they were troubled. Goest thou astray from thy Lord and Master? Yet mayest thou walk in the strength of this meat, even to the Mount of God.

These wonderful things doth the Holy Ghost in the Scriptures, and the Holy Ones of God, being inspired by the Holy Ghost, speak of this admirable Sacrament, whereof St. *Cyprian*, in his Sermon of the Lord's Supper most learnedly and religiously writeth: This unleavened bread which is the true and sincere meat doth by the Sacrament sanctify us by the receiving of it; it doth enlighten us with faith and confirmeth us with truth towards Christ. Therefore let all those who love the Lord's Passion come unto this most wholesome Bread, and let them not fear to eat of this most sweet Manna so often as they can, whereby they may be made able to pass through the wilderness of this world without danger of their life. Let him not fear to eat of this heathful bread whosoever desireth to have his heart made strong in the Lord, that he may overcome all those most wicked enemies, the devils, which daily lie in wait to hinder our salvation. Let no man doubt, so often as possibly he can, to eat this most sweet, delightful, comfortable Bread which was made in the womb of the Virgin and baked upon the Altar of the Cross, in the strength whereof we shall be made able, in forty days and forty nights (that is to say, in the short time of this transitory life), to walk not only to mount Horeb, which signifieth a desert, but even to mount Tabor, which is the brightness and glory of God.

---

(60) **Henry Hammond**
Archdeacon of Chichester, Canon of Christ Church, Oxford
Of Fundamentals in a Notion referring to Practice
1654

Those which are thus confirmed are thereby supposed to be fit for admission to that other Sacrament (in addition to Baptism) of the Body and Blood of Christ, instituted in the close of

His Last Supper. And that, whether it be considered, 1. as an Institution of Christ for the solemn Commemorating of His death; or 2. as a Sacrifice Eucharistical performed by the Christian to God; or 3. as the *koinonia*, 'Communication' of the Body and Blood of Christ, the means of conveying all the benefits of the crucified Savior unto all that come fitly prepared and qualified for them; or whether 4. as a Federal Rite betwixt the soul and Christ, eating and drinking at His Table, and thereby engaging our obedience to Him; or lastly, as an Emblem of the most perfect Divine charity to be observed among all Christians, in all and every of these respects, I say, it is doubtless an instrument of great virtue that hath a peculiar propriety to engage the receiver to persevere in all piety; and that yet further improved by the frequent iteration and repetition of that Sacrament.

First, as it is the commemorating the death of Christ, so it is the professing ourselves the disciples of the crucified Savior; and that engageth us to *take up His cross and follow Him,* and not to fall off from Him for any temptations or terrors of death itself, but to resist to blood, as Christ did, in our spiritual *agones,* our Olympics or combats against sin.

Secondly, as it is the Eucharistical Christian Sacrifice, so it is formally the practicing of several acts of Christian virtue: 1. of prayer, of thanksgiving, of all kind of piety towards God; 2. of charity to our brethren, both that spiritual of *interceding for all men, for Kings, etc.,* and corporal in the offertory, for the relief of those that want; and 3. the offering up and so consecrating *ourselves, our souls and bodies, to be a holy, lively, acceptable, sacrifice* to God, the devoting ourselves to His service all our days. And this last, a large comprehensive act of piety which contains all particular branches under it, and is again the repeating of the baptismal vow and the yet closer binding of this engagement on us.

Thirdly, as it is by God designed, and as an institution of His, blessed and consecrated by Him into a Sacrament, a holy rite, a means of conveying and communicating to the worthy receiver the benefits of the Body and Blood of Christ, that pardon of sin and sufficiency of strength and grace which were purchased by His Death and typified and consigned to us by the Sacramental elements, so it is again the ridding us of all our discouraging fears and the animating and obliging of us to make use of that grace which will carry us, if we do not willfully betray our succours, victoriously through all difficulties.

Fourthly, as it is a federal rite betwixt God and us, as eating and drinking both among the Jews and heathens was wont to be, so it is on our part the solemn undertaking of the condition required of us to make us capable of the benefit of God's new evangelical covenant, and that is sincere performance of all duties prescribed the Christian by Christ. And he that doth no longer expect good from God than he performs that condition is *ipso facto* divested of all those fallacious flattering hopes which pretended to make purifying unnecessary, and must now either live purely and piously, or else disclaim ever seeing of God.

Lastly, as this Supper of the Lord is a token and engagement of charity among the disciples of Christ, so it is the supplanting of all the most diabolical sins, the filthiness of the spirit, the hatred, variance, emulation, strife, revenge, faction, schism, that have been the tearing and rending of the Church of God—ofttimes upon pretense of the greatest piety—but were by Christ of all other things most passionately disclaimed and cast out of His temple. And if by the admonitions which this emblem is ready to afford us, we can think ourselves obliged to return to that charity and peaceable-mindedness which Christ so frequently and vehemently recommends to us, we have His own promise that the *whole body shall be full of light,* that all other Christian virtues will by way of concomitance or annexation accompany or attend them in our hearts.

(61) **Anthony Sparrow**
Bishop of Norwich
A Rationale upon the Book of Common Prayer
of the Church of England
1655/1657

[On the Gloria in Excelsis]

Then we say or sing the *Angelical Hymn, GLORY BE TO GOD ON HIGH, &tc.*, wherein the Ecclesiastical Hierarchy does admirably imitate the Heavenly, singing this at the Sacrament of his Body which the Angels did at the Birth of his Body. And good reason there is to sing this for Christ's being made *One with us* in the Sacrament, as for his being made *One of us* at his Birth. And if ever we be fit to sing this Angels song, it is then when we draw nearest to the estate of Angels, namely, at the receiving of the Sacrament. After the receiving of the holy Sacrament we sing a Hymn in imitation of our Savior, who *after his Supper sang a Hymn* to teach us to do the like. . . . And when can a Psalm or Hymn of thanksgiving be more seasonable and necessary than after we have received this heavenly nourishment? Is it possible to hear these words, *This is my Body, take and eat it; Drink ye all of this, This is my Blood,* and not be filled, as with a kind of fearful admiration, so with a sea of joy and comfort for the Heaven which they see in themselves? Can any man receive this Cup of Salvation and not praise and bless God with his utmost strength of soul and body?

(62) John Cosin
Bishop of Durham
Historia Transubstantiationis Papalis
1656/1675–1676

Those words which Our Blessed Savior used in the institution of the Blessed Sacrament of the Eucharist, *This is My Body, which is given for you, This is My Blood which is shed for you, for the remission of sins,* are held and acknowledged by the Universal Church to be most true and infallible. And if anyone dares oppose them, or call in question Christ's veracity or the truth of His words, or refuse to yield his sincere assent to them except he be allowed to make a mere figment or a bare figure of them, we cannot, and ought not, either excuse or suffer him in our Churches; for we must embrace and hold for an undoubted truth whatever is taught by Divine Scripture. And therefore we can as little doubt of what Christ saith, *My Flesh is meat indeed, and My Blood is drink indeed,* which, according to St. *Paul,* are both given to us by the consecrated elements. For he calls the bread *the communion of Christ's Body,* and the cup *the communion of His Blood.*

Hence it is most evident that the bread and wine (which according to St. *Paul* are the elements of the Holy Eucharist) are neither changed as to their substance, nor vanished, nor reduced to nothing, but are solemnly consecrated by the Words of Christ, that by them His Blessed Body and Blood may be communicated to us.

And further it appears from the same words that the expression of Christ and the Apostle is to be understood in a Sacramental and mystic sense; and that no gross and carnal presence of Body and Blood can be maintained by them.

And though the word *Sacrament* be nowhere used in Scripture to signify the Blessed Eucharist, yet the Christian Church ever since its primitive ages hath given it that name and always called the presence of Christ's Body and Blood therein mystic and Sacramental. Now a Sacramental expression doth, without any inconvenience, give to the sign the name of the thing signified. And such is as well the usual way of speaking, as the nature of Sacraments, that not only the names, but even the properties and effects of what they represent and exhibit are given to the outward elements. Hence (as I said before) the bread is as clearly as positively called by the Apostle *the communion of the Body of Christ.*

This also seems very plain, that Our Blessed Savior's design was not so much to teach what the elements of bread and wine are by nature and substance, as what is their use and office and signification in this mystery. For the Body and Blood of Our Savior are not only fitly represented by the elements, but also by virtue of His institution really offered to all by them, and so eaten by the faithful mystically and Sacramentally; whence it is that *He truly is and abides in us, and we in Him.*

This is the spiritual (and yet no less true and undoubted than if it were corporal) eating of Christ's Flesh, not indeed simply as it is flesh, without any other respect (for so it is not given, neither would it profit us), but as it is crucified and given for the redemption of the world. Neither doth it hinder the truth and substance of the thing that this eating of Christ's Body is spiritual, and that by it the souls of the faithful, and not their stomachs, are fed by the operation of the Holy Ghost; for this none can deny but they who, being strangers to the Spirit and the Divine virtue, can savour only carnal things, and to whom what is spiritual and Sacramental is the same as if a mere nothing.

As to the manner of the presence of the Body and Blood of Our Lord in the Blessed Sacrament, we that are Protestant and Reformed according to the ancient Catholic Church do not search into the manner of it with perplexing inquiries; but, after the example of the primitive and purest Church of Christ, we leave it to the power and wisdom of Our Lord, yielding a full and unfeigned assent to His words.

267

(63) **Anonymous**
(? Richard Allestree, Regius Professor of Divinity
at Oxford, Provost of Eton)
The Whole Duty of Man
1657

Now follows the Reverence due to the Sacrament of the LORD's Supper; and in this I must follow my first Division and set down, first, what is to be done *Before;* secondly, *At;* and, thirdly, *After* the Time of Receiving: For in this Sacrament we cannot be excused from any one of these, though in the former we are.

And first, for that which is to be done *Before:* St. *Paul* tells us it is Examination, I *Cor.* 11:28, *But let a Man examine himself, and so let him eat of that Bread, and drink of that Cup.* But before I proceed to the Particulars of this Examination I must in general tell you that the special Business we have to do in this Sacrament is to repeat and renew that Covenant we made with God in our Baptism; which we having many Ways grievously broken, it pleases God in his great Mercy to suffer us to come to the renewing of it in this Sacrament. Which if we do in Sincerity of Heart, he hath promised to accept us and to give us all those Benefits in this which he was ready to bestow in the other Sacrament, if we had not by our own Fault forfeited them. Since, then, the renewing of our Covenant is our Business at this Time, it follows that these three Things are necessary toward it: First, That we understand what the Covenant is; Secondly, That we consider what our Breaches of it have been; and, Thirdly, That we resolve upon a strict Observance of it for the rest of our Life. And the trying ourselves in every one of these Particulars is that Examination which is required of us before we come to this Sacrament.

And, First, we are to examine whether we understand what

this Covenant is. This is exceeding necessary, as being the Foundation of both the others; for it is neither possible to discover our past Sins, nor to settle Purposes against them for the future without it. Let this therefore be your first Business; try whether you rightly understand what that Covenant is which you entered into at your Baptism; what be the Mercies promised on God's Part and the Duties on yours. And because the Covenant made with each of us in Baptism is only the applying to our Particulars the Covenant made by God in Christ with all Mankind in general, you are to consider whether you understand that. If you do not, you must immediately seek for Instruction in it; and, till you have Means of gaining better, look over what is briefly said in the Entrance to this Treatise concerning the *second Covenant,* which is the Foundation of that Covenant which God makes with us in our Baptism. And because you will there find that Obedience to all God's Commands is the Condition required of us, and is also that which we expressly vow in our Baptism, it is necessary you should likewise know what those Commands of God are. Therefore, if you find you are ignorant of them, never be at rest till you have got yourself instructed in them and have gained such a Measure of Knowledge as may direct you to do that *Whole Duty of Man* which God requires. And the giving thee this Instruction is the only Aim of this Book; which the more ignorant thou art, the more earnestly I shall entreat thee diligently to read. And if thou hast heretofore approached this holy Sacrament in utter Ignorance of these necessary Things, bewail thy Sin in so doing; but presume not to come again till thou hast, by gaining this necessary Knowledge, fitted thyself for it, which thou must hasten to do. For though no Man must come to the Sacrament in such Ignorance, yet if he willfully continue in it that will be no Excuse to him for keeping from this holy Table.

• • •

I have now gone through those several Parts of Duty we are to perform *before* our Receiving: In the next Place, I am to tell you what is to be done *At the Time of Receiving.* When thou art at the holy Table, first, Humble thyself in an unfeigned Acknowledgment of thy great Unworthiness to be admitted there; and to that Purpose remember again, between God and thine own Soul, some of thy greatest and foulest Sins, thy Breaches of former Vows made at that Table, especially since thy last Receiving. Then meditate on those bitter Sufferings of Christ which are set out to us in the Sacrament: When thou seest the Bread broken remember how his blessed Body was torn with Nails upon the Cross; When thou seest the Wine poured out remember how his precious Blood was spilt there; and then consider it was thy Sins that caused both. And here think how unworthy a Wretch thou art to have done that which occasioned such Torments to him; how much worse than his very Crucifiers! They crucified him once, but thou hast, as much as in thee lay, crucified him daily. They crucified him because they knew him not, but thou hast known both what he is in himself, *The Lord of Glory,* and what he is to thee, a most tender and merciful Savior; and yet thou hast still continued thus to crucify him afresh. Consider this and let it work in thee, first, a great Sorrow for thy Sins past, and then a great Hatred and a firm Resolution against them for the Time to come.

When thou hast a while thus thought on these Sufferings of Christ for the increasing thy Humility and Contrition, then, in the second Place, think of them again to stir up thy Faith; look on him as the Sacrifice offered up for thy Sins, for the appeasing of God's Wrath and procuring his Favour and Mercies towards thee. And therefore believingly, yet humbly, beg of God to accept of that Satisfaction made by his innocent and beloved Son, and for the Merits thereof, to pardon thee whatever is past and to be fully reconciled to thee.

In the third Place, consider them again, to raise thy Thankfulness. Think how much both of Shame and Pain he there endured, but especially those great Agonies of his Soul, which drew from him that bitter Cry, *My God, my God, why hast thou forsaken me? Mt.* 27:46. Now all this he suffered only to keep thee from perishing. And therefore consider what inexpressible Thanks thou owest him and endeavour to raise thy Soul to the most zealous and hearty Thanksgiving: For this is a principal Part of Duty at this Time, the praising and magnifying that Mercy which hath redeemed us by so dear a Price. Therefore it will here well become thee to say with *David, I will take the Cup of Salvation, and will call upon the Name of the Lord.*

Fourthly, Look on these Sufferings of Christ to stir up this Love; and surely there cannot be a more effectual Means of doing it; for here the Love of Christ to thee is most manifest, according to that of the Apostle, 1 *Jn.* 3:16. *Hereby perceive we the Love of God towards us, because he laid down his Life for us,* and that even the highest Degree of *Love;* for as himself tells us, *Jn.* 15: 13, *Greater Love than this hath no Man, that a Man lay down his Life for his Friend.* Yet even greater Love than this had he; for he not only died, but died the most painful and most reproachful Death, and that not for his Friends but for his utter Enemies. And therefore if, after all this Love on his Part, there be no return of Love on ours, we are worse than the vilest Sort of Men; for even the *Publicans, Mt.* 5:46, *Love those that love them.* Here therefore chide and reproach thyself that thy Love to him is so faint and cool when his to thee was so zealous and affectionate, and endeavour to enkindle this holy Flame in thy Soul to love him in such a Degree that thou mayest be ready to copy out his Example: to part with all Things, yea, even Life itself whenever he calls for it; that is, whensoever thy Obedience to any Command of his shall lay thee open to those Sufferings; but in the meantime to resolve never again to make any League with his Enemies, to entertain or harbour any Sin in thy Breast. But if there have any such hitherto remained with thee, make this the Season to kill and crucify it; offer it up at this Instant a Sacrifice to him who was sacrificed for thee, and particularly for that very End that *he might redeem thee from all Iniquity.* Therefore here make thy solemn Resolutions to forsake every Sin, particularly those into which thou hast most frequently fallen. And that thou mayest indeed perform those Resolutions, earnestly beg of this crucified Savior, that he will, by the Power of his

Death, mortify and kill all thy Corruptions.

When thou art about to receive the consecrated Bread and Wine, remember that God now offers to seal to thee that new Covenant made with Mankind in his Son. For since he gives his Son in the Sacrament, he gives with him all the Benefits of that Covenant; to wit, Pardon of Sins, sanctifying Grace, and a Title to an eternal Inheritance. And here be astonished at the infinite Goodness of God, who reaches out to thee so precious a Treasure. But then remember that this is all on Condition that thou perform thy Part of the Covenant. And therefore settle in thy Soul the most serious Purpose of Obedience; and then, with all possible Devotion, join with the Minister in that short but excellent Prayer used at the Instant of giving the Sacrament; *The Body of our Lord,* &tc.

So soon as thou hast received, offer up thy devoutest Praises for that great Mercy, together with thy most earnest Prayers for such Assistance of God's Spirit as may enable thee to perform the Vow thou hast now made. Then, remembering that Christ is *a Propitiation not for our Sins only, but also for the Sins of the whole World,* let thy Charity reach as far as his hath done and pray for all Mankind, that everyone may receive the Benefit of that Sacrifice of his. Commend also to God the Estate of the Church, that particularly whereof thou art a Member; and forget not to pray for all to whom thou owest Obedience, both in Church and State, and so go on to pray for such particular Persons as either thy Relations or their Wants shall present to thee. If there be any Collection for the Poor (as there always ought to be at this Time), give freely according to thy Ability; or if by the Default of others there be no such Collection, yet do thou privately design something toward the Relief of thy poor Brethren, and be sure to give it the next fitting Opportunity that offers itself. All this thou must contrive to do in the Time that others are receiving, that so when the public Prayers after the Administration begin, thou mayst be ready to join in them; which thou must likewise take care to do with all Devotion. Thus much for Behaviour *At* the Time of Receiving.

Now follows the third and last Thing; that is, What thou art to do *After* thy Receiving. That which is immediately to be done is, as soon as thou art retired from the Congregation, to offer up again to God thy Sacrifice of Praise for all those precious Mercies conveyed to thee in that holy Sacrament; as also humbly to entreat the continued Assistance of his Grace to enable thee to make good all those Purposes of Obedience thou hast now made. And in whatsoever thou knowest thyself most in danger, either in respect of any former Habit or natural Inclination, there especially desire and earnestly beg his Aid.

When thou hast done thus, do not presently let thyself loose to thy worldly Cares and Business; but spend all that Day either in meditating, praying, reading, good Conferences, or the like; so as may best keep up that holy Flame that is enkindled in thy Heart. Afterward, when thy Calling requires thee to fall to thy usual Affairs, do it, but yet still remember that thou hast a greater Business than that upon thy Hands; that is, the performing of all those Promises thou so lately made to God; and therefore whatever thy outward Employments are, let thy Heart be set on that, keep all the Particulars of thy Resolutions in Memory, and whenever thou art tempted to any of thy old Sins, then consider this is the Thing thou so solemnly vowed against.

---

(64) **Jeremy Taylor**
*Chaplain to Lord Carbery, Bishop of Down and Connor and of
Dromore*
The Worthy Communicant
1660

[The Blessings and Graces of the Holy Sacrament]

This is the greatest solemnity of prayer, the most powerful Liturgy and means of petition in this world. For when Christ was consecrated on the cross and became our High Priest, having reconciled us to God by the death of the cross, he became infinitely gracious in the eyes of God and was admitted to the celestial and eternal Priesthood in heaven; where in the virtue of the cross he intercedes for us and represents an eternal sacrifice in the heavens on our behalf. That he is a Priest in heaven appears in the large discourses and direct affirmatives of St. *Paul;* that there is no other sacrifice to be offered but that on the cross, it is evident, because he hath but once appeared in the end of the world to put away sin by the sacrifice of himself; and therefore since it is necessary that he hath something to offer so long as he is a Priest, and there is no other sacrifice but that of himself offered upon the cross, it follows that Christ in heaven perpetually offers and represents that sacrifice to his heavenly Father, and in virtue of that obtains all good things for his Church.

Now what Christ does in heaven he hath commanded us to do on earth; that is, to represent his death, to commemorate this sacrifice by humble prayer and thankful record; and by faithful manifestation and joyful Eucharist to lay it before the eyes of our heavenly Father, so ministering in his Priesthood and doing according to his commandment and his example. The Church being the image of heaven, the Priest the Minister of Christ, the holy Table being a Copy of the celestial altar; and the eternal sacrifice of the Lamb slain from the beginning of the World being always the same, it bleeds no more after the finishing of it on the Cross. But it is wonderfully represented in heaven and graciously represented here; by Christ's action there, by his commandment here; and the event of it is plainly this, that as Christ in virtue of his sacrifice on the cross intercedes for us with his Father, so does the Minister of Christ's Priesthood here, that the virtue of the eternal sacrifice may be salutary and effective to all the needs of the Church both for things temporal and eternal. And therefore it was not without great mystery and clear signification that our blessed Lord was pleased to command the representation of his death and sacrifice on the cross should be made by breaking bread and effusion of wine; to signify to us the nature and sacredness of the Liturgy we are about and that we minister in the Priesthood of Christ; who is a Priest forever after the order of *Melchizedek.* That is, we are Ministers in that unchangeable Priesthood imitating *in the external Ministry* the prototype *Melchizedek:* Of whom it is said *he brought forth bread and wine and was the Priest of the most high God;* and *in the internal* imitating the antitype or the substance Christ himself; who offered up his body and blood for atonement for us, and by the Sacraments of bread and wine and the prayers of oblation and intercession commands us to officiate in his Priesthood, in the external ministering like *Melchizidek;* in the internal after the manner of Christ himself.

. . .

Let no man advance the preaching of the word of God to the disparagement or to occasion the neglect of the Sacraments. For though it be true that faith comes by hearing, yet it is not intended that by hearing alone faith is engendered; for the faith of the Apostles came by seeing and St. *Paul's* faith did not come by hearing, but by intuition and revelation; and *hearing* in those words of St. *Paul* does not signify the manner of ministration but the whole Economy of the word of God, the whole office of preaching; which is done most usefully to babes and strangers by sermon and homily, but more gloriously and illustriously to men by Sacraments. But however be it so or otherwise, yet one ordinance ought not to exclude the other, much less to disparage the other, and least of all to undervalue that which is the most eminent: but rather let every Christian man and woman think that if the word ministered by the spirit is so mighty, it must be more when the word and the spirit join with the Sacrament, which is their proper significatory. He that is zealous for the word of God does well; but let him remember that the word of God is a goodly ring and leads us into the circles of a blessed eternity; but because the Sacrament is not without the word, they are a jewel encased in gold when they are together. The Ministries of the Gospel are all of a piece;

though of several types, they work the same salvation by the conduct of the same spirit.

Let no man in the reception of the Sacrament, and in his expectation of blessings and events from it, limit his hopes and belief to any one particular, for that will occasion a littleness of faith and may make it curious, scrupulous and fantastical; rather let us adore the secret of God, and receive it with simple expectations, disposing ourselves to all the effects that may come rather with fear and indefinite apprehensions than with dogmatical and confident limitations; for this may beget scruples and diminution of value; but that hinders nothing but advances the reverential treatments and opinion.

He that guesses at the excellency and power of the Sacrament by the events that he himself feels must be sure to look for no other than what are *eminently* or *virtually* contained in it; that is, he must not expect that the Sacrament will make him rich, or discover to him stolen goods or cure the Toothache or Countercharm Witches or appease a Tempest if it be thrown into the Sea. These are such events which God hath not made the effects of religion, but are the hopes and expectations of vain and superstitious people. And I remember that Pope *Alexander* the third in the Council of *Lateran* wrote to the Bishop of St. *Agatha* advice how to treat a woman who took the Holy Sacrament into her mouth and ran with it to kiss her husband, hoping by that means to procure her husband's more intense affection. But the story tells that she was chastised by a miracle and was not cured but by a long and severe repentance.

He that watches for the effects and blessings of the Sacrament must look for them in no other manner than what is agreeable to the usual dispensation. We must not look for them by measures of nature and usual expectations: not that as soon as we have received the Symbols we shall have our doubts answered; or be comforted in our spirit as soon as we have given thanks for the holy blood; or be satisfied in the inquiries of faith as soon as the prayers of consecration and the whole ministry is ended; or prevail in our most passionate desires as soon as we rise from our knees. For we enter into the blessings of the Sacrament by prayer and the exercise of proper graces; both which being spiritual instruments of virtues work after the manner of spiritual things; that is, not by any measure we have but as God pleases; only that in the last event of things, and when they are necessary, we shall find them there. God's time is best, but we must not judge his manner by our measures nor measure eternity by time, or the issues of the spirit by a measuring line. The effects of the Sacrament are to be expected as the effect of prayers: not one prayer or one solemn meeting, but persevering and passionate, fervent and lasting prayers; a continual desire and a daily address is the way of prevailing. *In the morning sow thy seed and in the evening withhold not thy hand, for thou knowest not whether shall prosper either this or that, or whether they shall be both alike good.*

He that looks for the effects and blessings told of to be appendant to the Sacrament must expect them upon no other terms but such as are the conditions of a worthy Communion. If thou dost find thy faith as dead after the reception as it was before, it may be it is because thy faith was not only little but reprovable; or thou didst not pray vehemently, or thou art indisposed by some secret disadvantage; or thou hast not done thy duty. And he shall imprudently accuse that physic for useless and unfit that is not suffered to work by the incapacity, the ill-diet, the weak stomache, or some evil accident of the patient.

Let no man judge of himself or of the blessings and efficacy of the Sacrament itself, or of the prosperity and acceptation of his service in this ministry by any sensible relish, by the flavor and deliciousness which he sometimes perceives and other times does not perceive. For these are fine accidents and given to some persons often, to others very seldom; to all irregularly, as God please, and sometimes are the effects of natural and accidental dispositions and sometimes are illusions. But that no man may fall into inconvenience for want of them, we are to consider that the want of them proceeds from diverse causes. 1. It may be the palate of the Soul is indisposed by listlessness or sorrow, anxiety or weariness. 2. It may be we are too much immersed in secular affairs and earthly affections. 3. Or we have been unthankfull to God when we have received some of these spiritual pleasures and he therefore withdraws those pleasant entertainments. 4. Or it may be we are therefore without relish and taste because the Sacrament is too great for our weakness, like the bright Sun to a mortal eye; the object is too big for our perceptions and our little faculties. 5. Sometimes God takes them away lest we be lifted up and made vain. 6. Sometimes for the confirmation and exercise of our faith, that we may live by faith and not by sense. 7. Or it may be that by this dryness of spirit God intends to make us the more fervent and resigned in our direct and solemn devotions, by the perceiving of our wants and weakness and in the infinite inability and insufficiency of ourselves. 8. Or else it happens to us irremediably and inevitably that we may perceive these accidents are not the fruits of our labour but gifts of God, dispensed wholly by the measures of his own choice. 9. The want of just and severe dispositions to the Holy Sacrament may possibly occasion this uncomfortableness. 10. Or we do not relish the Divine Nutriment now as at other times for want of spiritual mastication; that is, because we have not considered deeply and meditated wisely and piously. 11. Or there is in us too much self-love, and delight in and adherence to the comforts we find in other objects. 12. Or we are careless of little sins and give too much way to the daily incursions of the smaller irregularities of our lives. If upon the occasion of the want of these sensible comforts and delightful relishes we examine the causes of the want, and suspect ourselves in these things where our own faults may be the causes, and there make amends; or if we submit ourselves in those particulars where the causes may relate to God, we shall do well and receive profit. But unless our own sin be the cause of it we are not to make any evil judgment of ourselves by reason of any such defect; much less diminish our great value of the blessings consequent to a worthy communion.

But because the pardon of sins is intended to be the great effect of a worthy communion, and of this men are most solicitous, and for this they pray passionately and labour earnestly and almost all their lives, and it may be in the day of their death have uncertain souls; and therefore of this men are most desirous to be satisfied if they apprehend themselves in danger; that is, if they be convinced of their sin and be truly penitent; although this effect seems to be least discernable and to be a secret reserved for the publication and trumpet of the Archangel at the day of Doom; yet in this we can best be satisfied. For because when our sins are unpardoned we are under the wrath of God, to be expressed as he pleases and in the method of eternal death; now if God intends not to pardon us he will not bless the means of pardon; if we shall not return to his final pardon we shall not pass through the intermedial; if he will never give us glory, he will never give us the increase of grace. If therefore we repent of our sins and pray for pardon: if we confess them and forsake them: if we fear God and love him: if we find that our desires to please him do increase, that we are more watchful against sin and hate it more: that we are thirsty after righteousness: if we find that we increase in duty, then we may look upon the tradition of the holy Sacramental Symbols as a direct indication of pardon. Not that it is then completed, for it is a work of time; it is as long in doing as repentance is in perfecting, it is the effect of that, depending on its cause in a perpetual operation; but it is then working, and if we go on in duty God will proceed to finish the methods of his grace and snatch us from eternal death which we have deserved, and bring us unto glory. And this he is pleased by the Sacrament all the way to consign: God speaks not more articulately in any voice from Heaven than in such real indications of his love and favour.

Lastly, since the Sacrament is the great solemnity of prayer and imitation of Christ's intercession in Heaven; let us here be both charitable and religious in our prayers, interceding for all states of men and women in the Christian Church and representing to God all the needs of ourselves and of our Relatives. For then we pray with all the advantages of the spirit when we pray in the faith of Christ crucified, in the love of God and of our neighbor, in the advantages of solemn piety, in the communion of Saints, in the imitation of Christ's intercession, and in the union with Christ himself Spiritual and Sacramental. And to such prayers as these nothing can be added but that which will certainly come, that is, a blessed hearing and a gracious answer.

· · ·

[Of the Manner of Reception of the Divine Mysteries]

Throw away with great diligence and severity all unholy and all earthly thoughts, and think the thoughts of heaven: for when Christ descends he comes attended with innumerable companies of Angels, who all behold and wonder, who love and *worship Jesus;* and in this glorious employment and society let thy thoughts be pure and thy mind celestial and thy work Angelical, and thy spirit full of love and thy heart of wonder; thy mouth all praises, investing and encircling thy prayers as a bright cloud is adorned with fringes and borders of light.

When thou seest the holy man minister, dispute no more, enquire no more, doubt no more, be divided no more; but believe and behold with the eyes of faith and of the spirit, that thou seest Christ's body broken upon the Cross, that thou seest him bleeding for thy sins, that thou feedest upon the food of elect souls, that thou puttest thy mouth to the hole of the rock that was smitten, to the wound of the side of thy Lord which, being pierced, streamed forth Sacraments and life and holiness and pardon and purity and immortality upon thee.

When the words of Institution are pronounced all the Christians used to say *Amen;* giving their consent, confessing that faith, believing that word, rejoicing in that Mystery which is told us when the Minister of the Sacrament in the person of Christ says, This is my body, This is my blood; This body was broken for you and this blood was poured forth for you; and all this for the remission of your sins. And remember that the guilt of eternal damnation which we have all incurred was a great and an intolerable evil, and unavoidable if such miracles of mercy had not been wrought to take it quite away; and that it was a very great love which would work such glorious mercy rather than leave us in so intolerable a condition. A greater love than this could not be; and a less love than this could not have rescued us.

When the holy Man reaches forth his hands upon the Symbols and prays over them, and intercedes for the sins of the people, and breaks the holy bread and pours forth the sacred chalice, place thyself by faith and meditation in heaven and see Christ doing in his glorious manner this very thing which thou seest ministered and imitated upon the Table of the Lord. And then remember that it is impossible thou shouldest miss of eternal blessings, which are so powerfully procured for thee by the Lord himself, unless thou wilt despise all this and neglect so great salvation, and choosest to eat with swine the dirty pleasures of the earth rather than thus to feast with Saints and Angels, and to eat the body of thy Lord with a clean heart and humble affections.

When the consecrating and ministering hand reaches forth to thee the holy Symbols, say within thy heart as did the Centurion, Lord I am not worthy: but entertain thy Lord as the women did the news of the resurrection, *with fear and great joy;* or as the Apostles, *with rejoicing and singleness of heart;* that is, clear, certain, and plain believing, and with exultation and delight in the loving kindness of the Lord.

---

(65) **Simon Patrick**
Bishop of Ely
**Mensa Mystica, or a Discourse concerning
the Sacrament of the Lord's Supper**
1660

The Sacraments being not unfitly called by an ancient Writer *the Garments that are cast about our Savior,* and it being the Profession of Divines to labour to see the naked Face of Truth, it is most worthy our Pains to open and reveal those Secrets that lie hid and veiled under Symbols and sensible Things.

And to say the Truth, these Vestments are so thin and transparent that the Truth doth shine thro' them and show itself to well-prepared Minds. They are but like to those thin Clouds wherein the Sun is sometimes wrapped, which render its Body the more visible to our weak and trembling Eyes.

I cannot pretend to have conversed much with barefaced Truth, yet having been drawn to publish a few Thoughts concerning Baptism I shall now further endeavour to unfold those Mysteries that lie hid under the Coverings of Bread broken and Wine poured out in the Sacrament of the Lord's Supper, that Men may not . . . embrace a mere Cloud instead of God himself. My Sight is not so sharp as to discern the very Flesh and Blood of Christ in those Forms and Shapes of Bread and Wine. . . . Yet I am so far from thinking that they are mere Signs of what Christ did for us, or only Representations of the Benefits we receive by him, that I am persuaded they exhibit our Lord himself unto believing Minds and put them into a surer Possession of him.

The Truth commonly lies between Two Extremes, and being a peaceable Thing cannot join itself with either of the directly opposite Parties. And therefore I shall seek for her in a middle Path, not bidding such a Defiance to the Corporeal Presence as to deny the real, nor so subverting the Fancy of a miraculous Change into a Celestial Substance as to level these Things into mere Shadows.

. . .

We must further consider this Action *as a Rite whereby we enter into Covenant with him.* This is included in our *taking* the Bread and Wine, as well as in our *eating* and *drinking* of them, and was expressed before when I said we must offer ourselves to God as the greatest Act of our Thanksgiving. That offering of ourselves is such a thing that it puts us out of our own Power; and besides we enter here into strict Engagements never to resume or draw back ourselves again, never to challenge any Right to have ourselves in our own Disposal; we make a solemn Agreement with the Lord Jesus that he shall dwell in us and possess himself of all our Faculties, as the sole Lord and Governor of our Souls. Tho' this hath been done once already when we were baptized, so that we cannot reverse the Deed nor cancel the Bond that is between us, yet seeing the Matter of the Covenant is always to be performed, and more than one World depends upon it, God thinks fit to take new Security of us and strengthen our Obligations lest we think of letting the Debt run on unpaid one Day after another, till we be quite Bankrupt and have nothing left whereby to discharge it.

. . .

The *Greek* Christians at this Day, when they take the Bread or Cup into their Hands, make this Profession, *Lord, I will not give thee a Kiss, like* Judas, *but I do confess unto thee, like the poor Thief, and beseech thee to remember me when thy Kingdom comes.* If we do touch the Body of Christ with traitorous Lips, and embrace him with a false Heart, we stain our Souls with the Guilt of that Blood which can only wash them from all their other Sins; and therefore we must come unfeignedly to bewail our Neglects and to settle our former Resolutions of strict Obedience. It is grown even to a Proverb . . . among the poor *Indians* who have entertained the Faith that . . . *He must never be guilty more of any Crime who hath once received the Eucharist.* And if they chance to commit any, they bewail it with such a Sorrow and Compunction that . . . he hath not found such Faith, no not in *Israel;* but it would be very sad if we should be sent to School as far as *India;* there are, I make no doubt, many pious Souls among ourselves that look upon it as a blessed Opportunity to knit their Hearts in greater Love to God, and that are more afflicted for an evil Thought after such Engagements than others are for a base and unworthy Action.

Whensoever therefore we come to celebrate the Memory of

Christ's Death in this manner, we must remember with ourselves that we are assembled to renew our Baptismal Vow and League and in the devoutest manner to addict ourselves to a more constant Love and Service of the Lord Jesus. We must look upon this Feast to which we are admitted as a disclaiming of all Enmity to him, and a Profession of our continuing a hearty Friendship so as never to do any hostile Act against him. And thence indeed it is called a *Sacrament* (according to *Tertullian,* and others with him) because we here take an Oath to continue Christ's faithful Soldiers, and never to do anything against his Crown and Dignity as long as there remains any Breath in our Bodies. We do repeat our Oath of Allegiance and swear Fealty again to him, or (as we ordinarily speak) we *take the Sacrament upon it* that we will be Christ's faithful Servants and Soldiers against the Devil, World and Flesh, and never fly from his Service.

Every Act of Sin then, after such Promises, is not only Treason but Perjury; not only the breaking of our Faith but of our Oath; yea, not only the Violation of a simple Oath but of Oath upon Oath; which we ought more to dread than we do to break our Bones.

. . .

The Distance being taken away between God and us, this Sacrament must be considered as a Means of our nearer Union with our Lord Christ. He doth not only kindly entertain us when we come to his Table, but he likewise knits and joins us to himself; he not only ties us with Cords of Love and binds us to his Service by Favours and Blessings conferred on us, but in some sort he makes us one with him and takes us into a nearer Conjunction than before we enjoyed; and who would not desire to be enfolded in his Arms? Who would not repose himself in his Bosom? But who durst have presumed to entertain a Thought of being married unto him and becoming one with him? And yet who would refuse such a Favour now that it is offered to us but they that neither know him nor themselves.

This Covenant into which we enter is a Marriage Covenant,

and our Lord promises to be as a Husband to us and we choose him as the best Beloved of our Souls. It is none of the common Friendships which we contract with him by eating and drinking at his Table, but the rarest and highest that can be imagined, and we are to look upon this as a Marriage Feast. What this Union then with Christ is, it need not be disputed, we may be sure that it is such a one as is between a Man and his Wife, the Vine and the Branches, the Head and the Members, the Building and the Foundation (as hereafter will more fully appear), yea, far beyond all sorts of Union, whether moral, natural, or artificial which the World affords Example of.

· · ·

As this Sacrament is a means of uniting us to our Lord by Faith, so likewise of uniting us to our Brethren by Love it knits us not only to our Head, but all the Members also thereby are more endeared unto each other, we enter here into a strict League of Friendship with them as well as into a Covenant with God.

For all true Christians are not only of the Family of God but his Children and nearest Relations, so that we cannot profess any Love to the Father of them all but we must at the same time embrace his whole Progeny as bearing his Character and having in them those very things which we love in him. When we take the Bridegroom, we contract a Kindred also with all the Friends of the Bridegroom; and Love indeed is of that nature that it is not only diffusive of itself but it runs forth with a certain Pleasure and fills our Hearts with Joy as it passeth from us, so that no Man would be excused from loving of his Brethren nor willingly want that part of this Christian Feast. We all grant that this Food would not be so full of Juice and Sweetness but that it tastes of the Love of our Lord; nor would this Cup be so pleasant but that it is the Cup of Charity. Now when the Heart is once filled with Love it wants nothing but Objects whereon to empty itself, and it is like new Wine that is ready to burst the Vessel unless it find some Vent; and therefore one good Man is glad at such a time to ease himself into the Bosom of others and to express himself to them in such charitable

Actions as cannot be done to God, who is all-sufficient of himself. This adds to the Grace of this Entertainment that there is nothing but Love to be seen in it; the Food is Love, the Master of the Feast glories in no greater Name than that *he is Love,* all the Guests are Brethren, they are all in their Father's House, they all receive the Tokens and Pledges of the Love of their Elder Brother, and his Love is so great that he is content to share his Inheritance among them. It must be therefore against Nature and the Course of Things not to love and to let our Brethren share in our Affections who have a Portion in the same Savior.

. . .

[*Of our Deportment at the Holy Table*]

When you see the Minister stand at the Table of the Lord to consecrate the Bread and Wine by Prayer and the Words of Christ's Institution; then send up *an Act of Wonder and Admiration that the Son of God should become the Food of our Souls by dying for us.* Then these words (so anciently used) *Sursum Corda, Lift up your Hearts,* should make a joyful noise in all our Souls; and they should spread their Wings that by the Divine Inspirations they may be mounted unto Heaven in adoring Thoughts. Nothing more becomes this Sacred Mystery than such a dumb Admiration; and the Love of our Lord is not better praised by anything than . . . by that most talkative Silence. When the Apprehensions of the Soul grow too big for the Mouth; when it lifts up itself in Speaking-Thoughts: and this is their Language, That they are not able to understand the Miracles of this Love; it shall not be long before it perceive how much God is pleased with its saying nothing. Let us therefore labour at the very Entrance to put ourselves into some degree of wonderment, to think what manner of Love this is wherewith he hath loved us. Wonder that he should die for thee when he was upon the Earth, and that he should nourish thee with himself now that he is in the Heavens. Be astonished that Heaven should so condescend to Earth and Man should be so united unto God. Lose thy Thoughts in Contemplation of the Strangeness of this

286

Kindness, that God should dwell in Flesh and that this Flesh should be our Food. Let it amaze thee that Christ can never think that he hath given himself enough to thee; but (as the Apostle saith) he gave himself to redeem us from our Sins and now he gives himself to be the Strength and Health of our Souls. He gave himself when he was among Men, he gives himself now that he is with God; and . . . he told a pious Man in a Vision that if it were necessary he would come and die again for the Sons of Men. This would be a rare good beginning of this Holy Service, and we should be fitter for all following Actions if we could put our Hearts into a kind of Ecstasy or Admiration at the stupendous Greatness of this Mystery. If our Thoughts were once got so high, we should be out of the reach of other things that are apt to thrust themselves in and interrupt us. If we had once climbed above ourselves and were ascended into Heaven, we should not be enticed, while the Solemnity lasted, to come down to the World again.

. . .

When we take the Bread into our Hands, it is a seasonable time to do that Act which I told you was one End of this Sacrament, *viz. Commemorate, and show forth or declare the Death of Christ unto God the Father.* Let us represent before him the Sacrifice of Atonement that Christ hath made; let us commemorate the Pains which he endured; let us entreat him that we may enjoy all the Purchase of his Blood, that all People may reap the Fruit of his Passion; and that for the sake of his bloody Sacrifice he will turn away all his Anger and Displeasure and be reconciled unto us. *Themistocles* (they say), not knowing how to mitigate and atone the Wrath of King *Admetus* and avert his Fury from him, snatched up the King's Son and held him up in his Arms between himself and Death, and so prevailed for a Pardon and quenched the Fire that was breaking out against him. And this the *Molossians* (of whom he was King) held to be *the most effectual way of Supplication,* and which of all others *could not be resisted or denied.* Of far greater prevalency is this Act, the holding up (as it were) the Son of God in our hands and representing to the

287

Father the broken Body and the Blood of his Only-begotten. Let us set this between the Heat of God's Anger and our Souls; let us desire he would have regard to his dearly-beloved, and the Lord cannot turn back our Prayers that press and importune him with such a mighty Argument.

. . .

And, *Secondly,* It is a seasonable time to *profess ourselves Christians* and that we will take up our Cross and follow after him. This *taking* of the Bread we should look upon as a receiving the Yoke of Christ upon our Neck and laying his Cross upon our Shoulder, if he think fit. We embrace a crucified Jesus and we are not to expect to lie in Pleasures unless they be spiritual; nor to rejoice with the World, but to endure Affliction and account it all Joy when we fall into manifold Temptations. Protest therefore unto him, that thou lovest him as thou seest him, *stript* and *naked, bruised* and *wounded, slain* and *dead;* and that thou art contented to take joyfully the spoiling of thy Goods, to be pleased with Pains, and to count Death the Way to Life.

When we eat, it is a fit season to put forth . . . Acts of Faith:

Let us *express our hearty Consent that Christ shall dwell within us,* that we will be ruled by his Laws and governed by his Spirit, that he shall be the alone King of our Souls and the Lord of all our Faculties; and that we will have no other Master but only him to give Commands within us. Eating, I told you, is a federal Rite; and therefore when we have swallowed this Bread we should think that we have surrendered all up into his hands and put him into full power over our Souls. And we should also think that we have given him the possession of our Souls forever and engaged never to change our Master. For *eating* is more receiving than *taking* a thing with our hands: It is, as it were, the incorporating of the Thing with the Substance of our Bodies and making it a part of ourselves that it may last as long as we. So should we meditate, that we receive the Lord Jesus never to be separated from his Service, forever to adhere unto him as our Prince and Captain, as our Head and Husband, wheresoever his Commands will lead us. And as we open our Hearts thus to receive him, so let us now fold him in our Arms and embrace him with a most cordial Affection. Let the Fire burn now and make us boil up, yea even run over with Love to him. Now is the time not only to give ourselves to him, but to make a Sacrifice of ourselves as a whole Burnt Offering unto God. Now should we lay ourselves on the Altar of the Lord, to be offered up entirely to him who made his Soul an Offering for Sin; that there may not only be a Representative but a real Sacrifice at this Feast unto Heaven; that is, that we may not only show forth the Sacrifice of Christ and represent it before God, but we ourselves may offer up our Souls and Bodies unto him and send them up in Flames of Love as so many Holocausts to be consumed and spent in the Service of our God. Then let us wish for the Flames of a *Seraphim* in the Love of God, for the Cheerfulness and Speed of a *Cherubim* in the Service of God, and for the Voice of an Angel that we may sing the Praises of God. Let us like our Choice so well and think we are so beholden to him that we may give ourselves to him, as to begin to leap for Joy that we have parted with ourselves, and are become his.

. . .

When we receive the Cup it is fit that we should again admire the wonderful Love of God that he would purchase us to himself by *his own Blood*. And we should consider the *great and inestimable value* of this Blood that could make Expiation and give God full satisfaction for such a World of Offenses. The *infinite Virtue* likewise, as well as *Value* of this Sacrifice, should be taken into our Thoughts, which lasts forever and is now as fresh and full of Efficacy as if the Blood were newly shed upon the Cross. For so the Apostle saith, *This Man after he had once offered for Sin, forever sat down on the right Hand of God.* And that you may wonder more at the Excellency of this Offering; consider how many Sins you have committed and then guess how many the Sins are which have been committed by all Men that have been, are, and shall be in the World; and yet that this *one*

Sacrifice is sufficient in God's account to take away all, being of an Everlasting Force and Power. And the better again to conceive of this admirable Thing, compare it with the Sacrifices of Old. One Sacrifice could take away but one Offense among the *Jews,* and that merely against a carnal Commandment; yet this, though but *one,* can take away all Offenses even against the eternal Law of God. And the strength of a Sacrifice under the Law continued no longer than just while it was offered, but was to be repeated again in case of a new Offense; but the Blood of Jesus endures forever, *and by one Offering he hath perfected forever them that are sanctified.* We that live at sixteen hundred Years distance from that Sacrifice may be as much expiated and receive as great benefit by it as they that saw him upon the Altar; or as he that put his Fingers into his Wounds and thrust his Hand into his Side. *For the Lord laid on him the Iniquity of us all;* and he bears the Sins not only of that Generation but of all succeeding Ages. Think then, now that the Cup is in thy Hands, now that thou drinkest of his Blood, that thou mayst receive as real Effects of his Sacrifice as if thou hadst been permitted to have laid thy Hands on his Head and put all thy Sins upon him, as *Aaron* did upon the Head of the Beast that was offered for the Congregation of *Israel.*

. . .

The next Festivity that we shall celebrate together must be in Heaven, in the very Presence of God when the Devil your great Enemy shall be overthrown and quite destroyed as *Pharaoh* was. And again he saith, *I will not drink of the Fruit of the Vine until the Kingdom of God shall come.* Which signifies no more but that he and they should not rejoice together any more till they came to drink of the Rivers of God's Pleasures. From all which we may well collect that the Wine here in the Kingdom of the Son is an Emblem of the Wine in the Kingdom of the Father. In this World is the Kingdom of Christ, in the World to come shall be the Kingdom of God; and what is done here is a Shadow of what shall be done in a more excellent manner hereafter; and therefore this Holy Feast should represent unto us those Heavenly Delights. From this Wine of the Grape we should endeavour to raise our Minds to . . . that which is apprehended by the Mind and tasted by the Palate of the Soul, which flows from God himself. We should think that these are but some *Foretastes* of those Pleasures that he will hereafter bestow upon us; but the *Antepasts* of the Eternal Supper, but the *Vigils* of the Everlasting Rest; and that now we rather fast than feast if we compare these Joys with those that are above. We should look upon these as an assurance of better Cheer, where our Appetites should be satiated and our Thirst quenched; where we shall see the Lord Jesus in his Glory and feast our Eyes with the sight of his Beauty; yea, where we shall be ravished with the sight of God himself and shall drink of the Pleasures that stream from the Light of his blessed Face. And after those Things in the World to come, should we strive to stir up the Longings of our Soul: We should desire to be in Heaven, we should thirst after larger Draughts to quench our thirst in the Ocean itself, and to pass from this dark Glass and this Veil of the Sacraments to the clear Vision of his Brightness. For if God do here satisfy his faithful Servants as with Marrow and Fatness, much more in the World to come will he replenish and fill them with Sweetness and Joy itself.

And in the Conclusion we should give God Thanks for these great Favours, for the Hopes of his Glory, for the Tastes which he gives us beforehand, for all the Fruits of his Son's Death, and the Earnests we have of the Eternal Inheritance. We should begin to praise him with the Heavenly Host and to join our Hearts and Voices with the Celestial Choir; we should wish that we could make all the World ring with his Praises, and that we could make all Men hear from the East to the West the sound of our Thanksgivings. We should sing that . . . which all the Churches of Christ throughout all Ages have sung, saying, *Holy, Holy, Holy Lord God of Hosts, Heaven and Earth are full of thy Glory.* And so we read that as soon as our Savior had spoken those Words, that he would not any more drink with them till the Kingdom of his Father should come, *they sung* a *Hymn,* or Psalm of Praise, and so went forth. And indeed who can sufficiently praise his Divine Majesty! The Tongues of Angels stammer in uttering of his Goodness; and we become dumb the more we endeavour to speak of it. The highest of our Praises is humbly and affectionately to acknowledge that we cannot sufficiently praise him; the greatest of our Endeavours is daily to admire him; the furthest we can strain our Souls is to long for Eternity wherein it may be our Employment to admire and praise him. Call upon the Armies of Angels and wish them to praise him, seeing thou canst not; call upon all Men and bid them praise him; wish thou couldst awake all the World that all Creatures might praise him. And make thine own Soul hear more plainly, call upon it more shrilly, call upon it again and again every Day to praise him: Say as the *Psalmist* doth,

Bless the Lord, ye his Angels which excel in strength, that do his Commandments, hearkening to the Voice of his words. Bless the Lord, all ye his Hosts: ye Ministers of his that do his Pleasure. Bless the Lord all his Works in all places of his Dominion. Bless the Lord, O my Soul.

---

(66) **Simon Patrick**
Bishop of Ely
The Christian Sacrifice. A Treatise Shewing the Necessity, End, and the Manner of Receiving the Holy Communion, together with Suitable Prayers and Meditations for every Month of the Year and the Principal Festivals in Memory of our Blessed Savior
1671

I hope the *Reader* will think fit to bring the like free and unprejudiced Mind to the Perusal of what I have writ; especially a Heart seriously desirous to have holy Devotion wrought in it to our Creator and Redeemer: and then neither of our

Pains, I presume, will prove unprofitable. But I do not mean, by Devotion, only some transient Thoughts and Passions arising at certain Seasons when we more solemnly address ourselves to God our Savior; but a settled Love to him, disposing us to present him alway with a Heart humble, pure, just, and charitable; which is the Oblation that all our other Sacrifices are to prepare for him and the greatest Honour that we are capable to do him.

For herein we express the high Esteem we have of him that we study, above all Things, to become like him. We show, indeed, that we think there is none better than he when we prefer his Wisdom, Goodness, Holiness, and Truth before all the Pleasures that Riches and Honours can raise us unto: Nay; when we choose, with the Loss of whatsoever is precious to us in this World, to conform ourselves to his blessed Nature and Will.

This is truly and substantially to glorify him before Men; to magnify his Name and to exalt his Praise. This proclaims him to be the most excellent Being; and that it is the supreme Happiness and Dignity of human Nature to be one of his Friends: But all the Praises and Doxologies we can bestow upon him, without this, are no better than Flatteries. They are but good Words and religious Compliments which we revoke and unsay again when we cross his Commands.

. . .

To make a true Feast, these four Things (in the Opinion of the most learned of all the ancient *Romans*) must conspire and meet together; *Chosen and select Persons, a choice and delicate Place, a choice Time and Season,* and *choice Provision;* proportionable to the Quality both of him that makes it and of those that are invited to it. Now in all these Regards, if we reflect a while on them, this Supper of the Lord which he makes for us will be found to be incomparably beyond the noblest Entertainment which the World ever saw.

For as concerning the Persons that here meet together, they are our blessed Lord, the Master of the Feast, and those *that believe on his name: to whom he hath given the right or privilege to become the sons of God, Jn.* 1:12. A Company of Souls that are larger than the World: *Heirs of a Kingdom; rich in Faith;* as full as they can hold of Love and Charity toward each other and toward all Men. So that there cannot either be more honourable or more sweet Society found under Heaven.

Then for the Place, you see it is prepared in the House of God: Where we *give unto the Lord the Glory due unto his Name and show forth his Salvation from Day to Day:* Where we *pay our Vows unto him in the Presence of all his People and make a joyful Noise unto him by singing of his Praises:* Where the Angels (as I may say) are Waiters and the heavenly Host are glad to attend upon us.

· · ·

As for the Time, you see likewise it is commonly the *Lord's Day:* On the Day when he rose from the dead, when he trampled under his Feet the great Enemy of Mankind; when the Angels not so glistering as he brought News that he had accomplished our Redemption; when the Host of Heaven was at a Gaze to see mortal Man made immortal and restored to the State of Paradise again; when we have nothing else to do but to rest and rejoice; to *declare the Works of the Lord; to give Thanks to his holy Name, and triumph in his Praise.*

And lastly, for the Provision itself, I have told you already what it is: The Body and Blood of the Lord of Life: Bread that excels the Angels Food: A Cup of Blessing of which those Sons of Glory never tasted. To these our Lord calls: Nay, beseeches and entreats us to come that we may feast ourselves on his Sacrifice of himself and be filled with his Love and satisfy ourselves with his Joys and everlasting Consolation.

Now what Soul is there that can be willing to lose his Share in such divine Food? That would be shut out from such Society or absent from such a Place; or desire to spend his Day better than in near Communion with our Lord? Either Men do not believe these Things, or they do not reflect on them and lay them to their Hearts; for otherwise there is none that reads this Writing but will be moved to make one at this holy Feast.

(67) Thomas Comber
Dean of Durham
A Companion to the Temple,
or A Help to Devotion in the Use of the Common Prayer
1672–76/1684

[Of the Communion Service in general]

Whatsoever Benefits we now enjoy or hope hereafter to receive from Almighty God, they are all purchased by the Death and must be obtained through the Intercession of the Holy Jesus. And for a perpetual memorial hereof we are not only taught to mention his Name in our daily Prayers, *John* 14:13 and 15:16, but are also commanded by visible signs to Commemorate and set forth his Passion in the Lord's Supper, 1 *Cor.* 11:26, wherein by a more forcible rite of Intercession we beg the Divine Acceptance. That which is more compendiously expressed in the Conclusion of our Prayers **[through Jesus Christ our Lord]** is more fully and more vigorously set out in this most Holy Sacrament; Wherein we intercede on Earth in Imitation of and Conjunction with the great intercession of our High Priest in Heaven; Pleading in the Virtue and Merits of the same Sacrifice here which he doth urge there for us. And because of this Sympathy and near Alliance between these two Offices of Praying and Communicating, we find the Eucharist in the purest Ages of the Church was a daily Companion of their *Common Prayer.* So that there is no Ancient *Liturgy* but doth suppose and direct the Celebration of this Sacrament as constantly as the use of Public Prayers: They being never separated but in the case of Novices or offending and secluded Christians who only had the benefit of the Petitions but were shut out before the Mysteries were begun.

. . .

[Of the Prayer for the Whole Church]

As the People of *Israel* were wont to bring their Gifts and Sacrifices to the Temple, and by the hands of the Priest to present them to Almighty God: So are we appointed to give our Oblations into the hands of the Minister of Christ, who by virtue of his Office may best recommend them with Prayers and Praises to the Majesty of Heaven. And yet we must not neglect to join with him in these Supplications, both to beg the acceptance of our Offering and to show that our Charity extendeth farther than our Alms can reach, for the benefit of these is received only by a few of our Neighbors but we ought to love all the World, especially our Christian Brethren, even those who do not need or cannot have profit by our gifts. And how can we express this better than by recommending them all to the mercies of God, who is able to relieve them all and of whose bounty all have need. Which excellent Duty, though it be to be done daily, yet at this holy Sacrament it is most proper because we here behold the universal love of Jesus and are declared lively Members of his mystical Body and conjoined in the strictest bonds of Union with all our fellow Christians: Besides, when can we more effectively intercede with God for the whole Church than when we represent and show forth that most meritorious Passion on Earth, by the virtue whereof our great High Priest did once redeem and doth ever plead for his whole Church even now that he is in Heaven. This Sacrament therefore hath been accounted the *great Intercession,* and accordingly all the ancient Liturgies did use such universal Intercessions and Supplications while this Mystery was in hand.

· · ·

[On the Sursum Corda]

Priest. **Lift up your Hearts:** *Answ.* **We lift them up unto the Lord.** Having searched and tried our ways by Repentance and by Faith turned again to the Lord, we are next by the method of the Holy Ghost advised to *Lift up our Hearts, Lam.* 3:40,41. They were oppressed with a load of guilt and fear before, but as soon as that burden is removed there is all possible reason to lift them up to praise our most gracious deliverer. Such was

296

David's practice, *Ps.* 25:1, such the Precept of the great Apostle, *Col.* 3:1, and from these Divine Fountains this pious Form of *Exhortation* was derived into all the ancient Liturgies: It is capable of a twofold sense, yet both do rarely agree to this place and to this Ordinance. *First,* As it requires a strict and entire attendance upon the Duty in hand: Thus St. *Cyprian* expounds this Preface, and St. *Chrysostom* and St. *Augustine* in like manner, *viz.,* That dismissing all Worldly thoughts we should wholly fix our minds upon the Mysteries and by Faith and Contemplation look into the Abyss of the Divine Mercy till we be even ravished and swallowed up with wonder and have forgotten all other things. The very Heathens in all their Holy Rites, (saith *Plutarch*) had a Cryer who with a loud Voice Proclaimed these words . . . By which they were warned to mind nothing but the Mystery, and that neither idleness nor business might interrupt them. And is not this much more necessary in this Celestial Feast where there are so many of the best objects in the World as will take up our whole Man and employ all our Power if we do attend them? *Secondly,* As it more directly respects the Duty of Praise which immediately follows after; and thus it admonisheth us to lift up our Hearts to contemplate the Infinite Majesty and Greatness, the admirable Mercy and Goodness of him whom we are to praise, that when our Souls are transported with the Divine Glories no base or mean Thoughts may dare to approach or disturb the holy pleasure. We are to praise God in the highest, to sing the Song of Angels. Let us therefore elevate our Thoughts to consider how that glorious Choir doth sing this Hymn, that we may do it with a fervency and pleasure almost unison to them and rejoice as if we were among them; we are now going to do the work of Angels, and so must be above the World.

. . .

[On the Preface and Sanctus]

"Therefore with Angels and Archangels, and all the Company of Heaven, we laud and magnify thy Glorious Name." That the Angels were present at the performance of Divine Mysteries hath been the Opinion of both Heathens and of Christians; but that they are especially present at the Lord's Supper is generally received. *Flesh and Blood* (saith St. *Chrysostom*) *is here made a part of the Angelic Choir:* And again, *Consider, O Man, near whom thou standest in these terrible Mysteries, with whom thou art about to worship God, with Cherubims and Seraphims, and all the Heavenly Powers.* And surely it will mightily exalt our affections and stir us up to the most vigorous devotion to consider with whom we are to bear a part, not only with the Priest, but with Angels and Archangels and all the Company of Heaven. For Jesus by his Death hath united Heaven and Earth, and designed all his redeemed ones to sing *Hallelujahs* with the blessed Spirits above forever. Wherefore it is fit that in this Commemoration of his Passion we should begin to unite our Voices with them with whom we hope to praise God to all Eternity. Only as we sing with them let us sing like them and not spoil their blessed Harmony by mingling flat and discordant Notes. O with what delight and pleasure, sincerity and joy, do they sing their Hymns while they are ravished with the prospect of the Divine Perfections! Could we but see their Felicity and hear their Music, it would transport us above ourselves and make us forget and despise all other pleasures to join with them. It may be we fear that we cannot sing in so high a Note, yet if we do it with like sincerity, our lower Key may grace the Harmony and complete the Concord. Behold those blessed Spirits who had no need of any Savior and who never did offend do praise God with incessant Voices for his Mercy and Love to us, and seem to invite us, saying, O ye Sons of Men, *praise the Lord with us,* and let us *magnify his Name* together. How then can we be silent? especially when our glorified Brethren, Prophets and Apostles, Saints and Martyrs, do also bear a part in this admirable Hymn. How justly do we style the object of these praises a *Glorious Name,* since all the World resounds its praise? To it Cherubim and Seraphim, Angels and Archangels, continually do cry, *Holy, Holy, Holy,* and all the Saints in Heaven and Earth do join to set forth the Glory thereof. . . .

"And did institute, and in his Holy Gospel command us, to continue a perpetual Memory of that his precious Death until his coming again." The work of our Redemption is so very excellent in itself that it deserves a perpetual Memorial, and who so fit to direct the particular manner of remembering it as he that did so nobly accomplish it? And this is that very way which he himself hath instituted, so that we have a most direct and powerful Argument to move our Lord to sanctify these Elements because we celebrate this Mystery in obedience to his own Commands. **Do this** (saith he) **in remembrance of me,** *Lk.* 22:19, and we are bid to show forth the Lord's death till he come, 1 *Cor.* 11:25, 26. And surely he will make these Symbols to be his Body and Blood to us because we are about to receive them purely by his Order; no doubt he will *establish that which he hath wrought for us, Ps.* 68:28, for otherwise he would seem (saith St. *Ambrose*) to abrogate that which he hath appointed. We are desirous as much as in us lieth to be partakers of his precious Body and Blood, and according to his command we are come thus far; but we can only strike the Rock, it is he must bring forth the Water; we must now stand still and see the Salvation of the Lord, for till he have blessed the Bread and Wine we can go no farther. Now if this holy Rite were a mere human device we could hardly expect to have so great a Grace and Power showed for its ratification; they that invocate God for those that are falsly called Sacraments cannot so rationally hope to be heard as we, who only desire him to be favourable to the work of his hands, and to prosper us in that which we undertake by express Commission from the Blessed Jesus. O let us then revere this Ordinance which hath so divine an Author on which the Image of God is so plainly stamped; let us with a mighty affection embrace our dying Savior's love who was so much afraid we should forget him and so desirous to be ever with us. Let us cheerfully go on without doubts or fears, knowing that he who hath bid us **Do this** is able to make it, whatsoever he will or whatsoever we need. Let us not startle at the difficulty of this

Sacramental change, but rest satisfied in the power of the Author and Enjoiner: Let us call on him earnestly and then believe that he will so be present by his Spirit and his Grace as that we shall feel the virtue and efficacy thereof from time to time, from one Communion to another, even till we come to see him unveiled and face to face at his coming again in glory.

. . .

Furthermore, lest we should be mistaken and either not understand or not believe the true worth of this incomparable Gift, he is pleased to tell us what it is, **This is my Body** (saith he) *which is given* for you and by that Word he makes it to be so to every true Believer. Wherefore the Minister ought to pronounce this so reverently and so deliberately that the Communicants may have time to exercise their Faith; because their Senses cannot discover any material alteration.

. . .

Meditations before the Receiving of the Bread
The Body of our Lord Jesus Christ
An Act of Faith

O Eternal Word of God, by whose power all things were made, I will not ask how thou canst give me thy Flesh to Eat, Because I am abundantly satisfied in thy saying, **This is my Body:** Since thou canst make it become to me whatsoever thou sayest it is. I believe, Lord, help my unbelief! What though my Senses assure me, the outward substance and its accidents still remain? Yet my Faith and my Experience tell me there is an efficacy therein, beyond the power of any other thing. Alas, the Flesh would profit me nothing, *Jn.* 6:63, for he that is joined to thee must be one spirit, 1 *Cor.* 6:17. O let these sacred Symbols therefore make me partaker of thy Nature and a partner in thy merits; let them unite me to thee, ingraft me in thee, and make that Body mine which did suffer Death for me, and then I shall seek no further but be more happy than if I could understand

300

all Mysteries. Sure I am, This is thy Body in Sacrament: it communicates to us the Blessings and Benefit thereof, and though presented in a Figure and by a holy Rite, yet it is to all its purposes that which it doth represent. I will therefore receive it as thy Body and esteem it infinitely above all other Food, that I may not be judged for not discerning thy Body. O let it be unto me according to my Faith. *Amen.*

. . .

[Post-Communion]

An Act of Thanksgiving

It is a mighty favour to me, O my God, that thou hast made Bread to grow out of the Earth to nourish my mortal Body, but O how far hast thou transcended that mercy in giving me the Bread of Life from Heaven to feed my immortal Soul. Whom was there in Heaven or Earth that I could have wished for in comparison of Jesus Christ! and now thou hast given him to me whom my Soul longed for, and in him thou hast given me all, for he is all in all. He is the fairest of Ten thousand, for whose sake I will trample upon all that this World accounts desirable: O my Soul bless thou the Lord. I came not to gaze at or taste of the outward part, but to satisfy the longings of my Sin-sick Soul by laying hold of the merits of a crucified Savior, yet I have received the Sacred Elements and thou hast made them to me that which I needed and desired, even the Body and Blood of thy Son. I have received his Flesh in Sacrament but his Grace in reality. And O how it fills my Soul with joy to behold thy Majesty appeased, my Sins expiated, my Peace made, and my Enemies vanquished. It revives my spirit and refreshes me more than comparisons can express, more than any can apprehend but they that feel the like. O praise the Lord with me and let us magnify his name together: We should have thought it a great felicity to have beheld the Glories of Jesus at a distance, but he hath now sent him home to our hearts, wherefore we will declare his mercy forever. *Amen, Hallelujah.*

"**And dost assure us thereby of thy favour and goodness**

toward us." When St. *John* was to introduce the Institution of this Sacrament he did it with this Preface, *chap.* 13:1, *Having loved his own, he loved them to the end,* or (as the word rather signifies) He loved them *in the highest degree,* intimating that this holy Communion is designed as a testimony that he loved us with a most *perfect love.* And there are many considerations which do most clearly show this to be an assured pledge of the favour of God unto us: 1. If we consider it only as a *Feast,* it hath always been a token of great respect and a symbol of entire friendship to admit (especially our inferior) to our Table. . . . Besides, Feasts have been esteemed a means to reconcile those who have been at variance, whence it is a Proverb in *Ben-Syra, Spread the Table, and the contention will cease.* And is it not matter of unspeakable joy to us who were Enemies, Rebels, and condemned Wretches to be thus invited to feast with the Lord of Hosts? Can we have a plainer Symbol of his favour than thus to be treated as his dear Friends? 2. But it is not an ordinary Feast, for it is *a Feast upon the Body and Blood of Christ* which was the great Sin-offering. Now it was not lawful of old for any to taste of the Expiatory Sacrifices, because those offerings could not wholly abolish Sin nor remove the Anger of God; he was not so perfectly reconciled by them as to give back the Offerers any part on which they might feast with him. But by the perfect Oblation of Jesus Christ it is evident that the Divine Justice is fully satisfied, and therefore the Flesh and Blood of Christ is given back to us by God in Sacrament that we may eat thereof before him and thereby be assured that he will remember our Sins no more. . . .

3. It will further appear to be a pledge of God's infinite Love to us if we consider *who* it is that in this Holy Rite he gives to us, even *Jesus Christ* his dearly beloved Son. May we not say (as God to *Abraham, Gen.* 22:12), Now know *we that thou lovest us,* because thou hast not withheld thy Son, thy only Son from us: And justly may we argue with St. *Paul, Rom.* 8:32, *He that hath* given us *his own Son, how shall he not with him also freely give us all things?* When he hath given the greatest and best to us to make

302

us his Friends, shall he deny us any lesser matters when we are reconciled? We may be confident there is nothing which God values more highly than his own dear Son, and that his design in giving him to us in this Sacrament is to be a testimony how infinitely he loveth us and how earnestly he desireth our Salvation. 4. That which adds weight to all the former is the consideration of *the Giver*, who is the God of Truth and is most sincere in all his dealings with us, so that we may be assured of all imaginable reality on his part. And now how should it fill our Minds with joy that we have such a pledge of his favour who is Almighty in power and governs all the World, whose goodness fills Heaven and Earth with joy. Were the gift never so mean that were bestowed in token of his favour and goodness, it ought to be esteemed above all things; therefore let us thus declare our gratitude for so excellent a gift, upon so blessed an account from so glorious a Majesty.

---

(68) **Daniel Brevint**
Dean of Lincoln
The Christian Sacrament and Sacrifice
1673

The blessed Communion was chiefly instituted by the Son of God for a *Sacrament* in the Church: But when it is received by the Christian People, if this *Receiving* of theirs be right, it must needs be attended with the Addition of such other Performances as will make it also a *Sacrifice*. As it is a Sacrament, this great Mystery shows three Faces, looking directly toward three Times, and offering to all worthy Receivers three Sorts of incomparable Blessings: that of *Representing* the true *Efficacy* of Christ's Sufferings, which are past, whereof it is a *Memorial;* that of *exhibiting* the first Fruits of these Sufferings in real and *present*

Graces, whereof it is a moral *Conveyance* and *Communication;* and that of *assuring* Men of all other Graces and Glories *to come,* whereof it is an infallible *Pledge.*

As this Sacrament looks back, it is an authentic *Memorial* which our Savior hath left in his Church of what he was pleased to suffer for her. For though these Sufferings of his were both so dreadful and holy as to make the Heavens mourn, the Earth quake, and all Men tremble: yet because great Objects, how terrible and magnificent forever they be, whilst they last are not less than the smallest things apt to be forgoten when they are gone: and so there was small Likelihood that the Passion of Jesus Christ, which was not seen upon the Cross above the space of some few Hours, could be well preserved in the Memory of Men throughout all Ages. Therefore our Savior was pleased at his last Supper to ordain this Sacrament, as a holy *Memorial, Representation,* and *Image* of what He was about to suffer for that short time to save his dear Church forever. So that when Christian Posterity, which had not seen the Crucifixion of their Savior, like the young *Israelites* that had not seen the killing of the first Passover, should come to ask after the Signification of those Things, this *Bread,* this *Wine,* the *breaking* of the one, the *pouring* out of the other, and the *Participation* of both; this sacred Mystery might expose to faithful Beholders as a present and constant Object, both the *Martyrdom* and the *Sacrifice* of this crucified Savior, giving up his *Flesh,* sheding his *Blood,* and pouring out his very *Soul* for the Expiation of their Sins.

Therefore, as in the Feasts of the Passover, the late *Jews* could say, *This is the Lamb, these are the Herbs, and this is the Bread of Affliction which our Fathers did eat in Egypt;* because their latter Feasts did so effectually represent the former, that the People who did partake of those had Ground enough both to act and speak as if they had been present at this: so at our holy *Communion,* which succeeds the Passover and is undoubtedly no less a blessed and powerful Sacrament to set before our Eyes *Christ our Passover who is sacrificed for us,* 1 Cor. 5:7, *Our Savior,* says St.

Austin, doubted not to say, This is my Body, when he gave to his Disciples the Figure of his Body. Because especially, besides the *Commemoration,* this Sacrament duly given and faithfully received, makes the thing which it represents as really present for our Use, and as really powerful in order to our Salvation as if the thing itself were newly done or in doing, *Eating this Bread, and drinking of this Cup, you set forth the Death of the Lord,* 1 Cor. 11. 26.

For certainly, not to mistake the Meaning of Christ nor to injure the Mystery, whensoever, with the Primitive Church, we call it a *Memorial* or a *Figure,* great care must be taken lest we confound these venerable Representations which God himself hath set up in his Church and for his Church, with those empty Figures and Marks which either some old Tradition or some private Fancy may by chance have put in our way. Men of ordinary Understanding do not regard with the Same Eye the Arms and Images of Princes which public Authority hath set up in a public eminent Place; and which a Painter, to please his Fancy, hath fixed in a private Room. Without all doubt a wise Traveler would be much more moved at the Sight of the *Salt Pillar* (if it did stand yet where it did) which God had set up purposely where *Lot*'s Wife looked toward *Sodom,* than at some Prints of her Feet (if they were to be seen yet) when she turned some other way. And if we credit the History, that Cross which the first Christian Emperor is reported once to have seen in the Air (which undoubtedly the Hand of God or an Angel had made appear with some Design) could not but cause a greater Respect than that ordinary Sign of the Cross which Christians have used on common Occasions. And what nobody can deny, that all sorts of *Signs* and *Monuments* become more or less venerable according to the greater or lesser Worth of the Objects which they are made to represent. It had been hard for *Abraham,* or for any devout Patriarch, not to feel some Motions of Reverence and holy Fear when they did chance to pass again by remarkable Places where God had appeared to them: and who doubts but the very Sight of *Bethlehem,* of the Mount of *Olives,* of *Calvary,* &tc., which Christ honoured with his Presence when he was born, when he suffered, and when he went up to Heaven, did heat the Primitive Christians with considerable Flames of Zeal, besides that usual *Faith* and *Knowledge* which they had got by their Reading? But when these Signs and Monuments, besides their ordinary Use, bear withal as it were on their Face the glorious Character of their Institution from above, and with this Institution the most express Design that God hath thereby to revive in a manner, and to expose, as full to all our Senses, his Passion and Sufferings as if they had still their true Being (as they have still the same Virtue), a discreet and pious Beholder must needs look on these Ordinances with these three Degrees of Devotion.

The first is when he considers those great and dreadful Passages which this Sacrament sets before him. I do observe on this Altar somewhat very like the *Sacrifice* and Passion of my Savior. For thus the *Bread of Life* was broken; thus the *Lamb of God* was slain; thus his most precious *Blood* was shed. And when I look upon the Minister who, by special Order from God his Master, distributes this *Bread* and this *Wine,* I conceive that thus verily God himself hath both given once his Son to die, and gives still the Virtue of his Death to bless and to save every Soul that comes unfeignedly to him.

The second is an Act of Adoration and Reverence when he looks upon that good Hand that hath consecrated for the Use of the Church the *Memorial* of these great Things. I cannot without some degree of Devotion look on any Object that in any wise puts me in mind of the Sufferings of my Savior; and if I did perceive but any Cloud, somewhat like them, although it were but casual, I would not neglect the Accident that had caused that Resemblance. But since the good Hand of my God hath purposely contrived it thus, to set before me what I see; and since by his special Appointment, these Representatives are brought in hither for this Church, and among all the rest for me; I must mind what *Israel* did when the Cloud filled the Tabernacle. I will not fail to worship God as soon as I perceive these Sacraments and *Gospel-Clouds* appearing in the *Sanctuary.*

Here I worship neither *Sacrament* nor *Tabernacle,* but I will observe the Manner that *Moses, David,* and all *Israel* have taught me to receive poor Elements with, after the Institution of God hath once raised them to the Estate of great Mysteries. Neither the Ark nor any Clouds were ever adored in *Israel,* though some brutish Heathens sometimes thought so: but sure it is, the Ark was considered quite otherwise than an ordinary *Chest,* and the Cloud than a Vapour, as soon as God had hallowed them both to be the Signs of his Presence. Therefore as the former People did never see the Temple or the Cloud, but that presently at that Sight they used to throw themselves on their Faces; I will never behold these better and surer Sacraments of the glorious Mercies of God, but as soon as I see them used in the Church to that holy Purpose that Christ hath consecrated them to, I will not fail both to remember my Savior who consecrated these Sacraments, and to worship also my Savior whom these Sacraments do represent. And God forbid that when I am able I should not receive them as my Savior himself was pleased to receive his own Baptism, with Devotion and *Prayer.* Lk. 3: 21.

The third, which is the Crown and the Completing of the two others, is such a vigorous and intense Act of Faith as may correspond to the great End which our Savior aimed at when he instituted this Sacrament. The main Intention of Christ was not here to propose a bare *Image* of his Passion, once suffered in order to a bare *Remembrance:* but over and above to enrich this *Memorial* with such an effectual and real Presence of continuing Atonement and Strength as may both *evidently set forth Christ himself crucified before our Eyes, Gal. 3: 1, and invite us to his Sacrifice, not as done and gone many Years since, but as to expiating Grace and Mercy, still lasting, still new, still the same that it was when it was first offered for us.*

All those Sacrifices under the Law, which had both their Use and their Strength limited, some to a Year, some to a Month, some to a Day, were not less powerful at the last than they were at the first Moment of their proper Duration: and they who lived or died within the twelfth

307

Month of the Year after the Feast of Propitiations had as much Benefit from that anniversary Sacrifice as they who were upon the Place and at the very Day when the High Priest did offer it. Upon the like but infinitely better Reason, the Sacrifice of Jesus Christ being appointed by God the Father for a Propitiation that should continue throughout all Ages to the World's End: and withal being everlasting by the Privilege of its own *Order,* which is *an unchangeable Priesthood, Heb.* 7: 24, and by his Worth who offered it, that is the Blessed Son of God, and by the Power of the *Spirit* by whom it was offered, which is the *Eternal Spirit,* Heb. ix. 14, all kinds of Eternity thus concurring together to the Sacrifice upon the Cross, it must in all respects stand everlasting and eternal; and *the same yesterday, today and forever, Heb. 13: 8.*

Therefore this Sacrifice being such, the holy Communion is ordained of Christ to set it out to us as such, that is, as effectual now at his holy Table as it was then at the very Cross: and by the same Proportion the Act of worthy Receivers (besides Remembrance and Worship) must needs be this; first to elevate their Faith and stretch their very Souls up to the Mount, with the blessed Virgin who stood nearest the Sacrifice; or at least with the Disciples who looked on it at some Distance: and then look up to the *Victim,* to *Jesus the Everlasting Mediator of the Everlasting Covenant,* and to the *Blood of Sprinkling that Speaks yet* and craves for *better Things* (Pardon and Blessing) *than Abel's did. Heb.* 12: 24. Here Faith must be as true a *Substance* of those Things past which we *believe,* as 'tis of those other Things yet to come which we *hope* for: *Heb.* 9: 1.

At the Approach therefore of this great *Mystery,* and by the Help of this strong *Faith,* the worthy Communicant being prostrated at the Lord's Table as at the very Foot of his Cross shall with earnest Sorrow confess and lament all his Sins, which were the Nails and Spears that pierced our Savior. We ourselves most chiefly, not *Pilate,* nor the *Jews* (for he would not have died for such alone), *we have crucified that Just One. Men and Brethren what shall we do? Acts* 2: 37. He shall fall amazed at that

Stroke of Divine Justice, that being offended but by *Men,* could not be satisfied nor appeased but by the Sufferings and Death of *God. How dreadful is the Place!* how deep and holy is this Mystery? Then he will fall again to worshiping, not less amazed at than thankful for those inconceivable Mercies of God the Father, who so gave up his only Son; and for the Mercies of God the Son, who thus gave himself up for us.

---

(69) **Robert Nelson**
layman and philanthropist
**The Great Duty of Frequenting the Christian Sacrifice,
and The Nature of the Preparation
Required, with Suitable Devotions**
1706

It is no Wonder that Men who are not serious in the *Business* of *Religion* and who frequent the Church only in Compliance with the Fashion of the World and in Obedience to an established Custom should neglect one of the greatest Advantages of the Christian Life: I mean the frequent receiving the *Holy Sacrament of Christ's Body and Blood.* But that Christians otherwise very devout and not lawfully hindered, who have the Fear of God before their Eyes and who aim at pleasing Him in all their Actions, should ever turn their Backs upon his *Holy Table,* and when invited to *commemorate* the meritorious *Sacrifice* of the *Death of Christ* should refuse to give such an easy Instance of a thankful Heart, is really Matter of Astonishment. Because they do thereby neglect the most effective Means of growing in Grace and overlook the best Method of attaining what they most sincerely purpose and desire.

. . .

And since we live in an Age that is disposed to make all the

309

inherent Powers in the *Priesthood* to be the Effects of *Priestcraft;* and that others take upon them to sign and seal Covenants in God's Name who have received no Commission to that purpose; It will be fit for any Man that prepares himself for this holy Ordinance to consider who has the Power of *administering* this *holy Sacrament,* whether *Laymen* as well as *Clergymen* who have received their Commission by Succession from the Apostles. This Consideration I am sure will be of great Comfort to the faithful Members of the Church of *England,* which has preserved the ancient Apostolical Government and the Primitive Orders in a due Subordination whereby they are secured of a right and truly *Canonical Ministry.*

Now to satisfy ourselves in these Enquiries we must observe that in the first Institution of this Sacrament it was celebrated by our Lord and Master *Jesus Christ;* He blessed the Bread and Wine and gave both to his Disciples; and he himself was, as the *Apostle* calls him, the *High Priest over the House of God.* And indeed, the Design of the Epistle to the *Hebrews* seems to be to show us the difference between the two *Covenants,* the Nature of the *Levitical* and *Evangelical* Priesthood, what Necessity there was of a change from the one to the other; that the Evangelical was after the Order of *Melchizedek;* that our *Savior* was the *High Priest* of that Order, and that this *Honour he took not to himself but was called of God* to it, as well *as Aaron was* to his. The Sacrament being thus instituted, and the Elements being consecrated by a Priest at the first Celebration of it; the Apostles kept close to their Master's Institution. Being commanded to *do the same in remembrance of him;* they consecrated the Elements and gave them to the People as he before did to them; and the same did the Bishops, their Successors after them, and those that they appointed. And this was so constantly and universally practiced in these early times that one Instance is not to be brought to the contrary.

Besides, the very Nature of a Sacrament requires commissioned Officers for the Administrations of it. For Sacraments being Seals of the Covenant of Grace, of that Covenant between God and Man, which our Savior purchased for us and confirmed with his Blood, Who can seal this Covenant unless such as are empowered by God to transact with us in his Name? On our part to offer up our Prayers and Supplications to him; and on his to bless us, to absolve us from our Sins upon Repentance, and to seal the Pardon of them by admitting us to partake of these holy Mysteries.

To this End the Apostles were careful in providing good Men to succeed them in their Ministry; St. *Paul* was earnest with *Titus* to *ordain Elders in every City,* and with *Timothy,* to *lay Hands suddenly on no Man;* and in his Epistles to both he describes, and that nicely too, the Qualifications of those that were to be admitted to Ecclesiastical Orders. In the Church of *Corinth* there were Prophets and Teachers, Helpers and Governors, which were their Bishops, Priests, and Deacons. Now what need was there of this Distinction and of this great care and caution in conferring Orders if they had no particular Powers to exercise and that every LayMan had an equal Right to dispense them?

---

(70) **William Beveridge**
Bishop of St. Asaph
The Great Necessity and Advantage of Public Prayer and Frequent Communion, designed to revive Primitive Piety, with Meditations, Ejaculations, and Prayers before, at, and after the Sacrament
1708

Thus we may employ our Thoughts while others are Receiving; but when it comes to our Turns to receive it, then we are to lay aside all Thoughts of Bread and Wine and Minister and everything else that is or can be seen, and fix our Faith, as it is *the Evidence of Things not seen,* wholly and solely upon our blessed Savior, as offering us his own Body and Blood to preserve our Bodies and Souls to everlasting Life, which we are therefore to receive *by Faith,* as it is *the Substance of Things hoped for,* steadfastly believing it to be, as our Savior said, *His Body and Blood;* which, as our Church teacheth us, *are verily and indeed taken and received by the faithful in the Lord's Supper.* By which Means, whatsoever it is to others, it will be to us who receive it with such a Faith the Body and Blood of CHRIST our Savior, the very *Substance of Things hoped for,* upon the Account of His Body that was broken and His Blood that was shed for us.

AND the better to excite and assist us in the Exercise of our *Faith* after this Manner, at our *receiving* the *Holy Sacrament,* the Minister, at the Distribution of it, first applies the Merits of CHRIST's Death to each particular Person that receives it, saying to everyone singly and by himself, *The Body of our Lord Jesus Christ* which was given for *THEE,* and the *Blood which was shed for THEE, preserve THY Body and Soul unto everlasting Life,* that so I may apply and appropriate it to myself as the Body and Blood of Him that loved *ME* and gave Himself for ME to preserve *MY* Body and *MY* Soul unto everlasting Life. And then he adds, at the Distribution of the Bread, *Take and eat this, in Remembrance that Christ died for THEE, and feed on him in thy Heart by Faith, with Thanksgiving.* Whereby I am put in Mind again to eat it, in Remembrance that CHRIST died for *ME* in particular; and then am taught how to feed upon Him, even *in my Heart by Faith, with Thanksgiving. In my Heart* because it is *not bodily* but *spiritual* Food: By *Faith,* as the only Means whereby the Heart or Soul can take in its proper Nourishment and receive *the Substance of Things hoped for,* even the *Body* and *Blood* of CHRIST, and then it must be with *Thanksgiving* too as the necessary Consequent of *Faith.* For as no Man can be truly thankful to CHRIST unless he actually believe in Him; so no Man can actually believe in Him but he must needs be truly thankful both to and for Him. And therefore at the Distribution of the Cup, after the Words *Drink this, in Remembrance that Christ's Blood was shed for thee,* it is only added *And be thankful.* Because this necessarily supposeth and implyeth our *Feeding upon* him in our Hearts by *Faith,* as without which it is impossible for us to be truly thankful.

---

(71) **Samuel Johnson**
Priest and missionary in Connecticut from the Society
for the Propagation of the Gospel,
first president of King's College (Columbia University)
On the Beauty of Holiness in the Worship
of The Church of England
1749

(In the) Communion Office, . . . what is there can more conduce to make us holy in all manner of conversation, than to have each of God's holy commandments rehearsed in a most grave and solemn manner, and for all the people, after every one of them, to pray for God's mercy to pardon their offenses against it, and his grace to incline their hearts to keep it for the future, and to write all his laws in their hearts? And, as the Holy Sacrament is the most divine and heavenly institution of our religion, and the most solemn act of our worship, the design of which is, to inspire our souls with a most grateful sense of the mighty love of our blessed lord and master in dying for us, in order to destroy both the power and guilt of sin; and to seal a pardon to us upon our true repentance, and fill us with the most ardent devotion to God and our Lord Jesus, and the most affectionate charity one towards another; so the manner of our administering and receiving it in the Church is excellent beyond that of any others. For which we are prepared, by a very suitable exhortation and confession of our sins, with the declaration of our pardon and the great and precious promises whereof this Sacrament is a seal. We are then called upon to lift up our hearts to God in the most seraphic form of thanksgiving, wherein the Church militant on earth joins, and, as it were, holds communion with the holy Church triumphant which is above; the angels and archangels, and all the company of heaven; saying, Holy, Holy, Holy, Lord God Almighty; Heaven and Earth are full of Thy Glory; Glory be to thee O Lord most High. Amen. The elements are then consecrated or set apart to represent the body and blood of Christ, in the gravest and most solemn manner, with the words of our blessed Lord's institution; and in the administration the inestimable benefits of his death are expressed in the delivery of them, to each particular person, receiving them in the devoutest manner upon his knees; which is the most decent posture wherein to receive the seal of our pardon. And lastly, the whole office is concluded with devoting ourselves to God both in body and soul, in our Lord's Prayer and others, the devoutest prayers and thanksgivings, and ends with an excellent benediction; than all which, I must think nothing can be imagined more conducive to train us up in all holiness, devotion and virtue for the glories of the heavenly state.

---

(72) **Thomas Secker**
Archbishop of Canterbury
Sermon XXIX, in Explanation and Defence of the Liturgy of the Church of England
c. 1758–1768

Then he exhorts them, thus comforted, to *lift up their hearts* and *give thanks to God:* which words, with the answers, and the substance of all that follows constantly, as far as *glory be to thee, O Lord most high,* appear to have been used in the Communion service 1500 years ago: and might probably descend from the

Apostolic times. Even the custom of appropriating particular prefaces to the more considerable festivals is 1200 years old, if not more.

And now approaching nearer to the act of receiving, we again solemnly acknowledge our own unworthiness, as all the old liturgies did, though not so fully: and pray, *that our sinful bodies may be made clean by Christ's body, and our souls washed through his most precious blood:* which expressions have been censured as if they implied that each of these, at least the latter of them (his blood), had some peculiar efficacy of which the other was destitute. But this cannot be intended, because very soon after the *preservation of our bodies and souls* also *unto everlasting life* is ascribed separately, both to his body and to his blood, as it is in Scripture also. Therefore the distinction made here was only meant for some kind of elegance in speech: and it much resembles what St. Clement the Roman, whom St. Paul entitles *his fellow-labourer,* hath said in his Epistle to the Corinthians, that Christ *gave his flesh for our flesh, and his soul for our souls.*

After this follows the Prayer of Consecration, or setting apart the bread and wine to the sacred purpose in which they are about to be employed. A prayer hath been used for that end at least 1600 years. And the mention which ours makes of the institution of the Lord's Supper, from the words *who in the same night that he was betrayed* to the conclusion is in every old liturgy in the world.

· · ·

The first part of the words which the minister speaks at delivering the elements is very ancient: the rest is added by our Church; and the whole is unexceptionable. The posture of kneeling which we use when we receive is a very proper one. Some indeed think that the Apostles received in the posture which they used at meals and that we ought to imitate them in this. Now if so, to imitate them strictly we must not sit (as these persons do), but lie all along: for so did the Apostles at table. But indeed we may rather suppose that when our Savior blessed the bread and wine, this being an address to God, both he and they were in some posture of adoration: and that they changed it before receiving is not likely considering how different that was from a common meal. Nor does it appear that any part of the Christian Church till of late years ever used any other posture than that of kneeling or standing; by each of which they meant to signify worship. We use the former: but with an express declaration inserted in all our prayer books that *no adoration is hereby intended or ought to be done, either to the sacramental bread and wine (for that were idolatry to be abhorred of all Christians), or to any corporal presence of Christ's natural flesh and blood: for they are in Heaven and not here.* We kneel therefore only to adore the invisible God, and to be in a fit posture for those prayers and praises which can never be more properly offered up to him.

Having communicated, we again repeat, after a long interval, the Lord's Prayer. For since, *to as many as* truly *receive him, he gives power to become the sons of God,* we may hope we have now strengthened our title to apply under that name to *Our Father, which is in Heaven, &tc.*

Then we *entirely,* that is with our whole hearts, *desire* him *to accept this our sacrifice,* or service, *of praise and thanksgiving* which we have offered up to him: begging leave at the same time to *offer up ourselves, body and soul,* as dedicated to his will: which is the great end of all our devotions. . . . We pray also once more for the whole Church: and lastly for our fellow communicants as well as ourselves that we may be *fulfilled,* that is, filled full, and as the Psalmist expresses it, *abundantly satisfied with God's grace and benediction.*

After this, as our blessed Lord sung a hymn with his disciples after the Passover (in imitation of whom the whole Christian Church hath used one in commemorating *Our Passover, sacrificed for us*), we use one likewise, as ancient in substance as the fourth century at least. It were better indeed that we sung it: if there did not, alas, often want numbers, and generally skill. The beginning of it is the song of the holy Angels in St. Luke: on which foundation we proceed to *glorify* God and *give thanks to him for his great glory;* meaning that of his goodness, wisdom and power displayed in the work of our redemption: fervently beseeching *the Son and Lamb of God* that his sufferings to *take away the sins of the world* and his *sitting at the right hand of the Majesty on* high may bring down *mercy upon us;* and acknowledging that we are all impure, *he only is holy;* men and angels are servants, *he only is the Lord; he only with the Holy Ghost,* united to the *Father in glory* unspeakable, is *most high* above all.

To this act of worship we subjoin (drawing now to a conclusion) one or more of those brief but comprehensive collects which are provided for that purpose. In the first of them some have objected against the phrase *chances of this mortal life* as implying somewhat irreligious. But our Savior hath not scrupled to say *and by chance there came down a certain priest.* Again in the fourth, which is also frequently used before sermon, some have stumbled at the expression *prevent us, O Lord, in all our doings,* because preventing most commonly signifies hindering. But the original meaning, and the true one here, is go before us: which may indeed be either to further us by opening the way or to obstruct us by stopping it. But surely it can no more be doubted, which we intend, than what David intended when he said *thou shalt prevent him with the blessings of goodness,* and again, *the God of my mercy shall prevent me.* The others, I think, have no difficulties.

What remains is the solemn and affectionate form of dismissal: most of which is taken from the words of holy writ. The minister of Christ in pronouncing it prays that *the peace of God, which passeth all understanding,* that inward sense of our Maker's goodness to us, which even now is delightful beyond the conception of those who have not experienced it, and shall hereafter be so heightened as vastly to exceed the present conceptions of the best of us, may *keep our hearts and minds,* our judgments and affections, *in the knowledge and love of God and his Christ:* and that every *blessing* of the holy Trinity may be distributed *amongst us and remain with us always.* Grant this, O heavenly Father, for the sake, &tc.

317

(73) **Anonymous**
The Companion or Spiritual Guide at the Altar
1783

After the *bread* and *wine* are deputed by holy prayer to God, to be used for a commemoration of Christ's death, though they do not cease to be what they were before, yet they become something which they were not before consecration: They become visible signs or pledges of that inward and spiritual grace which they are appointed by Christ himself to represent; which grace is no less than the *body and blood of Christ, which are verily and indeed taken and received by the faithful in the Lord's Supper.* For they have a real feel and portion given them in the death and sufferings of the Lord Jesus; whose body was broken and blood shed for the remission of sins. They truly and indeed partake of the virtue of his bloody sacrifice, whereby he hath obtained an eternal redemption for mankind. And it is the nature and office of these sacramental pledges to assure us of the good will of God, and of his truth in fulfilling his gracious promises. He engages to be faithful to us in *giving* them, as we engage ourselves to be faithful to him in *receiving* them. God bids us believe that we shall *be accepted in his beloved:* and he does after put us in possession of all that which the gospel promises and the sacrifice of Christ upon the cross obtained for us: no less than mercy, grace, and peace; remission of sins; the power of the Holy Ghost, and eternal life.

This sacrament is also a bond of union amongst Christians. They who believe in one common Savior and partake of the same sacrifice will never forget the duty of that lesson: *Beloved, if God so loved us* as to give his only begotten Son to die for our sins, *we ought also to love one another.* —The sacrifice here offered is declarative of Christian unanimity, knit together in a firm and inseparable charity. For when our Lord took the bread which is knead together and made up by the union of many corns, and called it his body, he thereby denoted all Christian people. In the same manner, when he took the wine which is pressed from many grapes and gathered together in one cup and called it his blood, he also denoted his flock, or the congregation of the faithful, joined by the mingling together of a united multitude.

Therefore, when we partake of the table of the Lord, let us consider that as we are thereby made one with Christ, so we are joined in close union one with another. And let us remember when we are preparing to receive this heavenly banquet, that as we are going to commemorate the dearest love of our Lord and to profess our love to him, so we at the same time engage to love all the members of that body of which Christ is the head. That we there enter into covenant one with another, as well as with Christ, by eating of the same bread and drinking of the same cup, never to be unreconciled unto each other and never to hate, revile, injure, backbite one another, or fall out any more; but to live for the time to come in the peace of God and in unity and godly love. As this is the effect of receiving the sacrament of Christ's body and blood; if it heals the breaches made amongst the faithful and promotes Christian love and charity; if it nourishes a loving kind disposition of mind and keeps the soul free from all base selfishness and covetous desires; the oftener anyone goes to the Lord's table with a true penitent heart and lively faith, the better Christian he will grow.

For this reason our blessed Savior instituted this sacrament, not for the rich and mighty but for the poor and weak also. He invites all states and conditions, and promises to receive them without distinction provided they do love one another with a sincere heart and unfeigned affection. Here the great are taught and engaged not to scorn them of low degree; and the poor are engaged not to envy the great. The rich are called upon to be merciful and liberal: the poor and needy to be thankful and contented. The learned and wise not to despise the ignorant and weak, and the weak not to judge the strong: but all to live together as loving brethren and members of the same body. That so *they may have the same care one for another. And whether one member suffer, all the members may suffer with it; or one member rejoiceth, all the rest may rejoice with it.* That as there is *one Lord and one Spirit, and one Baptism, and one Hope of our calling;* so *the multitude of believers may be of one heart and of one soul.* That *we may all speak the same thing,* and that *there be no divisions amongst us; but that we be perfectly joined together in the same mind and in the same judgment: and that we may with one heart and one mouth glorify God, even the father of our Lord Jesus Christ.*

To sum up all that has been said concerning the *nature, end,* and *use* of this *holy sacrament,* we must acknowledge and believe it to be a holy feast in commemoration of our Lord Jesus Christ, especially of his death; in which we, on our part, make a solemn profession of his religion as delivered to us and contained in the holy gospels, and tie ourselves in the strictest covenant to follow him unto death and to live in love and charity with all our Christian brethren. On the other part, Christ makes a representation of his dying love to us, and confirms the continuance of it, giving us pledges that he will make us heirs of all the blessings which were the purchase of his body broken and his blood shed for us. So that, when the minister gives the *bread* and the *cup* to us, we should receive them as tokens and assurances given by Christ of his continued and everlasting love and affection: and when we take, eat, and drink that which he gives us, we should receive it with resolutions to continue his faithful disciples, in hopes of that eternal life which God hath promised to them that believe in Jesus Christ whom he hath sent into the world to save sinners.

Having considered the premises, it will be no difficult matter to show that it is the duty of all Christians to *communicate* at the Lord's table. It was not instituted and ordained for the benefit of one church or nation, or for any peculiar state and condition of men; but for all that call upon the name of the Lord through Jesus Christ our Savior, who in his invitation to this feast makes no exception but extends his promise of its benefits unto all: *Come,* says the blessed Jesus, *unto me, all ye that travel and are heavy laden, and I will refresh you.* And, the Author of our Salvation, knowing how difficult it is for man to be drawn to anything by mere invitation, and that the devil, who tempted our first Parents to eat the forbidden fruit with so great success, was always diligent to prevent their posterity from receiving the means of grace and salvation, and, by assuming the form of an angel of light, to dissuade well-disposed Christians by scruples and groundless fears to reject so kind and loving an invitation, he has backed it with a special command:—*Take, eat; this is my body, which is broken for you—Drink ye all of this, for this is my blood shed for you.—Do this in remembrance of me.* For, *except ye eat the flesh of the Son of man, and drink his blood, ye have no life in you. But, whoso eateth my flesh and drinketh my blood hath eternal life, and I will raise him up at the last day.*

It is, therefore, beyond conception why so many excuse themselves, or rather seek for excuses to keep them from the communion of the body and blood of Christ. There is nothing which Christ enjoins with more solemnity and positiveness than this sacred action. Consequently, if we confess ourselves obliged to perform his other commands, there can be nothing invented by men sufficient to excuse us from obedience to this command—DO THIS—A command whereby our love and affection to Christ Jesus, our ever-blessed Redeemer, is tried and proved in a most particular manner. For, as the only reason why we should *do this* is because he would have us; so the doing of it is a piece of pure obedience arising wholly out of our respect and affection to him and his injunctions who laid down his life for us; instituted and ordained to keep up the memory of our Savior, and to perpetuate his love to the end of the world.

Thus, the oftener we receive the body and blood of Christ, we show forth the Lord's death till his coming again and approve our title to the covenant in Christ Jesus; because it is a peculiar mark of a Christian, a mark proper to him alone who is moved to this, not by nature and the common light of mankind, but purely by his religion and devotion to his Savior. For there is no part of divine worship in which he is interested so much as in this. It is more properly a Christian worship than any other part of his duty. All the world confess that they are in duty bound to pray to God, to praise him and to give him thanks; but to know him and acknowledge him through Jesus Christ, and to give him thanks by *doing this,* belongs only to believers in the Son of God.

The primitive Christians were so well convinced of this truth and of the necessity of frequenting the Lord's table that they never met to perform the duty of prayer but they communicated by *doing this in remembrance of* the death and passion of our Savior Christ. And as long as we have any need to grow in the grace of our Lord Jesus Christ, to increase in strength and power, to resist and conquer all temptations, and to perform our several duties; to renew the sense of our obligations to God and to bind ourselves faster to him; to heighten our love and gratitude and to stir up light and joy in God our Savior; so long it will be necessary to *do this,* without which we can't obtain those great ends and purposes.

For by these outward signs, instituted and ordained by Christ himself, we express our hearty consent to the new covenant made by Christ in his blood; and engage ourselves to stand on the terms and conditions of it. So that it is the same as if we refused to be of Christ's religion should we refuse or willfully neglect to come to this holy communion. He that made the new covenant with us made these outward rites and solemnities to be instruments of stipulation, whereby they who are willing to enter into that covenant and to be of that religion, should express their agreement and submission to it; and openly declare that they acknowledge Jesus to be the Lord and that they will perform due obedience to every one of his commands.

The command also includes a frequent repetition of the act of *doing this;* as *often,* says Jesus, *as ye do it.* When we have once done it we are to signify our continuance and steadfastness in that religion, to which by these means we have joined ourselves, by the repeated use of the same means. He that has put his hand to the plow will never reap the fruits of his labour should he draw back: neither can we hope to enjoy the benefits of this sacrament if we absent from the Lord's table upon any pretense whatsoever. They live as if they repented of the contract which they had made, and renounced our blessed Savior, who imagine it sufficient to partake of this sacrament once or twice in a lifetime: for Christ made the *doing this* a special evidence and ratification of our devotion to him and his service.

. . .

[On the Absolution by the Priest]

The priest is required to pronounce the absolution standing, *because it is an act of his authority in declaring the will of God whose Ambassador he is. But the people receive it* upon their knees *in token of that humility and reverence with which they ought to receive the joyful news of a pardon from* GOD.

Don't look upon this absolution *as a* presumptive act *of the priest, or that it receives more or less efficacy from the* intention *of the priest that pronounceth it: neither set so light by it as to imagine it to be* merely declarative, *or a* matter of form *that conveys no benefit to the people upon whom it is pronounced. But consider it* sacramentally, *conveying pardon to such only as come duly, or* worthily *prepared, to receive that absolution from their sins, which being freely forgiven by* GOD, *are, by* his authority, *ratified upon earth by his minister. Thus the* unworthy *petitioner partakes* not *of that blessing which is promised to such as come prepared for absolution, no more than the* unworthy communicant *is entitled to the benefits of a holy communion.*

Proportionable to the sincerity *of one's* repentance *is the forgiveness of his sins. If we with a true faith and hearty repentance turn to* GOD, *he will have mercy upon us; he will pardon and deliver us from all our sins; he will confirm and strengthen us in all goodness and bring us to everlasting life.*

These are the conditions *of our salvation and of our* absolution. *So that, if we be just and sincere to ourselves, God will ratify the priest's*

323

absolution of our sins and perform all the promises he has made to us in this sacrament.

---

(74) **Samuel Seabury**
*First Bishop of the Episcopal Church
in the U.S.A., Bishop of Connecticut*
An Earnest Persuasive to Frequent Communion
1789

The general practice in this country is to have monthly Communions, and I bless God the Holy Ordinance is so often administered. Yet when I consider its importance, both on account of the positive command of Christ and of the many and great benefits we receive from it, I cannot but regret that it does not make a part of every Sunday's solemnity. That it was the principal part of the daily worship of the primitive Christians all the early accounts inform us. And it seems probable from the Acts of the Apostles that the Christians came together in their religious meetings chiefly for its celebration. (*Acts* 2:42, 46; 20:7.) And the ancient writers generally interpret the petition in our Lord's prayer, "Give us this day," or day by day, "our daily bread," of the spiritual food in the Holy Eucharist. Why daily nourishment should not be as necessary to our souls as to our bodies no good reason can be given.

If the Holy Communion was steadily administered whenever there is an Epistle and Gospel appointed, which seems to have been the original intention—or was it on every Sunday—I cannot help thinking that it would revive the esteem and reverence Christians once had for it, and would show its good effects in their lives and conversations. I hope the time will come when this pious and Christian practice may be renewed. And whenever it shall please God to inspire the hearts of the Communicants of any congregation with a wish to have it renewed, I flatter myself they will find a ready disposition in their minister to forward their pious desire.

In the meantime, let me beseech you to make good use of the opportunities you have; and let nothing but real necessity keep you from the heavenly banquet when you have it in your power to partake of it.

May the consideration of this subject have its proper effect upon every one of you! And the God of peace be with you—"make you perfect in every good work to do His will" (*Heb.* 13:21)—keep you in the unity of His Church, and in the bond of peace and in all righteousness of life—guide you by His Spirit through this world, and receive you to glory through Jesus Christ our Lord. Amen.
All glory to God.

---

(75) **Samuel Seabury**
*First Bishop of the Episcopal Church
in the U.S.A., Bishop of Connecticut*
Discourses on Several Subjects, volume I
1793

The Eucharist is not only a memorial of the passion and death of Christ for the sin of the world, but also of that offering of himself—his natural body and blood—which, under the representation of bread and wine, he made to God at the institution of the holy ordinance. In this respect it exactly fulfills its type, the ordinance of the Jewish Passover. For that was not only a memorial of the deliverance of the Israelites from the bondage of Egypt, in the night when God slew the Egyptian firstborn, but also a memorial of the original Passover in Egypt, under the protection of the blood of which put upon the posts of their doors, they remained in safety when the firstborn of the Egyptians were slain.

Hence, also, it appears that the Eucharist is a memorial made not so much before man as before the Almighty Father. For before whom should the memorial of the offering and death of Christ be made but before him to whom the offering and death of Christ was a sacrifice for sin? If the offering was made to God, as has been proved, the memorial of that offering must also be made before God or it ceases to be a proper memorial. For a memorial is a monument or sensible sign intended to bring some event to remembrance: And the Eucharist being the memorial of Christ's offering himself to God, and of his passion and death for sin, it follows that the memorial of his offering and death must be made before God, that by it their merit and efficacy may be pleaded with him, for the remission of sin and for all other benefits and blessings which his passion and death procure for us.

In this respect, too, the Eucharist fulfills its type, the Jewish Passover. The memorial made by that was a memorial made before God by the people of Israel, as appears from their being commanded to *eat it before the Lord;* for if it were eaten or celebrated before the Lord then the memorial made by it was made before the Lord.

It appears, therefore, that the Eucharist is not only a sacrament in which, under the symbols of bread and wine, according to the institution of Christ, the faithful truly and spiritually receive the body and blood of Christ, but also a true and proper sacrifice commemorative of the original sacrifice and death of Christ for our deliverance from sin and death—a memorial made before God to put him in mind; that is, to plead with him the meritorious sacrifice and death of his dear Son, for the forgiveness of our sins, for the sanctification of his church, for a happy resurrection from death, and a glorious immortality with Christ in heaven.

From this account, the Priesthood of the Christian Church evidently appears. As a Priest, Christ offered himself a sacrifice to God in the mystery of the Eucharist; that is, under the symbols of bread and wine; and he commanded his apostles to do as he had done. If his offering were a sacrifice, theirs was also. His sacrifice was original, theirs commemorative. His was meritorious through his merit who offered it; theirs drew all its merit from the relation it had to his sacrifice and appointment. His, from the excellency of its own nature, was a true and sufficient propitiation for the sins of the whole world; theirs procures remission of sins only through the reference it has to his atonement.

When Christ commanded his apostles to celebrate the Holy Eucharist in remembrance of him, he, with the command, gave them power to do so; that is, he communicated his own priesthood to them in such measure and degree as he saw necessary for his church—to qualify them to be his representatives—to offer the Christian sacrifice of bread and wine as a memorial before God the Father of his offering himself once for all; of his passion and of his death—to render the Almighty propitious to us for his sake; and as a means of obtaining, through faith in him, all the blessings and benefits of his redemption.

And, as the Laity are permitted to partake of this sacrifice—the most holy thing—the shewbread, or bread of the presence of the Christian Church—which, under the law, was not lawful for any to eat but only for the priests; so it is evident that such portion of Christ's priesthood is given to them as qualifies them to join in offering the Christian sacrifice and to partake of it with the priests of the church. And, in this sense I take it, the whole body of Christians are called a holy priesthood, a royal priesthood—are said to be made not only *kings,* to reign with Christ in glory hereafter, but *priests* unto God. (It will by no means follow from hence that private Christians have a right or power to consecrate the Eucharist: that right or power being by the institution itself confined to the apostles and their successors, and those empowered by them—no others being present at the time but the apostles.)

From this view of the matter we may see in what sense the

consecrated, or eucharistized, bread and wine are the body and blood of Christ. They are so sacramentally or by representation—changed in their qualities, not in their substance. They continue bread and wine in their nature; they become the body and blood of Christ in signification and mystery—bread and wine to our senses; the body and blood of Christ to our understanding and faith—bread and wine in themselves; the life-giving body and blood of Christ in power and virtue; that is, by the appointment of Christ and through the operation of the Holy Ghost—and the faithful receive the efficacy of Christ's sacrifice and death to all spiritual intents and purposes.

There is, therefore, in this holy institution, no ground for the errors of transubstantiation, consubstantiation, or the bodily presence of Christ with which the Church of Rome, Luther, and Calvin have deceived, beguiled, and perplexed the church. The bread and wine are, in their nature, still bread and wine—They are not transubstantiated into the natural body and blood of Christ as the Papists teach—The natural body and blood of Christ are not consubstantiated with them so as to make one substance as the Lutherans teach—Nor are the natural body and blood of Christ infused into them nor hovering over them so as to be confusedly received with them as Calvin and his followers seem to teach; for they are far from being intelligible on the subject. The natural body and blood of Christ are in heaven, in glory and exaltation—We receive them not in the communion in any sense. The bread and wine are his body and blood sacramentally and by representation. And, as it is an established maxim that all who, under the law, did eat of a sacrifice with those qualifications which the sacrifice required, were partakers of its benefits; so all who, under the gospel, eat of the Christian sacrifice of bread and wine with those qualifications which the holy solemnity requires are made partakers of all the benefits and blessings of that sacrifice of his natural body and blood which Christ Jesus made, when, under the symbols of bread and wine, he offered them to God, a propitiation for the sin of the world.

(76) **John Henry Hobart**
Bishop of New York, founder of The General Theological Seminary
*** A Companion for the Book of Common Prayer***
1805/1827
(Footnotes are from the original text)

Of the First Part of the Communion Service

On Sundays and other Holy Days, though there be no actual communion, the Church enjoins the communion service to be read to the end of the gospel, concluding with the blessing.[1]

The proper place of performing the communion service is in the chancel, at the communion table.[2]

When the Communion is not administered, the American Church permits the part of the Communion which is always said on Sundays and holy days to be said in the usual place of morning and evening prayer. It was the opinion of Bishop Beveridge that this part of the Communion Service ought always to be said at the altar, with a view of reminding the people that it was the original practice and still the wish of the Church to administer the Communion *every* Sunday and holy day.

The Communion Service commences with the LORD's Prayer and with an excellent prayer for the purification of our hearts, that we may be fit to approach GOD in this most solemn office. While the minister pronounces these prayers he is supposed to stand at the north side of the altar looking toward it; when he pronounces the commandments he turns and addresses the people, who, in the humble and reverent posture of

---

[1.] Rubric at the end of the Communion service.

[2.] The chancel should be distinct from the desk and pulpit, and so elevated in front of them as that the railing of the chancel and the communion table may be seen from every part of the church. There should be a platform elevated at least eight or nine inches between the pews and chancel, and from this two or more steps to the rails of the chancel.

kneeling are to pronounce with sincere and contrite hearts the short supplication which follows each commandment.

After the commandments follow the Collect, Epistle, and Gospel for the day. The congregation, who are supposed to sit during the Epistle, as soon as the Gospel is announced stand up, as being the attitude of praise, and bless GOD for the glad tidings of salvation by pronouncing aloud, "Glory be to thee, O LORD."

After the gospel the minister announces the holy days that are to be observed during the ensuing week, and other matters to be published.

After some verses from the Psalms in metre are sung,

The Sermon

follows, which, it is to be supposed, will always be on some subject connected with the season, the particular festival or fast that may then be celebrated. Before and after Sermon, some Collect or Collects from the end of the Communion Service or other part of the Liturgy, is generally used, concluding, before Sermon, with the LORD's Prayer. As the ministering servants of the sanctuary bear the commission of GOD, their instructions should be heard with humble and earnest attention; and our prayers should be directed to GOD that he would impress on our hearts the truths which they may deliver.

After the solemn

Benediction

with which the service concludes is pronounced by the Bishop or Priest, the congregation should continue kneeling and offer a secret prayer to GOD for his mercy, his grace, and blessing.

The Communion Service[3]

[3.] The following brief explanation of the Office for the Holy Communion will be found in the 22d chapter of the *Companion for the Festivals and Fasts of the Protestant Episcopal Church;* for which it was originally drawn up by the author.

After the sermon, when there is a Communion, the Minister returns to the LORD's table and reads several sentences from Scripture which explain and urge the duty of charity. This part of the service, from being used while the people are *offering* their alms by oblation, is called

The Offertory

The bread and wine are then *placed upon the table by the Priest* as a solemn acknowledgement of GOD's sovereignty over the creatures.[4] To this offering of the bread and wine to GOD, the term *oblation* refers in the prayer for CHRIST's Church militant which follows the offertory. The bread and wine are here *offered* simply *as such;* they are afterward offered *as symbols* of the body and blood of CHRIST.

The *alms* for the poor, the *devotions* or *gifts* which used formerly to be made for the clergy, and the *oblations* of the bread and wine being now presented unto GOD and placed before him on his holy table, the Church then proceeds to the duty of intercession in a solemn and affecting PRAYER FOR CHRIST'S CHURCH MILITANT.

The Exhortations

to be used when *notice is given of the Communion* are designed to set forth the necessary preparation for this holy sacrament and the great danger and guilt of refusing to participate of it. The primitive Church did not need these exhortations; for then the communion was administered whenever public worship was celebrated and all the faithful partook of it.

The Exhortation

used at *the administration* of the Communion, in animating and affecting language, sets forth and enforces the dispositions with which we ought to approach the LORD's table.

---

4. The elements are commonly placed on the altar before morning prayer by the *clerk* or *sexton.* This is contrary to the rubric and to the custom of the primitive Church.

After the exhortation the Priest

Invites

the people to *draw near;* accordingly it would appear proper for all the communicants to come from the more remote parts of the church as near as possible to the LORD's table. And that they may come with *lively faith* in the merits of CHRIST, he calls upon them previously to

Confess

their sins; which is accordingly done in words the most solemn and pathetic. The Priest then, in a form of

Absolution

authoritatively declares the forgiveness of sins; thus conveying peace and consolation to the humble and contrite. And still further to strengthen the hopes of the penitent, he recites some

Sentences

from *Scripture* which, in the most lively manner, exhibit the mercy of GOD through JESUS CHRIST to all who truly turn to him.

The communicants having exercised their charity; having humbly confessed their sins, and received the comforting declaration of GOD's mercy in the absolution, they are now prepared for the solemn duty of

Thanksgiving,

the more appropriate design of the LORD's Supper, which was anciently called the *Holy Eucharist.* [5] Elevated, as it were, above the world, they seem prepared to enter into the heaven of

---

[5.] Nearly all of the remaining part of the Office for the Communion will be found *almost verbatim* in the most ancient writers of the Church. The members of the Episcopal Church enjoy the inestimable advantage of celebrating this most sublime ordinance of their religion according to a form handed down from the first and purest ages of the Church.

heavens, there to join with angels and glorified saints in adoring and praising the everlasting JEHOVAH. Accordingly, after
the Priest and people, in *short sentences,* mutually excite one
another to the duty of praise, the Priest, in the name of the
people, makes a solemn acknowledgment to GOD of their obligation to thank and praise him. And then both Priest and
people break forth in an animating act of thanksgiving used in
the most ancient liturgies; which, from the epithet *holy* being
thrice repeated, as addressed to the three persons of the TRIN-
ITY, is called the

Trisagion

or *thrice holy.* On certain festivals there are

Proper Prefaces

appointed, in which thanks are returned to GOD for the particular mercy of redemption that day commemorated. These prefaces are to be repeated *seven days;* in imitation, probably, of the
Jewish feasts which continued, some for seven and one for
eight days.[6]

   The nearer we approach these holy mysteries, the greater
reverence we ought to express: The Priest accordingly allays
the foregoing exultations by an

Act of Humiliation

highly expressive and affecting, taken from the most ancient
liturgies.

   The

Prayer of Consecration

is the most ancient and essential part of the whole communion.
This prayer, as it now stands in the Office of Communion
prescribed by our Church, is agreeable to the primitive model
and to the prayer of consecration in the first liturgy of King

---

[6.] Leviticus 23.

Edward VI, which was afterward materially altered. The Priest returns solemn *thanks* to God for the sacrifice of the death of Christ, the solemn *memorial* of which is now to be celebrated. He then solemnly sets apart the bread and wine to be *symbols of the body and blood of* Christ, repeating the words of Christ at the institution of them. They are then *offered* to God as a solemn memorial of the passion and death, the resurrection and ascension of Christ, whereby our redemption is effected. The blessing of God, through his word and Holy Spirit, is then *invoked* on the consecrated elements that they may be to every worthy receiver, *in power and efficacy,* the body and blood of Christ.[7] And in conclusion, the faithful, as a just return to God for the inestimable blessings of redemption, devote themselves, their souls and bodies, to his service; humbly imploring his mercy and grace. This prayer of consecration, formed on the model of the prayer of consecration in the primitive Church, is venerable for its antiquity: it presents the most just and impressive views of the efficacy and importance of the Holy Eucharist; and it is calculated to awaken the most solemn and tender affections of the soul.

After the mercy and goodness of God are celebrated in

A Hymn

the minister proceeds to *administer the consecrated elements* to the communicants, who devoutly kneel at the chancel.[8] The Church of Rome administers the *bread alone* to the laity. But such a partial sacrament, unauthorized by Scripture, was un-

[7] By the rubric in the Communion Office of the American Church, the minister, at the consecration of new elements, is to repeat the whole of the form of consecration from the words *All Glory be to thee,* &tc., to the words *partakers of his most blessed body and blood.*

[8] As our Savior blessed and gave thanks, both for the bread and wine, this, in the nature of it, must be supposed to have been performed in a posture of adoration, our Savior being remarkable for outward reverence in devotion. Had the table gesture been the one used at the institution of the Eucharist, yet it is very reasonable, since the circumstances are now different, our demeanour should also vary. The posture that might be suitable to the apostles is not now suitable in us. They conversed with Christ as man: we worship him in his glory; and do not converse with him in the sacrament, but as he is

known for a thousand years after CHRIST.

When the communicants have received these solemn pledges of the mercy of GOD, they are considered as restored to his favour and then address him in the *Lord's Prayer* as their reconciled Father. The *prayer* which follows is a solemn and devout acknowledgment of the goodness of GOD in this holy sacrament, and a humble supplication of his grace to preserve his people in their fellowship with him through JESUS CHRIST. After which the faithful proceed to praise GOD in the exulting and animating strains of the *Gloria in Excelsis*; and they are then dismissed by the Bishop or Priest with a solemn form of *benediction.* An Office for the Communion more solemn, appropriate, sublime, and affecting could not be devised.[9]

Christians are called to participate of the holy communion by the *command* of their blessed LORD, to whom they are bound by the dearest ties of *gratitude.* This holy ordinance is the instituted *mean* by which they are to derive from the Redeemer the consoling and strengthening succours of his grace and mercy. It is admirably calculated to excite and cherish every holy disposition in the soul. To abstain from it discovers the highest folly and the most criminal insensibility to the exalted displays of divine love. It should therefore be the business of every Christian to partake of this divine ordinance at every opportunity, with that sincere penitence and faith, love and devotion to GOD which will ensure to him the inestimable blessings it is designed to convey.

---

spiritually present there. The practice of *kneeling* has subsisted in the Western Church for above twelve hundred years. Anciently in the East, they received it standing, but then it was as Eusebius expresses, *with fear and trembling, with silence and downcast eyes, bowing themselves in the posture of worship and adoration.* The negligent posture of *sitting* was introduced by the Arians who, denying the divinity of CHRIST, thought it no robbery to sit with him at the table.

[9.] The rubric at the end of the Communion Office forbids any of the consecrated elements which may remain to be taken out of the church, and directs that the minister and communicants shall reverently eat and drink the same.

(77) Anonymous
The Companion to the Altar
1815

It may be proper to examine our faith in Christ and his gospel before we come to this Sacrament. *Examine yourselves* (saith *Paul) whether ye be in the faith;* that is, try whether you do believe and embrace Christianity upon a rational and full conviction of its excellency and truth.

Faith in, which supposes a knowledge of the gospel of Christ, is absolutely required, in order to salvation, from all those who have heard it. *Mk.* 16:15,16, *And he said unto them* (that is, *Jesus* said unto his eleven Apostles) *Go ye into all the world and preach the gospel to every creature; he that believeth and is baptized shall be saved, but he that believeth not shall be damned.* So that he who hears the gospel preached but will not enter into nor believe and embrace it, upon the evidences of its truth and divinity, which are sufficient to convince and gain every sincere and unprejudiced person, is justly excluded from the salvation that it proposeth. And that because his unbelief proceeds from the depravity of his mind and is a willful crime and sin; and as he is shut out from salvation who disbelieves the gospel through nothing but his own wicked negligence and prejudice, so he should be debarred from Christian communion. For what is the death of Christ to him who doth not believe or regard him as a teacher sent from God, nor credit anything which he and his Apostles declared to be the will of God concerning man's present duty or future happiness. His wicked unbelief doth wholly disqualify him for any of the benefits of Christ's mediation, and therefore must render him utterly unfit for the commemoration of his death in the symbols of it that he himself hath instituted.

By partaking of the Sacrament of Christ's body as broken

and his blood as shed for the remission of sins, we profess our faith in a crucified Savior, which he can never do that hath none. There must be a firm and rational belief of the gospel in those who would be safe at the Sacrament and saved after it. And hence the Church requires faith in all her members. *Draw near with faith* (saith the priest) *and take this holy Sacrament to your comfort.* There should be in every communicant an explicit belief of all the great things contained in the gospel; particularly "That God did, out of his abounding mercy and goodness, send forth in the fullness of time his only-begotten Son the Lord Jesus Christ to condemn sin in the flesh; and obtain the pardon of it by laying down his life. That in order to this, JESUS, who had a being with God before the world was created and was the brightness of his Father's glory and the express image of his person, was conceived by the power of the Holy Ghost in the womb of the Virgin *Mary* and born of her without sin. That he preached the will of God to men and set them an example of all holy living in the human nature. That at last he died for our sins, and rose again the third day from the dead for our justification. That after he had given his Apostles sufficient instructions about his kingdom, he ascended up into heaven and sat down at the right hand of God where he ever liveth to make intercession for us. That being ascended, he sent forth his Spirit to inspire the Apostles and sanctify his Church. That he will come again in the glory of his Father, with all the holy angels and the trump of God to judge the living and dead according to their deeds; when the wicked and ungodly shall go away into everlasting punishment, but the righteous into life eternal. That whoever repents of his former sins and believeth in him, leading a life of holiness and obedience here now, shall, through the mediation of Christ, be pardoned, accepted, and eternally saved as to both body and soul: but that all they shall forever perish who continue impenitent unto their lives' end." These are some of the great articles of faith which we must believe if ever we are saved hereafter or accepted here; yea, we must believe everything that is a fundamental of Christianity, whether it be here inserted or left out. It is only for persons that believe this that the Sacrament is administered, now, or was instituted at first; and therefore he who doth not believe the gospel nor was ever baptized in the name of Christ has no right to come to the Lord's table. And how is it, O my soul, with thee in this respect? Art thou a believer or an infidel? Thou wast very early taken into Christ's Church by *baptism:* but hast thou not forfeited thy relation to it through unbelief of the truth? Consider, O my soul! that to believe explicitly is a thing of very great moment and necessity. Thou hast the gospel of Christ, which containeth all things necessary to be known and believed in order to thine eternal salvation. Thou mayest read and hear it every day, but dost thou believe all things contained in it as divine truth? Dost thou believe that Jesus was a teacher and Savior appointed by God, in obedience to whom thou art to believe and submit to Christ? Dost thou believe that all sins (saving that against the Holy Ghost) are pardoned, and every offering accepted, all blessings imparted, and every sincere penitent saved, only through the mediation of our Lord Jesus Christ? Dost thou believe that thou shalt (willing or unwilling, a saint or a sinner) one day appear before the judgment seat of Christ that thou mayest receive the things done in the body, according to that thou hast done, whether it be good or bad? Dost thou fully believe the doctrine, miracles, and gospel of Jesus? If thou dost but live according to this faith, and worthily frequent this Sacrament, then through him whom thou believest thou shalt be justified and saved. But examination may be recommended and considered . . . as it respects our knowledge of the nature, end, and intention of this Sacrament. It is a good understanding of this Christian institution that must fit us to pursue and obtain the gracious designs of it. And therefore it is necessary in the nature of things that we should understand the holy Sacrament before we partake of it. How shall we *discern the Lord's body or look up to Jesus the author and finisher of our faith, who for the joy that was set before him endured the cross, despising the shame,* unless we know that it was instituted by

Christ and it is to be observed by us as a commemoration of him as dying? How shall we fix in our minds a lasting sense of God's being propitious to men (that is, inclined to pardon and save them upon their repentance of all past sin, and persevering in a course of virtue for the future) through the death of his Son, the Lord Jesus Christ, as a sacrifice for the expiation of all sin? I say, how shall we fix in our minds a sense of God's readiness to forgive and save reformed sinners through the death of Christ, without we know that this Sacrament was instituted and is to be kept up as a perpetual commemoration of that death of Christ through which God dispenses his mercy and forgiveth the sins of all that do unfeignedly repent? It is impossible that we should worthily partake of this solemn institution of Christ without we know and observe the ends of it.

---

(78) **Anonymous**
The Companion for the Altar (contained within
*The New Week's Preparation for a Worthy Receiving
of the Lord's Supper as Recommended
and Appointed by The Church of England)*
1818

When it comes to your turn to make your offering, do not let the basin pass by you without putting something into it: for this reason, among others, that you may join in that part of the prayer for the Church militant wherein you beseech God to accept your alms; and you may depend upon it he will accept them as given to himself if they bear a proportion to your ability and are done in obedience to his commands and with an eye to his glory, as a grateful acknowledgment of his mercies to yourself and as a testimony of your dependence upon him for the continuance of them. With such reflections your present offering and all your other gifts to the services of religion and the uses of charity ought to be accompanied.

They that are poor and cannot give as they are disposed in their hearts must remember that the alms given on this occasion are not a matter of necessity but a free gift; and that their small contributions will, like the poor widow's two mites, be preferred to the richest oblations of the wealthy. And even he that hath nothing at all to give is invited freely to partake of these spiritual blessings without money and without price.

---

(79) **Anonymous**
A Companion to the Altar
1826

With what joy and thankfulness then should every good Christian commemorate this exceeding love of God in the salvation of sinners by Jesus Christ! This was the proper end and design of this institution, to perpetuate this wonderful love of Christ in laying down his life for us. *Do this in remembrance of me* saith our Savior a little before his crucifixion, which being a solemn command of "our Master and only Savior thus dying for us," we cannot refuse obedience thereunto without being guilty of the most horrible ingratitude and contempt of his divine authority. He hath appointed it for a solemn commemoration of his great love to us, in laying down his life for us men and for our salvation: and therefore he commands us to do it *in remembrance of him:* And St. *Paul* tells us that *as often as we eat this bread and drink this cup, we do show forth the Lord's death till he come.* As for those men, then, amongst us who profess themselves Christians and hope for salvation by Jesus Christ, not to pay obedience to this his command is a downright affront to his sacred Majesty.

. . .

In this sacrament of the Lord's Supper we have the pardon and remission of all our sins, the grace and assistance of God's Holy Spirit, and the hopes of eternal life and happiness freely offered unto us: And therefore had we no love, no regard, or reverence to the dying words of our crucified Savior, yet surely the consideration of our own present and future advantage might prevail with us to be more frequent at the Lord's table than we usually are.

Hitherto a communicant has been directed to set his heart right toward God: but this is not all; he must proceed farther and inquire how it stands toward his neighbors, since we are expressly forbidden, *Mt.* 5:23,24, to offer up any gift or oblation to God if our hearts are leavened with malice, hatred, or revenge. "If thou bring thy gift unto the altar and there rememberest that thy brother hath aught against thee, leave there thy gift before the altar and go thy way; first be reconciled to thy brother and then come and offer thy gift." Here you see that Christ prefers *mercy* before *sacrifice.* And it is generally agreed on by the ancient fathers that these words of our Savior do directly point at this sacrament, on purpose to oblige all communicants to forgive all manner of injuries "before they presume to eat of that bread or to drink of that cup." And it is expressly said, *Mt.* 6:14,15, that our prayers are not accepted nor our pardon sealed in heaven until such time as we *forgive men their trespasses;* and, to be sure, we can never be welcome or worthy guests at this heavenly feast where Jesus the Savior of penitents and the Prince of Peace is spiritually present unless our repentance reconcile us to God, and our charity to all mankind.

And this charity of the heart in forgiving injuries must likewise show itself by the hand in relieving the wants and necessities of the poor. We read that when this sacrament was administered in the Apostles' days, large collections of monies were then gathered for the maintenance of the poor clergy and laity. *Acts* 2:44,45,46, and 1 *Cor.* 16:1. . . . It was not determined how much every man should give, but all men were

341

exhorted and enjoined to offer something according to their ability. . . . And to be sure nothing within our power can so effectively recommend our prayers and devotions as this of charity: it being well observed, *Matt.* 6, that our Savior hath enclosed *alms* between *prayer* and *fasting,* and therefore they are called its two wings, without which it will never fly so high as the throne of God. While *Cornelius* was fasting and praying we read that an angel from heaven was dispatched to him with this happy message: *Thy prayers and thine alms are come up for a memorial before God,* Acts 10:4. *He that hath pity upon the poor lendeth unto the Lord; and that which he hath given will he pay him again.* Prov. 19: 17. *Charge them that are rich in this world that they be rich in good works, ready to distribute, willing to communicate, laying up in store for themselves a good foundation against the time to come, that they may lay hold on eternal life.* 1 Tim. 6:17,18,19. *Do ye not know that they who minister about holy things live of the sacrifice, and they who wait at the altar are partakers with the altar? Even so hath the Lord also ordained that they who preach the Gospel should live of the Gospel,* 1 Cor. 9:13,14. *If we have sown unto you spiritual things, is it a great thing if we shall reap your worldly things?* 1 Cor. 11.

. . .

And when the communicant has thus far advanced toward the altar in his *examination, repentance,* &tc., he must not forget another excellent preparative belonging to this duty of communicating worthily, which although it be not mentioned in our church catechism, yet it is always implied as a necessary part of our sacramental preparation; that is, *prayer,* private and public—a duty upon which all our present and future blessings depend, *Mt.* 7:7,8, and 21,22. And so near a relation hath this duty of prayer with this sacrament that all those blessings therein contained and promised are only in return to our prayers. And no doubt but that man, who makes a conscientious practice of this duty in his closet and at church, can never be unprepared for this sacrament nor want a title to God's peculiar favour and blessing; *For the eyes of the Lord are over the righteous, and his ears are open unto their prayers,* 1 *Pet.* 3: 12. The constant exercise of *prayer* is the best method to get the mastery over all our evil inclinations and corrupt affections, and to overcome our vicious habits. It preserves a lively sense of God and religion in our minds and fortifies us against those temptations that assault us; it spiritualizes our nature, raises our souls above this world, and supports us under the troubles and calamities of this life by sanctifying such afflictions. It leads us gradually to the perfection of a Christian life and preserves that union between God and our souls which feeds our spiritual life with grace and goodness; without it, we in vain pretend to discharge those Christian duties incumbent on us or to prosper in our temporal affairs, which must have God's blessing to crown them with success. And as prayer in general has those great blessings and advantages attending it, so give me leave to suggest to you under this head that those public prayers and devotions which we offer unto God in our churches are not only more acceptable to him, but also much more edifying and advantageous to ourselves. They cannot but be more acceptable to God, because thereby his honour and glory is much more considerably advanced and maintained in the world than by our private devotions. By these outward *signs* and *tokens* we publicly declare to all the world that inward regard and esteem which we have for his divine perfections and goodness: Hereby we *let our light so shine before men that they may see our good works and glorify our Father which is in heaven, Mt.* 5:16. There is no duty in Scripture more frequently commanded, none more earnestly pressed upon us, than this of public prayer. We have the example of all good men in all ages for it, and of Christ himself, who was daily in the temple and in the synagogues and, no question, frequented those places at the usual hours of prayer, because then he had the fairest opportunity from those public assemblies to instruct and to exhort to *faith and repentance.* Secondly, we may expect greater blessings and success to our requests and desires when we join in the public prayers of our church than from private, because our Savior has, in a special manner, promised in such assemblies his immediate presence, that

343

"where two or three are gathered together in his name, there will he be in the midst of them." Which he hath nowhere said of private prayer, though both are very good; nay, both are absolutely necessary for the beginning and ending of a Christian life; and it is a very bad sign of some evil principle or other for any man to be much a stranger to the house of prayer, which is one of the greatest blessings and privileges (if we know how to value the same) that we can have in this world, and has always been accounted such among all wise and good.

---

(80) **Samuel Taylor Coleridge**
poet
Notes on the Book of Common Prayer
1827

The best preparation for taking this sacrament, better than any or all of the books or tracts composed for this end, is to read over and over again, and often on your knees—at all events with a kneeling and praying heart—the Gospel according to St. *John*, till your mind is familiarized to the contemplation of Christ, the Redeemer and Mediator of mankind, yea, and of every creature, as the living and self-subsisting Word, the very truth of all true being, and the very being of all enduring truth; the reality, which is the substance and unity of all reality; *the light which lighteth every man,* so that what we call reason, is itself a light from that light, *lumen a luce,* as the Latin more distinctly expresses this fact. But it is not merely light, but therein is life; and it is the life of Christ, the co-eternal Son of God, that is the only true life-giving light of men. We are assured, and we believe that Christ is God; God manifested in the flesh. As God, he must be present entire in every creature— (for how can God, or indeed any spirit, exist in parts?)—but he is said to dwell in the regenerate, to come to them who receive him by faith in his name, that is, in his power and influence; for this is the meaning of the word "name" in Scripture when applied to God or his Christ. Where true belief exists, Christ is not only present with or among us—for so he is in every man, even the most wicked—but to us and for us. *That was the true light, which lighteth every man that cometh into the world. He was in the world, and the world was made by him, and the world knew him not. But as many as received him, to them gave he power to become the sons of God, even to them that believe in his name; which were born, not of blood, nor of the will of the flesh, nor of the will of man, but of God. And the Word was made flesh, and dwelt among us.* John 1:9–14. Again—*We will come unto him, and make our abode with him. Jn.* 14:23. As truly and as really as your soul resides constitutively in your living body, so truly, really, personally, and substantially does Christ dwell in every regenerate man.

After this course of study, you may then take up and peruse sentence by sentence the communion service, the best of all comments on the Scriptures appertaining to this mystery.

---

(81) **J.P.K. Henshaw**
Rector of St. Peter's, Baltimore, Bishop of Rhode Island
**The Communicant's Guide, or, An Introduction
to the Sacrament of the Lord's Supper**
1831

Among the many causes of gratitude to Almighty God which distinguish our lot as Protestant Episcopalians, it is not one of the least that we are favoured with a scriptural and established LITURGY; which is entitled to the warmest commendation, not only as a directory for public worship, but also as a standard and preservative of sound doctrine.

The Prayer Book has been beautifully and appropriately styled "the daughter of the Bible"; and, probably, there is no other work of human composition which has embodied so much of the substance and spirit of the heavenly Oracles. Extracts from the Bible, in the form of Gospels, Epistles, and Psalter, constitute the greater part of the volume—and throughout the collects and prayers the spirit of the Divine Word breathes and glows and animates the whole. What can be more chaste and spiritual than its devotional services? What more humble and meek than its penitential confessions? What more fervent and comprehensive than its acts of intercession? What more full, ardent, and seraphic than its adorations and thanksgivings? How many of the followers of Christ in this day have felt their hearts glow with heavenly ardor—as if touched with a live coal from the altar—and experienced the sublime delights of spiritual communion in the use of those prayers and praises in which saints and martyrs of every age have poured forth their devotions to the Lord? And eternity only can disclose the multitude of instances in which the use of them has alleviated the pains of disease, assuaged the fears of the mariner amidst the terrors of the ocean, cheered the desolations of the prison, and softened the bed of death.

The Liturgy is entitled to veneration not only as a devotional work, but as a compendium of sound Christian theology. All the fundamental and important doctrines of the gospel are interwoven throughout its various offices; and while our congregations statedly use it they will be secured against the introduction of gross and flagrant heresy.

· · ·

What would have been the state of our branch of the Christian church had we been destitute of a fixed, sound, and spiritual Liturgy, God only knows. It has always preserved us from the open and avowed rejection of orthodox doctrine. And in former times, when the Pelagian and other heresies have been dealt out from some of our pulpits, evangelical prayers and scriptural instructions, as a sure antidote to the evil, continued to be administered from the desk. The pure flame which was first lighted up by Christ and his Apostles—and again rekindled at the reformation, has continued to burn in our Prayer Book, unquenched by the floods of heresy and false philosophy; and has, in successive ages, illuminated the path of many a traveler on his way to the heavenly Zion. We believe that the Liturgy is, under God, next to the Bible, the standard around which many of the soldiers of the cross who now disregard it will one day rally; next to the Bible, we believe it is the ark in which the truth as it is in Jesus will be preserved to the end of time.

Every office in our Liturgy is excellent in its kind, and may lay claim to as great a freedom from error as is consistent with the acknowledged fact that its authors were uninspired men, subject to the infirmities of our common nature. But the "order for the administration of the Lord's Supper" is a complete service in itself. Here we may find the excellencies of the ancient Liturgies condensed. It contains instruction as to the most important graces and duties of the Christian; acts of humiliation and confession; forms of supplication for ourselves and intercession for others; solemn professions of faith in the great doctrines of our holy religion—and the most fervent ascriptions of thanksgiving and praise for all the mercies we have received, whether temporal or spiritual.

If all the rest of the Prayer Book were lost, yet if this office were preserved, everything would be retained that is essential to public worship.

So admirably adapted is this service to its designed end that we might easily deduce from it all that is necessary to be known respecting the nature of the Lord's Supper, the benefits to be expected from it, the qualifications required in its recipients, and the obligations which it imposes upon them. There could not, perhaps, be a more useful treatise on the sacrament than a judicious and spiritual commentary upon this valuable office. But the preceding pages have been so much enriched by copious extracts from it that we must forego the pleasure and benefit of a particular analysis and content ourselves by giving, in this concluding chapter, a cursory glance at its different parts.[1]

The Church requires her children at all times, and especially when about to enter upon any important engagement, to realize their own ignorance and weakness and implore light and succour from above. Accordingly, this service is commenced upon our knees: and we are first required (the Lord's prayer having been previously used in the morning prayer) to beseech "Almighty God, unto whom all hearts are open, all desires known, and from whom no secrets are hid," that he would "cleanse the thoughts of our hearts by the inspiration of his Holy Spirit; that we may perfectly love him, and worthily magnify his holy name."

How important is it, that we should enter into the spirit of this affecting PRAYER! So manifold are our infirmities, so deep our corruptions, so fickle our minds, and so inconstant our purposes of good, that unless the thoughts of our hearts are cleansed by the inspiration of the Spirit, we can present nothing to God but an offering of pollution. And unless He works in us to will and to do of his good pleasure, even the glowing sentences of devotion contained in this service will come freezing from our lips; and our participation in the sacrament of the altar will be but a lifeless piece of formality and increase the already accumulated load of our transgressions. This feeling of dependence on the Holy Ghost, as the author of all good

[1.] The general usage of modern days is to introduce this service as a component part of the Morning Prayer on communion days; and in many churches a part of it is thus used on all Sundays and holy days. But originally it was a distinct service, and used at a different time from the Morning Prayer. It is worthy of reflection on the part of the authorities of the church whether the blending of separate services, each complete in itself, into one, does not extend our morning worship to an unreasonable length; and thus increase the difficulty of winning those who are now aliens from our communion, and at the same time lead many of our own members (the aged, the infirm and others) to view that as a penance which should be to them a source of satisfaction and delight? If there should be a return to primitive practice in this respect, might we not reasonably hope that our church would more rapidly "enlarge the place of her habitation," and that the comfort and edification of her members would be promoted thereby?

thoughts, holy affections, and righteous works with which we commence the service, should be kept up till its close: for without it we cannot hope for communion with God: without it we cannot possibly partake of the privileges of the true "circumcision, who worship God in the spirit, rejoice in Christ Jesus, and have no confidence in the flesh."

We are next called upon to listen to the TEN COMMANDMENTS, which the officiating minister, like another Moses, pronounces in our hearing in the name and by the authority of Almighty God. The moral law, which is a transcript of the divine perfections and a summary of the divine will, still performs the important office of a "schoolmaster to bring us to Christ." It is the most powerful instrument which the Holy Spirit employs in "convincing men of sin," and making them flee for refuge to the hope set before them in the gospel. While the different precepts are read, distinctly and solemnly, we should feel as if Jehovah himself were addressing to us the great things of his law. And if holy Moses at Sinai said, "I exceedingly fear and quake," how should our guilty souls tremble in the presence of that pure Lawgiver whose will we have so often, so deliberately transgressed! How profoundly should we meditate upon the spirituality and broad extent of the commandments! with what self-abhorrence and regret should we call to mind our numerous transgressions in thought, word, and deed! How fervently should we pray—"Lord have mercy upon us, and incline our hearts to keep this law!"

Then is given that admirable summary of the commandments in which He, "who came not to destroy the law, but to fulfil," teaches us that it is comprised in one word—LOVE. Every pious heart should here offer up some such ejaculation as this, "O that the wonderful act of God's love in the redemption of sinners by Jesus Christ, may constrain me to love Him supremely, and my fellow creatures for his sake!"

Immediately after this follows a most appropriate prayer that God would "direct, sanctify and govern both our hearts and bodies in the way of his laws and in the works of his commandments—and preserve us in body and soul, both here and ever." The Collect, Epistle, and Gospel for the day, are then read, and afterwards the sermon is delivered. These I shall pass over with this one remark: we should listen with profound attention, reverence, and faith to the truths of the gospel, whether read or expounded by the ministers of Jesus, and pray that they may be accompanied with power and that we may "receive with meekness that engrafted word which is able to save our souls."

We come next to that part of the office which is more immediately connected with the administration of the holy sacrament. And it seems peculiarly proper that the disciples of Christ, in celebrating this memorial of the most amazing act of God's love to man, should begin it with an exercise of love, and give proof of their discipleship by charity to their poorer brethren. This, accordingly, we are required to do, while the Minister reads several SENTENCES OF SCRIPTURE which in the clearest manner, and by the most affecting motives, teach us to "do good unto all men: and especially unto them that are of the household of faith."

The primitive Christians were in the habit of laying by on every Lord's-day, as God had prospered them, a portion of their substance to be used in holy charity, and "out of their deep poverty, the riches of their liberality abounded." But, alas! how many communicants in modern days give but a stinted offering at the monthly sacramental collections! It is true, there are various calls made upon their charity at other times which were unknown to the early disciples; but they should, notwithstanding, show at every communion season that they are disposed not only to remember, but also to imitate "the grace of our Lord Jesus Christ, who though he was rich, yet for our sakes became poor, that we through his poverty, might be rich."

It may be that in many congregations, a small gift from each communicant will be sufficient to supply the wants of the poor belonging to it. But this, though a primary, is by no means the

350

exclusive object of the contribution. The Rubric speaks of "alms for the poor, and *other devotions* of the people." If the amount collected be more than sufficient for the first named object, the balance may be very properly and usefully employed in the distribution of Bibles, prayer books, tracts and other useful publications among the needy; or be thrown as a consecrated offering into the treasury of the Missionary or some kindred society. Let each communicant, therefore, while the sentences of the *"Offertory"* are read, reflect upon this interesting department of Christian duty, and seek for the same commendation which was passed upon Cornelius: "thy prayers and thine alms are come up for a memorial before God."

The "PRAYER FOR THE WHOLE STATE OF CHRIST'S CHURCH MILITANT," which follows the offertory, is one of the most noble and comprehensive forms of devotion ever composed. As we have just before manifested our charity for the indigent members of the household of faith, we do now, in the use of this sublime prayer, exhibit our love for the whole human family by making intercessions for all men. We offer up our prayers, not only for our fellow worshipers of the same congregation, but for the widely scattered members of "the Universal Church"—that "all who confess God's holy name may agree in the truth of his holy word and live in unity and godly love." We intercede, not only in behalf of those in authority over us, but of "all Christian rulers"; that God would "so direct and dispose their hearts that they may truly and impartially administer justice, to the punishment of wickedness and vice, and the maintenance of true religion and virtue." We offer up our earnest petitions, not only for those who watch for our souls and are over us in the Lord; but for "all Bishops and other Ministers" of the gospel of every name; that God would "give them grace to set forth his true and lively word, and rightly and duly administer his holy sacraments." Nor do we forget to implore "comfort and succour for all those who, in this transitory life, are in trouble, sorrow, need, sickness, or any other adversity—and to bless God's holy name for all his servants

351

departed this life in his faith and fear; beseeching him to give us grace so to follow their good examples that with them *we* may be partakers of his heavenly kingdom."

In the offering up of this prayer, there should be, on the part of every communicant, the most lively exercise of devotion and charity. The Church here imitates the intercession of our Great High Priest; and all her Ministers and members should seek for a large portion of the spirit by which he is animated in pleading our cause before the throne of his Heavenly Father.

At the close of this admirable prayer, the communicants should rise from their knees, and, in a standing or sitting posture, reverently listen to the EXHORTATION which the officiating Minister, in the name of the Master of the feast, then addresses to all who propose to come to the holy communion.

The principal design of this exhortation is to guard the table against the intrusion of unworthy guests, and enforce the Apostolic exhortation, *"let a man examine himself, and so let him eat of that bread, and drink of that cup."* While it is being read, each communicant (who, it is to be presumed, however, has previously more carefully done it) should now briefly summon himself to trial again, and inquire as in the presence of the Searcher of hearts whether he has the repentance, faith, gratitude and love which are necessary to a profitable reception of this holy ordinance.

If our hearts condemn us not, and conscience bears witness that our self-inquisition has been sincere, we may listen with gratitude and joy to the following INVITATION: "Ye who do truly and earnestly repent you of your sins, and are in love and charity with your neighbors, and intend to lead a new life following the commandments of God and walking from henceforth in his holy ways; *draw near with faith, and take this Holy Sacrament to your comfort."*

This invitation, though spoken by the minister, is delivered in the name of his Master and therefore should be listened to as if coming from Christ himself. Who, on hearing it, can fail to exclaim—"behold, what manner of love is this?" Every communicant should say in his heart, "O blessed Jesus! how great is thy mercy—how infinite thy condescension—in asking me to appear as a guest at thy table! It is a distinction which angels might envy—and shall I dare to decline it? No, Lord, I accept it with cheerfulness and gratitude! 'I will go unto the altar of God: unto God, my exceeding joy!' "

But what are we, and what is our father's house, that the Lord should confer such honour upon us? Wherewith shall we come before the Lord and bow ourselves before the high God? Is there anything in us to entitle us to this privilege? Shall we proudly think ourselves worthy to draw nigh to God in this way of his appointment? Assuredly not. Every proud and self-righteous feeling should be banished from our minds. We must offer "the sacrifice of a broken and contrite heart"; and "make our humble CONFESSION to Almighty God, devoutly kneeling."

Since Christ's sufferings are here commemorated, it is very reasonable we should confess our sins which were the causes of them: and since we hope to have our pardon sealed, we ought first, with shame and sorrow, to own our transgressions, for his honour who so freely forgives them; which the congregation here does in words so apposite and pathetical that if their repentance be answerable to the form, it is impossible it should ever be more hearty and sincere.

In the use of this most appropriate and solemn form, our souls should be prostrated in the lowest self-abasement and penetrated with the deepest contrition. "Every tongue" also should "confess to God." How greatly would it add to the solemnity of this service if the whole body of communicants, bowed as a company of transgressors before God, would *audibly* "acknowledge and bewail their manifold sins and wickedness which they from time to time most grievously have committed, by thought, word, and deed, against the Divine Majesty; provoking most justly his wrath and indignation!" How striking would be the effect if they could be *heard* unitedly protesting, "we do earnestly repent, and are heartily sorry for these our misdoings; the remembrance of them is grievous unto us; the burthen of them is intolerable!" How would it appear like taking the kingdom of heaven by a holy "violence" which nothing could resist to hear a large company of penitent believers *"lifting up their voices with one accord,"* uttering the pathetic cry—"HAVE MERCY UPON US! HAVE MERCY UPON US, MOST MERCIFUL FATHER! for thy Son our Lord Jesus Christ's sake forgive us all that is past; and grant that we may ever hereafter serve and please thee in newness of life, to the honour and glory of thy name through Jesus Christ our Lord. Amen!"

While the body of communicants remain upon their knees, the Presbyter (or Bishop, if he be present) who has just united with them in the same penitential confession rises to pronounce the ABSOLUTION.

· · ·

If it be consolatory to humble penitents to listen to the declarations and prayers of him who is their "servant for Jesus's sake," how much greater must be their consolation when he directs their attention to Jesus himself; saying: "hear what COMFORTABLE WORDS our Savior Christ saith unto all who truly turn to him."

Every ear should be opened to hear the gracious language of the Redeemer: for the words that he speaks unto us, "they are spirit and they are life."

"Come unto me, all ye that travail and are heavy laden, and I will refresh you. (St. *Mt.* 11: 28.)

"So God loved the world, that he gave his only begotten Son, to the end that all that believe in him, should not perish, but have everlasting life." (St. *Jn.* 3: 16.)

Well, indeed, may these be called "comfortable words." That they may prove so to us, we should consider ourselves individually addressed and apply them to our hearts.

· · ·

After we have exercised our charity, repentance, and faith, the next part of the office is thanksgiving, which is so considerable a part of our present duty that it hath given name to the whole

354

and caused it to be called the *Eucharist,* or *Sacrifice of praise.*

• • •

Having, therefore, exercised our faith upon the foregoing sentences and so got above this world, we are now ready to go into the other and to join with the glorified saints and angels in praising and adoring that God who hath done so great things for us. In order to this, the Minister calls upon us to *lift up our hearts,* viz. by a most quick and lively faith in the most high God, the supreme governor of the whole world; which being ready to do, we immediately answer, *we lift them up unto the Lord;* and so casting off all thoughts of the world turn our minds to God alone.

And our hearts being now all elevated together, and in a right posture to celebrate the praises of God, the Minister invites us to join with him in doing it, saying, *let us give thanks unto our Lord God:* which the people having consented to and approved of by saying *it is meet and right so to do;* he turns himself to the Lord's table and acknowledgeth to the Divine Majesty— *it is very meet, right, and our bounden duty that we should at all times and in all places give thanks unto thee, O Lord, [Holy Father] Almighty, everlasting God.*

How can any Christian fail to give a warm response to this suitable acknowledgment by calling upon his soul and all that is within him to laud and bless God's holy name! If the Lord's redeemed ones should hold their peace upon such an occasion, surely "the stones would cry out!"

The Minister now looking upon himself and the rest of the congregation as communicants with the Church triumphant; and all of us apprehending ourselves, by faith, as in the midst of that blessed society; we join with them in singing forth the praises of the most high God, Father, Son, and Holy Ghost; saying—"THEREFORE WITH ANGELS, AND ARCHANGELS, AND WITH ALL THE COMPANY OF HEAVEN, WE LAUD AND MAGNIFY THY GLORIOUS NAME; EVERMORE PRAISING THEE AND SAYING, HOLY, HOLY, HOLY, LORD GOD OF HOSTS: HEAVEN AND EARTH ARE FULL OF THY GLORY; GLORY BE TO THEE, O LORD MOST HIGH. AMEN."

That the Angels are present in worshiping assemblies, and especially at the celebration of the Holy Communion, has been a generally received opinion among Christians. "For since Jesus by his death has united heaven and earth, it is fit that, in this commemoration of his passion, we should begin to unite our voices with the heavenly choir, with whom we hope to praise him to all eternity. For which end, the Christians of the very first ages took this Hymn into their office for the sacrament, being of divine original (*Is.* 6.3), and from the word *Holy* thrice repeated in it, called by the Greeks the *Trisagium*, or thrice Holy."

The PROPER PREFACES which follow have been provided that we may, when receiving the sacrament on a Festival, in addition to the general eucharistical offering, present our special thanks to God for the mercy commemorated at that season.

In the PRAYER which is directed to be said by the Minister "in the name of all who shall receive the Communion," there is a renewed call for the exercise of the same feelings of humiliation which have been previously expressed in the confession, accompanied by the most ardent desire for communion with Christ. With what cordial humility should we join in the acknowledgment: *"we are not worthy so much as to gather up the crumbs under thy table!"* With what holy importunity should we concur in the petition: *"Grant us, therefore, gracious Lord, so to eat the flesh of thy dear Son Jesus Christ, and to drink his blood, that our sinful bodies may be made clean by his body, and our souls washed through his most precious blood, and that we may evermore dwell in him, and he in us! Amen."*

The officiating Minister, having "so ordered the bread and wine that he may with the more readiness and decency break the bread before the people and take the cup into his hands," then offers up the PRAYER OF CONSECRATION, consisting of three parts—*the words of Institution, the Oblation,* and *the Invocation.*

Of this prayer, which is used by the Minister alone, we may safely remark that it is perfect in its kind and most admirably adapted to its end. While it is said, the people should fix the eye of faith upon the divine Institutor of this blessed memorial and mentally join in the petitions, intercessions, and thanksgivings contained in it; and especially in the consecration of "themselves, their souls, and bodies to be a reasonable, holy, and living sacrifice unto" God, which it avows on the part of all who are present at the solemnity.

All things being now so done that the sacrament may be "duly ministered according to Christ's ordinance, in all those things that of necessity are requisite to the same;" the communicants unite in singing a HYMN, or part of a hymn, that by the soothing influence of devotional music they may be prepared, with more perfect tranquility and self-possession, to engage in the solemn act of receiving the consecrated symbols.

• • •

The delivery of the elements to the people follows; and the form of words by which it is accompanied is of the most solemn and affecting kind. At giving the bread, the Minister says, *"The body of our Lord Jesus Christ, which was given for thee, preserve thy body and soul unto everlasting life: Take and eat this, in remembrance that Christ died for thee, and feed on him in thy heart by faith, with thanksgiving."* At the close of the petition contained in the former part of the sentence, the communicant may mentally ejaculate: "Amen—so be it! Merciful God, may I receive thy Son, and with him, eternal life!" And at the close of the direction given in the latter part; "blessed Jesus! I do gratefully remember thy dying love: O, for a lively faith to realize my personal interest in thy merits, and feed upon thee as the appropriate nourishment of my soul!" The bread should be received in the *open and naked hand* as an indication of our receiving Christ into our hearts by faith.

When delivering the cup, the Minister says: *"the blood of our Lord Jesus Christ, which was shed for thee, preserve thy body and soul unto everlasting life: drink this in remembrance that Christ's blood was shed for thee, and be thankful."* Here the recipient may again ejaculate: "Amen! May my soul be washed in the fountain opened for sin and uncleanness. May the precious blood of the everlasting covenant be sprinkled upon my conscience, cleansing me from dead works that I may serve the living God in this world—and in the world to come join in the heavenly song to Him who loved us and washed us from our sins in his own blood—be glory and dominion for ever and ever, Amen!"

Every communicant after having returned from the holy table to his seat should offer up fervent thanks to God for the privilege he has enjoyed; and keep his mind profitably exercised while others are partaking by reading portions of Scripture; meditating upon the mercies of redemption; and imploring blessings for himself, the Ministers of Jesus, the whole company of believers, and the world at large.

When all have communicated, we again assume the attitude of supplication and as with one heart and voice repeat the LORD'S PRAYER.

This divine form, being always appropriate, has a place in every distinct office of the Church; and never can it be more suitably used than when, after having received in this sealing ordinance fresh evidence of our adoption, we are enabled to say with filial confidence—*"Our Father who art in Heaven,"* &c.

Then follows the concluding THANKSGIVING: and assuredly, now if ever, we shall experience the emotions of a grateful heart. This form expresses the highest feelings of Christian confidence and joy. In it, we bless God that, in the rite which we have just celebrated, he has "assured us of his favour and goodness towards us, and that we are very members incorporate in the mystical body of his Son, which is the blessed company of all faithful people; and are also heirs through hope, of his everlasting kingdom." Are we indeed raised to such honours, and partakers of such privileges, in virtue of our "high calling of God in Christ Jesus?" Can we, then, love him with too much ardour? or serve him with too much fidelity? How earnestly should we say, "we most humbly beseech thee, O Heavenly Father, so to assist us with thy grace, that we may continue in that holy fellowship, and do all such good works as thou hast prepared for us to walk in, through Jesus Christ our Lord; to whom with thee and the Holy Ghost, be all honour and glory, world without end! Amen."

In imitation of our Lord, who after the institution of this ordinance sang a hymn with his disciples, we now join in singing or saying that sublime hymn "the GLORIA IN EXCELSIS; or, some proper hymn from the selection." No comment that I could make would serve to give to those who are in the habit of using it a more vivid conception of the inimitable beauties of this divine song. It would be like an attempt to improve the tints of the rainbow with earthly colours. I therefore abandon it in despair, presuming only to offer this one remark: if there are some parts of it which the humblest sinner upon earth would find appropriate to his feelings, there are others which the loftiest spirit in heaven would not find unsuitable to his enraptured acts of adoration.

In bringing this work to a conclusion, the author can indulge no better hope and offer no better prayer in behalf of its readers than that they may all enter into the spirit of the various parts of that admirable service which has now passed under our review.

Illustration from a
Book of Common Prayer, 1815.

CHAPTER EIGHT

Marriage

(82) **Anonymous**
Second Book of Homilies
An Homily of the State of Matrimony
1563 / 1571

The word of Almighty God doth testify and declare whence the original beginning of matrimony cometh and why it is ordained. It is instituted of God, to the intent that man and woman should live lawfully in a perpetual friendly fellowship, to bring forth fruit, and to avoid fornication: by which means a good conscience might be preserved on both parties in bridling the corrupt inclinations of the flesh within the limits of honesty; for God hath straitly forbidden all whoredom and uncleanness, and hath from time to time taken grievous punishments of this inordinate lust as all stories and ages hath declared. Furthermore, it is also ordained that the Church of God and his kingdom might by this kind of life be conserved and enlarged, not only in that God giveth children by his blessing, but also in that they be brought up by the parents godly in the knowledge of God's word; that thus the knowledge of God and true religion might be delivered by succession from one to another, that finally many might enjoy that everlasting immortality.

Wherefore, forasmuch as matrimony serveth as well to avoid sin and offense as to increase the kingdom of God, you, as all other which enter that state, must acknowledge this benefit of God with pure and thankful minds, for that he hath so ruled your hearts that ye follow not the example of the wicked world, who set their delight in filthiness of sin, where both of you stand in the fear of God and abhor all filthiness. For that is surely the singular gift of God, where the common example of the world declareth how the devil hath their hearts bound and entangled in diverse snares, so that they in their wifeless state run into open abominations without any grudge of their conscience. Which sort of men that liveth so desperately and filthily, what damnation tarrieth for them St. *Paul* describeth it to them, saying, *Neither whoremongers, neither adulterers shall inherit the kingdom of God.* This horrible judgment of God ye be escaped through his mercy, if so be that ye live inseparably according to God's ordinance.

But yet I would not have you careless, without watching. For the devil will assay to attempt all things to interrupt and hinder your hearts and godly purpose if ye will give him any entry. For he will either labour to break this godly knot once begun betwixt you, or else at the least he will labour to encumber it with divers griefs and displeasures. And this is his principal craft, to work dissension of hearts of the one from the other; that, whereas now there is pleasant and sweet love betwixt you, he will in the stead thereof bring in most bitter and unpleasant discord. And surely that same adversary of ours doth, as it were from above, assault man's nature and condition. For this folly is ever from our tender age grown up with us, to have a desire to rule, to think highly by ourself, so that none thinketh it meet to give place to another. That wicked vice

362

of stubborn will and self-love is more meet to break and to dissever the love of heart than to preserve concord. Wherefore married persons must apply their minds in most earnest wise to concord, and must crave continually of God the help of his Holy Spirit so to rule their hearts and to knit their minds together that they be not dissevered by any division of discord.

This necessity of prayer must be oft in the occupying and using of married persons, that ofttime the one should pray for the other lest hate and debate do arise betwixt them. And because few do consider this thing, but more few do perform it, (I say, to pray diligently,) we see how wonderfully the devil deludeth and scorneth this state, how few matrimonies there be without chidings, brawlings, tauntings, repentings, bitter cursings, and fightings. Which things whosoever doth commit, they do not consider that it is the instigation of the ghostly enemy who taketh great delight therein: for else they would with all earnest endeavour strive against these mischiefs, not only with prayer but also with all possible diligence; yea, they would not give place to the provocation of wrath, which stirreth them either to such rough and sharp words or stripes which is surely compassed by the devil: whose temptation, if it be followed, must needs begin and weave the web of all miseries and sorrows. For this is most certainly true, that of such beginnings must needs ensue the breach of true concord in heart, whereby all love must needs shortly be banished. Then cannot it be but a miserable thing to behold, that yet they are of necessity compelled to live together, which yet cannot be in quiet together. And this is most customarily everywhere to be seen. But what is the cause thereof? Forsooth, because they will not consider the crafty trains of the devil, and therefore give not themselves to pray to God that he would vouchsafe to repress his power. Moreover, they do not consider how they promote the purpose of the devil in that they follow the wrath of their hearts while they threat one another, while they in their folly turn all upside down, while they will never give over their right, as they esteem it, yea, while many times they will not give over the wrong part indeed. Learn thou therefore, if thou desirest to be void of all these miseries, if thou desirest to live peaceably and comfortably in wedlock, how to make thy earnest prayer to God that he would govern both your hearts by his Holy Spirit, to restrain the devil's power whereby your concord may remain perpetually.

But to this prayer must be joined a singular diligence, whereof St. *Peter* giveth his precept, saying, *You husbands, deal with your wives according to knowledge, giving honour to the wife, as unto the weaker vessel, and as unto them that are heirs also of the grace of life, that your prayers be not hindered.* This precept doth peculiarly pertain to the husband: for he ought to be the leader and author of love in cherishing and increasing concord; which then shall take place if he will use measurableness and not tyranny, and if he yield some things to the woman. For the woman is a weak creature, not endowed with like strength and constancy of mind: therefore they be the sooner disquieted and they be the more prone to all weak affections and dispositions of mind, more than men be; and lighter they be and more vain in their fantasies and opinions. These things must be considered of the man, that he be not too stiff; so that he ought to wink at some things and must gently expound all things and to forbear.

Howbeit, the common sort of men do judge that such moderation should not become a man: for they say that it is a token of a womanish cowardice; and therefore they think that it is a man's part to fume in anger, to fight with fist and staff. Howbeit, howsoever they imagine, undoubtedly St. *Peter* doth better judge what should be seeming to a man and what he should most reasonably perform. For he saith reasoning should be used and not fighting. Yea, he saith more, that the woman ought to have a certain *honour* attributed to her; that is to say, she must be spared and borne with, the rather for that she is *the weaker vessel,* of a frail heart, inconstant, and with a word soon stirred to wrath. And therefore, considering these her frailties, she is to be the rather spared. By this means thou shalt not only

364

nourish concord but shalt have her heart in thy power and will; for honest natures will sooner be retained to do their duty rather by gentle words than by stripes. But he which will do all things with extremity and severity, and doth use always rigour in words and stripes, what will that avail in the conclusion? Verily nothing but that he thereby setteth forward the devil's work; he banisheth away concord, charity, and sweet amity, and bringeth in dissension, hatred, and irksomeness, the greatest griefs that can be in the mutual love and fellowship of man's life. Beyond all this, it bringeth another evil therewith; for it is the destruction and interruption of prayer. For in the time that the mind is occupied with dissension and discord there can be no true prayer used. For the Lord's Prayer hath not only a respect to particular persons, but to the whole universal; in the which we openly pronounce that we will forgive them which hath offended against us even as we ask forgiveness of our sins of God. Which thing how can it be done rightly when their hearts be at dissension? How can they pray each for other when they be at hate betwixt themselves? Now, if the aid of prayer be taken away, by what means can they sustain themselves in any comfort? For they cannot otherwise either resist the devil, or yet have their hearts stayed in stable comfort in all perils and necessities, but by prayer. Thus all discommodities, as well worldly as ghostly, follow this perverse testiness and cumberous fierceness in manners; which be more meet for brute beasts than for reasonable creatures. St. Peter doth not allow these things, but the devil desireth them gladly. Wherefore take the more heed. And yet a man may be a man although he doth not use such extremity, yea though he should dissemble some things in his wife's manners. And this is the part of a Christian man which both pleaseth God and serveth also in good use to the comfort of their marriage state.

Now as concerning the wife's duty. What shall become her? Shall she abuse the gentleness and humanity of her husband, and at her pleasure turn all things upside down? No surely; for that is far repugnant against God's commandment. For thus doth St. *Peter* preach to them; *Ye wives, be ye in subjection to obey your own husbands.* To obey is another thing than to control or command; which yet they may do to their children and to their family; but as for their husbands, them must they obey, and cease from commanding, and perform subjection. For this surely doth nourish concord very much when the wife is ready at hand at her husband's commandment, when she will apply herself to his will, when she endeavoureth herself to seek his contentment and to do him pleasure, when she will eschew all things that might offend him. For thus will most truly be verified the saying of the poet, "A good wife by obeying her husband shall bear the rule": so that he shall have a delight and a gladness the sooner at all times to return home to her. But on the contrary part, when the wives be stubborn, perverse, and malapert, their husbands are compelled thereby to abhor and flee from their own houses, even as they should have battle with their enemies.

Howbeit, it can scarcely be but that some offenses shall sometime chance betwixt them: for no man doth live without fault; specially for that the woman is the more frail part. Therefore let them beware that they stand not in their faults and willfulness; but rather let them acknowledge their follies and say, My husband, so it is that by my anger I was compelled to do this or that: forgive it me, and hereafter I will take better heed. Thus ought women the more readily to do the more they be ready to offend. And they shall not do this only to avoid strife and debate, but rather in the respect of the commandment of God, as St. Paul expresseth it in this form of words: *Let women be subject to their husbands, as to the Lord: for the husband is the head of the woman as Christ is the Head of the Church.* Here you understand that God hath commanded that ye should acknowledge the authority of the husband and refer to him the honour of obedience. And St. *Peter* saith in that same place afore rehearsed, that *holy matrons did sometimes deck themselves,* not with gold and silver, but in *putting their whole hope in God,* and in *obeying their husbands; as Sara obeyed Abraham, calling him lord: whose daughters ye be,* saith he, if ye follow her example. This sentence is very meet for women to print in their remembrance. Truth it is that they must specially feel the griefs and pains of their matrimony in that they relinquish the liberty of their own rule, in the pain of their travailing, in the bringing up of their children; in which offices they be in great perils and be grieved with great afflictions, which they might be without if they lived out of matrimony. But St. *Peter* saith that this is the chief ornament of *holy matrons,* in that they *set their hope* and trust *in God;* that is to say, in that they refused not from marriage for the business thereof, for the griefs and perils thereof, but committed all such adventures to God in most sure trust of help after that they have called upon his aid. O woman, do thou the like, and so shalt thou be most excellently beautified before God and all his angels and saints. And thou needest not to seek further for doing any better works. For, obey thy husband, take regard of his requests, and give heed unto him to perceive what he requireth of thee; and so shalt thou honour God, and live peaceably in thy house. And beyond this, God shall follow thee with his benediction that all things shall well prosper both to thee and to thy husband, as the Psalm saith. *Blessed is the man which feareth God and walketh in his ways. Thou shalt have the fruit of thine own hands; happy shalt thou be and well shall it go with thee. Thy wife shall be as a vine plentifully spreading about thy house. Thy children shall be as the young springs of the olives about thy table. Lo, thus shall that man be blessed,* saith David, *that feareth the Lord.*

This let the wife have ever in mind, the rather admonished thereto by the apparel of her head, whereby is signified that she is under covert and obedience of her husband. And, as that apparel is of nature so appointed to declare her subjection, so biddeth St. *Paul* that all other of her raiment should express both *shamefastness and sobriety.* For, if it be not lawful for the woman to have her head bare, but to bear thereon the sign of her power wheresoever she goeth, more is it required that she declare the thing that is meant thereby. And therefore these ancient women of the old world called their husbands lords,

367

and showed them reverence in obeying them.

But peradventure she will say that those men loved their wives indeed. I know that well enough and bear it well in mind. But when I do admonish you of your duties, then call not to consideration what their duties be. For when we ourselves do teach our children to obey us as their parents, or when we reform our servants and tell them that they should obey their masters, not only at the eye but as to the Lord; if they should tell us again our duties, we would not think it well done. For when we be admonished of our duties and faults, we ought not then to seek what other men's duties be. For though a man had a companion in his fault, yet should not he thereby be without his fault. But this must be only looked on, by what means thou mayest make thyself without blame. For Adam did lay the blame upon the woman, and she turned it unto the serpent; but yet neither of them was thus excused. And therefore bring not such excuses to me at this time, but apply all thy diligence to hear thine obedience to thy husband. For when I take in hand to admonish thy husband to love thee and to cherish thee, yet will I not cease to set out the law that is appointed for the woman, as well as I would require of the man what is written for his law. Go thou therefore about such things as becometh thee only, and show thyself tractable to thy husband. Or rather, if thou wilt obey thy husband for God's precept, then allege such things as be in his duty to do but perform thou diligently those things which the Lawmaker hath charged thee to do: for thus is it most reasonable to obey God if thou wilt not suffer thyself to transgress his law. He that loveth his friend seemeth to do no great thing; but he that honoureth him that is hurtful and hateful to him, this man is worthy much commendation. Even so think thou, if thou canst suffer an extreme husband thou shalt have a great reward therefore; but if thou lovest him only because he is gentle and courteous, what reward will God give thee therefore? Yet I speak not these things that I would wish the husbands to be sharp towards their wives; but I exhort the women that they would patiently bear the sharpness of their husbands. For when either parts do their best to perform their duties the one to the other, then followeth thereon great profit to their neighbors for their example's sake. For when the woman is ready to suffer a sharp husband, and the man will not extremely entreat his stubborn and troublesome wife, then be all things in quiet as in a most sure haven.

• • •

Whereupon do your best endeavour that after this sort ye use your matrimony, and so shall ye be armed on every side. Ye have escaped the snares of the devil and the unlawful lusts of the flesh, ye have the quietness of conscience by this institution of matrimony ordained by God: therefore use oft prayer to him that he would be present by you, that he would continue concord and charity betwixt you. Do the best ye can of your parts to custom yourselves to softness and meekness, and bear well in worth such oversights as chance; and thus shall your conversation be most pleasant and comfortable. And although (which can no otherwise be) some adversities shall follow, and otherwhiles now one discommodity, now another, shall appear, yet in this common trouble and adversity lift up both your hands unto heaven; call upon the help and assistance of God, the Author of your marriage; and surely the promise of relief is at hand. For Christ affirmeth in his Gospel, *Where two or three be gathered together in my Name, and be agreed, what matter soever they pray for, it shall be granted them of my heavenly Father.* Why therefore shouldest thou be afeard of the danger where thou hast so ready a promise and so nigh a help? Furthermore, you must understand how necessary it is for Christian folk to bear Christ's cross; for else we shall never feel how comfortable God's help is unto us.

Therefore give thanks to God for his great benefit in that ye have taken upon you this state of wedlock; and pray you instantly that Almighty God may luckily defend and maintain you therein that neither ye be overcome with any temptation nor with any adversity. But before all things take good heed that ye give no occasion to the devil to let and hinder your prayers by discord and dissension. For there is no stronger defense and stay in all our life than is prayer: in the which we may call for the help of God and obtain it; whereby we may win his blessing, his grace, his defense, and protection, so to continue therein to a better life to come. Which grant us he that died for us all: to whom be all honour and praise for ever and ever. Amen.

---

(83) **Richard Hooker**
*Master of the Temple, Rector of Bishopsbourne (Kent),
chief apologist for Anglicanism under Queen Elizabeth I*
Of the Laws of Ecclesiastical Polity, book V
1597

[On The Celebration of Matrimony]

In this world there can be no society durable otherwise than only by propagation. Albeit therefore single life be a thing more angelical and divine, yet sith the replenishing first of earth with blessed inhabitants and then of heaven with saints everlastingly praising God did depend upon conjunction of man and woman, he which made all things complete and perfect saw it could not be good to leave man without a helper unto the fore-alleged end.

In things which some further end doth cause to be desired choice seeketh rather proportion than absolute perfection of goodness. So that woman being created for man's sake to be his helper in regard to the end before-mentioned, namely the having and the bringing up of children, whereunto it was not possible they could concur unless there were subalternation between them, which subalternation is naturally grounded upon inequality because things equal in every respect are never willingly directed one by another: woman therefore was even in her first estate framed by nature not only after in time but inferior in excellency also unto man, howbeit in so due and sweet proportion as being presented before our eyes might be sooner perceived than defined. And even herein doth lie the reason why that kind of love which is the perfectest ground of wedlock is seldom able to yield any reason of itself.

Now that which is born of man must be nourished with far more travail, as being of greater price in nature and of slower pace to perfection than the offspring of any other creature besides. Man and woman being therefore to join themselves for such a purpose, they were of necessity to be linked with some secure and insoluble knot. The bond of wedlock hath been always more or less esteemed of as a thing religious and sacred. The title which the very heathens themselves do thereunto oftentimes give is *holy*. Those rites and orders which were instituted in the solemnization of marriage, the Hebrews term by the name of conjugal *Sanctifications*.

Amongst ourselves because sundry things appertaining unto the public order of matrimony are called in question by such as know not from whence those customs did first grow, to show briefly some true and sufficient reason of them shall not be superfluous, although we do not hereby intend to yield so far unto enemies of all church orders saving their own, as though everything were unlawful the true cause and reason whereof at the first might hardly perhaps be now rendered.

Wherefore to begin with the times wherein the liberty of marriage is restrained. "There is," saith Solomon, "a time for all things, a time to laugh and a time to mourn." That duties belonging unto marriage and offices appertaining to penance are things unsuitable and unfit to be matched together, the Prophets and Apostles themselves do witness. Upon which ground as we might right well think it marvellous absurd to see in a church a wedding on the day of a public fast, so likewise in the selfsame consideration our predecessors thought it not amiss to take away the common liberty of marriages during the time which was appointed for the preparation unto and for exercise of general humiliation by fasting and praying, weeping for sins.

As for the delivering up of the woman either by her father or by some other, we must note that in ancient times all women which had not husbands nor fathers to govern them had their tutors, without whose authority there was no act which they did warrantable. And for this cause they were in marriage delivered unto their husbands by others. Which custom retained hath still this use, that it putteth women in mind of a duty whereunto the very imbecility of their nature and sex doth bind them, namely to be always directed, guided and ordered by others, although our positive laws do not tie them now as pupils.

The custom of laying down money seemeth to have been derived from the Saxons, whose manner was to buy their wives. But seeing there is not any great cause wherefore the memory of that custom should remain, it skilleth not much although we suffer it to lie dead, even as we see it in a manner already worn out.

The ring hath been always used as an especial pledge of faith and fidelity. Nothing more fit to serve as a token of our purposed endless continuance in that which we never ought to revoke. This is the cause wherefore the heathens themselves did in such cases use the ring, whereunto Tertullian alluding saith, that in ancient times "No woman was permitted to wear gold saving only upon one finger, which her husband had fastened unto himself with that ring which was usually given for assurance of future marriage." The cause why the Christians use it, as some of the fathers think, is either to testify mutual love or rather to serve for a pledge of conjunction in heart and mind agreed upon between them. But what rite and custom is there so harmless wherein the wit of man bending itself to derision may not easily find out somewhat to scorn and jest at? He that should have beheld the Jews when they stood with a four-cornered garment spread over the head of espoused couples while their espousals were in making, he that should have beheld their praying over a cup and their delivering the same at the marriage feast with set forms of benediction as the order amongst them was, might being lewdly affected take thereat as just occasion of scornful cavil as at the use of the ring in wedlock among Christians.

But of all things the most hardly taken is the uttering those words, "With my body I thee worship," in which words when once they are understood there will appear as little cause as in the rest for any wise man to be offended. First therefore inasmuch as unlawful copulation doth pollute and dishonour both parties, this protestation that we do worship and honour another with our bodies may import a denial of all such lets and impediments to our knowledge as might cause any stain, blemish, or disgrace that way, which kind of construction being probable would easily approve that speech to a peaceable and quiet mind. Secondly in that the Apostle doth so expressly affirm that parties married have not any longer entire power over themselves, but each hath interest in other's person, it cannot be thought an absurd construction to say that worshiping with the body is the imparting of that interest in the body unto another which none before had save only ourselves. But if this was the natural meaning the words should perhaps be as requisite to be used on the one side as on the other, and therefore a third sense there is which I rather rely upon. Apparent it is that the ancient difference between a lawful wife and a concubine was only in the different purpose of man betaking himself to the one or the other. If his purpose were only fellowship, there grew to the woman by this mean no worship at all but the contrary. In professing that his intent was to add by his person honour and worship unto hers, he took her plainly and clearly to wife. This is it which the Civil Law doth mean when it maketh a wife to differ from a concubine in dignity; a wife to be taken where conjugal honour and affection doth go before. The worship that grew unto her being taken with declaration of this intent was that her children became by this mean legitimate and free; herself was made a mother over his family; last of all she received such advancement of state as things annexed

unto his person might augment her with, yea a right of participation was thereby given her both in him and even in all things
which were his. This doth somewhat the more plainly appear
by adding also that other clause "With all my worldly goods I
thee endow." The former branch having granted the principal,
the latter granteth that which is annexed thereunto.

To end the public solemnity of marriage with receiving the
blessed Sacrament is a custom so religious and so holy, that if
the church of England be blameable in this respect it is not for
suffering it to be so much but rather for not providing that it
may be more put in use. The laws of Romulus concerning
marriage are therefore extolled above the rest amongst the
heathens which were before, in that they established the use of
certain special solemnities whereby the minds of men were
drawn to make the greater conscience of wedlock, and to esteem the bond thereof a thing which could not be without
impiety dissolved. If there be anything in Christian religion
strong and effectual to like purpose it is the Sacrament of the
holy Eucharist, in regard of the force whereof Tertullian
breaketh out into these words concerning matrimony therewith sealed, "I know not which way I should be able to show the
happiness of that wedlock the knot whereof the Church doth
fasten and the Sacrament of the Church confirm." Touching
marriage therefore let thus much be sufficient.

---

(84) **Thomas Comber**
Dean of Durham
A Companion to the Temple,
or A Help to Devotion in the Use of the Common Prayer
1672–76 / 1684

Matrimony is an honourable estate. In the New Testament it
is made the Symbol of an excellent Mystery, *viz.,* of the Union

between Christ and his Church, *Eph.* 5: 32.

. . .

A Venerable Rite indeed it is, instituted by God the Father, vindicated by God the Son, and explicated by God the Holy Ghost to signify the mysterious Love of Jesus to his Church; For our Lord forsook his Heavenly Father and did cleave to our Nature, becoming one Flesh with us, giving us his Spirit for a Dowry and Heaven for a Jointure, feeding us at his Table, adorning us with his Grace and protecting us by his Power, and from this Love of Christ to his Church are many Converts begotten unto God through the Gospel, and being born again of Water and of the Holy Ghost, they become Heirs of Glory. Now this is a great mystery, that Jesus should love us so exceedingly and unite us to him so nearly and provide for us so liberally: Yea, Marriage itself is Hallowed by being the Emblem of so Divine and mysterious a Mercy, and ought to be very seriously undertaken on that account lest we abuse the thing signified by profaning that which God hath made to be the sign thereof. He that represents a King must not be light and ridiculous while he wears that Character; and they that are to represent the King of Kings in the noblest act of his mercies had need be very grave and devout on so solemn an occasion.

Marriage is declared to be an honourable Estate from the practice of our Savior, who designing to do honour to this holy Rite was present at a Marriage and wrought his first Miracle there, *Jn.* 2, and doubtless his Presence at it testified his approbation of it. And it also gives us hope that if we call and invite him to this Marriage by fervent Prayers he will be spiritually present with us now, and by his Power and Mercy he will turn those Waters of Affliction, to which this (as well as other estates in this World) is liable, into the Wine of Joy. Nor is it without good Authority that we mention this act of our Lord's here, for the Greek Church did believe it to be so much for the honour of Marriage to have Jesus for one of its Guests, that they use this Portion of Scripture for the Gospel in this Office and mention it almost in every Prayer they make on this occasion.

Illustration from
*The New Week's Preparation for a Worthy
Receiving of the Lord's Supper,* 1818.

CHAPTER NINE

Reconciliation of a Penitent

(85) **Anonymous**
Second Book of Homilies
An Homily of Repentance
and of True Reconciliation unto God
1563 / 1571

The Second Part of the Homily of Repentance.

Hitherto have ye heard, well beloved, how needful and necessary the doctrine of repentance is, and how earnestly it is,
throughout all the Scriptures of God, urged and set forth, both
by the ancient Prophets, by our Savior Jesu Christ, and his
Apostles; and that, forasmuch as it is the conversion or turning
again of the whole man unto God, from whom we go away by
sin, these four points ought to be observed; that is, from
whence or from what things we must return, unto whom this
our returning must be made, by whose means it ought to be
done that it may be effectual, and, last of all, after what sort we
ought to behave ourselves in the same, that it may be profitable

377

unto us and attain unto the thing that we do seek by it. Ye have also learned that, as the opinion of them that deny the benefit of repentance unto those that, after they be come to God and grafted in our Savior Jesu Christ, do, through the frailness of their flesh and the temptation of the devil, fall into some grievous and detestable sin, is most pestilent and pernicious; so we must beware that we do in no wise think that we are able of our own selves and of our own strength to return unto the Lord our God from whom we are gone away by our wickedness and sin. Now it shall be declared unto you what be the true parts of repentance and what things ought to move us to repent and to return unto the Lord our God with all speed.

Repentance, as it is said before, is a true returning unto God, whereby men, forsaking utterly their idolatry and wickedness, do with a lively faith embrace, love, and worship the true living God only, and give themselves to all manner of good works which by God's word they know to be acceptable unto him. Now there be four parts of repentance which being set together may be likened unto an easy and short ladder whereby we may climb from the bottomless pit of perdition that we cast ourselves into by our daily offenses and grievous sins, up into the castle or tower of eternal and endless salvation.

The first is the contrition of the heart. For we must be earnestly sorry for our sins and unfeignedly lament and bewail that we have by them so grievously offended our most bounteous and merciful God; who *so* tenderly *loved us that he gave his only begotten Son* to die a most bitter death and to shed his dear heart blood for our redemption and deliverance. And verily this inward sorrow and grief, being conceived in the heart for the heinousness of sin, if it be earnest and unfeigned is as a sacrifice to God: as the holy Prophet David doth testify, saying, *A sacrifice to God is a troubled spirit; a contrite and broken heart, O Lord, thou wilt not despise.* But that this may take place in us, we must be diligent to read and hear the Scriptures and word of God, which most lively do paint out before our eyes our natural uncleanliness and the enormity of our sinful life. For unless we have a through feeling of our sins, how can it be that we should earnestly be sorry for them? Afore David did hear the word of the Lord by the mouth of the Prophet Nathan, what heaviness, I pray you, was in him for the adultery and murder that he had committed? So that it might be said right well that he slept in his own sin. We read in the Acts of the Apostles that, when the people had heard the sermon of Peter, they were remorseful and *pricked in their hearts.* Which thing would never have been if they had not heard that wholesome sermon of Peter. They therefore that have no mind at all, neither to read nor yet to hear God's word, there is but small hope of them that they will as much as once set their feet or take hold upon the first staff or step of this ladder, but rather will sink deeper and deeper into the bottomless pit of perdition. For if at any time through the remorse of their conscience, which accuseth them, they feel any inward grief, sorrow, or heaviness for their sins; forasmuch as they want the salve and comfort of God's word, which they do despise, it will be unto them rather a mean to bring them to utter desperation than otherwise.

The second is an unfeigned confession and acknowledging of our sins unto God; whom by them we have so grievously offended that, if he should deal with us according to his justice, we do deserve a thousand hells if there could be so many. Yet if we will with a sorrowful and contrite heart make an unfeigned confession of them unto God, he will freely and frankly forgive them and so put all our wickedness out of remembrance before the sight of his Majesty that they shall no more be thought upon. Hereunto doth pertain the golden saying of the holy Prophet David, where he saith on this manner: *Then I acknowledged my sin unto thee, neither did I hide mine iniquity: I said, I will confess against myself my wickedness unto the Lord, and thou forgavest the ungodliness of my sin.* These are also the words of John the Evangelist: *If we confess our sins, God is faithful and righteous to forgive us our sins and to make us clean from all our wickedness.* Which ought to be understanded of the confession that is made unto God. For these are St. Augustine's words: That confession

379

which is made unto God is required by God's law; whereof John the Apostle speaketh, saying, *If we confess our sins, God is faithful and righteous to forgive us our sins, and to make us clean from all our wickedness:* for without this confession sin is not forgiven. This is then the chiefest and most principal confession that in the Scriptures and word of God we are bidden to make, and without the which we shall never obtain pardon and forgiveness of our sins.

Indeed besides this there is another kind of confession which is needful and necessary. And of the same doth St. James speak after this manner, saying, *Acknowledge your faults one to another, and pray one for another, that ye may be saved:* as if he should say, Open that which grieveth you, that a remedy may be found. And this is commanded both for him that complaineth and for him that heareth, that the one should show his grief to the other. The true meaning of it is that the faithful ought to acknowledge their offenses, whereby some hatred, rancour, grudge, or malice have risen or grown among them one to another, that a brotherly reconciliation may be had; without the which nothing that we do can be acceptable unto God, as our Savior Jesu Christ doth witness himself, saying, *When thou offerest thine offering at the altar, if thou rememberest that thy brother hath aught against thee, leave there thine offering, and go and be reconciled, and when thou art reconciled come and offer thine offering.* It may also be thus taken that we ought to confess our weakness and infirmities one to another to the end that, knowing each other's frailness, we may the more earnestly pray together unto Almighty God, our heavenly Father, that he will vouchsafe to pardon us our infirmities for his Son Jesu Christ's sake, and not to impute them unto us when *he shall render to every man according to his works.*

And whereas the adversaries go about to wrest this place for to maintain their auricular confession withal, they are greatly deceived themselves and do shamefully deceive others. For if this text ought to be understanded of auricular confession, then the priests are as much bound to confess themselves unto the lay people as the lay people are bound to confess themselves to them. And if to pray is to absolve, then the laity by this place hath as great authority to absolve the priests, as the priests have to absolve the laity. This did Johannes Scotus, otherwise called Duns, well perceive, who upon this place writeth on this manner. "Neither doth it seem unto me that James did give this commandment or that he did set it forth as being received of Christ. For, first and foremost, whence had he authority to bind the whole Church, sith that he was only Bishop of the Church of Jerusalem? Except thou wilt say, that the same Church was at the beginning the head Church, and consequently that he was the head Bishop; which thing the see of Rome will never grant." "The understanding of it then is as in these words, *Confess your sins one to another,* a persuasion to humility, whereby he willeth us to confess ourselves generally unto our neighbors that we are sinners, according to this saying, *If we say we have no sin, we deceive ourselves, and the truth is not in us.* "

And where that they do allege this saying of our Savior Jesu Christ unto the leper, to prove auricular confession to stand on God's word, *Go thy way, and show thyself unto the priest,* do they not see that the leper was cleansed from his leprosy afore he was by Christ sent unto the priest for to show himself unto him? By the same reason we must be cleansed from our spiritual leprosy, I mean, our sins must be forgiven us afore that we come to confession. What need we then to tell forth our sins into the ear of the priest, sith that they be already taken away? Therefore holy Ambrose, in his second Sermon upon the hundred and nineteenth Psalm, doth say full well: *"Go show thyself unto the priest:* who is the true Priest but he which is *the Priest for ever after the order of Melchisedech?"* Whereby this holy father doth understand that, *both the priesthood and the law being changed,* we ought to acknowledge none other priest for deliverance from our sins but our Saviour Jesu Christ; who, being our sovereign Bishop, doth with the sacrifice of his body and blood, offered once for ever upon the altar of the cross, most effectively cleanse the

381

spiritual leprosy and wash away the sins of all those that with true confession of the same do flee unto him.

It is most evident and plain that this auricular confession hath not his warrant of God's word; else it had not been lawful for Nectarius, Bishop of Constantinople, upon a just occasion to have put it down. For when anything ordained of God is by the lewdness of men abused, the abuse ought to be taken away and the thing itself suffered to remain. Moreover, these are St. *Augustine's* words: "What have I to do with men that they should hear my confession, as though they were able to heal all my diseases? A curious sort of men to know another man's life, and slothful to correct or amend their own. Why do they seek to hear of me what I am, which will not hear of thee what they are? And how can they tell when they hear by me of myself, whether I tell the truth or not? sith that *no mortal man knoweth what is in man but the spirit of man which is in him.*" Augustine would not have written thus if auricular confession had been used in his time. Being therefore not led with the conscience thereof, let us, with fear and trembling and with a true contrite heart, use that kind of confession that God doth command in his word; and then doubtless, as *he is faithful and righteous, he will forgive us our sins, and make us clean from all wickedness.* I do not say but that, if any do find themselves troubled in conscience, they may repair to their learned curate or pastor, or to some other godly learned man, and show the trouble and doubt of their conscience to them that they may receive at their hand the comfortable salve of God's word: but it is against the true Christian liberty that any man should be bound to the numbering of his sins as it hath been used heretofore in the time of blindness and ignorance.

The third part of repentance is faith, whereby we do apprehend and take hold upon the promises of God touching the free pardon and forgiveness of our sins; which promises are sealed up unto us with the death and bloodshedding of his Son Jesu Christ. For what should avail and profit us to be sorry for our sins, to lament and bewail that we have offended our most bounteous and merciful Father, or to confess and acknowledge our offenses and trespasses, though it be done never so earnestly, unless we do steadfastly believe and be fully persuaded that God, for his Son Jesu Christ's sake, will forgive us all our sins and put them out of remembrance and from his sight? Therefore they that teach repentance without a lively faith in our Savior Jesu Christ do teach none other but Judas's repentance; as all the Schoolmen do which do only allow these three parts of repentance, the contrition of the heart, the confession of the mouth, and the satisfaction of the work. But all these things we find in Judas's repentance, which in outward appearance did far exceed and pass the repentance of Peter. For first and foremost we read in the Gospel that Judas was so sorrowful and heavy, yea, that he was filled with such anguish and vexation of mind for that which he had done, that he could not abide to live any longer. Did not he also, afore he hanged himself, make an open confession of his fault when he said, *I have sinned, betraying the innocent blood?* And verily this was a very bold confession which might have brought him to great trouble; for by it he did lay to the high priests' and elders' charge the shedding of innocent blood and that they were most abominable murderers. He did also make a certain kind of satisfaction when he did cast their money unto them again. No such thing do we read of Peter, although he had committed a very heinous sin and most grievous offense in denying of his Master. We find that *he went out, and wept bitterly:* whereof Ambrose speaketh on this manner. "Peter was sorry and wept because he erred as a man. I do not find what he said; I know that he wept. I read of his tears, but not of his satisfaction." But how chance that the one was received into favour again with God and the other cast away, but because that the one did, by a lively faith in him whom he had denied, take hold upon the mercy of God, and the other wanted faith, whereby he did despair of the goodness and mercy of God? It is evident and plain then that, although we be never so earnestly sorry for our sins, acknowledge and confess them, yet all these things shall be but means

383

to bring us to utter desperation except we do steadfastly believe that God our heavenly Father will, for his Son Jesu Christ's sake, pardon and forgive us our offenses and trespasses and utterly put them out of remembrance in his sight. Therefore, as we said before, they that teach repentance without Christ and a lively faith in the mercy of God do only teach Cain's or Judas's repentance.

The fourth is an amendment of life, or a new life, in bringing forth *fruits worthy of repentance*. For they that do truly repent must be clean altered and changed; they must become new creatures; they must be no more the same that they were before. And therefore thus said John Baptist unto the Pharisees and Sadducees that came unto his baptism: *O generation of vipers, who hath forewarned you to flee from the anger to come? Bring forth therefore fruits worthy of repentance.* Whereby we do learn that, if we will have the wrath of God to be pacified, we must in no wise dissemble, but turn unto him again with a true and sound repentance, which may be known and declared by good fruits, as by most sure and infallible signs thereof. They that do from the bottom of their hearts acknowledge their sins and are unfeignedly sorry for their offenses will cast off all hypocrisy and put on true humility and lowliness of heart. They will not only receive the physician of the soul, but also with a most fervent desire long for him. They will not only abstain from the sins of their former life and from all other filthy vices, but also flee, eschew, and abhor all the occasions of them. And as they did before give themselves to uncleanness of life, so will they from henceforward with all diligence give themselves to innocence, pureness of life, and true godliness.

We have the Ninivites for an example, which at the preaching of Jonas did not only proclaim a general fast and that they should every one put on sackcloth, but they all did *turn from their evil ways and from the wickedness that was in their hands.* But above all other the history of Zaccheus is most notable: for being come unto our Savior Jesu Christ, he did say, *Behold, Lord, the half of my goods I give to the poor; and if I have defrauded any man, or*

taken aught away by extortion or fraud, I do restore him fourfold. Here
we see that after his repentance he was no more the man that
he was before, but was clean changed and altered. It was so far
off that he would continue and abide still in his unsatiable
covetousness, or take aught away fraudulently from any man,
that rather he was most willing and ready to give away his own
and to make satisfaction unto all them that he had done injury
and wrong unto. Here may we right well add the sinful woman
which, when she came to our Savior Jesu Christ, did pour down
such abundance of tears out of those wanton eyes of hers,
wherewith she had allured many unto folly, that she did with
them wash his feet, wiping them with the hairs of her head
which she was wont most gloriously to set out, making of them
a net of the devil. Hereby we do learn what is the satisfaction
that God doth require of us, which is that we *cease from evil and do
good* and, if we have done any man wrong, to endeavour ourselves to make him true amends to the uttermost of our power;
following in this the example of Zaccheus and of this sinful
woman, and also that goodly lesson that John Baptist, Zach-
ary's son, did give unto them that came to ask counsel of him.

This was commonly the penance that Christ enjoined sinners, *Go thy way and sin no more.* Which penance we shall never
be able to fulfill without the special grace of him that doth say,
Without me ye can do nothing. It is therefore our parts, if at least
we be desirous of the health and salvation of our own selves,
most earnestly to pray unto our heavenly Father to assist us
with his Holy Spirit that we may be able to hearken unto the
voice of the true Shepherd and with due obedience to follow
the same. Let us hearken to the voice of Almighty God when he
calleth us to repentance. Let us not harden our hearts, as such
infidels do who do abuse the time given them of God to repent,
and turn it to continue their pride and contempt against God
and man; which know not how much they *heap God's wrath upon
themselves for the hardness of their hearts, which cannot repent, at the
day of vengeance.* Where we have offended the law of God, let us
repent us of our straying from so good a Lord. Let us confess

our unworthiness before him; but yet let us trust in God's free mercy for Christ's sake for the pardon of the same. And from henceforth let us endeavour ourselves to walk in a new life *as newborn babes,* whereby we *may glorify our Father which is in heaven,* and thereby to bear in our consciences a good testimony of our faith; so at the last to obtain the fruition of everlasting life through the merits of our Savior. To whom be all praise and honour forever. Amen.

---

(86) **John Jewel**
Bishop of Salisbury
An Apology of the Church of England
1564

Moreover, we say that Christ hath given to his ministers power to bind, to loose, to open, to shut; and that the office of loosing consisteth in this point, that the minister either by the preaching of the Gospel offers the merits of Christ and full pardon to such as have lowly and contrite hearts and do unfeignedly repent them, pronouncing unto the same a sure and undoubted forgiveness of their sins and hope of everlasting salvation; or else that the same minister, when any have offended their brothers' minds with some great offense or notable and open crime, whereby they have, as it were, banished and made themselves strangers from the common fellowship and from the body of Christ, then, after perfect amendment of such persons, doth reconcile them and bring them home again, and restore them to the company and unity of the faithful. We say also that the minister doth execute the authority of binding and shutting as often as he shutteth up the gate of the kingdom of heaven against the unbelieving and stubborn persons, denouncing unto them God's vengeance and everlasting punishment, or else when he doth quite shut them out from the bosom of the church by open excommunication. Out of doubt, what sentence soever the minister of God shall give in this sort, God himself doth so well allow of it that whatsoever here in earth by their means is loosed and bound God himself will loose and bind the same in heaven.

---

(87) **Richard Hooker**
Master of the Temple, Rector of Bishopsbourne (Kent),
chief apologist for Anglicanism under Queen Elizabeth I
Of the Laws of Ecclesiastical Polity, book VI
†1648

We are by repentance to appease whom we offend by sin. For which cause, whereas all sins deprive us of the favour of Almighty God, our way of reconciliation with him is the inward secret repentance of the heart; which inward repentance alone sufficeth, unless some special thing, in the quality of sin committed or in the party that hath done amiss, require more. For besides our submission in God's sight, repentance must not only proceed to the private contentment of men if the sin be a crime injurious; but also further, where the wholesome discipline of God's Church exacteth a more exemplary and open satisfaction. Now the Church being satisfied with outward repentance, as God is with inward, it shall not be amiss, for more perspicuity to term this latter always the Virtue, that former the Discipline of Repentance: which discipline hath two sorts of penitents to work upon, inasmuch as it hath been accustomed to lay the offices of repentance on some seeking, others shunning them; on some at their own voluntary request, on others altogether against their wills; as shall hereafter appear by store of ancient examples. Repentance being therefore either in the sight of God alone, or else with the notice also of men. Without the one, sometimes thoroughly performed but always practiced more or less, in our daily devotions and prayers we have no remedy for any fault; whereas the other is only required in sins of a certain degree and quality: the one necessary forever, the other so far forth as the laws and orders of God's Church shall make it requisite: the nature, parts, and effects of the one always the same; the other limited, extended, varied by infinite occasions.

. . .

God will have offenses by repentance not only abhorred within ourselves, but also with humble supplication displayed before him and a testimony of amendment to be given, even by present works, worthy repentance, in that they are contrary to those we renounce and disclaim. Although the virtue of repentance do require that her other two parts, confession and satisfaction, should here follow, yet . . . they belong as well to the discipline as to the virtue of repentance, and only differ for that in the one they are performed to man, in the other to God alone.

. . .

Our Lord and Savior in the sixteenth of St. Matthew's Gospel giveth his Apostles regiment in general over God's Church. For they that have the keys of the kingdom of heaven are thereby signified to be stewards of the house of God, under whom they guide, command, judge, and correct his family. The souls of men are God's treasure, committed to the trust and fidelity of such as must render a strict account for the very least which is under their custody. God hath not invested them with power to make a revenue thereof, but to use it for the good of them whom Jesus Christ hath most dearly bought.

And because their office herein consisteth of sundry functions, some belonging to doctrine, some to discipline, all contained in the name of the Keys, they have for matters of discipline, as well litigious as criminal, their courts and consistories erected by the authority of his most sacred voice. . . .

388

It standeth with us in the Church of England as touching public confession, thus:

First, seeing day by day we in our Church begin our public prayers to Almighty God with public acknowledgment of our sins, in which confession every man prostrate as it were before his glorious Majesty crieth guilty against himself; and the minister with one sentence pronounceth universally all clear, whose acknowledgment so made hath proceeded from a true penitent mind; what reason is there every man should not under the general terms of confession represent to himself his own particulars whatsoever, and adjoining thereunto that affection which a contrite spirit worketh, embrace to as full effect the words of divine Grace as if the same were severally and particularly uttered with addition of prayers, imposition of hands, or all the ceremonies and solemnities that might be used for the strengthening of men's affiance in God's peculiar mercy towards them? Such complements are helps to support our weakness, and not causes that serve to procure or produce his gifts. If with us there be "truth in the inward parts," as David speaketh, the difference of general and particular forms in confession and absolution is not so material that any man's safety or ghostly good should depend upon it.

And for private confession and absolution it standeth thus with us:

The minister's power to absolve is publicly taught and professed, the Church not denied to have authority either of abridging or enlarging the use and exercise of that power, upon the people no such necessity imposed of opening their transgressions unto men as if remission of sins otherwise were impossible; neither any such opinion had of the thing itself, as though it were either unlawful or unprofitable, saving only for these inconveniences which the world hath by experience observed in it heretofore. And in regard thereof, the Church of England hitherto hath thought it the safer way to refer men's hidden crimes unto God and themselves only; howbeit not without special caution for the admonition of such as come to the holy Sacrament and for the comfort of such as are ready to depart the world.

First, because there are but few that consider how much that part of divine service which consisteth in partaking the holy Eucharist doth import their souls; what they lose by neglect thereof and what by devout practice they might attain unto: therefore, lest carelessness of general confession should, as commonly it doth, extinguish all remorse of men's particular enormous crimes; our custom (whensoever men present themselves at the Lord's Table) is, solemnly to give them very fearful admonition what woes are perpendicularly hanging over the heads of such as dare adventure to put forth their unworthy hands to those admirable mysteries of life which have by rare examples been proved conduits of irremediable death to impenitent receivers; whom therefore as we repel being known, so being not known we can but terrify. Yet with us, the ministers of God's most holy word and sacraments, being all put in trust with the custody and dispensation of those mysteries wherein our communion is and hath been ever accounted the highest grace that men on earth are admitted unto, have therefore all equally the same power to withhold that sacred mystical food from notorious evil livers, from such as have any way wronged their neighbors, and from parties between whom there doth open hatred and malice appear, till the first sort have reformed their wicked life, the second recompensed them unto whom they were injurious, and the last condescended unto some course of Christian reconciliation whereupon their mutual accord may ensue. In which cases, for the first branch of wicked life, and the last which is open enmity, there can arise no great difficulty about the exercise of his power: in the second, concerning wrongs, there may, if men shall presume to define or measure injuries according to their own conceits, depraved oftentimes as well by error as partiality, and that no less in the minister himself than in any other of the people under him. The knowledge therefore which he taketh of wrongs must rise as it doth in the other two, not from his own opinion or conscience but from the evidence of the fact which is committed; yea, from such evidence as neither doth admit denial nor defense. For if the offender having either colour of law to uphold or any other pretense to excuse his own uncharitable and wrongful dealings shall wilfully stand in defense thereof, it serveth as a bar to the power of the minister in this kind.

. . .

Leaving therefore unto his judgment them whom we cannot stay from casting their own souls into so great hazard, we have in the other part of penitential jurisdiction, in our power and authority to release sin, joy on all sides, without trouble or molestation unto any. And if to give be a thing more blessed than to receive, are we not infinitely happier in being authorized to bestow the treasure of God than when necessity doth constrain to withdraw the same?

They which during life and health are never destitute of ways to delude repentance, do notwithstanding oftentimes, when their last hour draweth on, both feel that sting which before lay dead in them and also thirst after such helps as have been always till then unsavoury.

. . .

Yea, because to countervail the fault of delay, there are in the latest repentance oftentimes the surest tokens of sincere dealing; therefore upon special confession made to the minister of God he presently absolveth in this case the sick party from all his sins by that authority which Jesus Christ hath committed unto him, knowing that God respecteth not so much what time is spent as what truth is showed in repentance.

. . .

Repentance therefore, even the sole virtue of repentance without either purpose of shrift or desire of absolution from the priest; repentance, the secret conversion of the heart, in that it consisteth of these three and doth by these three pacify God, may be without hyperbolical terms most truly magnified as a recovery of the soul of man from deadly sickness, a restitution of glorious light to his darkened mind, a comfortable reconciliation with God, a spiritual nativity, a rising from the dead, a day-spring from out the depth of obscurity, a redemption from more than the Egyptian thraldom, a grinding of the old Adam even into dust and powder, a deliverance out of the prisons of hell, a full restoration of the seat of grace and throne of glory, a triumph over sin, and a saving victory.

Amongst the works of satisfaction, the most respected have been always these three, Prayers, Fasts, and Almsdeeds: by prayer we lift up our souls to him from whom sin and iniquity hath withdrawn them; by fasting we reduce the body from thraldom under vain delights and make it serviceable for parts of virtuous conversation; by alms we dedicate to charity these worldly goods and possessions which unrighteousness doth neither get nor bestow well: the first, a token of piety intended towards God; the second, a pledge of moderation and sobriety in the carriage of our own persons; the last, a testimony of our meaning to do good to all men. In which three, the Apostle by way of abridgment comprehendeth whatsoever may appertain to sanctimony, holiness, and good life: as contrariwise the very mass of general corruption throughout the world, what is it but only forgetfulness of God, carnal pleasure, immoderate desire after worldly things; profaneness, licentiousness, covetousness?

All offices of repentance have these two properties: there is in performance of them painfulness, and in their nature a contrariety unto sin. The one consideration causeth them both in holy Scripture and elsewhere to be termed judgments or revenges taken voluntarily on ourselves, and to be furthermore also preservatives from future evils, inasmuch as we commonly use to keep with the greater care that which with pain we have recovered. And they are in the other respect contrary to sin committed; contrition, contrary to the pleasure; confession, to the error which is mother of sin; and to the deeds of sin, the works of satisfaction contrary; therefore they all the more effectual to cure the evil habit thereof.

. . .

Wherefore concerning Satisfaction made to God by Christ only, and of the manner how repentance generally, particularly also, how certain special works of penitency, both are by the Fathers in their ordinary phrase of speech called satisfactory and may be by us so acknowledged; enough hath been spoken.

Our offenses sometimes are of such nature as requireth that particular men be satisfied, or else repentance to be utterly void and of none effect. For if either through open rapine or cloaked fraud, if through injurious or unconscionable dealings a man have wittingly wronged others to enrich himself; the first thing evermore in this case required (ability serving) is restitution. For let no man deceive himself: from such offenses we are not discharged, neither can be, till recompense and restitution to man accompany the penitent confession we have made to Almighty God.

. . .

Now although it suffice that the offices wherewith we pacify God or private men be secretly done; yet in cases where the Church must be also satisfied, it was not to this end and purpose unnecessary that the ancient discipline did further require outward signs of contrition to be showed, confession of sins to be made openly, and those works to be apparent which served as testimonies of conversion before men. Wherein, if either hypocrisy did at any time delude their judgment they knew that God is he whom masks and mockeries cannot blind, that he which seeth men's hearts would judge them according unto his own evidence, and, as Lord, correct the sentence of his servants concerning matters beyond their reach: or if such as ought to have kept the rules of canonical satisfaction would by sinister means and practices undermine the same, obtruding presumptuously themselves to the participation of Christ's most sacred mysteries before they were orderly readmitted thereunto, the Church for contempt of holy things held them incapable of that grace which God in the Sacrament doth impart to devout communicants; and no doubt but he himself did retain bound whom the Church in those cases refused to loose.

· · ·

The sentence therefore of ministerial absolution hath two effects: touching sin, it only declareth us free from the guiltiness thereof and restored into God's favour; but concerning right in sacred and divine mysteries whereof through sin we were made unworthy, as the power of the Church did before effectually bind and retain us from access unto them, so upon our apparent repentance it truly restoreth our liberty, looseth the chains wherewith we were tied, remitteth all whatsoever is past, accepteth us no less returned than if we never had gone astray.

For inasmuch as the power which our Savior gave to his Church is of two kinds, the one to be exercised over voluntary penitents only, the other over such as are to be brought to amendment by ecclesiastical censure; the words wherein he hath given this authority must be so understood as the subject or matter whereupon it worketh will permit. It doth not permit that in the former kind (that is to say, in the use of power over voluntary converts), to bind or loose, remit or retain, should signify any other than only to pronounce of sinners according to that which may be gathered by outward signs; because really to effect the removal or continuance of sin in the soul of any offender is no priestly act but a work which far exceedeth their ability. Contrariwise, in the latter kind of spiritual jurisdiction which by censures constraineth men to amend their lives; it is true that the minister of God doth more than declare and signify what God hath wrought. And this power, true it is, that the Church of Christ hath invested in it.

· · ·

Now the last and sometimes hardest to be satisfied by repentance are our minds; and our minds we have then satisfied when the conscience is of guilty become clear. For as long as we are in ourselves privy to our own most heinous crimes, but without sense of God's mercy and grace towards us, unless the heart be either brutish for want of knowledge, or altogether hardened by wilful atheism, the remorse of sin is in it as the deadly sting of a serpent.

· · ·

394

Are we not bound then with all thankfulness to acknowledge his infinite goodness and mercy which hath revealed unto us the way how to rid ourselves of these mazes; the way how to shake off that yoke which no flesh is able to bear; the way how to change most grisly horror into a comfortable apprehension of heavenly joy?

Whereunto there are many which labour with so much the greater difficulty because imbecility of mind doth not suffer them to censure rightly their own doings: some fearful lest the enormity of their crimes be so impardonable that no repentance can do them good; some lest the imperfection of their repentance make it ineffectual to the taking away of sin. The one drive all things to this issue, whether they be not men which have sinned against the Holy Ghost; the other to this, what repentance is sufficient to clear sinners and to assure them that they are delivered. Such as by error charge themselves of unpardonable sin, must think, it may be they deem that impardonable which is not.

. . .

For all other offenders, without exception or stint, whether they be strangers that seek access or followers that will make return unto God; upon the tender of their repentance, the grant of his grace standeth everlastingly signed with his blood in the book of eternal life. That which in this case overterrifieth fearful souls is a misconceit whereby they imagine every act which we do knowing that we do amiss, and every willful breach or transgression of God's law to be mere sin against the Holy Ghost; forgetting that the Law of Moses itself ordained sacrifices of expiation as well for faults presumptuously committed as things wherein men offend by error.

Now there are on the contrary side others, who doubting not of God's mercy toward all that perfectly repent, remain notwithstanding scrupulous and troubled with continual fear lest defects in their own repentance be a bar against them.

. . .

Notwithstanding, forasmuch as they wrong themselves with

overrigorous and extreme exactions, by means whereof they fall sometimes into such perplexities as can hardly be allayed, it hath therefore pleased Almighty God, in tender commiseration over these imbecilities of men, to ordain for their spiritual and ghostly comfort consecrated persons which by sentence of power and authority given from above may as it were out of his very mouth ascertain timorous and doubtful minds in their own particular, ease them of all their scrupulosities, leave them settled in peace and satisfied touching the mercy of God towards them. To use the benefit of this help for our better satisfaction in such cases is so natural that it can be forbidden no man; but yet not so necessary that all men should be in case to need it.

. . .

That which God doth chiefly respect in men's penitency is their hearts. The heart is it which maketh repentance sincere, sincerity that which findeth favour in God's sight, and the favour of God that which supplieth by gracious acceptation whatsoever may seem defective in the faithful, hearty, and true offices of his servants. "Take it" (saith *Chrysostom*) "upon my credit, Such is God's merciful inclination towards men, that repentance offered with a single and sincere mind he never refuseth; no not although we be come to the very top of iniquity. If there be a will and desire to return, he receiveth, embraceth, omitteth nothing which may restore us to former happiness; yea, that which is yet above all the rest, albeit we cannot in the duty of satisfying him attain what we ought and would, but come far behind our mark, he taketh nevertheless in good worth that little which we do; be it never so mean we lose not our labour therein." The least and lowest step of repentance in Saint *Chrysostom*'s judgment severeth and setteth us above them that perish in their sin. I will therefore end with St. Augustin's conclusion, "Lord, in thy book and volume of life all shall be written, as well the least of thy saints, as the chiefest. Let not therefore the unperfect fear; let them only proceed and go forward."

(88) **Herbert Thorndike**
Rector of Barley (Herts.), Fellow of Trinity College,
Cambridge, Prebendary of Westminster
The Service of God at Religious Assemblies
1642

That which this Church of England is to give account of in particular is the declaration of forgiveness upon the confession of sins, not used in other reformed Churches. In this he shall proceed upon the surest ground, that first shall resolve wherein the power of binding and loosing, of retaining and remitting sins, given by our Lord in the Gospel, under the symbol of the keys of His house, consisteth and how far it extendeth. For as there is no question that the ministers of the Church by this commission are authorized to declare forgiveness of sins to whomsoever they shall find disposed by serious contrition and true faith to receive it at God's hands: so to think that to bind and loose, to remit and retain sins, is nothing else but to declare them bound or loosed, remitted or retained, and that the charge whereof we speak consists in declaring this and nothing else is a thing which the property of no language will bear, seeing that in all use of speech all men understand it to be one thing to bind and loose, to retain and remit sins, another thing to declare that. Yet is it no part of my mind to make this power of the keys, by which sins are bound or remitted, to consist in the power of pronouncing sentence of forgiveness which God ratifieth: as resting well assured that God giveth pardon to whomsoever He sees disposed to receive it: and that thenceforth that disposition being brought to pass, the ministry of the keys consisteth only in declaring the pardon given by God: it seemeth nevertheless that the ministry of the keys is formerly seen otherwise, that is, in procuring that disposition of the hearts which is requisite to make men capable of forgive-

ness, in bringing them to the knowledge of their sins, in directing the course which they have to take in seeking their reconc-
ilement with God.

---

(89) Anonymous
(? Richard Allestree, Regius Professor of Divinity
at Oxford, Provost of Eton)
The Whole Duty of Man
1657

I shall add but one Thing more concerning the Things which
are to be done *Before* the Sacrament, and that is an Advice that
if any Person, upon a serious View of himself, cannot satisfy his
own Soul of his Sincerity and so doubts whether he may come
to the Sacrament, he do not rest wholly on his own Judgment in
the Case. For if he be a truly humbled Soul, it is likely he may
judge too hardly of himself; if he be not, it is odd, but if he be
left to the satisfying his own Doubts he will quickly bring himself to pass too favourable a Sentence. Or, whether he be the
one or the other, if he come to the Sacrament in that Doubt he
certainly plunges himself into farther Doubts and Scruples, if
not into Sin. On the other Side, if he forbear because of it, if
that Fear be a causeless one, then he groundlessly absents
himself from that holy Ordinance and so deprives his Soul of
the Benefits of it. Therefore in the midst of so many Dangers
which attend the Mistake of himself, I would, as I said before,
exhort him not to trust to his own Judgment but to make
known his Case to some discreet and godly Minister and rather
be guided by him, who will probably (if the Case be duly and
without any Disguise discovered to him) be better able to judge
of him than he of himself. This is the Counsel the Church gives
in the Exhortation before the Communion, where it is advised

that if any, by other Means there fore-mentioned, *cannot quiet his own Conscience but require farther Counsel and Comfort, then let him go to some discreet and learned Minister of God's Word and open his grief, that he may receive such ghostly Counsel, Advice and Comfort that his Conscience may be relieved, etc.* This is surely such Advice as should not be neglected, neither at the Time of coming to the Sacrament, nor any other, when we are under any Fear or Reasons of Doubt concerning the State of our Souls. And for want of this many have run into very great Mischief, having let the Doubt fester so long that it hath either plunged them into deep Distress of Conscience, or, which is worse, they have, to still that Disquiet within them, betaken themselves to all sinful Pleasures and so quite cast off all Care of their Souls.

---

(90) **Hamon L'Estrange**
lay theologian and historian
The Alliance of Divine Offices
1659

The Church (of England) approveth of, though she doth not command, Auricular Confession. Many times poor souls lie labouring under the pangs of a horrid reflex upon the number or greatness of their sins and the dreadful wrath of God deservedly expected for them. In this case, (there is) no remedy comparable to a humble and sincere confession at large, common to all, and sometimes restrained to some one particular predominant sin of whose pressure he finds the greatest weight. Upon which Confession, mixed with a vehement and earnest plying the Throne of God for mercy, it becomes the Minister instantly to interpose, to lay before him the inexhaustible treasure of God's infinite mercies, to assure him of his interest therein, and, upon the hypothesis of his contrition to be serious and unfeigned, to give him Absolution. Not that at the moment of such Absolution and not before the sinner's pardon is sealed in Heaven, which is done at the very first minute of his repentance, if to the great Critic of Hearts as He calls Himself, the all-seeing God, it appeareth cordial; but that that pardon be evidenced to him, and manifested by unspeakable comforts usually flowing into a disconsolate soul upon the pronouncing of such Absolution, God thereby countenancing and giving reputation both to His Word and Ministry. But there being two Absolutions mentioned in the former offices, one at Morning Prayer and the other in the Communion Service, it may be demanded why only this is in the first person, "I absolve thee"? The answer is, there are three opinions concerning Absolution. The first, entertained by a few, conceive it optative, precarious, or by petition only, as praying for the pardon of the sins of the penitent. The second think it declaratory only, that is, pronouncing the penitent absolved by applying God's promises to the signs of his contrition. Lastly, some contend that it is authoritative as deriving power and commission from God not to declare the party absolved, but for the priest to do it in words denoting the first person. All these three opinions our Church seemeth in part to favour. The first under these words, "Almighty God have mercy upon you, pardon and deliver you," etc. The second under these words, "Hath given charge and command to His Ministers, to declare and pronounce to His people, being penitent, the absolution and remission of their sins." The last by these words, "I absolve thee." Which authoritative Absolution is rather proper here because where the priest absolves in his own person his Absolution is not fitly applicable to any but such as have given him evident tokens of hearty sorrow for their sins, such as Divine chastisement usually causeth. Extendible it is not to whole congregations, as in the former instances, where the confession is too general to be conceived in all real; and a confession at large can at most pretend but to an Absolution at large, effectual only to such as truly and sincerely repent.

(91) **William Wake**
Archbishop of Canterbury
An Exposition of the Doctrine of the Church of England
1686

For *Penance* and *Confession,* we wish our Discipline were both more strictly required and more duly observed than it is. The *Canons of our Church* do perhaps require as much as the Primitive Christians themselves did: and it is more *the decay of Piety* in the People than any want of Care in her that they are not as well and regularly Practiced.

We do not believe *Penance* to be a Sacrament after the same manner that Baptism and the Holy Eucharist are, because neither do we find any Divine command for it, nor is there any Sign in it established by Christ, to which his Grace is annexed. We suppose that if the Ancient Church had esteemed it anything more than a part of Christian Discipline they would not have presumed to make such changes in it, as in the several Ages it is evident they did.

The Primitive Christians interpreting those places of *St. Matthew* and *St. John* (*Mt.* 18:18, *Jn.* 20:23) . . . of public Discipline, and to which we suppose with them they principally at least, if not only refer, *at first* Practiced no other. For private faults, they exhorted their Penitents to Confess them to God, and unless some particular Circumstances required the Communication of them to the Priest, plainly signified that this confession was not only in itself sufficient but in effect was more agreeable to Holy Scripture than any other.

If the Conscience indeed were too much burdened by some *Great fault,* or that the Crime committed was *notoriously Scandalous,* then they advised a Confession to the Priest too. But this was not to every Priest, nor for him just to hear the confession and then without more ado to say *I absolve thee.* They prescribed in every Church some Wise Physician of the Soul on purpose for this great charge; that might pray with the Penitent, might direct him what to do to obtain God's favour, might assist him in it, and finally, after a long Experience and a severe Judgment, give him Absolution.

. . .

The *Church of England* refuses no sort of Confession, either public or private, that may be any way necessary to the quieting of men's consciences; or to the exercising of that *Power of binding and loosing* which our Savior Christ has left to his Church.

We have our Penitential Canons for public Offenders; we exhort men if they have any least doubt or scruples, nay sometimes though they have none, but especially before they receive the Holy Sacrament, to confess their sins. We propose to them the benefit not only of Ghostly Advice how to manage their Repentance, but the great comfort of *Absolution* too, as soon as they shall have completed it.

Our form of Absolution after the manner of the Eastern Church at this day, and of the Universal Church for above 1200 Years, is *Declarative* rather than *Absolute*. While we are unable to search the Hearts of men, and thereby to infallibly differentiate the sincerely contrite from those that are not, we think it rashness to pronounce a *definitive Sentence in God's Name which we cannot be sure that God will always confirm.*

When we visit our Sick we never fail to exhort them to make a *Special Confession* of their sins to him that Ministers to them; and when they have done it, the *Absolution* is so full that the Church of *Rome* itself could not desire to add anything to it.

For the rest, we think it an *unnecessary torment to men's Consciences* to oblige them where there is no scruple to reveal to their Confessor every most secret fault, even of Wish or Desire, which the Church of *Rome* exacts. Nor dare we pronounce this Discipline *Sacramental* and *necessary to Salvation;* so that a contrite Sinner who has made his confession to God Almighty shall not receive a Pardon, unless he repeat it to the Priest too.

This we must beg leave with assurance to say is directly contrary to the Tradition of the Church, and to many plain and undoubted places of Holy Scripture. And if this be all our Reformation be guilty of, that we advise not that which may Torment and Distract but is no way apt to settle men's consciences, nor require that as indispensably necessary to Salvation which we find nowhere commanded by God as such, we . . . see no cause at all either to *regret the Loss* or to be *ashamed of the Change.*

Illustration from a
Book of Common Prayer, 1837.

CHAPTER TEN

Ministration to the Sick

(92) **Jeremy Taylor**
Chaplain to Lord Carbery, Bishop of Down and Connor and of Dromore
The Rule and Exercises of Holy Dying
1651

[Of visitation of the sick; or the assistance that is to be done to dying persons by the ministry of their clergy guides.]
God, who hath made no new covenant with dying persons distinct from the covenant of the living, hath also appointed no distinct sacraments for them, no other manner of usages but such as are common to all the spiritual necessities of living and healthful persons. In all the days of our religion, from our baptism to the resignation and delivery of our soul, God hath appointed his servants to minister to the necessities and eternally to bless and prudently to guide, and wisely to judge concerning souls; and the Holy Ghost, that, anointing from above, descends on us in several effluxes, but ever by the minis-

tries of the church. Our heads are anointed with that sacred unction, baptism (not in ceremony, but in real and proper effect), our foreheads in confirmation, our hands in ordinations, all our senses in the visitation of the sick, and all by the ministry of especially deputed and instructed persons: and we, who all our lifetime derive blessings from the fountains of grace by the channels of ecclesiastical ministries, must do it then especially when our needs are most pungent and actual. 1. We cannot give up our names to Christ, but the holy man that ministers in religion must enroll them and present the persons and consign the grace: when we beg for God's Spirit the minister can best present our prayers and by his advocation hallow our private desires and turn them into public and potent offices. 2. If we desire to be established and confirmed in the grace and religion of our baptism, the holy man, whose hands were anointed by a special ordination to that and its symbolical purposes, lays his hand on the catechumen and the anointing from above descends by that ministry. 3. If we would eat the body and drink the blood of our Lord, we must address ourselves to the Lord's table and he that stands there to bless and to minister can reach it forth and feed thy soul; and without his ministry thou canst not be nourished with that heavenly feast, nor thy body consigned to immortality nor thy soul refreshed with the sacramental bread from heaven, except by spiritual suppletories in cases of necessity and an impossible communion. 4. If we have committed sins, the spiritual man is appointed to restore us and to pray for us and to receive our confessions, and to inquire into our wounds and to infuse oil and remedy and to pronounce pardon. 5. If we be cut off from the communion of the faithful by our own demerits, their holy hand must reconcile us and give us peace; they are our appointed comforters, our instructors, our ordinary judges.

• • •

God, in compliance with our infirmities, hath of his own goodness established as a perpetual law in all ages of Christianity that God will speak to us by his ministers, and our solemn prayers shall be made to him by their advocation, and his blessings descend from heaven by their hands, and our offices return thither by their presidencies, and our repentance shall be managed by them, and our pardon in many degrees ministered by them. God comforts us by their sermons and reproves us by their discipline, and cuts off some by their severity and reconciles others by their gentleness, and relieves us by their prayers and instructs us by their discourses, and heals our sicknesses by their intercession presented to God and united to Christ's advocation: and, in all this, they are no causes, but servants, of the will of God, instruments of the divine grace and order, stewards and dispensers of the mysteries, and appointed to our souls to serve and lead, and to help in all accidents, dangers, and necessities.

And they who received us in our baptism are also to carry us to our grave and to take care that our end be as our life was or should have been: and therefore it is established as an apostolical rule, "Is any man sick among you? let him send for the elders of the church and let them pray over him."

The sum of the duties and offices respectively implied in these words is in the following rules:

1. Let the minister of religion be sent to not only against the agony of death, but be advised with in the whole conduct of the sickness: for, in sickness indefinitely, and therefore in every sickness, and therefore in such which are not mortal, which end in health, which have no agony or final temptations, St. *James* gives the advice; and the sick man, being bound to require them, is also tied to do it when he can know them and his own necessity. It is a very great evil, both in the matter of prudence and piety, that they fear the priest as they fear the embalmer or the sexton's spade; and love not to converse with him unless they can converse with no man else; and think his office so much to relate to the other world that he is not to be treated with while we hope to live in this; and, indeed, that our religion

407

be taken care of only when we die. And the event is this, of which I have seen some sad experience—that the man is deadly sick and his reason is useless, and he is laid to sleep and his life is in the confines of the grave so that he can do nothing toward the trimming of his lamp; and the curate shall say a few prayers by him and talk to a dead man, and the man is not in a condition to be helped but in a condition to need it hugely. He cannot be called on to confess his sins and he is not able to remember them; and he cannot understand an advice, nor hear a free discourse, nor be altered from a passion, nor cured of his fear, nor comforted on any grounds of reason or religion, and no man can tell what is likely to be his fate; or, if he does, he cannot prophesy good things concerning him, but evil. Let the spiritual man come when the sick man can be conversed withal and instructed, when he can take medicine and amend, when he understands or can be taught to understand the case of his soul and the rules of his conscience; and then his advice may turn into advantage: it cannot otherwise be useful.

2. The intercourses of the minister with the sick man have so much variety in them that they are not to be transacted at once; and therefore they do not well that send once to see the good man with sorrow, and hear him pray and thank him, and dismiss him civilly and desire to see his face no more. To dress a soul for funeral is not a work to be dispatched at one meeting: at first he needs a comfort and anon something to make him willing to die; and by and by he is tempted to impatience and that needs a special cure; and it is a great work to make his confessions well and with advantages; and it may be the man is careless and indifferent and then he needs to understand the evil of his sin and the danger of his person; and his cases of conscience may be so many and so intricate that he is not quickly to be reduced to peace. And one time the holy man must pray and another he must exhort, a third time administer the holy sacrament; and he that ought to watch all the periods and little portions of his life lest he should be surprised and overcome, had need be watched when he is sick, and assisted and called on and reminded of the several parts of his duty in every instant of his temptation.

. . .

4. Whether they be many or few that are sent to the sick person, let the curate of his parish or his own confessor be among them; that is, let him not be wholly advised by strangers who know not his particular necessities; but he that is the ordinary judge cannot safely be passed by in his extraordinary necessity, which in so great portions depends on his whole life past: and it is a matter of suspicion when we decline his judgment that knows us best, and with whom we formerly did converse either by choice or by law, by private election or by public constitution. It concerns us, then, to make severe and profitable judgments, and not to conspire against ourselves or procure such assistances which may handle us softly or comply with our weaknesses more than relieve our necessities.

5. When the ministers of religion are come, first let them do their ordinary offices; that is, pray for grace to the sick man, for patience, for resignation, for health, if it seems good to God in order to his great ends; for that is one of the ends of the advice of the Apostle: and therefore the minister is to be sent for, not when the case is desperate but before the sickness is come to its crisis or period. Let him discourse concerning the causes of sickness and by a general instrument move him to consider concerning his condition. Let him call on him to set his soul in order; to trim his lamp; to dress his soul; to renew acts of grace by way of prayer; to make amends in all the evils he hath done; and to supply all the defects of duty as much as his past condition requires and his present can admit.

6. According as the condition of the sickness or the weakness of the man is observed, so the exhortation is to be less and the prayers more, because the life of the man was his main preparatory; and therefore, if his condition be full of pain and infirmity the shortness and small number of his own acts is to be supplied by the acts of the ministers and standers-by who are, in such case, to speak more to God for him than to talk to him: for the prayer of the righteous, when it is fervent, hath a promise to prevail much in behalf of the sick person. But exhortations must prevail with their own proper weight, not by the passion of the speaker. But yet this assistance by way of prayers is not to be done by long offices but by frequent and fervent and holy; in which offices if the sick man joins, let them be short and apt to comply with his little strength and great infirmities: if they be said in his behalf without his conjunction, they that pray may prudently use their own liberty and take no measures but their own devotions and opportunities and the sick man's necessities.

---

(93) **Anthony Sparrow**
Bishop of Norwich
A Rationale upon the Book of Common Prayer of the Church of England
1655/1657

Then Shall the Priest examine the sick person concerning his Faith, whether it be **Christian**. And this is very necessary, for if that be wrong all is wrong. Christian Religion consists in these two, a right Faith and a righteous Life; and as a right Faith without a righteous Life will not save, so neither will a righteous Life without a right belief. He that hath said, *Do this and live,* hath said, *Believe and live:* and how then can we think him safe that lives indeed justly but blasphemes impiously? This then is a principal Interrogatory or question to be put to the sick person, whether he believes as a Christian ought to do? And this he does by rehearsing to him the **CREED.** And there

410

can be no better rule to try it by. For whatsoever was prefigured in the Patriarchs or taught in the Scriptures or foretold by the Prophets concerning God the Father, Son, and holy Ghost, is all briefly contained in the Apostles Creed.

. . .

In the next place holy Church directs the Priest to *examine* the sick person concerning his life and conversation; especially concerning these two particulars. 1. Whether he *forgives* all the World. 2. Whether he hath *satisfied* all injuries done to others: without which the medicine of repentance which is necessary to the sick person's salvation will not profit him. For the first, our Savior tells St. *Matt.* 6:14; that *unless we forgive others* neither our persons nor our Prayers will be accepted: *God will not forgive us.* And for the second . . . Repentance without restitution and reparation of injuries cannot be true and serious; or if it can, it cannot profit. *For if he that is injured by another cannot be forgiven of God unless he forgives him that injured him; how can he that injures others, and does not make him restitution, hope for pardon?* The Priest therefore is to advise him that whereinsoever he hath injured any, *he should make satisfaction to the uttermost of his power.* By the uttermost of his power is not meant that he must give to the injured persons all his estate, nor that he must restore fourfold for injuries done (which was required in some cases under *Moses's* Law, by way of punishment rather than of satisfaction), but that he be careful to the uttermost of his power that the person injured be so repaired that he be no loser by him; which is all that by the law of justice, which commands to give every man their due, is required.

. . .

Then the Priest is to admonish the sick person to settle his estate, **For the discharging of his own conscience, and quietness of his Executors.** But holy Church exhorts men to do this work in their health, that when they are sick they may not be troubled about the world but may bestow their whole time and care, as it is fit, about settling and securing their future estate. And were men possessed with that fear and trembling that St.

Paul speaks of, *Phil.* 2:12, they would be careful to gain all the time that might be then to work out their salvation.

The Minister **may not forget to move the sick person,** and that most earnestly, **to liberality toward the poor.** . . . For when the poor receives from us, Christ stands by and reaches out his hand to receive with them. *Inasmuch as ye have done it to one of these little ones, ye have done it to me, Mt.* 25:40. As it is always necessary to be put in mind of this duty, so especially at this time of sickness.

. . .

Here shall the sick person make a special Confession if he feel his conscience troubled with any weighty matter. It would be considered whether every deadly sin be not a weighty matter? After which Confession the Priest shall absolve him.

---

(94) **Thomas Comber**
Dean of Durham
A Companion to the Temple,
*or **A Help to Devotion in the Use of the Common Prayer***
1672–76 / 1684

It is agreeable enough to the changeable state of things in this uncertain World that so dolorous an Office as this should immediately succeed the Festivities of Holy Matrimony, for our delights are short and soon expire; and sometimes before our Nuptial Crowns wither they are wet with a shower of Funeral Tears. The Eastern Emperors thought it not incongruous to choose the Stones for their Sepulchre on the day of their Coronation. And it would make our very Mirth to be Innocent and Holy if by casting an Eye on this following Form we should call to mind that the next and the longer Scene must be Calamitous. 'Tis certain that Sickness doth always and everywhere lie in wait for us; no place nor condition of life can secure us from

412

it; our Bodies consist of contrary qualities which are continually in war with one another, and whether the heat or the cold, the dryness or the moisture become predominant, our Health falls under the Victor's Triumphs; so that we began to be sick when we began to live, *as soon as we were born we began to draw to our End;* and our whole life is but one continued Sickness, alleviated with some lucid intervals but ending in Death at last.

· · ·

And doubtless, since Men are so universally liable to Sickness, that sooner or later, in some kind or other, all shall come into this estate; it must be the duty of every particular Person to prepare for it, and it did well become the Prudence and Piety of the Church to provide a peculiar Office for those in this condition. No Man must forget that it will be his own lot, and all Men are concerned to pity and take care of those who at present lie under this common Calamity. *The Visitation of the Sick* therefore is a Duty incumbent upon all; we must remember them that are thus Afflicted as being ourselves also in body, *Hab.* 13:3. We are liable to the same miseries and likely to need the same Companion which we extend to others; we are Members of the same Body and must all conspire to succour and restore a weak and wounded Limb.

· · ·

But Christianity obligeth us to it by higher motives, St. *James* making it an Act of Religion, *Jas.* 1:27, and *David* assures us that he shall be blessed who visits the Sick and Needy, for God will comfort him in his Sickness and deliver him out of it, *Ps.* 41:1,2,3. Yea, our Lord Jesus adds that he will take thy Charity as done to his own Person and reward it at the last day with Eternal Glory, *Mt.* 25:34, 35. And who would not do so small a duty which shall be required, with so great a Recompense? The Jewish Doctors reckon it among the principal Acts of Mercy, calling it an imitation of the divine Compassion and a means to deliver from the flames of Hell. The Primitive Christians accounted the visiting the Sick and Weak Brethren among the solemn exercises of Religion; and the very Women among them did punctually observe this piece of Charity. But we are here to treat of visiting the Sick in a stricter sense, *viz.*, as it denotes the Religious Duties which the Clergy are to perform to those who lie on their Sickbed; for which use this Office was composed, and therefore of this we must give a fuller account.

. . .

"Look upon him with the Eyes of thy Mercy, give him comfort and sure confidence in thee." We proceed now more fully to express the blessed effects which we desire from God's gracious Visitation; and *First* we pray that God will *Look upon him with the Eyes of his Mercy,* which same Petition is used in the Greek Office, and the Phrase is very significant, for to look or set one's Eyes upon any is *to show a dear affection to them* and *to take a special care of them,* for we use to look often upon that which we love and value; and thence it is said, *The Eyes of the Lord are over the Righteous, and upon them that fear and love him.* So that when we pray that God will look upon the sick Man with the Eyes of his Mercy, we desire that he may signally express his love to him and care of him, that he may consider his misery and pity him.

. . .

[On the Commendatory Prayer for a
Sick Person at the point of Departure]
It is the Command of God in holy Scripture that whenever we are to *suffer anything according to his Will, we should commit the keeping of our Souls to him in well-doing, as unto a Faithful Creator,* 1 Pet. 4:19. And there is an Example preceding this Precept, even that of holy *David,* who in his great troubles saith, *Into thine hand I commend my Spirit, for thou hast redeemed me,* Psal.31:6. But there is the most need and greatest reason for us to do this in the last and highest kind of suffering, that is, at our Death; for having received our Soul from the hands of God, who lent it us for a time, we must like honest and grateful Creditors restore it and deliver it back again (when he calls) with all possible willingness: We know that though *the Body returns to the Earth whence it came, the Spirit must return to God that gave it, Ec.* 12:7.

414

Illustration from a
Book of Common Prayer, 1815.

CHAPTER ELEVEN

Burial of the Dead

(95) **John Jewel**
Bishop of Salisbury
An Apology of the Church of England
1564

To conclude: we believe that this our selfsame flesh wherein we live, although it die and come to dust, yet at the last day it shall return again to life by the means of Christ's Spirit which dwelleth in us; and that then verily, whatsoever we suffer here in the meanwhile for his sake, Christ will wipe from off our eyes all tears and lamentation; and that we through him shall enjoy everlasting life and shall forever be with him in glory. So be it.

(96) **Richard Hooker**
Master of the Temple, Rector of Bishopsbourne (Kent),
chief apologist for Anglicanism under Queen Elizabeth I
Of the Laws of Ecclesiastical Polity, book V
1597

The end of funeral duties is first to show that love toward the party deceased which nature requireth; then to do him that honour which is fit both generally for man and particularly for the quality of his person; last of all to testify the care which the Church hath to comfort the living and the hope which we all have concerning the resurrection of the dead.

(97) **Anthony Sparrow**
Bishop of Norwich
A Rationale upon the Book of Common Prayer
of the Church of England
1655/1657

When the unlearned or unbeliever hears us sing triumphant songs to God for our victory over death, when he hears holy Lessons and discourses of the Resurrection, when he hears us pray for a happy and joyful Resurrection to Glory: by all these he must be convinced that we do believe the Resurrection, which is a principal Article of Christian faith, and the same may be the means to convince him also and make him believe the same, *and so fall down and worship God.* And this is according to St. *Paul*'s rule, 1 *Cor.* 14:23, 24, 25, who thence concludes that all our publick religious services ought to be done, that the *unlearned or unbeliever may be convinced and brought to worship God.*

For the due performance of these holy public services, a Priest, ordained for men in things pertaining to God, *Heb.* 5:1, is required by the Church, as it ought to be and as it was of old.

It was an ancient custom after Burial to go to the holy *COMMUNION,* unless the office were performed after noon. For then, if men were not fasting, it was done only with Prayers.

---

(98) **Thomas Comber**
Dean of Durham
A Companion to the Temple,
or A Help to Devotion in the Use of the Common Prayer
1672–76/1684

Because the following a dear Friend to the Grave is Naturally accounted by us so sad and so afflicting an Office, the Church hath called in the aids of Religion to enable us to bear it the more easily. It was with this design that pious Antiquity carried out their Dead with Hymns of Triumph, as Conquerors that had finished their course and obtained their Crown of Victory. To this end were those Hallelujahs sung of old as they went toward the Grave, which Custom is yet retained in many parts of this Nation where they divert the grief of the Friends and Mourners by singing Psalms from the House of the Deceased to the very Gate of the Churchyard; and there our Rubric appoints the Priest to meet them clothed in White, which is the colour of Joy, and that in which the blessed Angels used to appear. And when the holy Man comes forth to meet us in this attire, we may very justly look upon him as an Emblem of the holy Angels who go out with joy to receive the Souls of the Faithful which they conduct to the Kingdom of Glory as we do their Bodies to the House of Rest.

419

. . .

First begin with the Promises and Sentences of Scripture and then pass to the proper Psalms. The subject of these Sentences, and the intent of them, is to teach us the three necessary Graces to be exercised at the Funeral, viz., Faith, Patience, and Thanksgiving, and these placed in the same order that they must be practiced; for by Faith we gain patience, and when Patience hath her perfect work it will produce Thanksgiving.

. . .

The time being now come to put the body into the Earth, or as *Abraham* expresseth it, *to bury our dead out of our sight, Gen.* 23:4, we will premise some general Considerations concerning the circumstances relating thereto, and then survey the words used on this occasion. *First,* We are now to take our last farewell of our Friend deceased, a Rite very solemnly observed in most parts of the World: The Gentiles took their leave by a certain form of words, bidding them *[Farewell forever]*; and then they added *[Let him go]*, by which they testified their submission to the Divine Will, and so departed to their homes. The Ancient Christians were wont to give a parting kiss of Charity to the body, just when it was about to be put into the Grave, to declare their affection and to evidence that he died in the unity and peace of the Church, for which reason we still say, *Our dear Brother or Sister:* Which pious custom is yet observed in the Greek Church and also in those Northern parts of *England* by the near Relations, who usually come near and kiss the Deceased before he be put into the Grave. *Secondly,* We may note the posture and position of the Corpse, which among the Christians hath always been to turn the feet to the East with the head toward the West that so they may be ready to meet the Lord, whom the Ancients did believe should appear in that Oriental part of Heaven.

. . .

All Nations had one certain way of placing the Corpse, from which they would not vary: And we Christians have so great reason and so good Antiquity for our custom that we ought not out of singularity to alter it. *Thirdly,* We consider the casting

420

Earth upon the body, esteemed of old, an act of great piety by the very Heathen, and to find a body unburied and leave it uncovered was judged a great Crime: And it seems there was some Religion in casting Earth upon it three times. The Christians had a peculiar order of Men to do this Office, although the Priest always put in the first Earth himself.

· · ·

"For as much as it hath pleased Almighty God to take unto himself the soul of our dear Brother here departed; we therefore commit his body to the ground, Earth to Earth, Ashes to Ashes, and Dust to Dust." When the Soul by which the Body lives is once recalled by him that first placed it therein, Death doth immediately follow that separation; and those several parts, the Body and Soul, go to receptacles as distant as those Originals are whence they had their beginning, *Ec.* 12:7. God disposes of the Soul himself and leaves the corruptible Carcass to our care. · · ·

And concerning that better and nobler part we have nothing to do now but only to acknowledge God hath disposed of that according to his good pleasure, which is seasonably intimated here because our Passions are usually at the very highest upon this last parting; but surely they will not resist nor be extravagant when it is considered it pleased God it should be so; and shall that displease us which pleases him? Again, we are told he is only *departed,* which is the phrase of holy Scripture and the sense of all good Christians concerning Death that it is but the entrance into a long Journey, the going a little before in that Path wherein we must all shortly follow them; so that we may comfort ourselves concerning them with *David,* saying, *We shall go to them, but they cannot come back to us,* 2 Sam. 12:23. Yea, the *Romans* of old were wont to say, *Farewell, for we (in the order that Nature appoints) shall all follow thee.* But we know more than they, we know the Soul is the principal part, and now that is gone the Man himself is not here, nothing but a Case is left behind; and yet for the Jewel's sake that once lodged in it we must not cast it away, for God himself will one day enquire for this Body again. We cannot be so imprudent to think that *this Body which is the work of God's Hands, the object of his Care, the house of the Soul, the principal of his Creatures, the Heir of his bounty, and the Priest of his Religion, should be suffered to perish forever;* wherefore we will decently lay it up and patiently wait for its restoration. In the Dust we lay it by God's own appointment and decree, *Gen.* 3:19; for Man was made of Dust at first, *Gen.* 2:7, and to Dust he will turn again as soon as the Soul is gone so that the committing his Body to the ground is no more than laying Earth to Earth and Ashes to Ashes. Our Bodies are called Houses of Clay and earthly Tabernacles, 2 *Cor.* 5:1, and their Foundation is said to be in the Dust, *Job* 4:9. Yea, St. *Bernard* notes that God not only threatens we shall be Dust but saith we are Dust just now, which should admonish us that are alive not be too confident of our strength, for God reckons us Dust at present and Nature will make us so very shortly.

The
Whole Duty
of
MAN
Necessary for
all
Families

With Private
Devotions
for Several
Occasions

Illustration: Title page from
The Whole Duty of Man, 1739.

CHAPTER TWELVE

Ordination

(99) **Richard Hooker**
Master of the Temple, Rector of Bishopsbourne (Kent),
chief apologist for Anglicanism under Queen Elizabeth I
Of the Laws of Ecclesiastical Polity, book V
1597

[On the Power given in Ordination]

The ministry of things divine is a function which as God did himself institute, so neither may men undertake the same but by authority and power given them in lawful manner. That God which is no way deficient or wanting unto man in necessaries, and hath therefore given us the light of his heavenly truth because without that inestimable benefit we must needs have wandered in darkness to our endless perdition and woe, hath in the like abundance of mercies ordained certain to attend upon the due execution of requisite parts and offices therein prescribed for the good of the whole world, which men thereunto assigned do hold their authority from him, whether they be such as himself immediately or as the Church in his name investeth, it being neither possible for all nor for every man without distinction convenient to take upon him a charge of so great importance. They are therefore ministers of God, not only by way of subordination as princes and civil magistrates whose execution of judgment and justice the supreme hand of divine providence doth uphold, but ministers of God as from whom their authority is derived, and not from men. For in that they are Christ's ambassadors and his laborers, who should give them their commission but he whose most inward affairs they manage? Is not God alone the Father of spirits? Are not souls the purchase of Jesus Christ? What angel in Heaven could have said to man as our Lord did unto Peter, "Feed my sheep: Preach: Baptize: Do this in remembrance of me: Whose sins ye retain they are retained: and their offenses in heaven pardoned whose faults you shall on earth forgive?" What think we? Are these terrestrial sounds or else are they voices uttered out of the clouds above? The power of the ministry of God translateth out of darkness into glory; it raiseth men from the earth and bringeth God himself down from heaven, by blessing visible elements it maketh them invisible grace; it giveth daily the Holy Ghost; it hath to dispose of that flesh which was given for the life of the world and that blood which was poured out to redeem souls; when it poureth malediction upon the heads of the wicked they perish, when it revoketh the same they revive. O wretched blindness if we admire not so great power, more wretched if we consider it aright and notwithstanding imagine that any but God can bestow it!

To whom Christ hath imparted power both over that mystical body which is the society of souls and over that natural which is himself for the knitting of both in one (a work which antiquity doth call the making of Christ's body); the same power is in such not amiss both termed a kind of mark or character and acknowledged to be indelible. Ministerial power is a mark of separation because it severeth them that have it from other men and maketh them a special *order* consecrated unto the service of the Most High in things wherewith others may not meddle. Their difference therefore from other men is in that they are a distinct *order*. So Tertullian calleth them.

· · ·

They which have once received this power may not think to put it off and on like a cloak as the weather serveth, to take it reject and resume it as oft as themselves list, of which profane and impious contempt these later times have yielded as of all other kinds of iniquity and apostasy strange examples; but let them know which put their hands unto this plough, that once consecrated unto God they are made his peculiar inheritance forever. Suspensions may stop and degradations utterly cut off the use or exercise of power before given: but voluntarily it is not in the power of man to separate and pull asunder what God by his authority coupleth. So that although there may be through misdesert degradation as there may be cause of just separation after matrimony, yet if (as sometime it doth) restitution to former dignity or reconciliation after breach doth happen, neither doth the one nor the other ever repeat the first knot.

· · ·

A thing much stumbled at in the manner of giving orders is our using those memorable words of our Lord and Savior Christ, "Receive the Holy Ghost." The Holy Ghost they say we cannot give, and therefore we "foolishly" bid men receive it. Wise men for their authority's sake must have leave to befool them whom they are able to make wise by better instruction. Notwithstanding if it may please their wisdom as well to hear what fools can say as to control that which they do, thus we have heard some wise men teach, namely that the "Holy Ghost" may be used to signify not the Person alone but the gifts of the Holy Ghost, and we know that spiritual gifts are not only abilities to do things miraculous, as to speak with tongues which were never taught us, to cure diseases without art, and such like, but also that the very authority and power which is given men in the Church to be ministers of holy things, this is contained within the number of those gifts whereof the Holy Ghost is author, and therefore he which giveth this power may say without absurdity or folly "Receive the Holy Ghost," such power as the Spirit of Christ hath endowed his Church withal, such power as neither prince nor potentate, king nor Caesar on earth can give. So that if men alone had devised this form of speech thereby to express the heavenly wellspring of that power which ecclesiastical ordinations do bestow, it is not so foolish but that wise men might bear with it.

If then our Lord and Savior himself have used the selfsame form of words and that in the selfsame kind of action, although there be but the least show of probability, yea or any possibility that his meaning might be the same which ours is, it should teach sober and grave men not to be too venturous in condemning that of folly which is not impossible to have in it more profoundness of wisdom than flesh and blood should presume to control. Our Savior after his resurrection from the dead gave his Apostles their commission saying, "All power is given me in Heaven and in earth: Go therefore and teach all nations, Baptizing them in the name of the Father and the Son and the Holy Ghost, teaching them to observe all things whatsoever I have commanded you." In sum, "As my Father sent me, so send I you." Whereunto St. *John* doth add farther that "having thus spoken he breathed on them and said, Receive the Holy Ghost." By which words he must of likelihood understand some gift of the Spirit which was presently at that time bestowed upon them, as both the speech of actual delivery in saying *Receive,* and the visible sign thereof his breathing did show. Absurd it were to imagine our Savior did both to the ear and also to the very eye express a real donation and they at that time receive nothing.

It resteth then that we search what especial grace they did at that time receive. Touching miraculous power of the Spirit, most apparent it is that as then they received it not but the promise thereof was to be shortly after performed. The words of St. Luke concerning that power are therefore set down with signification of the time to come: *"Behold I will send* the promise of my Father upon you, but tarry you in the city of Jerusalem until ye be endowed with power from on high." Wherefore undoubtedly it was some other effect of the Spirit, the Holy Ghost in some other kind which our Savior did then bestow. What other likelier than that which himself doth mention as it should seem of purpose to take away all ambiguous constructions and to declare that the Holy Ghost which he then gave was a holy and a ghostly authority, authority over the souls of men, authority a part whereof consisteth in power to remit and retain sins? "Receive the Holy Ghost: *whose sins soever ye remit they are remitted; whose sins ye retain they are retained.*" Whereas therefore the other Evangelists had set down that Christ did before his suffering promise to give his Apostles the keys of the kingdom of heaven, and being risen from the dead promise moreover at that time a miraculous power of the Holy Ghost, St. *John* addeth that he also invested them even then with the power of the Holy Ghost for castigation and relaxation of sin, wherein was fully accomplished that which the promise of the Keys did import.

Seeing therefore that the same power is now given, why should the same form of words expressing it be thought foolish? The cause why we breathe not as Christ did on them unto whom he imparted power is for that neither Spirit nor spiritual authority may be thought to proceed from us, which are but delegates or assigns to give men possession of his graces.

Now, besides that the power and authority delivered with those words is itself *charisma,* a gracious donation which the Spirit of God doth bestow, we may most assuredly persuade ourselves that the hand which imposeth upon us the function of our ministry doth under the same form of words so tie itself thereunto that he which receiveth the burden is thereby forever warranted to have the Spirit with him and in him for his assistance, aid, countenance, and support in whatsoever he faithfully doth to discharge duty. Knowing therefore that when we take ordination we also receive the presence of the Holy Ghost, partly to guide, direct, and strengthen us in all our ways,

429

and partly to assume unto itself for the more authority those actions that appertain to our place and calling, can our ears admit such a speech uttered in the reverend performance of that solemnity, or can we at any time renew the memory and enter into serious cogitation thereof but with much admiration and joy? Remove what these foolish words do imply and what hath the ministry of God besides wherein to glory? Whereas now, forasmuch as the Holy Ghost which our Savior in his first ordinations gave doth no less concur with spiritual vocations throughout all ages, than the Spirit which God derived from Moses to them that assisted him in his government did descend from them to their successors in like authority and place, we have for the least and meanest duties performed by virtue of ministerial power, that to dignify, grace, and authorize them, which no other offices on earth can challenge. Whether we preach, pray, baptize, communicate, condemn, give absolution, or whatsoever, as disposers of God's mysteries our words, judgments, acts and deeds are not ours but the Holy Ghost's. Enough, if unfeignedly and in heart we did believe it, enough to banish whatsoever may justly be thought corrupt, either in bestowing, or in using, or in esteeming the same otherwise than is meet. For profanely to bestow or loosely to use, or vilely to esteem of the Holy Ghost we all in show and profession abhor.

. . .

[On Degrees of Ministers]

Touching the ministry of the Gospel of Jesus Christ; the whole body of the Church being divided into laity and clergy, the clergy are either presbyters or deacons.

I rather term the one sort Presbyters than Priests because in a matter of so small moment I would not willingly offend their ears to whom the name of Priesthood is odious though without cause. For as things are distinguished one from another by those true essential forms which being really and actually in them do not only give them the very last and highest degree of their natural perfection, but are also the knot, foundation, and

430

root whereupon all other inferior perfections depend, so if they that first do impose names did always understand exactly the nature of that which they nominate, it may be that then by hearing the terms of vulgar speech we should still be taught what the things themselves most properly are. But because words have so many artificers by whom they are made, and the things whereunto we apply them are fraught with so many varieties, it is not always apparent what the first inventors respected, much less what every man's inward conceit is which useth their words. For anything myself can discern herein, I suppose that they which have bent their study to search more diligently such matters do for the most part find that names advisedly given had either regard unto that which is naturally most proper; or if perhaps to some other specialty, to that which is sensibly most eminent in the thing signified. And concerning popular use of words, that which the wisdom of their inventors did intend thereby is not commonly thought of but by the name the thing altogether conceived in gross, as may appear in that if you ask of the common sort what any certain word, for example, what a Priest doth signify, their manner is not to answer a Priest is a clergyman which offereth sacrifice to God, but they show some particular person whom they use to call by that name. And if we list to descend to grammar we are told by masters in those schools that the word *Priest* hath his right place "in him whose mere function or charge is the service of God." Howbeit because the most eminent part both of heathenish and Jewish service did consist in sacrifice, when learned men declare what the word *Priest* doth *properly* signify *according to the mind of the first imposer* of that name, their ordinary explanations do well expound it to imply sacrifice.

Seeing then that sacrifice is now no part of the church ministry how should the name of Priesthood be thereunto rightly applied? Surely even as St. *Paul* applieth the name of Flesh unto that very substance of fishes which hath a proportionable correspondence to flesh, although it be in nature another thing. Whereupon when philosophers will speak warily,

431

they make a difference between flesh in one sort of living creatures and that other substance in the rest which hath but a kind of analogy to flesh: the Apostle contrariwise having matter of greater importance whereof to speak nameth indifferently both flesh. The Fathers of the Church of Christ with like security of speech call usually the ministry of the Gospel *Priesthood* in regard of that which the Gospel hath *proportionable* to ancient sacrifices, namely the Communion of the blessed Body and Blood of Christ, although it have properly now no sacrifice. As for the people when they hear the name, it draweth no more *their minds* to any cogitation of sacrifice than the name of a senator or of an alderman causeth them to think upon old age or to imagine that every one so termed must needs be ancient because years were respected in the first nomination of both.

---

(100) **Anthony Sparrow**
Bishop of Norwich
A Rationale upon the Book of Common Prayer
of the Church of England
1655 / 1657

[On the word Priest]

The Greek and Latin words which we translate *Priest* are derived from words which signify holy: and so the word *Priest*, according to the Etymology, signifies him whose mere charge and function is about holy things: and therefore seems to be a most proper word to him who is set apart to the holy public service and worship of God: especially when he is in the actual ministration of holy things. Wherefore in the Rubrics which direct him in his ministration of these holy public services the word *Priest* is most commonly used, both by this Church and all the Primitive Churches Greek and Latin as far as I can find, and I believe it can scarce be found that in any of the old Greek or

432

Latin Liturgies the word Presbyter was used in the Rubrics that direct the order of service; but in the Greek and in the Latin, which we in English translate *Priest,* which I suppose to be done upon this ground that this word *Priest* is the most proper for him that ministers in the time of his ministration.

If it be objected that according to the usual acceptance of the word it signifies him that offers up a Sacrifice, and therefore cannot be allowed to a Minister of the Gospel who hath no Sacrifice to offer.

It is answered: that the Ministers of the Gospel have Sacrifices to offer, 1 *Pet.* 2: 5, *Ye are built up a spiritual house, a holy Priesthood to offer up spiritual Sacrifices* of prayer, praises, thanksgivings, &tc. In respect of these the Ministers of the Gospel may be safely in a metaphorical sense called *Priests;* and in a more eminent manner than other Christians are because they are taken from among men to offer up these Sacrifices for others. But besides these spiritual Sacrifices mentioned, the Ministers of the Gospel have another Sacrifice to offer, *viz.,* the unbloody Sacrifice as it was anciently called, the commemorative Sacrifice of the death of Christ which does as really and truly show forth *the death of Christ* as those Sacrifices under the Law did foreshow it, and in respect of this Sacrifice of the Eucharist the Ancients have usually called those that offer it up *Priests.* And if *Melchizedek* was called a Priest (as he is often by St. *Paul* to the Hebrews), who yet had no other Offering or Sacrifice that we read of but that of Bread and Wine, *Gen.* 14:18, *He brought forth Bread and Wine;* and, he was a *Priest;* that is, this act of his was an act of Priesthood, for so must it be referred, he brought forth Bread and Wine; for he was a *Priest.* And not thus, and he was a *Priest,* and blessed *Abraham.* If, I say, *Melchizedek* be frequently and truly called a *Priest* who had no other Offering that we read of but *Bread and Wine,* why may not they whose Office is to bless the people as *Melchizedek* did, and besides that to offer that holy Bread and Wine, the Body and Blood of Christ, of which his Bread and Wine, at the most, was but a type, be as truly and without offense called *Priests* also?

(101) **Thomas Comber**
Dean of Durham
A Companion to the Temple,
Or a Help to Devotion in the Use of the Common Prayer
1672–76/1684

And the weight of this Charge will still be more apparent if it be further considered of how great importance the affairs, and of how infinite value the things committed to their care are. 'Tis not the affairs of one earthly Kingdom, the safety of a fenced City or the Money and Goods of one great Man; but the concern of the King of Kings, the security of Christ's Church, and the Souls, the Immortal Souls of Men that are entrusted to their care. Thousands of Gold and Silver cannot buy one Soul; the precious Blood of Christ was the only thing in the World that could purchase them: And of these Souls his Church is composed, which is his Body and his Spouse; so dear to him that he loves it as himself, yea, better than his own life, *for he gave himself up to die for it.* Yet this Church and these Souls *that are a sort of Divine Beings lodged in Human Bodies;* and all that relates to their Salvation the Blessed Jesus is now about to commit to the care of those who are about to be Ordained: And if this be always printed in their remembrance, doubtless they will be faithful and very diligent to answer this mighty trust reposed in them by the Lord of Glory. For his and their Peoples' sakes they should manage it with their utmost skill and industry, for his Favour and their Peoples' eternal Welfare or Misery entirely depends upon it. But if this will not sufficiently work upon them, the Bishop charges them to be good Stewards *for their own sakes* because, as Human Masters do strictly call their Principal Servants to account for all things under their charge and make them answer or suffer for all that is lost by their default, So these Spiritual Stewards may be well assured

434

that their Heavenly and All-seeing Lord (the Judge of all Men) will certainly reckon with them for all that he hath entrusted them with. So that if the Church in general, or any Member of it in particular, be damaged by their Folly, Fraud, or Negligence; as the Sin is great to be false or negligent in such a Trust, so the punishment shall be very great also. He hath often declared that their Souls shall be condemned and suffer for all those poor Souls that perish and are lost by their willful neglect.

. . .

But if Ministers do warn their People of the danger of Heresy or Schism, and of such Vices as they perceive they are most likely to be drawn into, and they disregard or despise the notice and will go on to Ruin; then they are . . . guilty of their own Destruction, the Priest is clear of blame and shall not suffer for their Faults. So that this account his of undertaking need not discourage him from the Office, but only should make him resolve to be diligent in it because nothing can hurt him but his own neglect: And thus the Bishop goes on to apply it, charging them never to cease their Labour, but with their utmost care and diligence to do all that in them lies, according to their Duty, to bring all they have under their charge to such unity in the Faith and such perfection in their knowledge of God, and to that measure of the Stature of Christ that there may neither Error nor Vice be found among them.

. . .

Every Minister should cheerfully set about this noble design, firmly resolve to carry it on, and patiently endure all the difficulties thereof; and to excite him thereto the Bishop proposes two motives to engage the Candidate to apply himself with the greatest care and study to the rightly discharging this excellent and difficult Office. The first with respect to God; that is, out of Duty and Gratitude to him who hath placed them in so high a Dignity in his Family. As they have many Privileges above others, so they have also greater Obligations. The trust which God reposes in them and the honour he confers upon them binds them to more than ordinary diligence, *and it is required in Stew-*

435

ards that a Man be found faithful. Such Officers are accountable not only for their own but their Fellow-servants faults if their negligence or connivance occasion them, and therefore their personal innocence is no security with respect to their account with God. And secondly, the same care is to be taken with respect to Men; the Laity have but a single point to manage, *viz.,* to take care they do not offend God themselves, whereas a Minister must not only avoid that which is evil in itself, but also fly from the appearance of it and everything which may occasion his People to offend. So that there are several innocent Words and Actions which yet may be apt to be misconstrued that a Clergyman must abstain from lest others, taking the same liberty and wanting the like discretion, may stumble at the Stone which the other stepped over without hurt: So that his duty is nice and requires much Prudence as well as Virtue, for he must be Virtuous for his own sake, and unsuspected of Vice for the sake of others. Some company he may not keep, some places he must shun, some exercises he ought to forbear lest he give offense to weak but well-meaning People, or offer occasion to the wicked to speak evil of his sacred Profession. Now to take all the pains before spoken of with others, and keep so strict a guard constantly over a Man's self is so difficult an undertaking that none can naturally or of themselves have a mind or inclination to it. Nature delights in ease and freedom and would discourage Men from so laborious and strict a course of life; wherefore, since it appears these Candidates are willing to engage themselves to it, we conclude *this will is given them by God alone,* and he only can make them able to perform what his grace hath moved them to undertake.

· · ·

"Almighty God and Heavenly Father, who of thy infinite Love," &tc. Nothing can more fitly dispose us to praise Almighty God, who shows himself to be our Heavenly Father by providing a proper Ministry for his Spouse, the Church, our Mother, than serious reflection upon the whole Economy of our Redemption, and all the steps he hath made toward this mighty blessing. So that 'tis proper here to consider that when our first Parents fell from their Innocence they brought two evils upon their Posterity: First, The Guilt, and then the power of Sin. Now our Lord and Savior undertook the removing of both: First of our Guilt by his Death, and Secondly of our Bondage under its power, by his most holy Ordinances and his Word, and in order to this he left his Ministers in all Ages to apply these means to this great end: And therefore upon the ordaining new Pastors, 'tis very fit we should acknowledge.

---

(102) William Wake
Archbishop of Canterbury
An Exposition of the Doctrine of the Church of England
1686

The *Imposition of Hands* in Holy Orders, being accompanied with a Blessing of the Holy Spirit may perhaps upon that account be called a kind of *Particular Sacrament*. Yet since that Grace which is thereby conferr'd, whatever it be, is not common to all Christians, nor by consequence any part of that federal blessing which our Blessed Savior has purchased for us; but only a separation of him who receives it to a special Employ; we think it ought not to be esteemed a common Sacrament of the whole Church, as *Baptism* and the *Lord's Supper* are.

The outward sign of it we confess to have been usually *Imposition of hands,* and as such we ourselves observe it. Yet we do not read that Christ himself instituted that sign, much less tied the promise of any certain Grace to it. . . .

We confess that no man ought to exercise the Ministerial Office till he be first consecrated to it. We believe that it is the Bishop's part only to ordain. We maintain the distinction of the several Orders in the Church; and tho we have none of those below a Deacon, because we do not read that the Apostles had any, yet we acknowledge the rest to have been anciently received in the Church, and shall not therefore raise any controversy about them.

---

(103) **William Wake**
Archbishop of Canterbury
**The Principles of the Christian Religion explained
in a Brief Commentary upon the Church Catechism**
1699

Ordination is also a *Divine institution.* By the administration of it, authority is given to those who partake of it to minister in holy things: which otherwise it would not have been lawful for them to do. We do not at all doubt but that the *grace* of God accompanies this ordinance and the discharges of those ministers which are performed in consequence of it. But then this *grace* is only the *blessing* of God upon a particular employ; and is given to such persons rather for the *benefit* of *others* than for the furtherance of their own *salvation.*

---

(104) **Charles Simeon**
Fellow of King's College and Vicar of Holy Trinity, Cambridge
The Excellency of the Liturgy
1812 / 1813

There are three things to be noticed in the Ordination Service, Our *professions,* our *promises,* and our *prayers:* after consid-

438

ering which we shall endeavour to excite in all that desire which God has so tenderly and so affectionately expressed in our behalf.

Let me begin then with calling your attention to the *professions* which we make when first we become candidates for the ministerial office.

So sacred was the priesthood under the Law that no man presumed to take it upon himself but he who was called to it by God, as Aaron was. And though the priesthood of our blessed Lord was of a totally distinct kind from that which shadowed it forth, "yet did he not glorify himself to be made a high priest," but was so constituted by his heavenly Father, who committed to him that office "after the order of Melchizedek." Some call therefore, as from God himself, is to be experienced by all who devote themselves to the service of the sanctuary. Of this our Reformers were convinced; and hence they required the ordaining bishop to put to every candidate that should come before him this solemn interrogation: "Do you trust that you are inwardly moved by the Holy Ghost to take upon you this office?" to which he answers, "I trust so."[1]

Now I am far from intimating that this call, which every candidate for Orders professes to have received, resembles that which was given to the Apostles: it is certainly not to be understood as though it were a voice or suggestion coming directly from the Holy Ghost: for though God *may* reveal his will in this manner, just as he did in the days of old, yet we have no reason to think that he *does*. The motion here spoken of is less perceptible: it does not carry its own evidence along with

[1.] The church also insists on the necessity of a regular *external call* or *commission:* For the bishop demands of the candidate, "Do you trust that you are truly called, according to the will of our Lord Jesus Christ, and according to *the canons* of this church, to the ministry of the same." And the preface to the ordination offices declares, "No man shall be accounted or taken to be a lawful bishop, priest, or deacon in this church, or suffered to execute any of the said functions, except he be called, tried, examined and admitted thereunto, according to the form hereafter following, or hath had episcopal consecration or ordination." *(Footnote to the American edition.)*

it; (as did that which in an instant prevailed on the Apostles to forsake their worldly business and to follow Christ); but it disposes the mind in a gradual and silent way to enter into the service of God; partly from a sense of obligation to him for his redeeming love, partly from a compassion for the ignorant and perishing multitudes around us, and partly from a desire to be an honoured instrument in the Redeemer's hands to establish and enlarge his kingdom in the world. Less than this cannot reasonably be supposed to be comprehended in that question: and the way to answer it with a good conscience is to examine ourselves whether we have an eye to our own ease, honour, or preferment; or whether we have really a love to the souls of men and a desire to promote the honour of our God? The question, in this view of it, gives no scope for enthusiasm, nor does it leave any room for doubt upon the mind of him that is to answer it: every man may tell whether he feels so deeply the value of his own soul as to be anxious also for the souls of others; and whether, independent of worldly considerations, he has such love to the Lord Jesus Christ as to desire above all things to advance his glory. These feelings are not liable to be mistaken because they are always accompanied with corresponding actions and always productive of appropriate fruits.

Now in all cases where this profession has been made, it may be said, "They have well said all that they have spoken." For this profession is a public acknowledgment that such a call is necessary: and it serves as a barrier to exclude from the sacred office many who would otherwise have undertaken it from worldly motives. And though it is true that too many break through this barrier, yet it stands as a witness against them, and in very many instances an effectual witness; testifying to their consciences that they have come to God with a lie in their right hand, and making them to tremble lest they should be condemned at the tribunal of their God for having, like Ananias and Sapphira, lied unto the Holy Ghost. Yes, very many, who have lightly uttered these words when they first entered into the ministry, have been led by them afterwards to

440

examine their motives more attentively and to humble themselves for the iniquity they have committed, and to surrender up themselves with redoubled energy to the service of their God. Though therefore we regret that any should make this profession on insufficient grounds, we rejoice that it is required of all: and we pray God that all who have made it may reconsider it with the attention it deserves; and that all who propose to make it may pause till they have maturely weighed the import of their assertion, and can call God himself to attest the truth of it.

Let us next turn our attention to the *promises* by which we bind ourselves on that occasion.

In the service for the Ordination of Priests, there is an exhortation from the bishop which every minister would do well to read at least once every year. To give a just view of this part of our Liturgy, we must briefly open to you the contents of that exhortation, the different parts of which are afterwards brought before us in the shape of questions; to every one of which a distinct and solemn answer is demanded, as in the presence of the heart-searching God. The exhortation consists of two parts; in the first of which *we are enjoined to consider the importance of that high office to which we are called;* and in the second *we are urged to exert ourselves to the uttermost in the discharge of it.*

In reference to the former of these it speaks thus: "Now we exhort you in the name of our Lord Jesus Christ, that you have in remembrance, into how high a dignity, and to how weighty an office and charge ye are called: that is to say, to be Messengers, Watchmen, and Stewards of the Lord; to teach and to premonish, to feed and provide for the Lord's family; to seek for Christ's sheep that are dispersed abroad, and for his children who are in the midst of this naughty world, that they may be saved through Christ for ever."

Where in such few words can we find so striking a representation of the dignity of our office as in this address? We are "Messengers" from the Most High God to instruct men in the knowledge of his will, and to communicate to them the glad

441

tidings of salvation through the mediation of his Son: We are "Watchmen" to warn them of their danger, whilst they continue without an interest in Christ: And we are "Stewards" to superintend his household, and to deal out to every one of his servants from day to day whatsoever their respective necessities require. Now if we occupied such an office in the house of an earthly monarch only, our dignity were great; but to be thus engaged in the service of the King of kings is an honour far greater than the temporal government of the whole universe. Should we not then bear in mind what an office is devolved upon us?

From speaking thus respecting *the dignity of the ministry,* it proceeds to speak of *the importance of the trust* committed to us: "Have always therefore printed in your remembrance how great a *treasure* is committed to your charge. For they are the sheep of Christ which he bought with his death, and for whom he shed his blood. The congregation whom you must serve, is his spouse, and his body." What a tender and affecting representation is here! The souls committed to our care are represented as "the sheep of Christ, which he bought with his death, and for which he shed his blood." What bounds would there be to our exertions if we considered as we ought that we are engaged in that very work for which our Lord Jesus Christ came down from the bosom of his Father and shed his blood upon the cross; and that to us he looks for the completion of his efforts in the salvation of a ruined world? Further still, they are represented as "the spouse and body of Christ," whose welfare ought to be infinitely dearer to us than life itself. We know what concern men would feel if the life of their own spouse or of their own body were in danger, though they could only hope to protract for a few years a frail and perishable existence: what then ought we not to feel for "the spouse and body of Christ," whose everlasting welfare is dependent on our exertions!

After thus impressing on our minds the importance of our office, the exhortation proceeds in the next place to urge us to a diligent performance of it. It reminds us that we are answera-

442

ble to God for every soul committed to our charge: that there must be no limit to our exertions except what the capacity of our minds and the strength of our bodies have assigned. It calls upon us to use all the means in our power to qualify ourselves for the discharge of it by withdrawing ourselves from worldly cares, worldly pleasures, worldly studies, worldly habits, and pursuits of every kind in order to fix the whole bent of our minds on the study of the Holy Scriptures, and of those things which will assist us in the understanding of them. It directs us to be instant in prayer to God for the assistance of his Holy Spirit, by whose gracious influences alone we shall be enabled to fulfill our duties aright. And, finally, it enjoins us so to regulate our own lives, and so to govern our respective families, that we may be patterns to all around us; and that we may be able to address our congregations in the language of St. Paul, "Whatsoever ye have heard and seen in me, do: and the God of peace shall be with you." But it will be satisfactory to you to hear the very words of the exhortation itself: "If it shall happen the same church, or any member thereof, to take any hurt or hindrance by reason of your negligence, ye know the greatness of the fault, and also the horrible punishment that will ensue. Wherefore consider with yourselves the end of your ministry towards the children of God, towards the spouse and body of Christ; and see that you *never cease your labour, your care and diligence,* until you have done *all that lieth in you,* according to your bounden duty; to bring all such as are or shall be committed to your charge unto that agreement in the faith and knowledge of God, and to that ripeness and perfectness of age in Christ, that there be no place left among you, either for error in religion, or for viciousness of life."

"Forasmuch then as your office is both of so great excellency, and of so great difficulty, ye see with how great care and study ye ought to apply yourselves, as well that ye may show yourselves dutiful, and thankful unto that Lord who hath placed you in so high a dignity; as also to beware that neither you yourselves offend, nor be occasion that others offend.

443

Howbeit ye cannot have a mind and will thereto of yourselves; for that will and ability is given of God alone: therefore ye ought and have need to pray earnestly for his Holy Spirit. And seeing that you cannot by any other means compass the doing of so weighty a work, pertaining to the salvation of man, but with doctrine and exhortation taken out of the Holy Scriptures, and with a life agreeable to the same, consider how studious ye ought to be in reading and learning the Scriptures, and in framing the manners both of yourselves and of them that specially pertain unto you, according to the rule of the same scriptures: and for this selfsame cause, how ye ought to forsake and set aside (as much as you may) all worldly cares and studies."

Here let us pause a moment to reflect what stress our Reformers laid on the Holy Scriptures as the only sure directory for our faith and practice and the only certain rule of all our ministrations. They have clearly given it as their sentiment that to study the word of God ourselves, and to open it to others, is the proper labour of a minister; a labour that calls for all his time and all his attention: and by this zeal of theirs in behalf of the Inspired Volume they were happily successful in bringing it into general use. But if they could look down upon us at this time and see what an unprecedented zeal has pervaded all ranks and orders of men amongst us for the dissemination of that truth, which they at the expense of their own lives transmitted to us; how would they rejoice and leap for joy! Yet, methinks, if they cast an eye upon this favoured spot and saw that, whilst the Lord Jesus Christ is thus exalted in almost every other place, we are lukewarm in his cause; and whilst thousands all around us are emulating each other in exertions to extend his kingdom through the world, we, who are so liberal on other occasions, have not yet appeared in his favour; they would be ready to rebuke our tardiness, as David did the indifference of Judah from whom he had reason to expect the most active support; "Why are ye the last to bring the king back to his house, seeing the speech of all Israel is come to the king, even to his house?" (2 *Sam.* 19:11). But I am persuaded that there is

444

nothing wanting but that a suitable proposal be made by some person of influence among us; and we shall soon approve ourselves worthy sons of those pious ancestors: I would hope there is not an individual among us who would not gladly lend his aid that "the word of the Lord may run and be glorified," not in this kingdom only but, if possible, throughout all the earth.

But to return to the bishop's exhortation. "We have good hope that you have well weighed and pondered these things with yourselves long before this time; and that you have clearly determined, by God's grace, to *give yourselves wholly to this office,* whereunto it hath pleased God to call you; so that, as much as lieth in you, you will *apply yourselves wholly* to this one thing, and draw all your cares and studies this way; and that you will continually pray to God the Father, by the mediation of our only Savior Jesus Christ, for the heavenly assistance of the Holy Ghost; that by daily reading and weighing of the Scriptures, ye may wax riper and stronger in your ministry, and that ye may so endeavour yourselves from time to time to sanctify the lives of you and yours, and to fashion them after the rule and doctrine of Christ, that ye may be wholesome and godly examples and patterns for the people to follow."

After this, the bishop calling upon the candidates in the name of God and of his church to give a plain and solemn answer to the questions which he shall propose to them puts the substance of the exhortation into several distinct questions; two of which only, for brevity sake, we will repeat: "Will you be diligent in prayers, and in reading of the Holy Scriptures, and in such studies as help to the knowledge of the same, laying aside the study of the world and the flesh?" To which we answer, "I will endeavour myself so to do, the Lord being my helper." Then he asks again: "Will you be diligent to frame and fashion your own selves and your families, according to the doctrine of Christ, and to make both yourselves and them, as much as in you lieth, wholesome examples and patterns to the flock of Christ?" To which we answer, "I will apply myself thereto, the Lord being my helper."

These are the promises which we make before God in the most solemn manner at the time of our Ordination. Now I would ask, Can any human being entertain a doubt whether in making these promises, we have not "well said all that we have spoken?" Can any of us say that too much has been required of us? Do we not see and feel that, as the honour of the office is great, so is the difficulty of performing it right, and the danger of performing it in a negligent and heartless manner? If a man undertake any office that requires indefatigable exertion and that involves the temporal interests of men to a great extent, we expect of that man the utmost diligence and care. If then such be expected of the servants of *men,* where temporal interests only are affected, what must be expected of the servants of *God,* where the eternal interests of men and the everlasting honour of God are so deeply concerned? I say again, We cannot but approve the promises we have made; and methinks God himself, when he heard our vows, expressed his approbation of them, saying, "They have well said all that they have spoken."

We come, lastly, to mention our *prayers,* which were offered to God on that occasion.

And here we have one of the most pious and affecting institutions that ever was established upon earth. The bishop, who during the preceding exhortation and questions has been seated in his chair, now rises up and, in a standing posture, makes his earnest supplication to God in behalf of all the candidates, in these words: "Almighty God, who hath given you this will to do all these things, grant also unto you strength and power to perform the same; that he may accomplish his work which he had begun in you, through Jesus Christ our Lord. Amen." After this a request is made to the whole congregation then present to offer up their prayers in secret to God, and to make their supplications to God for all these things. And that they may have time to do so, it is appointed that *silence shall be kept for a space;* the public services being for a while suspended in order to give the congregation an opportunity of pouring

446

out their souls before God in behalf of the persons who are to be ordained.

What an idea does this give us of the sanctity of our office and of the need we have of Divine assistance for the performance of it! And how beautifully does it intimate to the people the interest they have in an efficient ministry! Surely, if they felt as they ought their need of spiritual instruction, they would never discontinue their prayers for those who are placed over them in the Lord but would plead in their behalf night and day.

After a sufficient time has been allowed for these private devotions, a hymn to the Holy Ghost is introduced *(the candidates all continuing in a kneeling posture),* a hymn which in beauty of composition and spirituality of import cannot easily be surpassed.

. . .

In this devout hymn the agency of the Holy Spirit, as the one source of light and peace and holiness is fully acknowledged, and earnestly sought as the necessary means of forming pastors after God's heart.

. . .

Passing over the remaining prayers, we conclude this part of our subject with observing that no sooner is the imposition of hands finished, and the commission given to the candidates to preach the gospel, then the newly ordained ministers consecrate themselves to God at his table; and seal, as it were, their vows, by partaking of the body and blood of Christ, into whose service they have been just admitted, and whom they have sworn to serve with their whole hearts.

Illustration from a
Book of Common Prayer, 1837.

CHAPTER THIRTEEN

Catechetical Instruction and Preaching

(105) Richard Hooker
Master of the Temple, Rector of Bishopsbourne (Kent),
chief apologist for Anglicanism under Queen Elizabeth I
Of the Laws of Ecclesiastical Polity, book V
1597

[On Preaching and Catechising]

Places of public resort being thus provided for, our repair thither is especially for mutual conference, and as it were commerce to be had between God and us.

Because therefore want of the knowledge of God is the cause of all iniquity amongst men, as contrariwise the very ground of all our happiness and the seed of whatsoever perfect virtue groweth from us is a right opinion touching things divine; this kind of knowledge we may justly set down for the first and chiefest thing which God imparteth unto his people, and our duty of receiving this at his merciful hands for the first of those religious offices wherewith we publicly honour him on earth. For the instruction therefore of all sorts of men to eternal life, it is necessary that the sacred and saving truth of God be openly published unto them. Which open publication of *heavenly mysteries* is by an excellency termed Preaching. For otherwise there is not anything *publicly notified* but we may in that respect, rightly and properly say it is "preached."

---

(106) **George Herbert**
Rector of Fugglestone with Bemerton (Wilts.)
A Priest to the Temple, or The Country Parson
1633 / 1652

The Country Parson values Catechizing highly: for there being three points of his duty, the one, to infuse a competent knowledge of salvation in every one of his Flock; the other, to multiply and build up this knowledge to a spiritual Temple; the third, to inflame this knowledge, to press and drive it to practice, turning it to reformation of life by pithy and lively exhortations. Catechizing is the first point, and but by Catechizing the others cannot be attained. Besides, whereas in Sermons there is a kind of state, in Catechizing there is a humbleness very suitable to Christian regeneration, which exceedingly delights him as by way of exercise upon himself, and by way of preaching to himself, for the advancing of his own mortification. For in preaching to others he forgets not himself, but is first a Sermon to himself and then to others; growing with the growth of his Parish. He useth and preferreth the ordinary Church Catechism, partly for obedience to Authority, partly for uniformity sake, that the same common truths may be everywhere

450

professed, especially since many remove from Parish to Parish, who like Christian Soldiers are to give the word and to satisfy the Congregation by their Catholic answers. He exacts of all the Doctrine of the Catechism; of the younger sort, the very words; of the elder, the substance. Those he Catechizeth publicly, these privately, giving age honor according to the Apostle's rule (1 Tim. 5:1). He requires all to be present at Catechizing: First, for the authority of the work; Secondly, that Parents and Masters, as they hear the answers prove, may when they come home either commend or reprove, either reward or punish. Thirdly, that those of the elder sort who are not well grounded may then by an honorable way take occasion to be better instructed. Fourthly, that those who are well grown in the knowledge of Religion may examine their grounds, renew their vows, and by occasion of both enlarge their meditations. When once all have learned the words of the Catechism, he thinks it the most useful way that a Pastor can take to go over the same, but in other words: for many say the Catechism by rote, as parrots, without ever piercing into the sense of it.

---

(107) William Wake
Archbishop of Canterbury
The Principles of the Christian Religion explained in a Brief Commentary upon the Church Catechism
1699

Q. FROM whence is the word *Catechism* derived?
A. From a *Greek* word which signifies to teach by word of mouth; and has been used particularly to signify such a kind of instruction as is made by way of *Question and Answer*.
Q. What is that you call your *Church Catechism?*
A. It is a short, but sufficient, institution of the principles of

the Christian religion, set forth by authority, and required to be learned of every person, in order to his being confirmed by the Bishop; and prepared both for the profitable reading and hearing of God's word, and for the worthy receiving of the Lord's Supper.

Q. What do you look upon to be the proper subject of such institution?

A. It ought to comprehend all such things as are generally necessary to be known of all persons, in order to their due serving of God here, and to their being saved hereafter.

---

(108) **Anonymous**
The New Whole Duty of Man
1747

First, CATECHISING is a peculiar method of teaching the ignorant by question and answer; adapted to the meanest capacities for their more ready instruction in the first and necessary rules or principles of our holy religion; and is of very ancient date in the practice of the Christian church. And as to the great usefulness of it, catechising hath a particular advantage as to children because they are subject to forgetfulness and want of attention. Now catechising is a good remedy against both these; because, by questions put to them, children are forced to take notice of what is taught and must give some answer to the question that is asked; and a catechism being short and containing in a little compass the necessary principles of religion, it is the more easily remembered. Again, the great usefulness, and indeed the necessity of it, plainly appears by experience: for as Solomon observes, Train up a child in the way he should go, and when he is old he will not depart from it; so it very seldom happens that children who have not been catechised have any clear and competent knowledge of the principles of religion ever after; and, for want of this, are incapable of receiving any great benefit by preaching, which supposes persons to be in some measure instructed beforehand in the main principles of religion. Besides, if they have no principles of religion fixed in them, they become an easy prey to seducers. And therefore

I would recommend this way of instruction to parents and masters of families with respect to their children and servants. For I do not think that this work should lie wholly upon ministers. You must do your part at home, who, always living with your families, have better and more easy opportunities of fixing the principles of religion upon your children and servants. Neither must such as have been so unfortunate as to grow in years without this instruction imagine they are exempt from it; for, as soon as they are able to see their own danger and discover their own ignorance, they must apply in good earnest to this means of obtaining the first things to be known in the Christian religion. Therefore, whoever he be, of what age and condition soever, that finds his own ignorance in the mysteries of his religion and service of God, or in any such degree thereof, as he feels a want of any part of necessary saving knowledge; let him, as he loves his soul and would rescue it from eternal death, seek out for instruction, first by the means of catechising, and then he shall profit through God's grace by the word preached. For,

Secondly, PREACHING is not only a publication of God's mercy, favour, blessings, grace, and promises to those who love him and keep his commandments, but it is also a declaration of those threats and punishments recorded in the word of God against the obstinate and evildoer. Its use is to put us in mind of our duty, and to exhort and assist us to withstand those lusts and temptations which set us at enmity with God. Consequently we honour God by attending to his holy word, read and preached to us, with a resolution of mind to perform what we shall be convinced is our duty; with such submission of our understanding as is due to the oracles of God; and with a

453

particular application of general instructions to the state of our own minds, that we may grow in grace and in the knowledge of God the Father, and of our Lord and Savior Jesus Christ. Therefore, at hearing the word preached, we should give our attention with great reverence and take heed how we hear, lest our negligence be interpreted as a contempt of that authority which speaks to us; and not, as the manner of some is, who at church place their public worship, not in their hearts and knees but in lolling, gazing, and unseemly gestures; and employ their ears, the channel by which faith is conveyed into our souls, not to hear their duty but to find some unreasonable fault with their teacher: for instead of improving the word of God preached for their instruction, when they return home their whole discourse turns upon the man and not his sermon. And such hearers never want subject of complaint against the preacher, that they may in some measure screen their own neglect of duty to God, their neighbor, and themselves. Thus at one time they find fault with his memory, because too short; or with his sentences, because too long: if he be young, they despise his youth, and say that he does but prate: if he is aged, they seldom scruple to term his zeal for their souls and good instructions the dictates of one in his dotage that knows not what he says. Again, if he preaches in a plain style suitable to weak capacities, they call him a sloven, a bad master of languages; if he is solid, then he preaches flat: but, if he be not plain, then he is too witty; and, if not solid, he is certainly accused of levity and ridiculing the word of God: if he be unlearned, they justly say he is not worthy of so great a calling; and, if he be endowed with the qualifications of a good pastor and teacher, he is immediately proclaimed unfit for so plain and ignorant a people. In fine, when the sermon must be confessed to be very excellent, then they say he preaches for gain; and, if it be but ordinary, they cry they can read as good at home. But now

What can be thought to be the end of such men? God may justly give them up to a reprobate mind, and withdraw that grace which they have abused; and then it is no wonder they turn the most serious things into ridicule and hear the terrors of the Lord without the least sense of their own guilt. Pray God that this may not be the case of many who stay from church under a pretense that they cannot benefit under such and such a minister! And let not those who constantly attend on stated days to hear God's word preached, and still continue in their habitual sins, think they have honoured God: No. The way to reverence God by honouring his word is not to imagine, when we have been affected with a sermon, that the great end of hearing is fulfilled; for we must apply those good instructions and exhortations in such a manner as to enable us to conquer our most secret sins. Sins are the distempers of the soul, and God has prescribed this as a means of its cure: therefore, as no patient can hope for the cure of his bodily infirmities by talking with or only looking upon the physician, and his prescriptions and medicines; so neither can anyone hope to be released of his sins that never applies God's word to enable him to eschew evil and to do good. The main matter then of hearing a sermon is putting useful instructions into practice; for, when God enlightens our minds, it is our business to walk as children of light. We must never despair of conquering our evil habits, nor be discouraged in prosecuting the convictions of our own consciences; for a mighty resolution, with the assistance of God's grace, will overcome great difficulties. Let us therefore never measure our godliness by the number of sermons which we are present at, as if that outward mark of reverence to God was any sure mark of a good Christian; but let us estimate our obedience to God and reformation of our manners by the quantity of the good fruit which the dew of God's grace has, through the ministration of the word, enabled us to bring forth; without this disposition of the heart, all our hearing will only draw the heavier judgment of God upon us, because we hear and know our master's will and do it not.

(109) John Henry Hobart
Bishop of New York, founder of The General Theological Seminary
A Companion for the Festivals and Fasts
of the Protestant Episcopal Church
1804

Q. *When a sermon is delivered, with what dispositions ought we to hear it?*

A. However frail and unworthy the ministering servants of the sanctuary may be, yet, as they bear the commission of God and are appointed by him to promulgate the terms of salvation, we should listen to their instructions with humble and earnest attention; and our prayers should be directed to God that he would impress the truths which they may deliver on our hearts, to our conviction, our consolation, and our growth in holiness and virtue.

Select Bibliography

G.W.O. Addleshaw. *The High Church Tradition: A Study in the Liturgical Thought of the Seventeenth Century,* chapter 2. London, Faber and Faber, 1941.

Charles Bodington. *Books of Devotion.* London, Longmans, Green and Co., 1903.

John Booty. *Three Anglican Divines on Prayer: Jewel, Andrewes, and Hooker.* Privately printed, Society of St. John the Evangelist, Cambridge, Massachusetts, 1978.

John Dowden. *Outlines of the History of the Theological Literature of the Church of England from the Restoration to the Close of the Eighteenth Century.* London, S.P.C.K., 1897.

Faye L. Kelly. *Prayer in Sixteenth Century England.* Gainesville, University of Florida Monographs, Humanities no. 22, 1966.

J. Wickham Legg. *English Church Life from the Restoration to the Tractarian Movement,* chapter 11. London, Longmans, Green and Co., 1914.

Paul Elmer More and **Frank Leslie Cross,** eds., *Anglicanism: The Thought and Practice of the Church of England, Illustrated from the Religious Literature of the Seventeenth Century.* London, S.P.C.K., 1935.

Darwell Stone. *A History of the Doctrine of the Holy Eucharist,* volume 2. London, Longmans, Green and Co., 1909.

C.J. Stranks. *Anglican Devotion: Studies in the Spiritual Life of the Church of England Between the Reformation and the Oxford Movement.* London, SCM Press Ltd., 1961.

Martin Thornton. *English Spirituality,* chapter 20. London, S.P.C.K., 1963.

Helen C. White. *The Tudor Books of Private Devotion.* Madison, University of Wisconsin Press, 1951.

William J. Wolf, ed. *Anglican Spirituality* (esp. Harvey H. Guthrie, "Anglican Spirituality: An Ethos and Some Issues," David Siegenthaler, "The Literature of Anglican Spirituality," and Daniel B. Stevick, "The Spirituality of the Book of Common Prayer"). Wilton, Ct., Morehouse-Barlow, 1982.

Table of Sources

1. **Richard Hooker**, *Of the Laws of Ecclesiastical Polity*, book V, 1597. Excerpted from Everyman's Library edition (New York, 1907/1965), vol. II, pp. 105, 107–109.

2. **George Herbert**, *A Priest to the Temple, or The Country Parson*, 1633/1652. Excerpted from *George Herbert: The Country Parson, The Temple*, ed. John N. Wall Jr. (New York, 1981), pp. 74–75.

3. **Herbert Thorndike**, *The Service of God at Religious Assemblies*, 1642. Excerpted from *Theological Works*, vol. I (Oxford, 1844), pp. 103, 211–212.

4. **Anthony Sparrow**, *A Rationale upon the Book of Common Prayer of the Church of England*, 1655/1657. Excerpted from edition of London 1672, pp. 317–321, 333–335, 9.

5. **Thomas Comber**, *A Companion to the Temple, or A Help to Devotion in the Use of the Common Prayer*, 1672–76/1684. Excerpted from edition of London 1701, vol. I, preface (pages unnumbered).

6. **Daniel Brevint**, *The Christian Sacrament and Sacrifice*, 1673. Excerpted from edition of London 1756, pp. 1–2.

7. **Anthony Horneck**, *The Crucified Jesus, or, A Full Account of the Nature, End, Design and Benefits of the Sacrament of the Lord's Supper*, London 1686, pp. 36–39, 41–42.

8. **Robert Nelson**, *The Practice of True Devotion, in Relation to the End, as well as the Means of Religion, with an Office for the Holy Communion*, 1698. Excerpted from edition of London 1726, pp. 5–9.

9. **William Beveridge**, *The Great Necessity and Advantage of Public Prayer and Frequent Communion, designed to revive Primitive Piety, with Meditations, Ejaculations, and Prayers before, at, and after the Sacrament*, 1708. Excerpted from edition of London 1721, pp. 78–83.

10. **Anonymous**, *The New Whole Duty of Man*, 1747. Excerpted from edition of London 1853, pp. 166–167.

11. Samuel Johnson, *On the Beauty of Holiness in the Worship of the Church of England,* 1749. Excerpted from *Samuel Johnson: His Career and Writings,* ed. Herbert and Carol Schneider (New York, 1929), vol. III, pp. 533–534.

12. John Henry Hobart, *A Companion for the Book of Common Prayer,* 1805. Excerpted from edition of New York 1827, pp. 18–21.

13. Richard Hooker, *Of the Laws of Ecclesiastical Polity,* book V, 1597. Excerpted from Everyman's Library edition (New York, 1907/1965), vol. II, pp. 110–111.

14. Herbert Thorndike, *The Service of God at Religious Assemblies,* 1642. Excerpted from *Theological Works,* vol. I (Oxford, 1844), pp. 267–268.

15. Anonymous (John Gauden, later Bishop of Exeter, and/or King Charles I), *Eikon Basilike,* 1648. Excerpted from *Anglicanism,* ed. P.E. More and F.L. Cross (London, 1935), pp. 622–624.

16. John Durel, *The Liturgy of the Church of England Asserted,* London 1662, pp. 20–28.

17. William Beveridge, *A Sermon on the Excellency and Usefulness of the Common Prayer.* 1681/1682. Excerpted from *Anglicanism,* ed. P.E. More and F.L. Cross (London, 1935), pp. 624–627.

18. William Beveridge, *The Great Necessity and Advantage of Public Prayer and Frequent Communion, designed to revive Primitive Piety, with Meditations, Ejaculations, and Prayers before, at, and after the Sacrament,* 1708. Excerpted from edition of London 1721, pp. 55–58.

19. Thomas Bisse, *The Beauty of Holiness in the Common Prayer,* 1716. Excerpted from edition of Cambridge 1842, pp. 1–7.

20. Samuel Johnson, *On the Beauty of Holiness in the Worship of the Church of England,* 1749. Excerpted from *Samuel Johnson: His Career and Writings,* ed. Herbert and Carol Schneider (New York, 1929), vol. III, pp. 520–523.

21. Thomas Secker, *Sermon XXIV, on the Lawfulness and Expediency of Forms of Prayer,* c. 1758–1768. Excerpted from *Works* (London, 1825), vol. III, pp. 383–394.

22. John Henry Hobart, *A Companion for the Festivals and Fasts of the Protestant Episcopal Church,* 1804. Excerpted from edition of New York 1862, pp. 72–74.

23. John Henry Hobart, *A Companion for the Book of Common Prayer,* 1805. Excerpted from edition of New York 1827, pp. 5, 10–14.

24. Thomas C. Brownell, *The Family Prayer Book, or the Book of Common Prayer . . . accompanied by a General Commentary, Historical, Explanatory, Doctrinal, and*

460

Practical, 1823. Excerpted from edition of New York 1857, pp. 5–14.

25. Richard Hooker, *Of the Laws of Ecclesiastical Polity*, book V, 1597. Excerpted from Everyman's Library edition (New York, 1907/1965), vol. II, pp. 352–353.

26. Anthony Sparrow, *A Rationale upon the Book of Common Prayer of the Church of England*, 1655/1657. Excerpted from edition of London 1672, pp. 88–96.

27. John Durel, *The Liturgy of the Church of England Asserted*, London 1662, pp. 29–30.

28. Thomas Comber, *A Companion to the Temple, or A Help to Devotion in the Use of the Common Prayer*, 1672–76/1684. Excerpted from edition of London 1701, vol. I, pp. 523–525.

29. Robert Nelson, *A Companion for the Festivals and Fasts of the Church of England*, 1703. Excerpted from edition of London (n.d., 1850), pp. 1–9, 401, 64–65, 235–236.

30. Anonymous, *The New Whole Duty of Man*, 1747. Excerpted from edition of London 1853, pp. 50–53.

31. John Henry Hobart, *A Companion for the Book of Common Prayer*, 1805. Excerpted from edition of New York 1827, pp. 35–36.

32. Lancelot Andrewes, *Sermons on the Lord's Prayer*, probably given at Cambridge in the 1580s. Excerpted from *Ninety-Six Sermons*, vol. V (Oxford, 1843), pp. 363–364, 388–389.

33. Richard Hooker, *Of the Laws of Ecclesiastical Polity*, book V, 1597. Excerpted from Everyman's Library edition (New York, 1907/1965), vol. II, p. 145.

34. Anthony Sparrow, *A Rationale upon the Book of Common Prayer of the Church of England*, 1655/1657. Excerpted from edition of London 1672, pp. 56–57.

35. John Pearson, *An Exposition of the Creed*, 1659. Excerpted from edition of London 1676, pp. 26–27, 178–179.

36. Thomas Comber, *A Companion to the Temple, or A Help to Devotion in the Use of the Common Prayer*, 1672–76/1684. Excerpted from edition of London 1701, vol. I, pp. 1–2, 37, 40, 71, 83, 88, 117, 118, 135, 145–146, 167.

37. William Wake, *The Principles of the Christian Religion explained in a Brief Commentary upon the Church Catechism*, 1699. Excerpted from edition of London 1849, pp. 26–28.

38. Samuel Johnson, *On the Beauty of Holiness in the Worship of the Church of England*, 1749. Excerpted from *Samuel Johnson: His Career and Writings*, ed.

461

Herbert and Carol Schneider (New York, 1929), vol. III, pp. 523–528.

39. Thomas Secker, *Sermon XXV, in Explanation and Defence of the Liturgy of the Church of England,* c. 1758–1768. Excerpted from *Works* (London, 1825), vol. III, pp. 402–411, 447–451.

40. John Henry Hobart, *A Companion for the Book of Common Prayer,* 1805. Excerpted from edition of New York 1827, pp. 17–18, 21–35.

41. Charles Simeon, *The Churchman's Confession, or, An Appeal to the Liturgy,* 1805. Excerpted from edition of New York 1813, pp. 146, 150–154, 157–158, 166, 174.

42. Frederick Denison Maurice, *Sermons on the Prayer Book and the Lord's Prayer,* 1848–1849. Excerpted from edition of London 1902, pp. 283–293.

43. Anthony Sparrow, *A Rationale upon the Book of Common Prayer of the Church of England,* 1655/1657. Excerpted from edition of London 1672, pp. 81–83.

44. Thomas Comber, *A Companion to the Temple, or A Help to Devotion in the Use of the Common Prayer,* 1672–76/1684. Excerpted from edition of London 1701, vol. I, pp. 198, 291–292.

45. Samuel Johnson, *On the Beauty of Holiness in the Worship of the Church of England,* 1749. Excerpted from *Samuel Johnson: His Career and Writings,* ed. Herbert and Carol Schneider (New York, 1929), vol. III, p. 528.

46. Thomas Secker, *Sermon XXVIII, in Explanation and Defence of the Liturgy of the Church of England,* c. 1758–1768. Excerpted from *Works* (London, 1825), vol. III, pp. 452–462.

47. John Henry Hobart, *A Companion for the Book of Common Prayer,* 1805. Excerpted from edition of New York 1827, pp. 31–32.

48. Frederick Denison Maurice, *Sermons on the Prayer Book and the Lord's Prayer,* 1848–1849. Excerpted from edition of London 1902, pp. 163–166.

49. John Jewel, *An Apology of the Church of England,* 1564; ed. J. E. Booty (Ithaca, 1963), pp. 30–31.

50. Richard Hooker, *Of the Laws of Ecclesiastical Polity,* book V, 1597. Excerpted from Everyman's Library edition (New York, 1907/1965), vol. II, pp. 244, 309.

51. Anonymous (? Richard Allestree), *The Whole Duty of Man,* 1657. Excerpted from edition of London 1739, pp. 51–58.

52. Simon Patrick, *Aqua Genitalis: A Discourse concerning Baptism.* 1659. Excerpted from edition of London 1717, pp. 426–427, 443–444.

53. John Durel, *The Liturgy of the Church of England Asserted*, London 1662, pp. 28–29.

54. Thomas Comber, *A Companion to the Temple, or A Help to Devotion in the Use of the Common Prayer*, 1672–76/1684. Excerpted from edition of London 1701, vol. I, pp. 607, 627.

55. John Henry Hobart, *A Companion for the Book of Common Prayer*, 1805. Excerpted from edition of New York 1827, pp. 56–58.

56. Anonymous, *Second Book of Homilies*, 1563/1571. *An Homily of the Worthy Receiving and Reverent Esteeming of the Sacrament of the Body and Blood of Christ* (John Jewel). Excerpted from edition of London 1899, pp. 472–484.

57. John Jewel, *An Apology of the Church of England*, 1564; ed. J. E. Booty (Ithaca, 1963), pp. 31–32.

58. Richard Hooker, *Of the Laws of Ecclesiastical Polity*, book V, 1597. Excerpted from Everyman's Library edition (New York, 1907/1965), vol. II, pp. 318–322.

59. Christopher Sutton, *Godly Meditations upon the Most Holy Sacrament of the Lord's Supper*, 1613/1630. Excerpted from edition of Oxford 1839, pp. 1–2, 8–9, 257–262.

60. Henry Hammond, *Of Fundamentals in a Notion referring to Practice*, 1654. Excerpted from *Anglicanism*, ed. P.E. More and F.L. Cross (London, 1935), pp. 461–462.

61. Anthony Sparrow, *A Rationale upon the Book of Common Prayer of the Church of England*, 1655/1657. Excerpted from edition of London 1672, pp. 242–243.

62. John Cosin, *Historia Transubstantiationis Papalis*, 1656/1675–1676. Excerpted from *Anglicanism*, ed. P.E. More and F.L. Cross (London, 1935), pp. 467–468.

63. Anonymous (? Richard Allestree), *The Whole Duty of Man*, 1657. Excerpted from edition of London 1739, pp. 59–61, 77–82.

64. Jeremy Taylor, *The Worthy Communicant*, 1660. Excerpted from edition of London 1667, pp. 54–56, 70–76, 382–384.

65. Simon Patrick, *Mensa Mystica, or a Discourse concerning the Sacrament of the Lord's Supper*, 1660. Excerpted from edition of London 1717, pp. 1–2, 40, 56–58, 78–79, 97–98, 227–228, 240–243, 249–250, 262–264.

66. Simon Patrick, *The Christian Sacrifice. A Treatise Shewing the Necessity, End, and Manner of Receiving the Holy Communion, together with Suitable Prayers and*

Meditations for every Month of the Year and the Principal Festivals in Memory of our Blessed Saviour, 1671. Excerpted from edition of London 1732, pp. A3, 94–96.

67. Thomas Comber, *A Companion to the Temple, or A Help to Devotion in the Use of the Common Prayer*, 1672–76/1684. Excerpted from edition of London 1701, vol. I, pp. 413, 450, 519, 521, 535, 539, 547, 564–565.

68. Daniel Brevint, *The Christian Sacrament and Sacrifice*, 1673. Excerpted from edition of London 1756, pp. 4–15.

69. Robert Nelson, *The Great Duty of Frequenting the Christian Sacrifice, and the Nature of the Preparation Required, with Suitable Devotions*, 1706. Excerpted from edition of London 1718, pp 23–24, 48–51.

70. William Beveridge, *The Great Necessity and Advantage of Public Prayer and Frequent Communion, designed to revive Primitive Piety, with Meditations, Ejaculations, and Prayers before, at, and after the Sacrament*, 1708. Excerpted from edition of London 1721, pp. 206–208.

71. Samuel Johnson, *On the Beauty of Holiness in the Worship of the Church of England*, 1749. Excerpted from *Samuel Johnson: His Career and Writings*, ed. Herbert and Carol Schneider (New York, 1929), vol. III, pp. 529–530.

72. Thomas Secker, *Sermon XXIX*, in *Explanation and Defence of the Liturgy of the Church of England*, c. 1758–1768. Excerpted from *Works* (London, 1825), vol. III, pp. 476–481.

73. Anonymous, *The Companion or Spiritual Guide at the Altar*. Excerpted from edition of 1783, pp. iv–ix, 20–21, bound in with *A New Family Prayer-Book, containing the Book of Common Prayer, . . .*, ed. James Cookson (Winchester, 1783).

74. Samuel Seabury, *An Earnest Persuasive to Frequent Communion*, New Haven 1789, pp. 27–28.

75. Samuel Seabury, *Discourses on Several Subjects*, New York 1793, vol. I, pp. 176–180.

76. John Henry Hobart, *A Companion for the Book of Common Prayer*, 1805. Excerpted from edition of New York 1827, pp. 33–34, 53–56.

77. Anonymous, *The Companion to the Altar*. Bound in with *The Book of Common Prayer*, Oxford 1815, pp. 516–519.

78. Anonymous, *The Companion for the Altar*. Bound in with *The New Week's Preparation for a Worthy Receiving of the Lord's Supper as Recommended and Appointed by the Church of England*, London 1818, p. 98.

79. Anonymous, *A Companion to the Altar*. Excerpted from edition of London 1826, pp. 18–23, bound in with *The Book of Common Prayer*, Cambridge 1823.

464

80. Samuel Taylor Coleridge, *Notes on the Book of Common Prayer*, 1827. Excerpted from *The Complete Works*, ed. W.G.T. Shedd (New York, 1853), vol. V, p. 22.

81. J.P.K. Henshaw, *The Communicant's Guide, or, An Introduction to the Sacrament of the Lord's Supper*, Baltimore 1831, pp. 185–211.

82. Anonymous, *Second Book of Homilies*, 1563/1571. *An Homily of the State of Matrimony*. Excerpted from edition of London 1899, pp. 534–542, 548–549.

83. Richard Hooker, *Of the Laws of Ecclesiastical Polity*, book V, 1597. Excerpted from Everyman's Library edition (New York, 1907/1965), vol. II, pp. 391–397.

84. Thomas Comber, *A Companion to the Temple, or A Help to Devotion in the Use of the Common Prayer*, 1672–76/1684. Excerpted from edition of London 1701, vol. I, pp. 642–643.

85. Anonymous, *Second Book of Homilies*, 1563/1571. *An Homily of Repentance and of True Reconciliation unto God*. Excerpted from edition of London 1899, pp. 572–581.

86. John Jewel, *An Apology of the Church of England*, 1564, ed. J. E. Booty (Ithaca, 1963), pp. 26–27.

87. Richard Hooker, *Of the Laws of Ecclesiastical Polity*, book VI (†1648). Excerpted from *The Works of that Learned and Judidious Divine, Mr. Richard Hooker*, ed. John Keble, Oxford 1874, vol. III, pp. 6–7, 12–13, 49–54, 62–64, 66, 78–79, 101–107.

88. Herbert Thorndike, *The Service of God at Religious Assemblies*, 1642. Excerpted from *Theological Works*, vol. I (Oxford, 1844), pp. 364–365.

89. Anonymous (? Richard Allestree), *The Whole Duty of Man*, 1657. Excerpted from edition of London 1739, pp. 74–76.

90. Hamon L'Estrange, *The Alliance of Divine Offices*, 1659. Excerpted from *Anglicanism*, ed. P.E. More and F.L. Cross (London, 1935), pp. 519–520.

91. William Wake, *An Exposition of the Doctrine of the Church of England*, London 1686, pp. 40–43.

92. Jeremy Taylor, *The Rule and Exercises of Holy Dying*, 1651. Excerpted from *The Works of Jeremy Taylor, D.D.*, ed. T.S. Hughes (London, 1831), vol. V, pp. 521–526.

93. Anthony Sparrow, *A Rationale upon the Book of Common Prayer of the Church of England*, 1655/1657. Excerpted from edition of London 1672, pp. 282–286.

94. **Thomas Comber**, *A Companion to the Temple, or A Help to Devotion in the Use of the Common Prayer*, 1672–76/1684. Excerpted from edition of London 1701, vol. I, pp. 701–702, 714–715, 768.

95. **John Jewel**, *An Apology of the Church of England*, 1564, ed. J.E. Booty (Ithaca, 1963), p. 39.

96. **Richard Hooker**, *Of the Laws of Ecclesiastical Polity*, book V, 1597. Excerpted from Everyman's Library edition (New York, 1907/1965), vol. II, p. 401.

97. **Anthony Sparrow**, *A Rationale upon the Book of Common Prayer of the Church of England*, 1655/1657. Excerpted from edition of London 1672, pp. 306–307.

98. **Thomas Comber**, *A Companion to the Temple, or A Help to Devotion in the Use of the Common Prayer*, 1672–76/1684. Excerpted from edition of London 1701, vol. I, pp. 784, 808, 812, 813.

99. **Richard Hooker**, *Of the Laws of Ecclesiastical Polity*, book V, 1597. Excerpted from Everyman's Library edition (New York, 1907/1965), vol. II, pp. 416–433.

100. **Anthony Sparrow**, *A Rationale upon the Book of Common Prayer of the Church of England*, 1655/1657. Excerpted from edition of London 1672, pp. 317–339.

101. **Thomas Comber**, *A Companion to the Temple, or A Help to Devotion in the Use of the Common Prayer*, 1672–76/1684. Excerpted from edition of London 1702, vol. II, pp. 217, 270–272, 288.

102. **William Wake**, *An Exposition of the Doctrine of the Church of England*, London 1686, pp. 45–46.

103. **William Wake**, *The Principles of the Christian Religion explained in a Brief Commentary upon the Church Catechism*, 1699. Excerpted from edition of London 1849, p. 148.

104. **Charles Simeon**, *The Excellency of the Liturgy*, 1812. Excerpted from edition of New York 1813, pp. 110–130.

105. **Richard Hooker**, *Of the Laws of Ecclesiastical Polity*, book V, 1597. Excerpted from Everyman's Library edition (New York, 1907/1965), vol. II, pp. 55–56.

106. **George Herbert**, *A Priest to the Temple, or The Country Parson*, 1633/1652. Excerpted from *George Herbert: The Country Parson, The Temple*, ed. John N. Wall Jr. (New York, 1981), pp. 82–83.

107. William Wake, *The Principles of the Christian Religion explained in a Brief Commentary upon the Church Catechism*, 1699. Excerpted from edition of London 1849, pp. 1–25.

108. Anonymous, *The New Whole Duty of Man*, 1747. Excerpted from edition of London 1853, pp. 57–59.

109. John Henry Hobart, *A Companion for the Festivals and Fasts of the Protestant Episcopal Church*, 1804. Excerpted from edition of New York 1862, p. 88.

Authors and Titles

Anonymous *Second Book of Homilies*, 1563/1571.
An Homily of the Worthy Receiving and Reverent Esteeming of the Sacrament of the Body and Blood of Christ (John Jewel).
An Homily of the State of Matrimony.
An Homily of Repentance and of True Reconciliation with God.

John Jewel, Bishop of Salisbury.
An Apology of the Church of England, 1564.

Lancelot Andrewes, Bishop successively of Chichester, Ely, and Winchester.
Sermons on the Lord's Prayer, probably given at Cambridge in the 1580s.

Richard Hooker, Master of the Temple, Rector of Bishopsbourne (Kent), chief apologist for Anglicanism under Queen Elizabeth I.
Of the Laws of Ecclesiastical Polity, book V (1597); book VI (†1648).

Christopher Sutton, Canon of Winchester and Lincoln.
Godly Meditations upon the Most Holy Sacrament of the Lord's Supper, 1613/1630.

George Herbert, Rector of Fugglestone with Bemerton (Wilts.).
A Priest to the Temple, or The Country Parson, 1633/1652.

Herbert Thorndike, Rector of Barley (Herts.), Fellow of Trinity College, Cambridge, Prebendary of Westminster.
The Service of God at Religious Assemblies, 1642.

Anonymous (John Gauden, later Bishop of Exeter, and/or King Charles I).
Eikon Basilike, 1648.

Jeremy Taylor, Chaplain to Lord Carbery, Bishop of Down and Connor and of Dromore.
The Rule and Exercises of Holy Dying, 1651.
The Worthy Communicant, 1660.

Henry Hammond, Archdeacon of Chichester, Canon of Christ Church, Oxford.
Of Fundamentals in a Notion referring to Practice, 1654.

Anthony Sparrow, Bishop of Norwich.
A Rationale upon the Book of Common Prayer of the Church of England, 1655/
 1657.

John Cosin, Bishop of Durham.
Historia Transubstantiationis Papalis, 1656/1675–1676.

Anonymous (? Richard Allestree, Regius Professor of Divinity at Oxford,
 Provost of Eton).
The Whole Duty of Man, 1657.

Hamon L'Estrange, lay theologian and historian.
The Alliance of Divine Offices, 1659.

John Pearson, Bishop of Chester.
An Exposition of the Creed, 1659.

Simon Patrick, Bishop of Ely.
Aqua Genitalis: A Discourse concerning Baptism, 1659.
Mensa Mystica, or a Discourse concerning the Sacrament of the Lord's Supper,
 1660.
*The Christian Sacrifice. A Treatise Shewing the Necessity, End, and Manner of
 Receiving the Holy Communion, together with Suitable Prayers and Medita-
 tions for every Month of the Year and the Principal Festivals in Memory of
 our Blessed Saviour,* 1671.

John Durel, Minister of the French Church in the Savoy, Dean of Windsor.
The Liturgy of the Church of England Asserted, 1662.

Thomas Comber, Dean of Durham.
*A Companion to the Temple, or A Help to Devotion in the Use of the Common
 Prayer,* 1672–76/1684.

Daniel Brevint, Dean of Lincoln.
The Christian Sacrament and Sacrifice, 1673.

William Beveridge, Bishop of St. Asaph.
A Sermon on the Excellency and Usefulness of the Common Prayer. 1681/1682.
*The Great Necessity and Advantage of Public Prayer and Frequent Communion,
 designed to revive Primitive Piety, with Meditations, Ejaculations, and Prayers before, at, and after the Sacrament,* 1708.

Anthony Horneck, Vicar of All Saints, Oxford, Chaplain to William III,
 Prebendary of Westminster.

The Crucified Jesus, or, A Full Account of the Nature, End, Design and Benefits of the Sacrament of the Lord's Supper, 1686.

William Wake, Archbishop of Canterbury.
An Exposition of the Doctrine of the Church of England, 1686.
The Principles of the Christian Religion explained in a Brief Commentary upon the Church Catechism, 1699.

Robert Nelson, layman and philanthropist.
The Practice of True Devotion, in Relation to the End, as well as the Means of Religion, with an Office for the Holy Communion, 1698.
A Companion for the Festivals and Fasts of the Church of England, 1703.
The Great Duty of Frequenting the Christian Sacrifice, and the Nature of the Preparation Required, with Suitable Devotions, 1706.

Thomas Bisse, Preacher at the Rolls Chapel, Chancellor of Hereford Cathedral.
The Beauty of Holiness in the Common Prayer, 1716.

Anonymous
A Companion to the Altar.
The Companion to the Altar.
The Companion for the Altar.
The Companion or Spiritual Guide at the Altar.
Several various texts with similar titles, of anonymous authorship, and of rather different contents, were published throughout the eighteenth and nineteenth centuries and bound within various editions of the Book of Common Prayer.

Anonymous
The New Whole Duty of Man, 1747.

Samuel Johnson, Priest and missionary in Connecticut from the Society for the Propagation of the Gospel, first president of King's College (Columbia University).
On the Beauty of Holiness in the Worship of the Church of England, 1749.

Thomas Secker, Archbishop of Canterbury.
Sermons, c. 1758–1768.

Samuel Seabury, First Bishop of the Episcopal Church in the U.S.A., Bishop of Connecticut.
An Earnest Persuasive to Frequent Communion, 1789.
Discourses on Several Subjects, volume 1, 1793.

John Henry Hobart, Bishop of New York, founder of The General Theological Seminary.

470

A Companion for the Festivals and Fasts of the Protestant Episcopal Church, 1804.

A Companion for the Book of Common Prayer, 1805/1827.

Charles Simeon, Fellow of King's College and Vicar of Holy Trinity, Cambridge.

The Churchman's Confession, or, An Appeal to the Liturgy, 1805/1813.

The Excellency of the Liturgy, 1812/1813.

Anonymous

The New Week's Preparation for a Worthy Receiving of the Lord's Supper as Recommended and Appointed by the Church of England, 1818.

Thomas C. Brownell, Bishop of Connecticut.

The Family Prayer Book, or the Book of Common Prayer . . . accompanied by a General Commentary, Historical, Explanatory, Doctrinal, and Practical, 1823.

Samuel Taylor Coleridge, poet.

Notes on the Book of Common Prayer, 1827.

J.P.K. Henshaw, Rector of St. Peter's, Baltimore, Bishop of Rhode Island.

The Communicant's Guide, or, An Introduction to the Sacrament of the Lord's Supper, 1831.

Frederick Denison Maurice, Professor of Theology at King's College, London; Professor of Moral Philosophy at Cambridge.

Sermons on the Prayer Book and the Lord's Prayer, 1848-1849.

Index of Selections